YET WIT

Biographies

With every good wish
Charles L. Hoskins

Charles Lwanga Hoskins

2001

Cover design by Crystal L. Watts

First Printing, February 2001

ISBN: 0-9708215-0-6

Published by The Gullah Press
P.O. Box 994, Savannah, Georgia 31402

Funding for this publication provided by

The City of Savannah's

Department of Cultural Affairs/

Leisure Services Bureau's

To

Florencia, Evalena, Cecille, Tyra, Tia,

The Women of St. Matthew's Episcopal Church

And

The Sons and Daughters of Mother Africa, Herein Recorded

CONTENTS

1. TRAILBLAZERS

2. MAAFA *(unspeakable horror)* IN SAVANNAH

3. THE STRUGGLE BEGINS

4. WHEN JIM CROW WAS KING

ACKNOWLEDGMENTS

Over the past twenty-five plus years I have been unusually fortunate to be surrounded by many incredible storytellers, especially "Nellie" Pollard, Amanda Parker, Earl Ashton, Marion O. Johnston, and Frank Bynes, to mention only a few. None of them, however, seemed to have had the inclination to put their stories in writing. Unfortunately history, as we normally understand it, is not what happened, but what someone has written, actually took place. I have tried to record their stories and what I have discovered on my own. I owe a deep debt of gratitude to the many, many persons, whose stories I have borrowed, and used.

I thank especially, Lucy Gadsden Solomon, Margaret Gadsden Caution, Martha Wright Wilson, Mary Bradley McDew, Yvonne Taylor, General and Lazola Cope, Noel Wheeler and Jocelyn Poole, Chalmus and Martha Hicks, Richard and Clemontine Washington, Dorothy Canty Bass, Jewel Henry, Janie Evans Fowles, Lee Grant and Margaret A. Pearson, Sam and Marian Parker, Willie Mae Robinson, Felix and Gloria Villarin, Ethel Burke Shelton, Charles and Joenelle Gordon, Ernest and Annette Brown, and Willie and Georgette Kelly, for their financial assistance in publishing this book.

Without the interest of Mayor Floyd Adams, Jr., and the help of the staff of the Weave-A-Dream program, this book would simply not have seen the light of day. Thank you all very much.

Charles Lwanga Hoskins

FOREWORD

The African-American community in Savannah, Georgia has traveled a long, arduous road, in its attempt to overcome the legacy of slavery and Jim Crowism. The community's thirst for education as a means of advancement can be traced back to the time when the Freedmen of Savannah met with Secretary of War Edwin M. Stanton and General William T. Sherman to request the Government's assistance in maximizing their new freedom. Evidence of our achievements can be seen in the ever-changing face of our local power structure.

As the first Mayor of Savannah of African descent, it has been my personal objective to unite all of the citizens of Savannah under the common goal of improving our city, both economically and socially. This study demonstrates that the African-American community has survived and has truly come into its own.

Floyd Adams, Jr.,
Mayor of Savannah

Telling Our Stories

Remembering and Living Our Truths

Horace, the Roman lyric poet, once wrote that many brave men lived before Agamemnon but remained "unwept and unknown for lack of a sacred bard." In 1977, at the mature age of 103, a sacred bard, Mrs. Eleanor "Nellie" Pollard, gave the author four taped hours of her recollections of the lives of African Americans in Savannah. One got the distinct impression that she was very anxious to pass on to me the lore of her people, which she had harbored in her memory for well nigh a century. It therefore fell to me to expand her database and put her story in this more accessible written form.

Eleanor "Nellie" Reid Scott Pollard was born in Savannah, August 18, 1874. The Rev. Joseph S. Atwell baptized her at St. Stephen's (later called St. Matthew's) Episcopal Church, Monday, March 8, 1875. Duncan S. Scott and Susie M. Scott were her parents and Kate Middleton, Florida O'Byrne and Enoch R. Spaulding were her Godparents.[1] Eleanor Scott and Lachlan Pollard were married at St. Stephen's, November 28, 1901. The rector, the Rev. Richard Bright, solemnized their marriage.[2] The author officiated at the burial of Mrs. Eleanor Pollard, November 14, 1978.

This study, volume one of a projected two volume series, covers the period from 1733 to 1920. It is neither a history of Savannah nor the definitive record of African Americans in Savannah. Rather, it is some missing pages of Savannah's written history. In 1837, Firmin Cerveau's painting of Savannah ignored several parts of the city, even hiding the "source of the city's wealth."[3] Cerveau surely did not "see" black Savannah. In 1856, William M. Thackeray "saw" Andrew Low's blacks as "happy Negroes sauntering here and there."[4]

This book presents a collection of profiles, in the style of Mrs. Pollard, that young Andrew Bryan, Andrew C. Marshall, Jane Deveaux, Mary Woodhouse, Alexander Harris, James M. Simms, John H. Deveaux, and hundreds of others must have heard at home, and which helped to frame their exceptional lives and in part accounts for their remarkable resilience.

Commenting on the obstacles African Americans have confronted in Savannah, the Rev. Emanuel K. Love remarked, "These hardships developed wonderful characters. Whatever the Negroes have learned, they have paid for it dearly."[5] Editor Sol C. Johnson of the *Savannah Tribune* stated, "History is one of the foundation stones of a race. It is left to us to retain ours as a heritage."[6] To put it another way, if we forget who will remember?

Sol Johnson remarked, "The recording of Negro history and the propagation of the same, is dear to us. We deem it one of the best means to arouse a consciousness in the youths that will give them a proper complex."[7] He recognized that written history of the people could instill the youth "with the spirit that will thwart every inferior complex."[8] He admonished parents, "teach your children to read about the achievements of successful men of the race, have the pictures of them in your homes, thereby instill in that which will give the children ambition and a desire for uplift."[9]

The author leaned very heavily on the files of that treasure trove of Savannah's black history, the *Colored Tribune*, later called the *Savannah Tribune*, located in Savannah State University's Library and those of the *Herald*, kept at Barnard Street. The *Savannah Morning News* and earlier papers, located in the Georgia Historical Society, and the Bull Street Public Library, were also used.

The following books were consulted: James M. Simms' *The First Colored Church in North America,* (1888); Emanuel K. Love's *The First African Baptist Church*, (1888); Edgar G. Thomas' *The First African Baptist Church of North America,* (1925); Kermit O. Smalls *Year Book of Colored Savannah,* (1934); Robert E. Perdue's *The Negro in Savannah; 1865-1900*, (1973). William A. Byrne's unpublished *The Burden And Heat Of The Day: Slavery And Servitude In Savannah, 1733-1865,* (1979); Donald L. Grant's great classic history of blacks in Georgia, *The Way It Was In The South*, (1993); Whittington B. Johnson's authoritative *Black Savannah: 1788-1864*, (1996), Gaye Hewitt's magisterial but unpublished *Black Savannah: A Century Of Social Struggle;* Charles J. Elmore's, *An Historical Guide To Laurel Grove Cemetery South* (1998); and my own publications, *Black Episcopalians In Georgia* (1980), *Black Episcopalians In Savannah* (1983); *The Trouble They Seen* (1989), and *African American Episcopalians In Savannah* (1995).

Sixty-seven years ago Kermit O. Smalls declared, in the preface to his book,

> "This attempt was made on the assumption that somebody who has the time and the talent will come along and engineer a high powered, scientific research, which will pry into all the various avenues of Negro life. Nevertheless no apology will be made for this experiment."[10]

Even though this author lacks the "time," the "talent," and above all, the resources, to "engineer a high powered, scientific research," into "all the various avenues of Negro life," this study is offered to the public in order to remind some, and expose others, to many remarkable profiles of black life, often omitted in the written telling of Savannah's history. It hopes to have in one book, information that is scattered in several locations. In that sense it attempts to expand and update Kermit Smalls' *Year Book of Colored Savannah,* published in 1934 and long out of print.

The odyssey is presented with a minimum of interpretation in an attempt, to the extent possible, to retain our elders' perception of the Savannah experience. As Dr. John Duncan remarked, "Black history has traditionally been recorded through the eyes of white people."[11] This account attempts to "see" Savannah mainly through black eyes. Partly for that reason, the terms, African, black, colored, Negro, to mention only the polite ones, though obviously dated, and the more recent, African American, are used throughout the text.

The author is grateful to many people for their assistance in the preparation of this book. Dr. J.W. Jamerson 111, John B. Collier, Lucy G. Solomon and Margaret G. Caution, allowed the author use their *Family Papers*. Frank Mahitab Librarian, Savannah State University, was very helpful and generous with his time and advice. Dr. John Duncan valiantly bore the burden of filling the lacunae in my knowledge of Savannah's history. Dr. Luetta C. Milledge graciously provided some editorial and copy reading assistance.

Finally, I thank my wife Evalena, for her constant encouragement while this work was in progress. I lay sole claim to all the mistakes.

Charles Lwanga Hoskins

Endnotes:

[1] St. Stephen's Register, 1868, 79.

[2] *Savannah Tribune,* November 30, 1901.

[3] Joseph F. Waring, *Cerveau's Savannah*, Georgia Historical Society, 1973, 6.

[4] Quoted in Joseph F. Waring, 26.

[5] Emanuel K. Love, *History Of The First African Baptist Church, From Its Organization January 20th, 1788, to July 1st, 1888,* Savannah 1888, 32.

[6] *Savannah Tribune,* February 3, 1938.

[7] *Savannah Tribune,* February 9, 1939.

[8] *Savannah Tribune,* January 25, 1940.

[9] *Savannah Tribune*, February 23, 1907.

[10] Kermit O. Smalls, *Year Book of Colored Savannah*, Savannah, 1934.

[11] *Savannah Morning News,* June 9, 1998.

TRAILBLAZERS
Africa to the Rescue

The Federal Writers Project in 1937 reported the existence of a legend among the city's African Americans, that a ship of black men from Santo Domingo came up the Savannah River and conquered Spaniards on the coast long before James Edward Oglethorpe founded Georgia.[1] Historian Jane Landers states that Spaniards and Africans in 1526 landed in the area of Sapelo Sound.[2] There seems to be no doubt that African Americans were with Oglethorpe in 1733, when he founded the colony. The Trustees asked Governor Johnson of South Carolina to hire twenty slaves and four pairs of sawyers to help them clear the land for building homes.

At least three of these slaves escaped on their way to the town.[3] Not surprisingly, one account states that they "did the heaviest work."[4] Though imported into the colony, against their will and solely for their labor, African Americans were destined to remain "a troublesome presence" for their fellow Georgians. White Georgians were obsessed with the compulsion to keep blacks "under due order and subjection."[5] As historian Donald Grant stated, most of Georgia's whites believed that to use blacks as "work animals," they had to be "treated" as such.[6]

That African Americans survived the harsh yoke of slavery, the inhumane ordeal of Jim Crow and its aftermath testifies to their incredible stamina.[7] These pioneer blacks were subsequently returned to South Carolina,[8] but soon several other slaves appeared in Savannah and Augusta. Some were smuggled in; others were sailors aboard boats docking at the port or slave prisoners.[9] Two slaves were jailed in the town in 1734.[10] England's thirteenth colony in North America was conceived as the solution to problems facing the colonists in South Carolina and urban society in Britain. Georgia was to be a bulwark against Spanish attacks from the south and a peculiar nursery for the cultivation of exotic crops. Finally, the colony was to serve as a refuge for indigent Englishmen.[11] Since large land holdings were forbidden, the Trustees believed that a lily white Georgia could manage without slaves.[12]

A scant two years after its founding, some settlers petitioned the trustees for the use of slaves, claiming that the climate of Georgia was more suited for slave labor, and that South Carolina would always be able to out produce Georgia because of the use of slave labor.[13] The authorities also feared that a slave presence would grow to represent a fifth column among the colonists.[14] Partly as a reaction to this pressure, on April 3, 1735, the Trustees published the first explicit prohibition against slavery. This Negro Act was styled, *An Act for Rendering the Colony of Georgia more defensible by Prohibiting the Incorporation and use of black slaves or Negroes into the same.*[15] The colonists were not against the system of slavery. James Oglethorpe himself owned slaves in South Carolina and was a Director and Deputy Governor of the Royal African Company, a slave trading enterprise, which contributed to his fortune.[16] The Negro Act also imposed a fine of fifty pounds sterling on anyone importing slaves into the colony. Some colonists claimed that slaves had been surreptitiously introduced and that the officials had looked the other way.[17]

On December 9, 1738, another 117 freeholders petitioned the Trustees to use rum and slaves and to have a "fee-simple land policy.[18] Any black found in the colony was to become the property of the Trustees. Permission of the Trustees was required to hire, keep, lodge, board, or employ "any person or persons being black or blacks or Negro or Negroes on any account whatsoever." Some settlers petitioned to repeal this new law. Patrick Tailfer claimed that it was next to impossible to progress in the colony without the use of Negroes.[19] A settler from South Carolina introduced slaves into Wilmington Island around 1737. The next year a Savannah Grand Jury requested the repeal of the ban on the use of slaves.[20] In February 1740, one slave was sold by auction in Savannah, and another slave was sold in June.

The presence of slaves, with their penchant to desert to freedom in Florida, made the colonists even more insecure. After 1693, the Spanish crown promised freedom and lands to all slaves who deserted the British and were willing to become Catholics. Hundreds of slaves from South Carolina and Georgia escaped to Spanish Florida. Governor Manuel de Montiano gave some ex British slaves Gracia Real de Santa Teresa de Mose, a village two miles north of St. Augustine.[21]

In 1740, James Oglethorpe, who had earlier used about 200 slaves to work on the fortifications of St. Simon's Island,[22] invaded this village and a contingent of Spaniards and about 800 former slaves from South Carolina and Georgia fighting under the Spanish flag, with their own officers, resisted his attack. Francisco Menendez, a fugitive slave from South Carolina, led part of the contingent. Though routed at first, they regrouped and repelled the English. One report claimed that this victory was due largely to the "Negroes who were aiding the Spanish." Oglethorpe's victory, almost by default,[23] over the Spaniards, two years later in the battle of Bloody Marsh, finally rid the colonists of any further fear of Spanish attack from the south.

The clamor for slaves continued to increase. Two Anglicans the Reverend George Whitefield, one of the principal propagandists of the Great Awakening religious revival then sweeping the country, and his friend James Habersham, played major roles in reviving the colonists' desire for slaves. In 1747, Whitefield bought a plantation in South Carolina and used the profit from slave labor there to subsidize his Savannah orphan home.[24] He was of the opinion that slavery "benefited" the slave, and felt that the presence of slaves in Georgia was part of

God's "providence."

Whitefield claimed that to settle white people in Georgia without the labor of Negroes was like tying their legs and then bidding them to walk. He was convinced that the future of the colony of Georgia and his orphan home was dependent on the labor of slaves.[25] Peter Gordon opined that it was "morally impossible" to advance in Georgia without the use of slaves. Some of the Trustees even conceded that the worsening economic conditions were pressuring them to grant the petition to repeal the Negro law.

In 1740, some settlers requested the right "to use Negroes."[26] Seven years later about 121 "malcontents" signed a petition demanding the right to use slaves. Oglethorpe objected to this move and perhaps agreed with those who claimed: "the idle ones are indeed for Negroes." He believed that the introduction of slaves would ruin the colony.[27] The malcontents wrote a book laying out their views on the advisability of using slaves.[28] Many settlers were leaving the colony for more prosperous areas. Meanwhile, on the cusp of Britain's victory over Spain, the fragile colony's appetite for slaves grew ever stronger. They had gone "stark mad" to use Negroes. By 1747 the presence of slaves in the town was "practically recognized."[29] Savannah's whites were surely aware of the 1739 Stono slave rebellion in neighboring South Carolina where twenty-one whites and forty-four blacks were killed.[30] The proslavery forces were clearly in the ascendancy.

Thomas Stephens, one of the malcontents wrote that it was "essentially necessary" as the very tools the colonists used, to have slaves. Some settlers complained that the white poor, who had been "useless" in England, were equally "useless" in Georgia. As a group, they were said to have "low morality" and "unsatisfactory industry."[31] Some colonists hired or leased slaves from South Carolina.[32] The use of slaves was said to be the "one thing needful" for the survival of the colony. Some even claimed that the colony was "decaying and desolate." As late as 1748, the Trustees were resolved "never to permit the introduction of Negroes into the Colony of Georgia."[33] Yet another petition in 1749 this time instigated and fostered by James Habersham and the Rev. George Whitefield and others accomplished the desired change. By January 1, 1750, slavery was lawful in Georgia.[34]

The Reverend Bartholomew Zouberbuhler, rector of Christ Church, was obviously concerned about the spiritual welfare of the slaves. On Saturday, July 7, 1750, he baptized a black woman, one of the first black baptisms in the colony, and dedicated the newly built church. Zouberbuhler wrote: "I have the pleasure to see many Negroes decently join our Service."[35] He conducted a school for some slaves and stated: "Our school in Savannah at present consists of 41 children and might increase to many more if masters of slaves would show a greater concern to have young Negroes instructed and brought up in the knowledge and fear of God." Moreover, the rector was anxious to obtain the services of a catechist/headmaster for his school. He contacted the associates of Dr. Bray in England and the Trustees assisted him financially in engaging the services of Joseph Ottolenghe, (sometimes written, Ottolenghi), a Jewish convert who was born in Casale, Italy.[36]

The new headmaster/catechist arrived in Savannah in July 1751,[37] and for the next eight years educated slaves. Classes were held three nights each week after work. The permission of the owners was required. Ottolenghe[38] taught his students to read and learn the Lord's Prayer and other prayers "appropriate" for their inferior status in the society, as well as portions of the catechism[39] He reported that many began to read, "Tolerably well." In 1758, Ottolenghe built a large house and used part of it as a schoolroom. This was Georgia's first attempt at integrated education since the headmaster also taught some of "ye white people who could not read or were ignorant of the faith."[40] Writing to the Rev. John Warring on July 12, 1758, 0ttolenghe gave his assessment of the school and his students. He found the slaves "naturally stupid," generally "ill fed," and "barbarously treated."[41]

He found that slave owners bought slaves to profit from their labor.[42] The slaves were said to "behave decently and devoutly joined in the prayers and singing," when they attended services at Christ Church. Ottolenghe soon bought two slaves, "a young fellow and his wife."[43] When the Reverend Zouberbuhler died in 1766, his will provided for the education of his forty-nine slaves.[44] Zouberbuhler also stipulated that any male slave who desired to evangelize his fellow slaves was to be manumitted and employed as a catechist. Cornelius Winter later carried on this work of educating slaves. William Knox engaged two Moravians to instruct slaves, and James Habersham, an ardent supporter of slavery in Savannah, taught many of his slaves to read but in 1775, regretted that many did not demonstrate any "real conversion." Within a few years, interest in educating slaves fell into disfavor. The colony's population experienced a precipitous decline of several thousand by 1742, and in 1752, the authorities surrendered their charter to the crown.

Them Dark Days

"Chattels personal in the hands of their owners and possessors"

In one sense the repeal of the *Negro Act* signaled the failure of Oglethorpe's wild utopian dream of creating a lily-white colony in North America. The new law was entitled, *An Act for repealing and for permitting the importation and use of black slaves or Negroes into the same.*[45] This law also introduced affirmative action legislation into Savannah, as slaves were prohibited from being apprenticed to almost all occupations except that of coopers, for fear that many whites would be unable to compete with slaves for those jobs. The petitioners stated that they did not intend to "employ Negroes" in any "mechanic business," but only in felling trees etc. Marriage between whites and blacks was outlawed. Those whites convicted of "lying with a black could be fined or whipped, but blacks were always to be whipped."[46] Slaves were to be instructed in the Christian faith. The Privy Council in England never approved this 1750 law.[47]

The first slaves came in small batches mainly from South Carolina and the West Indies. Many of the white South Carolinians had actually come from the West Indies and brought their fear of slaves with them.[48] This sharp increase of the slave population partly triggered the first comprehensive slave code of 1755. That law was styled: *An Act for the better ordering and Governing Negroes and other Slaves in the Province.*[49] It adopted all the harshness of South Carolina's code. This law effected a critical change in the lives of African Americans in Savannah. It framed, defined and established the contours of race relations and the power relationship between the two groups. This legal and social foundation enabled those in power to order society in a way which would guarantee white supremacy, the complete subjugation of blacks, and ensured the subsequent exploitation of black labor that was to last for a very, very long time.

The code stipulated that all blacks in the Province and their issue and offspring "born or to be born shall be and they are hereby declared to be and remain forever hereafter absolute slaves and shall follow the condition of the mother and shall be deemed in law to be chattels personal in the hands of their owners and possessors."[50] Other codes followed in 1765 and again in 1770.[51] The 1770 addition guaranteed that the offspring of a white male and a black female would be born a slave.[52] The colonial government placed a minimum bounty of five pounds sterling on slaves caught trying to escape, and the scalps of slaves dead or alive, with ears still attached, went for one pound. The Indians received a gun and three blankets for each returned slave. The economic upswing of the 1760's and the Indian concessions accompanied a very large increase of the slave population. Blacks were to be submissive and were forbidden the use of drums, horns or loud instruments. Whites were to restrain the wanderings and meetings of slaves, and it was illegal for a slave to keep guns or pistols. Slaves needed passes for travel, and it was unlawful for more than seven of them to travel together. They were not allowed to keep boats, canoes, horses, cattle, or to sell goods. Selling goods carried a penalty of twenty lashes, but Savannah slaves could obtain a license to sell fruits or vegetables.[53] The death penalty could be applied to slaves convicted of "carrying poison to others."

African Americans were declared in law to be a species of property transferable at will. An Act passed April 7, 1763, proved clearly that the authorities were having trouble controlling the slaves. [54] Blacks never accepted this definition of their humanity. We have no written documents of what these forerunners thought of their slave condition. Available reports however, give us some idea of what they actually did in response to their slave status. Austin D. Washington[55] chronicled several attempts by slaves to revolt or run away. In 1759, the Royal Legislature established a City Guard to protect the inhabitants.[56] This group used the pass and curfew to regulate the movements of blacks. In 1795, a plot was reported to Major-General Jackson and Colonel Tattnall. As Gamble stated "This fear of the San Domingo Negroes increased rather than diminished with the passing of the years."[57]

Slaves could be put to death for killing a white person, inciting a riot, enticing another slave to run away, or burning property. The owner of an executed slave was compensated for his loss of property. A less serious infraction could result in whipping or being kept in irons. Slaves who committed murder could be executed in public by burning at the stake. About seventeen Georgia slaves suffered this fate from 1755 to 1773.

Slaves resisted slavery by running away.[58] Between 1763 and 1775, over 453 advertisements for runaway slaves were placed in the Georgia Gazette.[59] By 1765, several runaways banded together and established a camp on the north side of the Savannah River, in the pattern of the maroons in Surinam, Jamaica, and other parts of the West Indies. They killed a white man and an Indian. From that location, they attacked plantations on the Savannah River. About three years later, a grand jury complained that a few owners were allowing their slaves to live "at large." In 1766, a grand jury protested that slaves were gathering in large numbers at night for funerals,[60] and had rioted and frequented tippling houses. A Savannah grand jury in 1768 complained about slaves living apart from their owners. Six years later yet another grand jury complained of frequent meetings of slaves in large numbers on Sundays and holidays. A 1783 grand jury complained about slaves roaming the streets without tickets and that they were idle and disorderly. In 1769, a serious attempt at revolt failed because the participants could not agree on tactics.

Later, about three hundred slaves living below the Trustees Garden Bluff attempted to revolt. In 1771, acting Governor James Habersham, a slave owner, dispatched troops to attack some maroon settlements. The next year yet another grand jury reported that runaways were "raining depredations on the inhabitants in that neighborhood with Impunity." Before his death in 1775, the Rev. George Whitefield bequeathed his slaves to the Countess of Huntingdon. Slaves at his orphan home armed themselves, imprisoned the overseer and threatened to die rather surrender and be sold. Several eventually escaped. Further trouble broke out in 1771 between Savannah and Ebenezer.

In June 1772, a grand jury was presented with information that a number of slaves were attacking whites from the Savannah River.[61] A group of British trained slaves, calling themselves, King of England Soldiers, in May of 1786 fled into the swamps.[62] In 1774, Jack, a slave was burnt on the Savannah Commons for setting his owner's house on fire. He denied the charge.[63] Up to 1790 grand juries were one of the means used by the authorities to keep slaves "in due order and subjection."

The authorities reported in 1772, that another posse of slaves was congregating around the Savannah River terrorizing the inhabitants.

Slaves revolted in St. Andrew's Parish in 1779. They killed their overseer, three other whites and wounded many more. Two of the instigators were burned alive.[64] In 1795, Major General James Jackson and Colonel Josiah Tattnall discovered a plot among the slaves in Savannah. The Legislature passed an Act on February 23, 1796, making it "unlawful to import any Negro, mustee or mulatto, free or slave, from any West India or Bahama Island into Georgia."[65] Some slaves even fled to the Cherokees. From 1759, the surveillance of the City Guard helped to keep blacks in control, but by 1806, a permanent City Guard was established.

Two years later a rumor was running through Savannah that a slave revolt was being planned. The Marshal was directed to warn shopkeepers not to sell any powder or lead to slaves.[66] Six years later a committee banned the book, "An Historical Journal of the Revolution of St. Domingo," for fear it would fall into the hands of free people of color and might "inflame in them a desire to repeat on Georgia soil the atrocities of the island." The ordinance was further amended in 1839 when the Guard was empowered to arrest "all slaves and free persons of color who may be found out of his or her house or enclosure after the ringing of the Guard House bell without a pass."[67] In 1839, the City Guard ordinance was amended. Slaves and free persons of color were subject to arrest if found to be "in any streets, lanes, alleys or other places in Savannah without a ticket from his or their owner or overseer."[68] By the late 1850's a bell was installed at President and Whitaker Streets and it was rung "every night at eight o'clock in the winter and nine in o'clock in the summer." As the Federal Writers' Project put it, blacks sang, "Oh Mister Watchman don't ketch me, Ketch that Negro behind dat tree."[69] No general uprising ever took place in Savannah.

It was not until 1766 that slaves were imported from Africa. In that year, about 1,000 slaves were imported into the colony, and during the next six years about 4,718 were imported. From 1750 to 1764, about 1,238 slaves entered the colony and from 1766 until 1775, about 7,950 slaves entered, with the largest group, 1,162, coming in 1774. By 1773, nearly half of Georgia's population was black. Slaves, even those from Africa, as human beings, could not and did not arrive in Savannah "culturally naked." In other words, they brought with them their cultural mores, belief systems and life coping skills. Not surprisingly, a grand jury in Savannah pleaded for the enforcement of the Negro Act in order to prevent slaves from singing, dancing and performing strange funeral rites. Present day Gambia and Sierra Leone accounted for 2,466 or 44.5% of the slaves brought in at one period. The Gold coast, Gambia and Angola were considered the best locations of origin for slaves; Eboes of Nigeria were considered the least desirable. Slaves were expected to work a sixteen-hour day on the neighboring plantations in cultivating rice and indigo and were fed and clothed by their owners. Prime slaves, those fourteen to twenty-five years of age, fetched a higher price than others.

April to September was considered the best time to deliver slave cargoes. Many prominent white Savannah families engaged in the importation, sale and use of slaves. Cowper and Telfair Company was one of the first firms to import slaves. The slave trade also positively affected other parts of Savannah's business activity. Slavers John Graham, Joseph Clay and James Habersham did a brisk trade but perhaps the most aggressive were John Inglis and Nathaniel Hall who brought in nine shiploads between 1766 and 1770. An Act of April 1763 required the captain of a slave ship to obtain a health certificate under a penalty of 500 pounds sterling.[70] Such was the fear of diseases, especially when more slaves were imported from Africa, that in the 1760's, the authorities bought a 104-acre estate on the north western end of Tybee Island near the mouth of the Savannah river and constructed a Lazaretto for the quarantine and hospitalization of slaves.[71] They built a two-story tabby structure 40 feet by 20 with 20-foot walls. A keeper's house 16 by 24 feet also of tabby was built nearby.[72]

All vessels with ten or more slaves had to stop at the Lazaretto for about ten days. Those slaves who had survived the "middle passage" across the Atlantic Ocean, had to disembark, often still in shackles, and remain on the shore for several hours, for cleansing and purifying them of any malignant or contagious distempers.[73] Slaves who died at the Lazaretto were buried on the Island at least five feet under ground. A doctor had to certify the health of the cargo before the captain was allowed to proceed to the port of Savannah. When cleared, the ship then proceeded to the city where many slaves were kept in yards until sale. Some slaves were rubbed down with oil before sale. An agent, who usually received five per cent of the gross, would advertise the sale in the local paper. Later another Lazaretto was built at Cedar Hammock near Sunbury. The price of slaves varied according to their sex, health condition and age. A healthy male slave could be sold for between 30 and 40 pounds sterling.[74] West Indian planters were accused of dumping some of their unruly slaves on the Savannah market. The price of slaves rose in the late 1760's. Most of the slaves landing in the town were sold to the neighboring plantations. Every arriving slave ship was taxed.

Slaves working in the neighboring rice fields, the staple crop of the day, experienced great difficulty during the winter months. Some slaves committed suicide, apparently with the expectation of resurrection in their homeland. Others were lost during the seasoning process. Many slaves brought in from other locations had experience in several trades. Timber products were very profitable during this period. Slaves worked as sawyers, felling trees, splitting shingles, or making barrel staves and tanning. In the tidewater area of South Georgia where slaves were the majority of the population, most of them worked in agriculture. Within three years, the colonists exported more than three thousand barrels of rice. The economic advantage of slavery thus needed no further proof.

Advertisements in the local press about runaways or requests for workers give a clear picture of the importance of blacks to the economy. Savannah's slaves worked on the waterfront loading the trading ships and were employed as skilled and unskilled laborers. Some worked as shipwrights, caulkers, sawyers, coopers, brick makers, carpenters, artisans and seamen on the boats plying the Savannah River. A few slaves became very proficient pilots. Others were hired out,[75] from dawn until dusk for one shilling and six pence. Those who dared to refuse to work under these conditions could receive thirty lashes "on the bare back." These slaves had to wear a public badge or ticket to work away from their owners. Slaves who had experience in planting rice in Africa were sold at a higher price. Rice was planted in March and harvested in September. Men, women and children all worked in the production of this crop.[76]

The Ethiopian Regiment

Someone once said: "to the victor falls the lot of writing the history." White authors have usually slighted or ignored the contributions of blacks to Savannah and American history thereby unwittingly distorting both accounts in the process. Part of the problem in this instance, was caused by the fact that a fire destroyed the National Palace in Haiti in 1869. French and British reports deal mainly with the activity of their own nationals. Partly to remedy this situation, Theophilus G. Steward, a black army chaplain, in 1899, published a seminal account of black Haitians in the battle for Savannah. The siege of Savannah in 1779, found the town populated by about 2,000 whites, 5,000 slaves and a few hundred Indians, perched on a bluff ringed by rice fields and swamps.

Both sides used slaves under their control in some form during the decisive battle for Savannah. John Murray, the Earl of Dunmore, Governor of Virginia, had promised freedom to slaves who supported the British against the colonials. The colonial government passed a law in 1777, to utilize slaves in the event of hostilities, promising slaves freedom in exchange for their support.[77] This Ethiopian Regiment, as it was called, was to be part of the British effort to maintain control of the Colonies in North America. In the Savannah theatre, a year later, Lt. Col. Archibald Campbell with the help of slaves expelled the American troops under General Robert Howe and Great Britain regained control of Savannah. The British authorities amassed a force of regulars, loyalists, Indians, and blacks. Major General Augustin Prevost had about 250 armed blacks, some brought in from South Carolina, whom he found "very useful in Savannah." Slaves were hired out each day at a set fee to work as carpenters, sawyers and wheelwrights. Governor James Wright "impressed" or forced, 500 slaves to work on the fortifications and batteries around the city, especially the southeastern section of the city, near East Broad and Liberty Streets.

The British used blacks as spies and their wide knowledge of the waterways proved incalculably beneficial. The slave Sampson piloted the British into Savannah. Slaves received bounties for capturing Hessian soldiers who deserted their British officers. They were paid two guineas per head, dead or alive, and slave children were paid to recover inoperative French explosives. It seems certain from several reports that many blacks were armed and fought alongside the British. Mark King testified under an oath that 150 blacks were armed and equipped as infantry by the British in this area. Blacks composed about one-third of the British forces in the siege of Augusta in May 1781.[78] Blacks also served as musicians in the British Army.[79] Governor Wright was of the opinion that blacks contributed "vastly to our defense and safety." The American leader Colonel Andrew Pickins reported killing sixty black soldiers in an encampment near Savannah. African Americans who supported the British were also greatly influenced by the Savannah experience. In 1779, the Governor's Council was asked to suppress the large number of slaves who roamed the town and the countryside, many with firearms and other offensive weapon.

The British recaptured Savannah in 1778, due in part, to information provided by Quamino Dolly,[80] a black oyster man, sometimes called Quash, who showed them, for a price,[81] a secret path through the swamp.[82] Thomas L. Stokes wondered why Dolly "betrayed" the American side,[83] as though slavery itself was not a sufficient grievance to trigger a dash for freedom. The British then attacked the patriots from the rear and captured Savannah.[84] Dolly was the patriarch of a remarkable local black family. He bought his own freedom and that of some of his relatives and owned a slave and a lot in the Trustees Garden. When he died in 1810, he left four slaves and cows to his wife. From 1786 to 1810, four members of his family bought their freedom and three bought 12 slaves, while two members owned two parcels of land.[85]

About 200 were drafted into fatigue duty for the British forces.[86] Over 300 slaves worked on the fortifications to defend the town from attack.[87] When the British finally left Savannah in July 1782, they took with them, between 3,500 and 5,000 loyal blacks. No one knows the exact number. This first black exodus had the effect of sending about 1,568 African Americans to Jamaica, other parts of the West Indies, Canada and Africa. Some African Americans ended up as the nucleus of black British troops in the West Indies. Several who went to England suffered abuse at the hands of the English, though many became free in the process.

Later a contingent of about 300 slaves, from Georgia and South Carolina, who formerly fought with the British under Major Moncrief, reorganized and one group under Captain Lewis took the name King of England Soldiers. Captain Cudjoe led another faction. They took advantage of the almost total fog and chaos of the times, and attempted to safeguard their freedom[88] and avoid a return to slavery.

They established a base near the swamps of the Savannah River, a piece of land in Belle Isle Swamp, about 20 miles west of the town. This area was 700 yards long and 120 yards wide. From that location, they wreaked havoc on settlers on both sides of the Savannah River for several years until the combined militia of Georgia, and South Carolina and by some Catawba Indians routed them in 1786. In this and many other ways, African Americans proved themselves to have been more than simply spectators in the drama then unfolding in Savannah.

French Admiral Count Jean Baptiste d'Estaing sought volunteers in Saint Domingue, later called Haiti, for his continental army. Between 545 and 800 free mulattoes and blacks left the Island with him on August 15, 1779, for Savannah. These men were part of a militia, which the Marquis de Chateau-Mornad organized in 1716. They were well trained and had proven themselves disciplined soldiers. Their motto was "to die rather than fail." These soldiers were also called Fontages, since they were under the command of Viscount de Fontages. They formed part of a flotilla of some forty ships with about 3,500 troops which arrived off the coast of the city on September 12, 1779,[89] and joined Polish Count Casimir Pulaski and more than 1,000 continentals.

The presence of these black soldiers[90] under French command must have inflated the hearts of local African Americans. Count d'Estaing decided to delay his attack on the English and perhaps, thereby, probably doomed his likelihood of success.[91] According to Gerard M. Laurent, the Haitian forces saved the continental army from "a massacre" by the English troops. They did not let themselves be intimidated by the enemy bullets nor by the furious attack ordered by General Augustin Prevost.

One thing seems certain, however, this motley contingent of black Haitians learned a great deal from their Savannah experience. They returned home, and in 1791, carried out the first successful slave revolt in the Americas. Henri Christophe, was born a slave in Grenada in 1767, and participated in the Siege of Savannah.[92] He became President of Haiti in 1806 and king of Northern Haiti in 1811. Jean Baptiste Villatte, Louise Jacques Beauvais, Martial Basse, Andre Rigaud, and others who also fought in Savannah, and later joined Simon Bolivar to liberate Mexico and several South American countries. This slave revolt in Haiti also contributed to the influx of French-speaking blacks into the city.

In 1779, the American Continental Congress approved a plan for the slaves that would give them their freedom with their swords. Delegates from Georgia and South Carolina vehemently resisted this approach. A few slaves captured by the patriots were put to work at Tybee. African Americans, Austin Dabney and David Monday, received their freedom for service to the American side. Dabney was given 112 acres of land. Slave kidnapping occurred on both sides of the conflict. The American patriots confiscated the British Governor's 523 slaves valued at 27,586 pounds sterling. After the departure of the English the Americans decided to pay government debts using confiscated slaves as currency. Various officers received about 70 slaves under this system. Slaves also functioned as booty during the war. The American Revolution had a considerable impact on African Americans in Savannah. For the first time they saw themselves as having some ability to influence events in their lives. They had performed roles as soldiers, support forces and even as a medium of commerce.

The 1779 battle for the Springhill Redoubt had blacks fighting on the side of the British, fighting other blacks on the side of the Americans, and simultaneously, one assumes, fighting for their own freedom. The black population fell as percentage of the population, from 36% in 1773, to 36% in 1776. The absence of a stable slave labor force had a very negative effect on the economy. Rice production suffered as perhaps thousands of slaves escaped during the war. Planting rice never regained its importance for by the 1790's cotton was about to dominate the scene. By this time, Georgia had begun to savor the profitability of slave labor, and though they fought for their own freedom from British domination, even the venerated Tondee Tavern crowd, saw nothing incongruous in keeping these benighted Africans in servitude.

Forgotten Confederates?

Slavery and Confederacy are the two uncomfortably yoked Siamese twins of Southern history. Focusing on them as agents of a shared past has always been difficult. The authorities of British Savannah successfully used some armed slaves in their attempt to regain control of the town. Confederate Savannah, however, could not bring itself to arm blacks even when its very existence was in jeopardy. Vice President Alexander H. Stephens in his March 21, 1861, speech in Savannah stated his understanding of the issue at hand. He asserted that contrary to Northern views on the issue, the Confederacy was,

> "Founded upon exactly the opposite idea; its foundations are laid, its cornerstone rests, upon the great truth that the Negro is not equal to the white man; that slavery, subordination to the superior race, is his natural and moral condition. This our new Government, is the first, in the history of the world, based on this great physical, philosophical, and moral truth."[93]

William H. Fleming found a "fatal flaw in the logic," of Stephen's racial superiority doctrine as the justification of black slavery.[94] Nevertheless, it is also true that hundreds of African Americans contributed to the cause of

Confederate Savannah.

In May 1861, a free person of color and a slave visited the local Counting Room. After they left it was discovered that "two ten-dollar subscriptions were voluntarily contributed, one by a free Negro and the other by a slave of this city. They desired to the extent of their ability to prove their devotion to the cause of the South."[95]

That same month a number of slaves were sent to Tybee to work on the fortification. The response of the owners was said to have been "most generous and patriotic."[96] A writer, "commonwealth," in a letter to the editor of the local paper, had occasion to refer to free blacks as "drones in the hive."[97] Two days later the following reply was published,

> "The remarks of your correspondent "commonwealth," in your issue of the 4th Inst., are worthy of consideration. I am willing to be taxed, even to my last dollar, for the defence of the honor and rights of the South. The burdens should be borne by all-All classes of the community are bound to contribute their aid to the public defence. The allusion to the "free Negro population," as "drones in the hive," is not altogether well merited.
>
> As early as April last, sixty odd of the free colored men of this city made a written tender to his Excellency the Governor, of their services in any capacity in which he would employ them. It was not their fault that their services were not accepted. These were not the men who spend their time in "grog-shops, and in indolence and vice," but the best men of their class in the city, who are always ready to volunteer their labor and services for the good of the community.
>
> The free colored women, actuated by the same public spirit, have tendered their services to General Lawton to make up one hundred suits of clothes for our brave volunteers, and are now actually engaged at the work. They are also ready to act as nurses for the sick, and willing to work so long as a Southern soldier shall need a garment.
>
> The loyalty of this class of our population has never been questioned. No people were ever more attached to the government that protects them.
>
> During the war of 1812 the free colored men of this city rendered signal services as a corps of pioneers and in working on the fortifications. The present colored population will require no compulsion to labor in the public service. When required, they will cheerfully engage in any labor, which may be assigned to them."—Justice [98]

In the early part of July the local press listed the names of the free colored volunteers who worked on the fortifications around the city. The officer in charge at Fort Pulaski discharged,

> "Simon Mirault, Levy Moore, Robert Low, Geo Bulloch, Robert Woodhouse, Eugene Treuchhholet, James Bourke, Henry Jenckes, Prince Kandy, James Clarke, Alex Gunn, William Kiverns, Sampson Richards, Scipio Gordon, Geo Jones, Adam Dolly, James Williams, Geo Thompson, Benjamin Murel, Henry Savoy, Matthew Jones, William Woodhouse and Mitchell Boufillet." They had "faithfully served the time for which they volunteered." The paper further added: "We understand that another detachment of twenty four will go down to the fort on Thursday.[99]

General David Hunter of the Union Forces "signalized his occupation of Fort Pulaski by issuing an order freeing the slaves on Cockspur Island and in Fort Pulaski."[100] In June, a published advertisement informed the public that 1,000 Negroes were needed for "important works in the neighborhood of Savannah." Owners were requested to "furnish this force without delay."[101] The army requested one-fourth of the "working force of planters" to report at Savannah "or otherwise measures will be taken to impress in this section of the state."[102] The government held itself responsible for the value of such slaves should they be killed or fall into the enemy's hands. During the period, about 3,000 slaves and free blacks worked for the Confederate cause. Some worked on boats plying the rivers as wagon drivers, hospital helpers or body servants. Both sides used slaves.

The authorities estimated that about one-tenth of the slave population would be needed.[103] Brig. Gen. W. H. Mercer received several requests from slave owners to return their slaves working on the fortifications around Savannah.[104] A letter of the Confederate Secretary of War making a "requisition upon the State of Georgia for fifteen hundred able-bodied Negroes to work on the defenses of Savannah were also received.[105] To make matters even worse slaves were running away from the fortifications. Bob, the slave of R. A. Allen of Richmond County, runaway and his owner offered a reward of $25 for his return.[106]

By November, General H. M. Mercer made requisition for 1,500 slaves to work on the Savannah fortifications.[107] The Southern Confederacy claimed "our Negroes have been an element of strength in this struggle, in cultivating our fields, whilst our laboring white men have taken up arms in the cause of freedom."[108]. In early October, the local paper carried the advertisement "Negroes Wanted." The authorities offered to pay owners $16 per month "for good men," and $13 per month "for good women." The government also offered to pay for those slaves who absconded from the work detail or deserted to the enemy.[109] By December 26, no tickets were counter-signed for slaves or free persons of color to travel by rail.[110] The mayor banned the issuance of passes for slaves or free people of color to travel on either of the two railroads in the city.[111]

In April 1863 Senator Gordon of Chatham County supported a bill that sought to repeal the ban on teaching blacks to read or preach. He claimed that the older generation saw slavery as a "necessary evil," and in their judgment it was their mission to improve and ameliorate it. Later the notion that slavery was of divine disposition gained some credence.[112] In March 1863 a call went out for 25 Negro teamsters and laborers.[113] Brig. Gen. Mercer requested one fourth of the working force of planters to report to Savannah or else they would be impressed.[114]

In August 1863, General Hugh Mercer, a slave owner himself, informed other slave owners that he had received authority from the Secretary of War to "impress," i.e. order, a sufficient number of slaves, to construct fortifications necessary for the defense of the city. The owners were asked to send one fifth of their able-bodied male slaves for whom transportation will be furnished and wages paid at the rate of $25 per month. Ten able-bodied Negroes to "run on my boats," were needed.[115] A "citizen" in a letter to the editor of the *Daily Morning News* complained to the city fathers that it was impossible to walk the streets without encountering a Negro with a cigar in his mouth and blowing smoke in the faces of passersby. [116]

The authorities at Proctor's Point captured a boat full of Negroes attempting to escape to the Union forces.[117] Twenty blacks attempted to escape from the city. All but two drowned in this effort. Three days later, a pilot discovered two canoes filled with nineteen Negroes.[118] The local paper was somewhat agitated about the possibility of arming slaves as a last resort. All freepersons of color of sixteen years and over were required to register their names in the ordinary's office.[119] In October the Milledgeville Recorder was quoted advocating using blacks in a subordinate position but "never, never, we say, with arms in their hands."[120] The Connecticut Times reported that the Union's "Negro regiment from St. Mary's has just returned after burning the town."[121]

Through it all, some white Savannahians were making a brisk dollar, selling slaves. J. A. Stevenson announced that he had "Negroes for sale privately at my mart. 108 Bryan Street." General Wylly, Esq., "sold before the Court House, eighty-one Negroes belonging to the estate of John S. Montmollin, the entire lot bringing ninety thousand four hundred dollars." The General sold at the Court House, "Ninety Negroes of all ages and sizes, belonging to the estate of Randolph Spalding, deceased." The total amount of the sale was $114,930. The average price was $1,277.[122] A. H. Sadler and James M. Hines used the *Daily Morning News* of July 2, 1864 to announce that they had taken over the Negro Mart of the late Captain Joseph Bryan near Monument Square and would "buy and sell Negroes and other property on commission."

A clash erupted between white and colored troops at the lower end of Bay Street between detachments of the 153rd New York Volunteers and the 103 U.S., S.C. Troops, who were detailed to assist in unloading government vessels.[123] Governor Jenkins requested the Federal government to remove the Negro troops from the South.[124] Former provisional Governor Johnson went to Washington with the same request.[125] As to why the war was fought, we have seen a war begun for the perpetuation of slavery result in the declaration by the most powerful of the nations of the earth, that it shall no longer exist."[126]

Jackson B. Shefthall, a mulatto butcher, who supplied beef to the Confederate forces for a fee, later claimed that he was forced to do so. He worked at Fort Pulaski. Several other black butchers also aided the Confederate cause.[127] The largest black slave owner in the area, Anthony Odingsells[128] earned money from the Confederates but lost his slaves when Fort McAllister surrendered to Sherman's forces.

Black Frank, [129] a slave of the Stiles family, was born around the same time as his close friend and owner George Stiles. They were inseparable as children growing up, Frank played drums and George played the piano. Frank and George went off to war together where Frank's music "brought cheer to the men in camp." They both returned to the city after the war and continued to be inseparable.[130] It was said that Frank "held his head high and walked as if he owned cotton in Augusta." Frank became active in the local black militia. George Stiles preceded him in death.[131] In life not even the Civil War could separate Frank and George.

In death however, Savannah's race mores accomplished the impossible. Frank now lies in black Laurel Grove South Cemetery, while George lies in white Laurel Grove North Cemetery. And it may be, as the Negro Spiritual has it, "their eyes are watching God" for an explanation of the separation. Another slave David Footman also went off to war with his owner Neal Habersham, but he never returned to the city. Several black musicians served in the Confederate cause.[132] Henry J. Kennedy wrote that before the Civil War the fife and drum units were "all blacks."[133] These African American musicians "participated in all of the functions of the Guards from its founding." Their best-loved piece of music was the "Savannah Volunteer Guards Quick Step," composed by David Bell.

Joe Parkman, "old Joe,"[134] a slave fifer, was the leader of music for the Savannah Volunteers.[135] During the Civil War, he was mustered with Company A and saw service, among other places, at Sailor's Creek near the Appomattox Court House. The thirsty Parkman picked up a bottle, drank its contents, and died soon afterwards. He was buried "with military honors," in an unmarked grave in Virginia. As Henry Kennedy wrote, "there was never a man more devoted to the Guards than he. Faithful to the last, he died in their service."[136] Free blacks Joe Verdery and Jack Bolton, were kettle drummers while Louis DuBross, was a fifer. Slave Dave

Ellison was a bass drummer.

Louis DuBross and Joe Verdery withdrew from the Guards when they were called up for service in the Civil War. Free persons of color Henry McCleskey and George Postell also served with the Guards while Dave Ellison's health prevented him from serving.[137] These blacks served at Fort Boggs, Savannah, Battery Gregg, South Carolina, and in Virginia. William Starr Basinger claimed, "When the writer of these pages recalls the unswerving fidelity of these Negroes, the cheerfulness with which they encountered dangers, hardships and privations common to all, he feels that it would be most unjust, in narrating the history of the Corps during the eventful period of the War, to omit honorable mention of these, its faithful servants."

William Waters, born in 1832, a drum sergeant with the Republican Blues, went off to war with the group.[138] Cyrus Robinson, Hamilton, Praylor, Weeks, Burney Houston served the Union cause. Josiah Jenkins of Savannah, a 23-year-old farmer, enlisted in the Union Navy in Philadelphia. Joseph De Villars, a 28-year-old Savannah carpenter, enlisted in New York. Savannahian Alexander Anderson, a 22-year-old, enlisted in Philadelphia. Prince Beatty, a 17-year-old steward from Savannah, enlisted in Philadelphia. Old Tom, born in 1808 in Savannah was the slave of Captain John Wheaton and served with him during the Civil War. A Southern Cross was placed on his grave in Laurel Grove Cemetery South.[139]

Edward Wicks was born in Savannah in March 1842 and joined First Bryan Baptist Church in 1859. Wicks served as a deacon of his church for 50 years and clerk for 34 years. He served in the Union forces during the Civil War and after the war was adjutant of the Robert G. Shaw Post of the Grand Army of the Republic. He was a member of Myrtle Lodge of Odd Fellows and the Deacons' Union.[140] The contribution of two other African American Savannahians was even more remarkable. John H. Deveaux, while still a youngster, served with the Confederate Mosquito Fleet which protected the city by attacking Union ships in the area. He was with Lieutenant Thomas Postell Pelot when the Water Witch was attacked on December 19, 1864. Pelot lost his life in the attack and it fell to Deveaux to transport Pelot's body back to the city.

Moses Dallas, a slave pilot, was perhaps the most spectacular black individual involved on the side of the Confederates and apparently also on the side of the Union forces. One account claims that he was born in Duval County, Florida, but lived in Savannah where he and his wife eventually bought their freedom. They were apparently fairly well off and he was reputed to be one of the "best pilots in the area." Dallas was involved in the incident with the USS Water Witch in Ossabaw Sound, with John Deveaux and Lieutenant Thomas Postell Pelot. One report of the incident states that Dallas died during the altercation. Another account claims that he was a Florida slave who joined the Union Navy but later deserted to the Confederate side and served as a pilot. Other sources also, postulate that he escaped from the Confederates and enlisted in the Union Navy. Valuska reports that one, Moses Dallas, a 23-year-old Savannahian waiter, enlisted in New York. After the war, Dallas and his wife Harriet lived in Florida. Richard Riley, in an unpublished article, refers to Moses Dallas as the "forgotten, black Savannah Confederate hero."

Governor Charles Jenkins contacted the President "importuning him, in the name of people who are quiet and orderly and need no military restraint of any kind, to remove the Negro troops from the state."[141] A week later, the Columbus Enquirer reported that ex-provisional Governor W. B. Johnson was intervening with the Federal Government regarding the "pernicious effects of keeping garrisons of colored troops in the South."[142] At least four black Union regiments troops were stationed in the city during 1865, including the 54th Massachusetts. In addition, in March 1865 the 1st. South Carolina Volunteers, renamed the 33rd United States Colored Troops in 1864, arrived in Savannah.[143] There were about 2,300 black Union troops in the city.[144] The Savannah Republican reported that the black troops exhibited "a soldierly manner" and showed a "high state of perfection" at military parades. The companies C., D., and G of the 103rd United States Colored Troops left by steamer for Fort Pulaski.[145]

Historian Henry W. Grady wrote in 1889, "history has no parallel to the faith kept by the Negro in the South during the war."[146] have both presented a more balanced view of the role of blacks. Unfortunately, very few African Americans have left us written reports on their experiences in Savannah.

According to Ed Jackson, several black Federal troops were stationed in Savannah and its environs, although "no black troops served with General Sherman." The first black regiment, the First South Carolina, was formed May 9, 1862 in Beaufort, South Carolina after the fall of Hilton Head Island. In January 1865, the 55th Massachusetts moved to Savannah. Many of the companies "taking up command in the batteries around the city." Company "F" "of the 55th Massachusetts "was stationed at Old Fort Jackson from early January until February 2, 1865."[147] Members of the ex-Union soldiers organization composed of colored men who had served in the Federal army held a meeting at their Hall. Abraham Burke was appointed secretary.[148]

Captain Franklin F. Jones was born in Savannah during the dark days of slavery. He conducted a successful business in the city market, "having as his patrons many of the more prominent families." This accommodating butcher at stall 31 in the city market and always kept "on hand a supply of best Beef etc.,"[149] His strict application to business and excellent service rendered won him high praise.

Jones received his commission as captain of the Savannah Hussars in 1887.[150] In his early years, Jones was prominent in many civic movements and encouraged African Americans to enter business. He was an ardent supporter of the Savannah Tribune and one of its consistent advertisers. Captain Jones fought in the Civil War having enlisted in his teens in the Union forces. His ability was soon recognized and he was promoted to the rank of Sergeant in his Company.

First Battalion Colored

The arrival of black Union soldiers in Savannah in 1865 must have frayed the edges of both sides of the city's racial nerve center. For local African Americans, their presence must have represented an important symbol of citizenship and new status in society. They must have marveled at the manner in which black soldiers conducted themselves in relations with their white officers and the self-confidence with which they interacted with the white citizenry.

Whites, on the other hand, must have been horrified that one of their worst fears had been realized: blacks appeared to be their equals. For a time they accepted what, under the circumstances, could not be avoided. Within months after the departure of the black troops in 1866, the Republican-Party-affiliated Union leagues began organizing groups in and around Savannah. By February 1868, blacks had held an unauthorized meeting in Chippewa Square. This meeting was disbanded but continued at First African Baptist Church. The authorities intervened and a small riot broke out in which pistols, rock, and clubs were freely used. Some twenty-six persons were arrested.[151]

In July, a riot started in Yamacraw. The local press traced this action to the riotous disposition of blacks and the assembling of about 800 of them on King's Plantation, some five miles from the city. There, the blacks listened to what were called inflammatory speeches by black scoundrels, and then, accompanied by fifes and drums, with many armed with muskets or shot guns, they drilled in military formation. A reporter was particularly upset at "the number of white villains who teach the Negroes to believe that they are superiors of the whites and that the lands belong to them and urged them to assert what they call their rights." It was felt that these assemblies "bode no good for white people of this section and should be stopped, no matter what the cost." A white attorney, Elias Yulee, admonished blacks to put aside "your guns and pistols and quit drilling." Shortly thereafter, a young white leader, Captain John R. Dillon, scion of a well-known Catholic family, went to Tennessee took a secret oath and was inducted in the Ku Klux Klan. On his return to the city, Dillon established a local chapter of the Ku Klux Klan.[152]

However, the spark lit by the presence of black Union troops and Savannah's love affair with soldiers and parades were not to be snuffed out. Almost spontaneously, black military entities sprouted into existence. Some emerged out of former fire companies. A group of butchers produced a military unit. These new militia organizations soon came to the attention of the state. The legislature passed a law August 24, 1872, to regulate all military companies. Priority was given to those units established before 1861. Black units were, of course, constituted after that date. The United States War Department, on March 21, 1873, issued general order

#39 which provided funding for all state units. By then, some 1,500 men were organized in Savannah's black militia and those in Augusta, Macon and Atlanta. Captain John Gardner headed the Chatham Light Infantry, Captain William Woodhouse the Forest City Light Infantry and Captain Charles E. West the Hunter Zouves. Captain Robert H. Goodman commanded the Union Lincoln Guards.

The white press reported "Some fifty colored men with muskets and fantastic dress, calling themselves the Lincoln Guards and Chatham Light Infantry paraded themselves through several streets. The Lincoln Guards marched into the customhouse during business hours to obtain a speech from Col. James Atkins, collector of the Port. The collector declined to speak and dismissed the deluded people from his presence. The demonstration was in commemoration of the anniversary of freedom in Liberia."[153] The Grant Calvary of Charleston visited the Savannah Hussars of Savannah. The two groups paraded around town followed by "the usual crowds of gleeful colored folks." Captain William Woodhouse of the Forest City Light Infantry led the Savannah contingent. After the parade, the colored troops retired to Woodlawn Park, beyond the canal, where the day was "pleasantly spent."

Oddly enough the paper complimented the black troops, stating: "the appearance of the Savannah colored companies was quite credible."[154] The paper probably later regretted that out of character compliment to the colored troops. Louis B. Toomer and Richard (most likely John) Deveaux made speeches, at a collation black troops held at McIntire Hall and advised their listeners to "stick together and get control of the offices." The paper continued, Deveaux "said many naughty things" about the Savannah press. We "emphatically deny any injustice done his race. He has adopted the wrong method of rectifying the imaginary evil."[155] Around that time the white paper reported without comment: "The first detachment of Negro soldiers enlisted in this city for the colored regiment off on the frontier service left this afternoon via the western and southern Railroad."[156] The Savannah Light Infantry was the second oldest company in the First Battalion Infantry Georgia State Troops Colored. Francis Mc Neil, Henry Taylor and Isaiah Castelow were foremen in an Ax company. In 1872 the group formed itself into the Colored Volunteers and later changed their name to the Savannah Light Infantry with Captain Isaiah Castelow as commander. First lieutenant William H. Royall, Charles Jackson, Anderson Wiggins and William Raiford were the junior lieutenants. Later Major William Royall was elected captain.[157]

The first statewide prize drill of African American troops took place May 27, 1878. The Savannah Morning News regarded the event as "an eventful day in the history of the colored people of Savannah, and will long be remembered by them and their friends from neighboring cities." Governor Alfred H. Colquitt took part and was escorted to Pulaski House by the Savannah Hussars. The visiting troops from Macon and Augusta together with the locals, assembled on South Broad Street under the sharp eye of their commander, Captain William H. Woodhouse. At four o'clock, the drill began. Each contest lasted about thirty minutes. At the end of the drill, Chatham Light Infantry was declared the winner. This Company was the second oldest of the black troops and had a long and honorable record. Soon after the Civil War, the men were members of an ax company of the city's fire department. After the official events "the various companies with their guests indulged in social enjoyment at balls and suppers."

In 1872, the group became the Colored Volunteers and afterwards the name was changed to the Savannah Light Infantry with Captain Isaiah Castelow as commander. First Lieutenant William H. Royall was Captain, and Charles Jackson, Anderson Wiggins and William Raiford were Junior Lieutenants. Finally, all partook of a round of suppers, balls and games. The Forest City Light Infantry was the only black group to receive arms from the state. Chatham Light had built a two-story armory on Montgomery Street, between Gaston and Huntington Streets. They drilled at least once each week and held parades each month.

Black musicians even serenaded the press: "The Morning News office was yesterday complimented by a serenade from the Braham Club, composed of Negro men in this city. The compliment evinces the sentiments entertained for the Morning News by the respectable class of colored people." [158] In 1876, a legislative committee was set up to regulate troops in Georgia. No blacks were on the committee. On July 20, 1880, special order #59 constituted all black troops into the First Battalion Georgia Volunteers Colored, with William H. Woodhouse, a Lieutenant Colonel, in command.

William H. Woodhouse was born in Charleston South Carolina, July 5, 1830 and was a charter member of the Mutual Benevolent Society, and one of the founders of Mount Mariah Masonic Lodge. He helped organize the Republican Party in Savannah. The captain was a member of a well-known black family and was a carpenter by trade. At a meeting of the officers of the First Colored Battalion Georgia Volunteers at the Lincoln Guards Hall, with Captain J. H. Gardner in the chair and Louis B. Toomer acting secretary, Woodhouse was unanimously chosen as the candidate for Lieutenant Colonel, to be voted for at the election ordered by the governor Colquitt.[159] Justice William H. Woodhouse, Justice of the peace of the Fourth District, was on trial in Superior Court for malfeasance in office. The jury found him guilty.[160] Woodhouse later resigned his military position and John H. Deveaux took command of the troops.

Though black troops were now a Battalion, they were still besieged by two inescapable handicaps. The local press relentlessly ridiculed the slightest foible committed by any black soldier but remained silent when the state disbursed grossly inadequate allotments to the black troops in the provision of supplies and opportunities for training. James R. Middleton was elected captain of the Forest City Light Infantry and Joseph L. Mirault second lieutenant. The Oglethorpe brass band played for the event.[161] The Colquitt Blues received 32 Springfield rifles and the Lone Star Cadets 8 additional guns.[162]

On May 29, 1887, the First Battalion paraded in honor of the anniversary of the passing of the 15th amendment. Lieutenant Colonel John H. Deveaux commanded his troops and A.K. Des Verney was Adjutant. A Bowman was Quartermaster, and T. Sanders was Paymaster. The Union Lincoln Guards were commanded by Lieutenant J.H. Hammund: The Colquitt Blues by Captain J.H. Carter; The Lone Star Cadets were led by Captain P. A. D. Lloyd and the Chatham Light Infantry by Captain Julius Maxwell. Lieutenant Williams headed the Forest City Light Infantry. Captain W.H. Royal headed the Savannah Light Infantry. Captain W.H. Stiles led the Georgia Light Infantry. Captain W. H. Bell headed the Savannah Hussars.

From the days of slavery, blacks were known for their love of clothes and their sense of fashion. The black troops were true to this tradition. The Colquitt Blues wore dark blue uniforms trimmed with light blue and gold lace and white cross belts. The beaver hat was fitted with a white plume with a blue tip. Wanamaker & Brown of Philadelphia made the uniforms. Most military groups had a lady's auxiliary and never failed to seize an opportunity to enjoy a good parade and the sheer fun and social prestige connected with soldiering. Participating in this organization gave the black troops a very high degree of stature and an opportunity to show their skills, and develop a sense of race pride and unity. Dr. T. James Davis received his commission as Surgeon of the First Battalion Georgia Volunteers in 1888.[163]

During the 1890's, African Americans experienced a period of increased racism and deprivation. In Georgia, African Americans lost the little political leverage they exerted as Democrats and Populists competed for their votes. White primaries finally excluded blacks from political activities. Though they barely met standards in 1892 and 1893, the writing was on the wall. Deveaux and his men used their own money to support themselves. In 1895, black troops received a negative report from inspection. The Union Lincoln Guards, the Lone Star Cadets, the Savannah Hussars, and the Georgia Artillery fell below the minimum requirement and were recommended for disbandment. Colonel John H. Deveaux frequently complained against the injustice. In April 1899, the Lone Star Cadets and the Savannah Hussars made up mostly of butchers were disbanded. The Forest City Light Infantry and the Lincoln Union Guards were consolidated, and the Georgia artillery was granted a reprieve. Deveaux's offer to lead his troops in the Spanish American War was refused.

The Forest City Cadets were organized for boys 12 to 14 years. G.W. Rhan was captain; B. Lewis and Edward W. Middleton were lieutenants. The well laid plans of the authorities came to fruition and by 1892 only four of twenty units, from a high of 20 earlier survived in 1889, and by 1901, the Georgia Artillery was the only one in the country.[164] The First Battalion paraded in honor of the Fifteenth

Amendment, under the command of major William H. Royall. Captain F. F. Jones was in command of the Savannah Hussars.[165]

Judge George A. Davison (1854-1893) was born in Savannah August 2, 1854. He was elected magistrate of the 5th. G. M. district in 1889 and was re-elected in the subsequent election and showed himself "a faithful and true guardian of the trust conferred in him by his constituents." He amassed "considerable property and his relations with the legal fraternity were of the most cordial kind."

Davison was connected with the newspaper the Weekly Echo. Judge Davison was very interested in military affairs and organized the Georgia Cadets, a juvenile company that subsequently became "the pride of the city." He was a member of the Forest City Light Infantry and held the rank of Sergeant Major of the First Battalion. He was a member of First Congregational Church. At his funeral service the "church was thronged with the family and friends; and surrounding the church were also crowds, even the streets leading to the cemetery were lined with people." The Forest City Light Infantry and Middleton's band participated in the procession. A very large crowd witnessed the last rights of the military. A wife, two children and a mother, several sisters and a brother survived him.[166]

Black troops participated in the inauguration of President William McKinley in Washington, D.C., in 1897. That same year the legislature voted to restore Deveaux to the personal rank of Lieutenant Colonel. It had previously stripped him of the title. Two white men were found guilty of driving through the ranks of the Colquitt Blue while they were drilling on Liberty and East Broad. One pleaded guilty and apologized for his action. Col. Deveaux then requested the recorder to be lenient with him. He was fined $50. The other man was fined $10.[167]

Col. John H. Deveaux, Captains E. A. Williams of the Forest City Light Infantry, L. A. Washington, Lone Star Cadets, Robert Simmons of the Union Lincoln Guards, F. F. Jones of the Savannah Hussars, and J. C. Simmons of the Georgia Artillery attended the meeting of the Military Advisory Board in 1896. They attempted to prove to the board why their companies should not be disbanded. Col. Deveaux was of the opinion that the troops "would not be disbanded,"[168] and was assured that the "military companies of Savannah are all right. The boys can rest assured on this fact and go to work in building up the several companies better than ever."[169]

The Forest City Light Infantry celebrated its 25th anniversary. Captain J. L. Mirault commanded the company. They assembled at their armory on Harris Street at 4 o'clock headed by Prof Middleton's brass band paraded through the main streets of the town. All forty fully uniformed men "with their fine soldierly bearing and fine marching attracted the most favorable comment by all friends of the military." The ceremonies concluded with a grand banquet at night at the company's armory. Sergeant E. E. Desverney was master of ceremonies and introduced "veteran member Col. William H Woodhouse who made a welcome address. Captain Mirault gave the history of the company. At a late hour the bands struck up "Home Sweet Home."[170]

By the end of the month however news came that the colored troops were not asked to increase their numbers as the white troops were asked to do. As if to reaffirm their commitment to the state, the paper added: "The loyal spirit that exists among the colored military is an admirable one, notwithstanding the fact that the state has done nothing toward fully equipping them and the guns etc., given them are second-handed and in some instances unserviceable."[171] Meanwhile the white press continued its bombardment on the colored troops. As the Savannah Tribune reported: "The newspapers are ever ready to chronicle the least unlawful act that the colored soldier may commit, but the many escapades of the other fellows are either applauded or not spoken about."[172]

Captain Joseph Mirault (1859-1898) was born in Savannah January 18, 1859.[173] He rose through the ranks as a "marker" for the company, to the command of the Forest City Light Infantry. He was "greatly devoted to his company and was chief of rifle practice for the First Battalion of Georgia Volunteers. He was a letter carrier for many years and was president of the Carrier's Association. Mirault, a member of the "advisory board of St. Benedict's Catholic Church and also a member of the Independent Club of this city," he died suddenly in October 1898. His Sunday funeral took place at St. Benedict's Church. The remains escorted by the Forest City Light Infantry and the board of officers of the company. A "large concourse of sorrowful friends attended the funeral rites at Laurel Grove."[174] The First Battalion Infantry, Georgia State Troops, Colored, celebrated its 21st anniversary in 1901. The Chatham Light Infantry was the oldest unit of the First Battalion Infantry, Georgia State Troops, Colored. The unit was an ax company of the black firemen of the city. Captain Barcus Davison was the first commander.

In 1902, the state Adjutant General recommended that all colored troops be disbanded since they were unsuited to quell riots involving whites. Never daunted, but having naught for their comfort, Deveaux and his men began building an armory on Cuyler Street near Duffy Street. Lieutenant Sol C. Johnson was Adjutant, Lieutenant J. H. Bogg Inspector of rifle practice. Thomas headed Chatham Light Infantry; Lieutenant R.L. West led the Colquitt Blues. Captain John C. Simmons led the Georgia Artillery. Captain W.J.Pinckney led the Lincoln Guards, and Lieutenant John Maxwell led the Savannah Light Infantry. The Dick Act passed by Congress came into effect on January 21, 1903. This Act proved to be the perfect instrument for the Georgia legislature to destroy black troops. Not surprisingly, the Dick Act sought to accomplish the opposite. The Act was intended to equalize the treatment of black and white troops, and to raise the standards of all troops and to pay them the same salary. A series of inspections between 1903 and 1905 practically finished off the African American troops and then on August 19, 1905, the legislature disbanded them.

Sol C. Johnson commented,

> "It has been asserted that a large amount of money has been expended on Negro troops. This is erroneous. During the past twenty-five or thirty years the Negro troops have maintained themselves. Within the past two or three years the state became ashamed for the past treatment and assayed to give each company the paltry sum of $144 a year for armory rent, etc. A local white officer who fathered the sentiment for disbandonment of the troops was sufficiently fair to credit them with efficiency but claimed that they would be of no service to the state in event of riot, etc. When he made the assertion, he undoubtedly had forgotten Statesboro. This same officer claims that in war the Negro is no good. His mind is of a kindergarten sort and any person who knows the least about wars in this country would readily agree with us, for they yet have vividly on their minds the action of the Negro troops at San Juan Hill." [175]

The *Savannah Tribune* reported: "Until recently these troops were not molested, especially under the regime of those state house officers who were broad minded and willing to give a helping hand to the race." The writer expressed the opinion that "Within the past few years strenuous efforts have been made by a few young officers to have the troops disbanded. Each of these efforts have proven futile until last week." The paper expressed the crushing blow as: "The most brutal and unjust action that has ever been inflicted upon our people in the state."[176]

Captain W. D. Armstrong (1861-1914) for many years "one of the leading Negro politicians of the district," was born in Owens Ferry, Georgia in 1861 but lived most of his life in Savannah. He was chairman of the Republican Party County committee. Captain Armstrong held a pilot's license and "was well known all along the Savannah River." In addition, he was for some years "on the custodian force of the post office."

Armstrong was the "leading Odd Fellow of the city holding the position of Deputy of the twelfth division and a member of Armenia Lodge." He was also "among the first members of Olympia Lodge, K. of P. but later joined the J.W. Armstrong Lodge K. of P. He was a member of Eureka Lodge, Masons and Solomon Temple and Eastern Star. His funeral was held at St. Phillip's Church at Charles and West Broad Streets. [177] He was a member of the Savannah Hussars. He went up the ladder from Private to Lieutenant and when Captain W. H. Bell resigned Jones was elected as commander. He was said to have a "dashing soldiery appearance." In the mid 1920's, he retired from the business. The *Savannah Tribune* wished that his sterling qualities would be "profitably emulated by all of our young men." [178]

A year before he died editor Johnson reflected on the black troops in a piece entitled, Savannah's Military Glory. He stated,

> "The existence of eight military organizations was the pride of Negro citizens who looked forward to New Year's Day when they would witness the parade of their soldiers and festivities that took up a whole day and culminated with maneuvers and speech making in Forest City Park Extension... one of the bands had the distinction of being the band that played for the Savannah Volunteer Guards, a white company whenever that organization went out on parade... As is usual in Southern thinking, there was only one thing to do, one choice to make, to solve the problem of what to do about Negro officers who have attained senior rank; abolish the Negro militia. An important and unifying influence in Negro life was destroyed when this was done. .. These actions are taken in spite of the fact that Negroes were expected to and did fight in every war, including the Spanish war, World War 1, and World War 11. They will be expected to fight in future (?) wars. Fairness dictates that they should have the same opportunity of becoming as well prepared as any other citizens who volunteer or are drafted to serve their country in time of need.
>
> This comment would be incomplete if it omitted to name Sol C. Johnson, adjutant to Col. J. H. DeVeaux and the one Negro Confederate soldier we knew, the late (Rev.) Alexander Harris. Only the memory of the Negro's participation in the military glory of Savannah remains."[179]

World War 1

Sol C. Johnson was appointed chief registrar of black troops in 1917 and registration stations were at Cuyler Street School and the Carnegie Library. About 4,979 blacks and 3,665 whites registered. Earl Ashton, Arthur Dilworth and L. G. Middleton were among several black youths who left for training camp at Camp Des Moines, Iowa. In March 1918, 53 more draftees left for Camp Gordon and 124 more left the city in April. In May, over 1,200 soldiers returned and were given a rousing welcome. In June, the black Toussaint L'Overture Branch of the Red Cross distributed refreshments to about 16 carloads of colored soldiers as they passed through the city.

Another 135 men left for Camp Gordon, and African Americans subscribed $200,000 to war savings on Pledge Day. About 163 colored soldiers left for Camp Gordon and the names of the 800 selectmen who left for Camp Wheeler were published. [180] About 225 draftees were given a rousing send off as they left for Camp Jackson, Columbia in South Carolina. Pierce M. Thompson was selected a first lieutenant. He was with the machine gun Company at Fort Dodge, Iowa. The Rev. J. Henry Brown vicar of St. Augustine's Episcopal Church entered the army chaplain training school at Camp Zachary Taylor.[181] The announced that Dr. C. B. Tyson and Dr. O. C. Clayborn were sworn as medical examiners for the eastside draft board.[182] (They were regarded as "among the leading Negro physicians of the city." Dr. Tyson had practiced medicine in the city for about twenty years and Dr. Clayborn for five years. The paper stated: "only two Negro doctors in the state to be appointed to such positions and their selection is one, which should carry with it much appreciation by the Negroes of this city."

Paul J. Steele returned to the city in early 1919. He was mustered out at camp Jackson in South Carolina. He was a member of the 371st Infantry and took part in the assault on Hill No. 188, in Champagne Sector where his regiment won undying fame and the title Black Tigers. It was in this fight that Vance Allison and Robert Steele, two other local boys, lost their lives.

The welcome home celebration for returning black soldiers was said to be the "grandest and most dignified demonstration ever held in this city by Negroes." It was many thousands short of the mammoth Thrift Stamps parade of May 1918but more than 1,000 returned soldiers paraded. The parade started at 11:00 a.m. from West Broad and Henry streets going north on West Broad to Broughton, east to Bull Street, and south to the park extension where exercises were held. There were six companies of uniform rank Knights of Pythians, under Col. C.S. Andrews and his staff headed by the K. of P. band. The men were dressed in brand new cream flannel suits. They received much applause throughout the entire line of March. The 1,200 returned soldiers were next in line. Captain Austin T Walden, of Atlanta, First Lieutenant Pierce Mc Neal Thompson of Albany, formerly of Savannah, both of whom saw active service in Europe, were at the head of this section. Next was First Lieutenant Father J. Henry Brown, vicar of St. Augustine Episcopal Church, who was commissioned at Camp Zachary Taylor and was the only Savannah minister to serve as a chaplain during the war.

The men were formed into six companies, each under the command of a sergeant. The *Savannah Tribune* reported that as the parade passed, these men were given one continuous round of applause. There were men in line from nearly every one of the Negro combat regiments, which saw service in the trenches overseas. Seven wounded men in a car brought up the rear. John T. Preston, Parish Hamilton led about 500 longshoremen, all headed by Middleton's marching band. The Compress Workers Association, the Young Boys Aid and Social Club, Young Sons and

Daughters of Savannah, Hickman's Union and the Friendly Brothers Aid and Social Club were all decked out in their uniforms.

J. Rivers commanded two Companies of the Ladies Drill Corps of the Imperial Club, under the leadership of Captain Jos. J. Rivers. Next came the Union Brotherhood, Fountain City Aid and Social Club and the Evening Call Aid and Social Club. About 150 members of the Savannah Home Association were dressed in Palm Beach suits, white shoes, straw hats and white ties. They carried large white umbrellas with the letters: S.H.A., and led by Allen's band from Beaufort, South Carolina. Last in line were the five floats, one depicting a Negro soldier who had given his life on the battle field for democracy, another showing the monument of Crispus Attucks of Revolutionary fame, and a third was that of a massive gold star for the number of Chatham county Negroes who made the supreme sacrifice in World War I.

Next came three veterans of the Civil War, members of the Shaw Post No. 8, Grand Army of the Republic. The *Savannah Tribune* reported that "the old gentlemen whose heads were snowy white and whose frames were slightly bent from the passing years, marched steadily and were accorded a big hand as they passed through the crowded streets dressed in their dear old blue uniform which brought freedom to four million black souls over a half century ago." After the exercises, the soldiers marched to the old baseball park where a barbecue was served. The festivities closed with the planting of an elm tree at First Bryan Church in honor of the soldiers of Chatham County, who had given their lives for democracy.

The Rev. W.G.Alexander gave the principal address and Prof. Robert W. Gadsden directed the Community Chorus. Negroes and all the black business houses observed the day as a general holiday and schools were closed. In April 1918 the Savannah army recruiting station was said to be seeking an "unlimited number of qualified Negroes, for its Stevedore Regiments of colored men." Men between 18, 21, and 30 to 40 who were physically qualified were especially needed.[183] A big welcome was planned for the returning soldiers.[184] Private Williams was a member of the famous 300th Infantry, formerly the old Fifteenth New York National Guard regiment, which was the first Negro combat regiment to go overseas and which "won undying fame not only because of its almost unendurable record of 191 days on the firing line." Williams took part with his regiment in the attack on Snake Hill in the Champagne sector where he exhibited the valor which won him the high French medal of bravery. His mother lived at Perry and East Broad Streets. Corporal George W. Barcly died in France February 21, 1919.

A beautiful bronze tablet containing the names of the 85 white and 24 black soldiers who made the "supreme sacrifice," was erected. Vance Allison, Richard Ancrom, Remus Bacon, James Bailey, George Barclay, Joseph Bembry, Neptune Bobin, Willie Cuspard, Isaac Gillison, Charles H. Green, Alex Gray, Harmon Jones, Marshall Mallard, George Mulligan, Richard Norhern, Clarence Powell, Isadore

Pinckney, Sheppard Sears, Charles H. Shavers, William Simmons, Robbie Steele, James S. Stephens and James Williams, were the African Americans who made the "supreme sacrifice."[185]

A Rock In A Weary Land

Although freedom of worship was one of the platitudes contained in the Georgia slave code of 1750, and owners were expected to be "solicitous for the religious education of their slaves," from the beginning whites were never comfortable with blacks meeting by themselves even for worship. White ministers used the Bible as part of a matrix constructed to keep blacks "in due order and subjection." However, religion by its very nature is a two edged-sword. While whites were able to use it to oppress blacks, conversely blacks used religion to survive and eventually, to the extent possible, overcome the oppression.

Joseph F. Waring attributed the absence of any "threat of servile rebellion in Savannah" to the religious leadership of Andrew Bryan, Andrew Marshall and Henry Cunningham who produced in their large congregations "a spirit of Christian patience with their lot," but remarked that, "underneath the pleasant surface there was gnawing anxiety."[186]

As has often happened in the history of religion, and the story of David Margate at Bethesda Orphan Home magnified, many black practitioners reinterpreted the Christian religious teachings, symbols and metaphors from the perspective of their own "life situation"[187] and not surprisingly transformed the received doctrine into their own effective "tool for survival."[188] It was the genius of black religion to be the "conveyor belt" of black survival. Nowhere in the New World African Diaspora does history record mass suicide of the people.

The black church provided its members with a level of social organization, and temporarily assuaged their "dreary existence."[189] It was the "soul power" that gave them "staying power." One of the earliest recorded spirituals, published in America in 1867, has the words: "Come along, Moses, don't get lost don't get lost. Come along Moses, don't get lost we are the people of God."[190] Karl Marx could possibly have been thinking of black religion when he defined religion as "the heart of a heartless situation."

In 1836, Episcopal Bishop Meade published his Sermons, Dialogues and Narratives for Servants, to be Read to them in Families. The following year the Rev. Charles C. Jones, a Georgia slave owner, published a Catechism for Colored Persons. In addition, in 1842 Jones published The Religious Instruction of the Negroes in the United States. In the hands of black religious leaders, however, these and similar teachings took on a very different meaning. Both Denmark Vessey and Nat Turner used their religious congregations as the "hard core" of true believers, in their planned revolts. Even after slavery was abolished, the white church kept up its propaganda of black inferiority.

The Rev. C. F. McRae, rector of St. John's Episcopal Church, Savannah, preached a "forcible and Christian sermon," in which he reminded his congregation that "a great and radical change has taken place in our social system...which indeed was the stay and prop of our of our social structure, has been suddenly removed." The rector went on to say "mutual dependence does not beget an equality of station. Our social relations are not leveled because all are politically free." He thought the "God of nature has thus given the white race those superior intellectual endowments ...to the exclusion of the black race."[191]

The results of the government election in 1884 and the return of the Democrats to power caused quite a dither in the town. It was reported that most black clergy were telling their members that it was God's punishment, and that great harm would come to the people and that there was a danger of reverting back to slavery. The press claimed that the black people should have confidence in the white Southerners to protect the rights of blacks. Louis A. Faligant, M.D., wrote the editor of the *Savannah Morning News* reminding blacks that their children are educated through taxes paid mostly by whites, that the white run dispensaries furnish blacks with medicine and white physicians look after them when they are sick. He felt that such ministers are unworthy of their calling and that if the preachers would not do it then the better educated among the blacks should set matters straight.[192]

David Margate, a black Trevecca College trained Anglican missionary from England, arrived in Charleston South Carolina, in January 1775, en route to Bethesda Orphan Home near Savannah. While in Charleston he preached to whites and blacks and in the course of his sermon stated that he was convinced that God would liberate the slaves, as he had freed the Israelites from their "Egyptian bondage." Whites interpreted Margate's sermon as an attempt to foment "rebellion" among the slaves, and a grand jury lodged a presentment against Margate's host. White missionary John Cosson and his wife accompanied Margate to Savannah. Cosson thought Margate looked "pious and devoted," and hoped that God would use Margate to bless the "heathens around us."[193] Two weeks after his arrival at the Rev. George Whitefield's Bethesda Orphan Home, much to the chagrin of the white missionary, Margate claimed that God had told him to marry a slave who was already married to another. Margate also asserted that he was a second Moses about to bring salvation to his captive people. Cosson warned Margate to change his approach less he "lose his life," and defeat his mission.[194] A great panic broke out as Margate continued to preach his "inflammatory doctrine" to the slaves. Within seven months in the area, Margate had become inimical to the best interest of whites. [195]

James Habersham wrote to Robert Keen relating information he had obtained from the letters of other persons. David Margate was said to have exhibited "imprudent Airs." He definitely did not plan to preach a gospel of submission on the part of blacks. Habersham was glad that David Margate was leaving Bethesda because his approached would have caused havoc among "her Ladyships Negroes." Margate, in Habersham's view, lacked the true spirit of a missionary. Habersham felt that Margate's obligation was to preach about "spiritual deliverance" not civic or political freedom. This first black missionary in the area was put on a boat bound for England.[196] African American missionary activity along the Savannah River produced a unique quartet of leaders: clerics George Liele, David George, Andrew Bryan, and lay leader, William J. Claghorn (sometimes written Cleghorn). Their Christian evangelization in the hostile environment of slavery is truly remarkable. Equally astounding is the fact that the work continues to the present.

The argument could be made that the contemporary congregations, First African Baptist, First Bryan Baptist, Second African Baptist, Bethlehem Baptist and St. Matthew's Episcopal, all originated from pioneer black missionary endeavors along the Savannah River. These five congregations went through "the valley of the shadow of death," slavery, and survived relatively intact. Therefore, they are the "elder daughters" of "old Jerusalem."[197] As the Savannah Tribune noted, "Old Jerusalem is the name that the First Bryan Church used to be called by the old citizens, and is now fondly called old Bryan by its admirers and loyal members." [198]

George Liele was born a slave in Virginia in 1751.[199] His owner Henry Sharpe a pro-British Baptist deacon, brought him to Georgia sometime in 1773. Liele, who had a "natural fear," of God,[200] soon fell under the religious influence of the Rev. Matthew Moore, was baptized and became a member of the interracial Buckhead Creek Baptist Church in 1774.[201] Once converted, he felt "called by grace," and after a trial sermon judged by the quarterly meeting of some white ministers, was "licensed" on a temporary basis to preach to the slaves.[202]

Liele was ordained a Baptist minister May 20, 1775.[203] The Georgia Slave Act of 1770 with its prohibition of loud noises and gatherings of slaves by themselves hindered the evangelization of slaves. Henry Sharpe freed his slave Liele in 1777, and Liele devoted himself to the evangelization of his fellow blacks and a few whites. Liele used hymns as a means of spreading the gospel. He would read the hymns then encouraged the people to sing. He also practically took over the evangelization of blacks and encouraged David George to preach. Exhorter the Rev. Wait Palmer formed David George, George's wife, Jesse Galpin and others into a congregation at Silver Bluff, South Carolina.[204]

Robert Scott Davis viewed the American Revolution as an "unexpected boon" to Baptists.[205] It surely seemed to have been a windfall for black Baptists, especially the Rev. George Liele, the first black ordained minister in the area. Liele and Brother Palmer, a white, made frequent visits to George Galpin's plantation, Silver Bluff, on the South Carolina side of the Savannah River and subsequently baptized eight slaves and formed them into a church.[206]

During preaching missions on the Savannah River banks and Yamacraw in 1778, Liele converted several slaves on Tybee and the Brampton plantation and baptized Andrew Bryan; his wife Hannah and Kate and Hager.[207] A letter dated September 15, 1790 credits Liele with planting establishing the first Baptist Church in Savannah.[208] Whatever the actual story was it seems clear that Liele was the leader of the nucleus of what would later became a full-fledged congregation. Liele's ministry on the Savannah River gave him experience working with slaves who lived away from their owners. Many of these blacks had apparently preserved some of their African customs since they were a higher percentage of the population and were more isolated than the slaves in Burke County. This experience was of great benefit to him later in Jamaica.

The heirs of Liele's former owner attempted to repossess him but through the efforts of Colonel Moses Kirkland a British officer, [209] Liele decided to leave with the British forces in 1782, and went to Jamaica,[210] paying his passage as an indentured servant. Liele arrived in Jamaica in December 1783, and was employed by the Governor Archibald Campbell who served with the British forces in Georgia. After repaying his indebtedness, he and his family were fully free.[211] Liele started his evangelistic work in Jamaica "by preaching in a private house to a small congregation."[212]

Liele subsequently "organized" a church with four other Americans.[213] The congregation soon numbered about 1,500 persons. He also started a free school "for the instruction of the children, both free and slaves."[214] In Jamaica Liele farmed the land and operated a drayage business and kept a stable of horses.[215] By 1791, Liele wrote that he had "baptized four hundred in Jamaica." His wife and four children seemed to have settled down well in Jamaica. Liele was the first black preacher from the Savannah River area to take the gospel to Africans in the diaspora.

During the 1790's, partly in response to the slave revolt in Haiti, the black Baptists in Jamaica suffered many privations.[216] Liele was even imprisoned for indebtedness. He nevertheless maintained a high social standing on the island. His ability to read and write as well as his fluency in English and his leadership gifts served him well. Liele adapted his evangelization methods to the rigors of the slave system. Slaves had to get permission of their owners and their consent before baptism.

In 1789, Liele's congregation bought about three acres in east Kingston for a church.[217] Liele never received any payment for his missionary work in Georgia or Jamaica;[218] He occupied a "privileged-position" in the local society. By 1793, he had over one thousand converts on the Island.[219] Much of the data on the original black Baptists in the Savannah area was taken from the recollections and letters of

George Liele in his declining days. Robert S. Davis found the letters "not those of a polished writer nor student of the American Revolution. Rather they are the work of an old man who took justifiable pride in writing the story of his ministry."[220] However, the magazine's editor seems to contradict Davis' harsh assessment of Liele's letters.[221] In 1916, African American Baptists erected a monument to the Rev. George Liele at First Bryan Baptist Church.[222]

David George was born about 1743, in Essex County, Virginia, to John and Judith both African born slaves. He witnessed the lynching of his brother who had run away and the flogging of his mother. George was flogged sometimes "till the blood has run down over my waistband." He soon ran away and finally, after two escapades with Indian tribes, ended up as a slave on George Galpin's plantation in Silver Bluff, in Aiken County on the Savannah River twelve miles from Augusta.[223]

Irish born George Galpin came to America in the 1730's and eventually settled in Augusta near the Savannah River. The town at that time was home to a very diverse collection of nationalities. Though married and with two children, Galpin fathered children with mulatto and Indian women and provided for them in his will. He allowed blacks to use his mill as a meeting place and permitted David George to be ordained,[224] sometime before 1777.[225] Galpin's children taught David George to read, and Cyrus, a slave, instructed him in the tenets of religion and he was appointed an elder in a congregation. George was also very inspired by the preaching of his childhood friend George Liele.

Experiencing "a call," around 1773, David George began to preach at the Silver Bluff gathering and the congregation increased from 8 to 30.[226] As soon as hostilities between the British and local patriots began in earnest, this motley nucleus of about forty slaves, black Baptists, and possibly pro-British as well, headed for British controlled Savannah.[227] Since itinerant missionaries were banned from preaching to the slaves, local black preachers took control of the religious endeavor. On his way to Savannah, David George was imprisoned for allegedly "misleading" some slaves. By 1778, David George, his wife whom he married in 1770, two children and more than fifty others, were in Savannah along with George Liele and Jesse Peter.

Brooks credits Liele with being the leader of this Silver Bluff congregation while it was in exile in Savannah. Soon after he got to Savannah, David George opened a butcher's stall, while his wife was the washerwoman for British General Henry Clinton.[228] A French-American cannonball destroyed part of his home, and George contracted smallpox. During the Revolution, George continued preaching to the slaves and was "one of the founders of the African American church."[229] Jesse Peter, sometimes called Jesse Galpin, eventually took over the work and restored the Silver Bluff congregation.[230] This Savannah "Babylonian captivity" of the Silver Bluff congregation must have been quite an experience for their Savannah co-religionists as they rubbed shoulders for several months, with the three leading black evangelists of the area, George Liele, David George and Jesse Galpin.[231]

David George eventually left for Charleston and later went with British sympathizers to Nova Scotia, Canada. There he founded a Baptist church in Shelburne.[232] Most of the former American slaves were not treated fairly by the British. They got the worst parcels of land, and George endured many indignities in his effort to preach the gospel in Canada. Later, in 1792, the Reverend David George and about 1,000 African Americans migrated to the British colony Sierra Leone, in Africa and established the Baptist church there.[233] Once again, George had to contend with raw racism, this time coming from the Sierra Leone Company. Thus, a ministry that began on the Savannah River banks was completed in the evangelization of some of the children of Mother Africa. His was truly a vocation full of "adventure."[234]

Andrew Bryan (1716-1812) was born a slave of Jonathan Bryan, in Goose Creek, South Carolina, in 1716. His father Caesar was born in Africa but came from a plantation in Barbados, West Indies.[235] Bryan was the coachman and body servant of his owner[236] and learned to read.[237] The Rev. George Liele, preaching from chapter 3 verse 7 of St. John's gospel, "Ye must be born again," baptized Andrew and his wife Hagar, the property of Jonathan Bryan.[238] Sometime after 1782, Bryan began to "exhort his colored brethren and friends and a few whites that assembled to hear him."[239] Bryan had apparently filled the vacuum left by Liele's departure for Jamaica.[240] William Bryan, a British sympathizer, allowed these black Baptists to establish their first place of worship on his barn on the Brampton estate, three miles from Savannah.[241]

Whites feared that blacks were meeting to plot "mischief and insurrection" under the cover of religious worship. A grand jury in 1788 made a presentment which stated in part, "We present as a grievance Negroes in different parts of this county being permitted to assemble in large bodies under pretence (sic) of religion, by which holy institution is not only become a mere mockery, but a cloak for every species of blasphemy, theft, and debauchery."[242] Bryan, his brother Samson, and about fifty members were "severely whipped" and imprisoned.[243] Bryan was also imprisoned because he refused to "discontinue his work."[2.44] He was inhumanly cut and bled abundantly: "But while under the lashes he held up his hands and told his persecutors that he rejoiced not only to be whipped but would freely suffer death for the cause of Christ."[245] Several prominent whites interceded for them and "Chief Justice Osborne gave them permission to continue their worship any time between sunrise and sunset."[246]

The Rev. Abraham Marshall a white from Kiokee in Columbia County, assisted by the Rev. Jesse Peter, sometimes called Jesse Galpin, a black, ordained Bryan January 19, 1788 and the next day established the group of about sixty-seven persons as, the Ethiopian Church of Jesus Christ in Savannah.[247] This motley gathering of black Baptists was increased when the Rev. Thomas Barton, visited them and "on creditable profession of faith baptized eighteen of their number."[248] Within four years this nucleus of a congregation increased to about 235 persons. Another 350 had been accepted as converts, but many "had not received the permission of their owners to be baptized."[249] Slaves had to obtain tickets or passes from their owners to attend these services.[250]

In 1789, Andrew Bryan purchased his freedom for 50 pounds sterling.[251] The group occupied their second place of worship when in 1790. Bryan bought a lot on Mill Street in Oglethorpe ward and built a church for twenty-seven pounds sterling.[252] Bryan also ordained four deacons including his slave brother Sampson whom he made his assistant. The 1792 legislature, partly influenced by events in Haiti, forbade blacks, except under certain controlled conditions, from assembling even for worship.

By 1800, the congregation reached 800 members[253] and became an accepted part of the respectable religious milieu of Savannah. The Sunbury Association organized in 1818 included the two all-black congregations. By 1857, thirteen of the twenty-five congregations were all black. Whites amounted to 537 of the 6,507 members. The Rev. Andrew Bryan informed Dr. Rippon that he had been: "well provided for, as to worldly comforts, (though I have had very little given me as a minister), having a house and lot in this city, besides the land on which several buildings stand, for which I receive a small rent, and a fifty-six-acre tract of land, with all buildings, four miles in the country, and eight slaves, for whose education and happiness I am enabled thro mercy to provide."[254]

The Rev. Dr. Henry Holcombe, pastor of the white Savannah Baptist Church, recorded this impression of Andrew Bryan: "His fleecy and well-set locks have been bleached by eighty years; and dressed like a Bishop of London. He rides, moderately corpulent, in his chair and with many features of a jetty hue, fills any person to whom he gracefully bows with pleasure and veneration, by displaying in smiles even rows of natural teeth white as ivory and a pair of fine black eyes sparkling with intelligence, benevolence and joy."[255] Father Andrew Bryan died October 6, 1812,[256] reportedly at 96 years of age. The Rev. Edgar G. Thomas listed Father Bryan's death as October 12, 1812.[257] Bryan served as pastor of the church for 24 years[258] and though born a slave, at his death he left an estate valued at $3,000.

One divine regarded him as "a man of good sense and great zeal and some natural elocution."[259] Membership in the church had reached 1498 souls. Father Bryan was the last of the original memorable black clerical leaders to come from the banks of the Savannah River and was "loved and honored by white and black."[260] An official local marker in memory of the Rev. Andrew Bryan was installed at First Bryan Baptist Church in 1979.[261] Bryan's plan was to divide his congregation when it became too large to function and he facilitated the organization of Second African Baptist Church in Savannah and the Ogeechee Colored Baptist.[262] Towards the end of 1812, the members began to build a place of worship, with "the assistance of a number of benevolent gentlemen of different denominations." The frame building was 42 x 40 feet and "stood the storms of many years until it was torn down to give place to the present structure in 1873."[263] Council authorized the congregation to build a church on lot No. 11, Yamacraw, August 25, 1831.[264] Thomas Gamble, 481. In 1832 the congregation under Marshall, bought a larger frame building that the white Baptists vacated, on Montgomery Street, and moved into its third church home.[265]

The first major discord in the congregation occurred when the Rev. Andrew Cox Marshall, son of the sainted Andrew Bryan's sister, and Andrew Bryan's successor, was pastor of Old Jerusalem. This doctrinal "holy war" broke out in 1832, over the "new theology" teachings of the Rev. Alexander Campbell. Some followers claimed that the Rev. Andrew Marshall "was favorable to the Campbellite doctrine" and "for some time the church was in a state of thorough disorganization." The fracas pitted the Rev. Andrew Cox Marshall against West Indian born, deacon Adam Arguile Johnson. In the end, the congregation split into two parts. The Rev. Andrew C. Marshall headed one faction with 2, 640 members housed in the unused former white Baptist Church on Montgomery Street, which before the split, the congregation had made arrangements to purchase. Deacon Adam Arguile Johnson led the smaller group of about 155 persons housed in the building on the original lot on Bryan Street.[266]

FIRST AFRICAN BAPTIST: The Rev. William J. Campbell (1812-1880) a mulatto slave was born in Savannah January 1, 1812.[267] The Rev. Andrew C. Marshall baptized Campbell around 1830 and he joined the choir. Marshall made Campbell his assistant in 1855. The congregation sent Campbell to Richmond to accompany Marshall's body back to Savannah.[268] Campbell was the body servant of his owner and in that capacity made several trips outside of Savannah and he developed into a "prodigious reader."[269] He remained a slave until he was liberated by the will of his owner Mrs. Mary Maxwell in 1849,[270] but was married to a free mulatto woman.[271] The Executive Board of the Sunbury Baptist Association ordained Campbell and he succeeded the venerable Father Andrew Marshall as pastor of First African Baptist Church in 1857.[272]

It fell to Campbell to fulfill the dream of his mentor, the Rev. Andrew Marshall, to demolish the wooden building and replace it with "the beautiful brick edifice, which was in the heart of Father Marshall to do before he left the walks of men."[273] The new brick building had a seating capacity of 700, and inside had a white pulpit, oak pews and the aisles were sometimes covered with "oil cloth." The building was described as a "tasteful house of worship on Franklin Square." The Rev. S. C. Daniel, pastor the First Baptist Church (white), laid the cornerstone of the First African Baptist Church on July 5, 1859.[274] The building cost $10,000 and "all but $1,500 having been paid."[275] The Rev. Edgar Thomas put the cost at $26,000.[276]

Campbell was known as "a man of keen foresight, iron will, and wonderful executive ability."[277] Early in his ministry he was falsely accused of stealing cotton on the Bay. He survived that ordeal and led his church to reach 4,000 members. The congregation rallied around him the same way it had supported his predecessor and it was said: "no man ever had more influence over people than Reverend Campbell."[278] He received a salary of $100 per month, three months vacation and "everything he wanted."[279] In his old age however Campbell experienced some opposition from certain cliques in the congregation. The Rev. William J. Campbell, the third pastor of First African Baptist Church died in 1880. The members erected a tablet on his grave with the words, "this memorial is erected by the Ruth Association and the church in token of their love and veneration for him." A news reporter recorded the fact that "the veneration of their churches for their pastors is more pronounced among colored people than among the whites."[280]

Charles L. DeLamotta (1822-1887) was born in South Carolina. However there is no agreement on the date of his birth. Emanuel K. Love claims DeLamotta was born in 1822, but he does not list the month or day.[281] Eric Foner[282] puts the date at 1817/8,[283] and Charles Elmore gave the date as March 30, 1822.[284] Delamotta was baptized by the venerable Andrew C. Marshall and was ordained a deacon October 12, 1862.

According to Love, Delamotta opposed the election of the Rev. William V. Campbell and this difference of views caused the stubborn Delamotta and the congregation much grief. Delamotta was twice expelled from the church in 1858 and again in 1876. He organized a Sunday school in 1861and became Church School Superintendent. This school "won for him laurels that will be carried far into the future by his little flock, and a name that will ever live in the community." It was "through his labors that the Sunday school erected the beautiful marble tablet to the memory of Rev. Andrew Cox Marshall."[285] During the disturbance following his removal from office, his seventeen teachers refused to teach in his absence. The Colored Tribune expressed the view that his removal was "a most serious blow at the Sunday School interests of our people."[286]

By the following month the matter seemed to have been cleared up and the editor published a letter from Delamotta in which he claimed to have a Sunday school with "an average attendance of about 200 scholars divided into twenty-three classes." The newly introduced International series of Bible Lessons were found to have been "just the thing for the Sabbath schools."[287] Delamotta was a delegate to the Georgia Freedmen's Convention in 1866 and served as a U. S. detective in the city in 1870. The following year he worked in the custom house. That year he owned $350 personal property according to the census of 1870.[288] Charles L. Delamotta died in 1886 and was buried January 1, 1887. His remains were placed in First African Baptist Church on Friday afternoon "in order that the thousands who desired to take a last look might be accommodated." On Saturday morning the Sabbath School conducted an appropriate remembrance of their leader. The regular funeral service then followed. The Grand Lodge of Free and Accepted Masons, the Sabbath School and a "large concourse of sorrowing friends" followed the body to the cemetery.[289]

The Rev. Emanuel K. Love (1850-1900) was born a slave July 27, 1850 in Perry County, Alabama.[290] As a youngster he had "a burning desire to get an education," and studied privately at home then went to Lincoln University, Marion, Alabama.[291] In October 1884, a year before he became pastor of First African Baptist Church, the Rev. Emanuel K. Love offered a resolution to the executive board of the state Baptist convention in Milledgeville calling for an adequate celebration of the coming centennial of black Baptist worship in Georgia.[292]

In 1885 at 35 years of age, he accepted the pastorate of First African Baptist Church of Savannah. Some doubted whether such a "young pastor," could "handle" a congregation with a tradition of strong pastors and equally strong deacons accustomed to older leadership. His brother Dr. Phillip Love had lived in the city for many years and had a successful medical practice here.

After Love came to Savannah he began collecting material to write a history of First African Baptist Church, the mother church of black Baptists in the state. The Rev. James M. Simms was one of his collaborators in this quest. Love was described as "congenial, jovial and commanding, he was easily the center of attraction of almost any group."[293] Not surprisingly, soon First African Baptist Church and its pastor, the Rev. Emanuel K. Love, were on the cusp of yet another rift. The Rev. Dr. Goowon, pastor of the white First Baptist Church, presided over the discussion. Love was cleared "of every charge made against him," and his friends were jubilant.[294]

Love celebrated his tenth pastoral anniversary at First African Baptist Sunday, October 3, 1895 with full pomp and circumstance. Prof. Samuel B. Morse was in charge of the special music for the occasion. I. M. Jackson, a student at the Georgia College for Colored Youth in Thunderbolt, wrote an anniversary ode, which was first read by College President Richard Wright, then sung by the congregation. The Rev. Alexander Harris preached a special anniversary sermon from the text, "And Lo I am with you always."

In the course of his sermon, the Rev. Harris recalled the history of the early pastors of "old Jerusalem." The sainted patriarch Andrew Bryan, "who was thrice whipped and imprisoned, but remained firm and baptized many." The "very able minister," the Venerable Andrew Marshall, who "had much trouble being whipped and imprisoned. He was stopped from preaching several times and the church was closed for many months." Marshall's successor, the Rev. W. J. Campbell, "who had similar troubles, but baptized several thousands." During Campbell's pastorate, the church split into two factions with one group leaving to form another church. Then there was the Rev. George Gibbons, “a quiet and dignified Christian, who presided over the church without trouble until his death in November 1884.”

And finally, Harris came to the honoree, the Rev. Emanuel K. Love, who was installed as pastor October 1, 1885. The preacher summed up Love’s tenure, up to that point, with the cryptic words “He has had much trouble in the church, but has triumphed over dissension.” Church membership “increased one-third under his pastorate.” Love had baptized 1,758 and received 187 by letter of transfer making a total addition of members during his term of 1,945 new members. The membership in 1895 was estimated to be 5,000.[295] The church added 26 ° feet to the rear at a cost of $18, 000. Galleries were installed and a 100 foot steeple with a bronze bell weighing 1, 000 pounds was put in place. The church also received a thorough “face-lift.”[296]

A storm in September 1893 toppled First African Baptist Church’s steeple. Scipio Americanus writing in the *Savannah Tribune* described the scene; “never in my life have I beheld such a spectacle as the one on Monday morning. Trees torn up by the roots, houses unroofed and general desolation everywhere.” The only sanguine note was the laconic phrase, “The Negroes were fortunate, as a whole only one life was lost in the city and he was killed not by the storm directly, but by an electric wire. Very little of the property of Negroes were destroyed.” The writer went on to state, “we sympathize with Dr. Love and his people in their misfortunes.”[297]

The Young men of First African Baptist Church organized a Young Men’s Christian Association. Writer Scipio hoped “that the young will extend an invitation to all young men of the city to join them that denomination lines will be broken and an effort made to save young men and bring them into the fold of Christian love and fellowship.”[298] First African Baptist Church had had four pastors up to Love’s anniversary celebration. The Rev. Andrew Bryan served for 24 years; Rev. Andrew Marshall 54 years; Rev. William J. Campbell 20 years and Rev. Emanuel K. Love 15 years. Love’s successor, the Rev. J. W. Carr, became pastor in 1901 and served for 6 years. During Carr’s pastorate the congregation bought a parsonage at 717 West Broad Street, “the most attractive Negro Baptist pastorium in Georgia.”[299] The Rev. W.L. Jones, served for 4 years. [300]

The Executive Board of the Mount Olive Baptist Association organized the First African Baptist Church of East Savannah Thursday August 26, 1897. The 34 members of the new congregation, formerly members of First African Baptist on Montgomery Street, obtained ‘regular and peaceful letters of demission for the purpose of organizing a church at East Savannah, where all the members reside.” The covenant was read and “each member subscribed to it.”[301] The Rev. Alexander Harris was moderator of Mt. Olive Baptist Association.

The Rev. Alexander Harris organized Mount Tabor Baptist Church in October 1893.[302] First African Baptist Church on Russell Street bought the O’Connor property on West Broad and Bolton Streets and renovated the building as their church.[303] Several ministers met and organized the Evangelical Ministers Association.[304] The Rev. J. H. N. Sengstacke and Miss Lizzie Fleming of the *Savannah Tribune* were engaged in a "heated debate on the topic-Was Christ A Baptist.[305] The opening services of College Park Baptist Church with pastor H. R. Thomas officiating were held in December 1895.[306] The cornerstone of the Mt. Olive Baptist Church on Burroughs Street was laid in March 1896. The Rev. Alexander Harris, moderator of the Mt. Olive Baptist Association, organized First African Baptist Church of East Savannah.[307]

FIRST BRYAN BAPTIST: West Indian born Deacon **Adam Arguile Johnson** was baptized by the Rev. Andrew Bryan in the late 1790's and was "a diligent student of the bible." He was "pious and upright" a man who believed in the right as he saw it. The Rev. Emanuel K. Love gave this bleak analysis of Johnson's role in the conflict: "to him is due more than any one else the split of the church in 1832. He must be credited with waging one of the most disastrous wars that has ever disgraced a Christian Church."[308] Johnson became the official leader of the 155 souls gathered on Bryan Street and the church "remained in continuous operation under the deacons led by Deacon Adam Johnson.[309] Johnson died March 18, 1853 after serving his church for 40 years. Love expressed the view that "Deacon Johnson will always be remembered in Savannah. He was always after the split, the leader of the Third African Baptist Church (now First Bryan Baptist Church), which was the result of the split and which was organized under him as leader."[310]

In 1835 the Presbyterian Church discontinued the operation of the Sunday school and the members First Bryan took over that responsibility. A church brochure described the period between 1836-1916 as "a period of struggle, decline in membership and a series of six ministers but still continuous operation."[311] The Rev. Ulysses L. Houston became pastor in 1861 and served the congregation for 26 years, the longest pastorate in the church's history. During his ministry the congregation splintered again when the Rev. Alexander Harris and a small number of members left and founded First Bryan Baptist Church on West Broad Street near Walburg Street.

First Bryan was charted by the state in 1866. After many years of raising funds a new building was constructed on the site in 1874. The Grand Lodge of Masons laid the cornerstone October 13, 1873.[312] The white paper proclaimed peace between the warring factions at the church, only to have to retract the statement. It reported that "the same breach exists and the matter of church property is still in litigation. The proposed new building is to be constructed by the Simms-Houston faction, while those members of the congregation who desire to have the Rev. Alexander Harris officiate as their pastor, are now endeavoring to raise means for the purpose of building a church on the corner of Bolton and West Broad Streets.[313]

In 1885 First Bryan Baptist Church invited the state Baptist convention to meet at First Bryan for the centennial celebration in 1888. William Rivers, Church School Superintendent of First Bryan, celebrated the school's 65th anniversary. The Rev. Ulysses H. Houston gave a reading of scripture and teachers and students then recited poems or presented essays. J. H. Brown, Superintendent of First African Baptist's Church School, delivered the principal address. Rivers was said to have done "much toward bringing the school up to its present good standing." The school had an enrollment of about 400 pupils.[314]

A large crowd of about 5,000 to 8,000 witnessed the baptism of 138 new members, on the banks of the Ogeechee canal.

The Rev. Ulysses L. Houston was assisted by three deacons.[315] In 1887, committee chairman, the Rev. Alexander Harris, with the Revs. U. L. Houston, James M. Simms, David Waters, Emanuel K. Love and deacon J.H. Brown secretary, announced that the Missionary Baptist Convention of Georgia and the State Baptist Sunday School Convention would hold a one month long celebration of the centennial of the Negro Baptist of Georgia, in June 1888 in Savannah. About 75,000 of the 159,690 black Baptists in the state were expected to visit the city during the festivities. The Baptists hoped that the event would "reflect with pleasing credit upon Savannah and her citizens white and black."[316]

On Friday evening January 20, 1888, First Bryan Baptist Church celebrated the congregation's 100th anniversary. The members began entering the church at sunset and by 7:30 p.m., "the building was packed and late comers accommodated themselves as best they could in the aisles and about the doorways." The pastor, the Rev. Ulysses Houston presided.

The Rev. James M. Simms read his history of the founding of The First Colored Church in North America. The *Savannah Morning News* reporter stated that the task was "well performed." He added that it was a feat that a man "of more literary pretensions than the reader might be proud, to have woven the history of a church for 100 years with its various ups and downs embodying statistical data in such a manner as to keep the perfect attention of his audience." The "immense throng of colored people" listened with "the most wrapped attention."[317] Love traced the history of the First Colored Church from its founding by the Rev. Andrew Bryan in 1788. Bryan bought some property for 30 pounds sterling, which was held in trust by some whites since blacks were not able to hold property in their own name.

By 1802 the membership had grown so large that it was divided into two congregations. A storm in 1804 killed twenty-one members. When Bryan died in 1812 about 5,000 persons attended his funeral. He left an estate worth $3,000 after having purchasing his freedom as well as that of his wife and daughter. In 1832, while the Rev. Andrew Marshall was pastor, the congregation split. Marshall was silenced and the church was reorganized as a branch of the white church. Love claimed that the congregation numbered 2, 000 persons in 1888.

Towards the close of the service, the presiding officer called on Dr. J. E.

Holmes, a white minister, to address the congregation. Holmes said that he had not expected to be called on to give remarks but told the congregants that they had "abundant reason to be grateful not only for the history but for the cause in which the history has been written." Holmes concluded, "Let us begin with quickened ardor, feeling assured that He who led the fathers will lead the children." He congratulated the black Baptists for having clung to the faith and claimed that they had "set a good example to the whites."[318] The *Savannah Tribune*'s editor received a copy of the Rev. James M. Simms' book, *The First Colored Church in North America*, and found it: "a most valuable contribution to the race's history and it should be in every body's library."[319]

The African Missionary Baptist State Convention met in May 1888, to celebrate the centennial of Baptist worship in the state and grappled with the question, "which is the oldest church organization in the state?" The matter was referred to a special committee. This committee composed of the Rev. F. M. Simmons of Stone Mountain, the Rev. W. S. Ramsey of Columbus, the Rev. S.R. Hamilton of Walthourville, the Rev. S.R. McNeil of Augusta, the Rev. E. J. Fisher of LaGrange, the Rev. C. T. Walker of Augusta, the Rev. N.B. Williams of Quitman, the Rev. G. T. Johnson of Arlington and the Rev. G. H. Brightharp of Milledgeville, presented a report in favor of the primacy of First African Baptist Church of Savannah. The *Savannah Morning News* article did not indicate how many of these clergy were trained historians.

The committee's unanimous ruling stated in part: "We find that the church organized at Brampton's barn three miles southwest of Savannah, January 20, 1788 is the First African Baptist Church of today. This fact is admitted by the work which Rev. Simms has written." And concluded,

> "We feel honor bound to decide that the First African Baptist Church at Franklin Square is the original First African Baptist Church organized at Brampton Barn January 20, 1788, by the Rev. Abraham Marshall and Rev. Jesse Peter, whose centennial anniversary we have gathered together to celebrate. We decide therefore that the claim of priority of the First Baptist Church (which has given itself this name since emancipation) and the claim of the book written by Rev, J. M. Simms of being the oldest colored church in North America is without foundation."[320]

First African Baptist presented a deed "yellow with and honeycombed by Andrew Bryan, a free white man to the trustees of the First African Baptist Church of lot 7 in Yamacraw village for a consideration of thirty pounds sterling. Also a sketch of the church written by Rev. Simms when he was friendly to it." When the report was read, the Rev Simms sprang to his feet "with blood in his eyes," and accused the committee of being stacked in the interest of First African Baptist Church.[321] This issue was destined to remain a moot point for at least the next 113 years.

This author is utterly incapable of answering the question, which church is older, First African Baptist or First Bryan Baptist? The correct answer has eluded greater minds than his that have grappled with the issue for more than a century. Part of the problem stems from the fact that the two camps use different dates and concepts that have several meanings.

The authors of *A History Of The Georgia Baptist Association, 1784-1984*, claim that "probably" the first black Baptist church in Georgia was the Silver Bluff Baptist Church organized by slaves in 1773 with David George as pastor and Jesse Galpin (Jesse Peter) and George Liele as members. This congregation reached 180 by 1790. In 1782 the pro-British colonists moved to the safety of British held Savannah and several slave and free black Baptists, perhaps of the same political persuasion, accompanied them. These historians speculate that Savannah was the second center of black Baptist activity although there could possibly have been earlier black Baptist preaching in the area. It is also possible that an unofficial congregation could have been established, "without white notice or approval." It is possible that Andrew Bryan took over the leadership of one of these cells.[322]

Historian Walter Brooks wrote about several "sui generis," self-starting or "spontaneous" churches in Virginia, Georgia, South Carolina, the West Indies or even Africa. Black Methodists broke away from the white Methodist Church in Philadelphia in 1787, but it was not until 1794 that Bishop Francis Asbury "constituted them" a Methodist congregation. Black Episcopalians in Philadelphia had a somewhat similar experience. St. Thomas African Church was "founded" when Bishop William White recognized them in 1794 as an Episcopal congregation, even though they were an already existing group. Liele's work in Savannah and Jamaica possibly fell under this category.[323] Brooks puts Liele in Savannah from 1779 to 1782 as part of the "Babylonian captivity" of the Silver Bluff Church. It is not known why Jesse Peter alone decided to stay with the American side when David George, and George Liele wagered their future on the British.[324]

In 1925, while the Rev. Edgar Thomas was pastor, a monthly conference of the First African Baptist Church adopted a resolution that fixed May 20, 1775, as "the official date of our birth."[325] By 1928 the *Savannah Tribune* carried a blazing headline: F.A.B. Church Rumpus Being Aired in Court. The congregation was convulsed by yet another conflict. On that occasion the "breach between the contending forces at the First African Baptist Church, Franklin Square, was aired in the Superior Court room last Friday night." One faction claimed that the Rev. Thomas was "not the right man to lead the church, that he was contentious and that the church had not made the proper headway under his leadership." A Superior Court judge appointed a panel of three Special Masters, all white Baptist ministers, to hear the matter. The hearing was "witnessed by a very large crowd, every available seat and all standing room being taken long before the case was adjourned at 11 o'clock to be continued on Friday night, May 4th." The first witness called was Emanuel K. Greene, a bailiff of the city court.[326] One week later the *Savannah Tribune* ran the headline: Fight On Pastor Comes Up Sunday. The monthly conference was due to vote on whether to retain their pastor.

The moderator of the Mt. Olive Baptist Association, the Rev. R. D. Arline, presided over the hearing. There was much controversy over whether the financial status of members or the new constitution and by-laws of the church should be operative.[327] The denouement was a vote of 170 to remove and 131 to retain the Rev. Edgar Thomas as pastor. The meeting "was attended by about six hundred of the several thousand members which the church has on roll." Sol Johnson editorialized that the church was in a state in which the membership was "disrupted and the future of the church threatened, all because of differences in its ranks which might have been worked out amicably had not some of the leaders been so nearsighted."[328]

The Rev. Edgar G. Thomas entitled his last sermon as pastor of the First African Baptist Church, "God's Song of Desolation." The *Savannah Tribune* carried the full text. Thomas regarded his five years as pastor as years of "genuine gratification," the "most conscientious most zealous and most fruitful labors of my whole career." He began his sermon by disclaiming any "spirit of revenge," but soon said of the congregation: "With size and power it grew vain and arrogant." Thomas continued,

> "Father Campbell, the builder of this edifice was driven out with a few followers and organized a new church in the Beach Institute. At his death his body was not allowed in the edifice he built to be funeralized. The illustrious E. K. Love died with a broken heart, and his wife had to sue the church for the remainder of her husband's salary. Dr. J. W. Carr died with an injunction in court pending against him.
>
> Dr. W. L. Jones after burning the mortgage passed from the church in turmoil and in the midst of all kinds of rumors as to how he came to his death. The humiliating manner in which Dr. T. J. Goodall was forced out is still the talk of the town. And now I go the way of all the rest. It is my turn I take it for my part." (He concluded that the history of First African Baptist Church since slavery was), "a record of successive pastoral persecutions. Instead of following your shepherds you have fought them."[329]

In 1930 Dr. D. D. Crawford, executive secretary at the Colored Baptist Headquarters in Atlanta, claimed that Dr. Abraham Marshall organized the First Church in 1788 and Dr. Marshall and Jesse Peters organized the second church known as the Springfield Baptist Church of Augusta. He reported that Marshall established the second church "about 1840." The good doctor opted for the primacy of First Bryan Baptist.[330]

In 1938 editor Sol Johnson retold the story of black churches in Savannah. Referring to the split at First African Baptist, Johnson stated,

> "This was the beginning of the old contention of the two churches. On this point we will not touch, but simply to say that both of these churches have rendered honorable service to the glory of God and for civic and racial advancement. The observance of the sesqui-centennial of these two honorable churches should be an inspiration to their members for more effective service."[331]

Sometime around 1950, deacon, later pastor, Matthew Southall Brown of First African Baptist and deacon "Fish" Brown, with the co-operation of the respective pastors, organized a joint celebration between the two churches.[332] Both churches claimed 1788 as their founding date. The first joint service was held at the Municipal Auditorium.[333] As the *Savannah Tribune* reported,

> "For many years these two churches had a veritable feud over which church was the older of the two, both claiming the honor of being the oldest Negro church in North America. In 1950 this difference was resolved by both churches deciding to hold their anniversary jointly, going to one edifice one year and to the other church the next."[334]

On a NAACP pilgrimage to Brampton Plantation in 1972, as part of the Georgia week celebration, W. W. Law stated that Bryan bought a lot in Yamacraw in 1793 and constructed a frame building there the following year.[335] Another account states that the Rev. George Liele came to the Savannah area in 1778 with British sympathizers.[336]

J. Fred Waring, onetime president of the Georgia Historical Society, called the issue "a touchy little thing." In a tape recording made in 1972 shortly before his death, Waring recorded the fact that First African Baptist asserted that it was "a continuance of the First Church" and prided itself as "the true congregation." The First Bryan folks lay hold to the reality that they occupy one of the earlier locations of the congregation. Waring stated "they continued to squabble over this thing for the next hundred years, of course." Eventually both groups, "somehow or other," finally considered the verbal jousting futile and began holding joint anniversary celebrations. Waring commended this move because "no one can really say one church is the first church." In that year the two churches celebrated a joint commemorative service in memory of their 188th anniversary and later had their own individual anniversary celebrations.[337]

Westley W. Law wrote the Parks Department stating that the Savannah Church was older than the first black one in Philadelphia. Law wrote: "On September 4, 1793, Rev. Andrew Bryan bought for the price of thirty pounds Lot No. 7 in the village of St. Gall, fronting Bryan Street and that he erected a church there in 1794."[338] An advertisement of First African Baptist Church in 1987, states: "the 'heroic age' of George Liele marks the beginning of the church in 1773. He was ordained May 20, 1775 and enjoyed absolute freedom. He constituted the church December 1777 and thus became the first pastor of the First African Baptist Church of Savannah, Georgia."[339]

In 1988, the *Atlanta Constitution* ran an article entitled, "Which Was First Black Church? Two Savannah Congregations With Shared History Vie For U.S. Distinction." This was the 200th anniversary of the two churches, according to some sources. The reporter discovered the existence since 1832, of a scholarly and religious debate that rages today." When questioned about the quality of the relationship between the two churches, the Rev. Thurmond Tillman, pastor of First African Baptist Church stated "I don't known if it's friendly," and the reporter concluded that "Tillman and his congregation regard First Bryan as a new church formed after the schism of 1832." W. W. Law, the curator of the King-Tisdell House, was of the opinion that "both congregations can share the distinction of being the first black church. They all come from the same beginnings and have equal claim to being part of that first congregation. That's all we can say about it."[340]

The First African Baptist Church published an anniversary book entitled, *First African Baptist Church 200th Celebration*. The unsigned Foreword ends: "This 200 th Souvenir Journal reveals much that can be told in words and pictures the beginnings of this great church from 1773-1988 "But thanks be to God, which giveth us the victory through our Lord Jesus Christ. 1 Corinthians 15:57." The Rev. Thurmond N. Tillman's letter of Greetings and Salutations, states,

> "It is important to understand as we have this Bicentennial Celebration that this congregation's beginnings start as early as 1773 when Brother George Liele was called and licensed to preach the gospel of Jesus Christ. On May 20, 1775 he was ordained into the gospel ministry. It is important to note that in 1786 in a letter to W. H. Leicestershire, the Rev. George Liele states that he constituted the church in Savannah in December of 1777." (No advice was given on solving the obvious discrepancy of dates.) [341]

One of the latest public skirmishes took place at First African Baptist Church in June 1999, when Dr. Charles Elmore of Savannah State University and author of a forthcoming book on the history of First Bryan Baptist Church and Dr. Andrew Billingsley of the University of South Carolina and author of *Mighty Like A River*, grappled with the priority issue between the two churches. Not surprisingly neither side "won" the dispute.[342]

Meanwhile over at First Bryan Baptist on Bryan Street the congregation bought the large organ formerly used by the Independent Presbyterian Church. The Sunday school gave a "dime party at Chatham new Hall," to raise funds for the organ.[343] The Sunday School also "had a very pleasant concert" in the evening. The "recitations by the various classes were interesting and fine." Eleven little girls sung "Little Bright Eyes," which was judged to have been "exceptionally grand." Miss Kate Benjamin was the "excellent" organist. The church was "crowded and many had to go away being unable to gain admission."[344] In 1892, First Bryan on West Broad Street was making great efforts to "have pews put in the church. They have offered a handsome gold watch scarf pin and bracelet to the person who gets the largest amount of votes. These articles can be seen at the window of Sternbergs on Broughton Street." The paper ended this report with: "It is very seldom that this church comes before the public for aid, therefore let everybody assist."[345]

The Rev. Frank Keating (1820-1893) was born a slave around 1820. The Rev. Thomas Anderson, pastor of Second African Baptist Church, baptized Keating in April of 1841. Keating soon became a choir member under the leadership of the Rev. John Deveaux and later William Rose and earned the reputation as "an excellent singer." When mayor Richard Wayne died in June 1858, the family requested that Keating sing at the cemetery. He did so and led "a large number of the colored people at the gate of Laurel Grove Cemetery, as the funeral cortege passed with such solemn beauty and effectiveness that the press and whole community praised and spoke of it for years after, and brother Keating was ever afterwards commended by the white citizens for this mark of esteem toward them."[346]

Bishop Elliott conducted the funeral which was "confessedly the greatest funeral pageant ever witnessed in our city and participated in by all classes of citizens. At the cemetery the congregation of the First African Baptist Church of which Mayor Wayne had been a trustee, sang the funeral hymn."[347] After he became free, Keating was ordained and functioned as a missionary in the Zion Baptist Association. He regularly participated in revivals in several churches of Savannah and neighboring counties for about twenty years and was pastor of St. Matthew's Baptist Church of South Carolina. Keating was buried from First Bryan Baptist Church and the Rev. Alexander Harris conducted the service. The singing was "notably appropriate and well rendered" and the leaders of Bethlehem Baptist Church "literally covered his grave with flowers."[348]

SECOND AFRICAN BAPTIST: Henry Cunningham (1759-1842), a free mulatto, was born a slave in McIntosh County in 1759, but came to Savannah as a free person of color.[349] He married mulatto Elizabeth in 1792 and was a cooper by trade. Sometime between 1788 and 1798, he joined the First Colored Church under the Venerable Andrew Bryan and was duly baptized and ordained a deacon. One version of the story of the establishment of Second African Baptist Church has it that the white Baptist minister, the Rev. Henry Holcombe, suggested that the Colored Baptist Church split into three churches. Black Baptists have a parallel story. They contend that they had already decided to establish another church.

In 1952, Second Baptist Church celebrated its 150th anniversary and Catherine Hunt recounted the history of the congregation. She stated,

> "It was in the year 1802, December 26, when Second Baptist was formally organized by Rev. Henry Cunningham, brethren Scippio Gordon, Richard Houston, Thomas Anderson, Sisters Betty Cunningham, Leah Simpson, Silvia Whitfield, Charlotte Walla, Silvia Manox, Susan Jackson and Rev. John B. Deveaux. The Rev. Cunningham pastored the church for thirty years. Following him in order were, Rev. Thomas Anderson, Rev. John Cox, Father Simpson, Rev. Alexander Ellis, Dr. J. J. Durham, Revs. W. Bolivar, Davis., May, Wrenn and Reid."[350]

Second African Baptist Church historian Gertrude Lark, in an interview with correspondent Debby Luster, claimed that Henry Cunningham and Evans Grate, were competing for the position of pastor of the soon to be established congregation. Fearing he might not be chosen, Henry Cunningham left the colored church and joined the white Baptist church. Such was Cunningham's stature that many other members followed him and joined the white Baptist church. In the end, Henry Cunningham was chosen pastor of the new congregation.[351] During the scramble, some white Baptists bought their favored candidate, the slave Henry Francis and gave him his freedom. Francis eventually became pastor of the Ogeechee Baptist Church. Both white and black Baptist churches dismissed members to form the Second African Baptist Church.

Cunningham was ordained January 1, 1803,[352] and pastored Second African Baptist Church, which he founded December 26, 1802, until his death on March 29, 1842, at 83 years of age. He could both read and write and was a charter member of the Savannah River Association and the Sunbury Association. He built the church on lot 19 on Greene Square. The original one-story building "was remodeled and expanded in 1812"[353] On May 20, 1816, City Council granted lot 19, Greene ward to the Second Colored Baptist Church, which released it from paying taxes on the property.[354]

Second African Church proved to be the foremost seminary for local black Baptist clergy. John Benjamin Devous, later written Deveaux, became the first deacon of Cunningham's church. One report asserts that the Rev. Henry Cunningham served as pastor of the African Baptist Church in Philadelphia from 1809 to 1811[355] Historian Whittington Johnson claims that another Savannahian of the same name, and not the pastor of Second African Baptist Church, was the pastor of a Baptist church in Philadelphia.[356]

Pastor Henry Cunningham seemed to prosper in his new position. He advertised the hire of two carriages and operated a drayage business. In 1812, it fell to Cunningham to officiate at the funeral of the sainted Andrew Bryan. At Bryan's request, the funeral was conducted according to the Episcopal rite of burial. By the next year, Cunningham owned a lot at the corner of Broughton and Houston Streets and slaves whom he hired out and relied on for his income. Cunningham received and baptized Andrew Marshall, Bryan sister's son and the second pastor of First African Baptist Church. From 1817 to 1835, Cunningham owned five slaves. In 1822 Cunningham changed the name of the church to Second African Baptist Church.

Historian Julia Floyd Smith claims that Second African Baptist was the first black Baptist Church in Savannah to build a "baptismal pool" in the church.[357] By 1818, the Sunbury Association had succeeded the Savannah River Association as the umbrella organization of both white and black Baptists. The Rev. Andrew Cox Marshall was pastor of his uncle's church, the First Colored Church, the Rev. Henry Cunningham was pastor of the Second Colored Church, and the Rev. Henry Francis was pastor of the Great Ogeechee Church. Sometime in 1822, the word African in the title of the church, replaced Colored.

David Walker's *Appeal to the Colored Citizens of the World*, which called on slaves to revolt against their white oppressors, appeared in Savannah on December 21, 1829. The police seized 60 copies of the *Appeal*.[358] Walker was a former North Carolina slave who lived in Massachusetts and was part of the antislavery movement. Whites placed a bounty on his head. A white steward aboard one of the boats docked in the port was reported to have given a copy of the Appeal to Cunningham for distribution to other African Americans. At least that was one version of the story.

Another version of the incident holds that Cunningham gave the document to the mayor. Ida Martin alleges that the Governor sent the legislature a copy of the document[359] As an astute manipulator of Savannah's racial fault lines, Cunningham perhaps sought to protect himself and his congregation from the fallout, by secretly seeking the protection of the white authorities. In response to this commotion the Georgia Legislature passed an act, providing for the death penalty for anyone caught circulating written material calling for "insurrection, conspiracy or resistance among the slaves, Negroes, or citizens of this state."[360]

The ever-present fear of black revolt and the age-old white obsession to keep blacks "under due order and subjection" took a sinister turn after the discovery of Denmark Vesey and Nat Turner's attempted revolts. Black preachers had to obtain permission to preach. The legislature passed a law, which seriously restricted the activities of black ministers. It stated that "no person of color, whether free or slave, shall be allowed to preach to, exhort, or join in any persons of color, there being more than seven Negroes present." In that year, Cunningham's church had 736 members. All black preachers had to obtain a written permit from three ordained white ministers of their denomination, which attested to their good moral character to preach the gospel. County and city officials also had to issue appropriate permits.

Cunningham, though not a wealthy man, lived comfortably with perhaps little financial support from his church members and owned his own home. He reportedly had "the confidence and esteem of all classes of the community in which he has lived so long, so vigorously and so usefully."[361] Joseph F. Waring wrote that in 1837, though enfeebled, Cunningham "held his people."[362] After losing his wife of 46 years in July 1838, Henry Cunningham survived another three years and ten months. He died March 29, 1842 and was buried in the colored cemetery in Calhoun Ward. Later in 1853, his remains, along with those of several other blacks including the sainted Andrew Bryan, were exhumed and reburied in Laurel Grove Cemetery South, the black section of Laurel Grove Cemetery. The Rev. Thomas Anderson, a son of the church who had helped organize Second African Baptist and was at the time pastor of First Bryan Baptist Church, replaced Cunningham as pastor in 1842 and served until 1848.

Mrs. Nancy Cox, wife of the Rev. John Cox, pastor of Second African Baptist Church, died Sunday October 19, 1856. Her funeral was attended by a "very large number of friends." About 55 carriages and a large number of members on foot followed her remains to the cemetery.[363] The Rev. John H. Cox pastored Second African Baptist during the Civil War. The famous meeting to explain the consequences of field order # 15 was held in the church during his administration.

In 1889 the one story building was elevated to make a second level. The upper level became the sanctuary with a balcony and an indoor baptismal pool. The following year the name African was removed from the church's title. In 1910 the choir loft was moved from the rear balcony to a position facing the congregation. Members of the Monroe family donated an organ to the church in memory of their mother, the late Matilda Monroe former organist of the church. In 1886 the black paper reported: "Some of the colored churches of our city have been visited by a class of white rowdies who seem to have no other object to view than to interrupt the services and annoy the worshippers."[364]

The Rev. Alexander Ellis was born in Jamaica, West Indies in 1838. He completed his early education on the island and graduated from Calabar College in Kingston. Ellis immigrated to the United States around 1864 and pastored a church in Boston. He accepted a call to become pastor of Second African Baptist Church and was regarded as one of the "most scholarly ministers" to have served the church.[365] In March 1889, the Rev. Alexander Ellis reported that the work on the church addition was almost complete. Services were held in the basement during the building.[366] The cost of repairs including the new organ amounted to $15,000.[367]

The renovated two-story complex was dedicated August 1889.[368] Soon however, the Rev. Ellis and members of the choir were engaged in a serious conflict that resulted in his tentative deposition. A council of white ministers was invited to mediate the disagreement. They presented their conclusion to the church but the Rev. Ellis refused to accept that decision and on December 13, 1889, he was officially deposed as pastor.[369] Around this time the word African was dropped from the church's title.

The Second African Baptist Church split into two parts when the pastor, the Rev. Alexander Ellis, and about 400 members left the congregation and organized Beth-Eden Baptist Church, December 28, 1890, at Duffy Street Hall.[370] This was the third time that a West Indian born cleric was the principal protagonist in the breakup of a church in Savannah. The conflict landed in city court and was settled "by compromise." The church agreed to pay him $500 with interest, for "salary due as its late pastor."[371] The first service of the new congregation was held at the Mozart Hall St. James Street near the Savannah Tribune office. The congregation worshipped for some time in the old Ford's Hall on Whitaker Street.

In April 1891, the congregation bought a lot at the northeast corner of Lincoln and Gordon Streets for their new church.[372] One year later the Rev. Ellis and Second African Baptist Church settled their dispute "for salary due" by an agreed upon compromise.[373] Beth Eden celebrated Easter Sunday 1892 "with a superb program in the morning. The children "were out in large numbers and bright colors and acquitted themselves admirably." Miss Mamie F. Mill's class won a handsome banner for raising "the largest amount of money."[374] By May 1892, Beth-Eden had made the following payments on its lot: in April 1891, $1,000, 1892, $1,472.03 and had a balance due of $375.[375] During 1894, Beth-Eden sponsored a "rare musical treat" in the chapel on St. Julian Street. The Rev. Dr. J. H. Manley, otherwise known as the "Black Sankey," assisted by "Blind Tom No 2, and others."

The Rev. Alexander Ellis celebrated his fifteenth pastoral anniversary in 1896. The *Savannah Tribune* reported that, "The members and friends showed their appreciation by turning out in large numbers." ur city. He and The paper considered Rev. Ellis "among the divines that have done much for the spiritual, dignified and refined growth of churches in o all on his order will ever have the hearty support of the citizens."[376] The corner stone of Beth-Eden Baptist Church at Lincoln and Gordon Streets, the Rev. Alexander Ellis pastor, was laid in March 1897 before "a large and interested crowd of people." The Rev. W.J. White of Augusta was the master of ceremonies.

A "commodious platform had been erected on the north side of the church, on which were seated a number of prominent divines and citizens together with the fine choir of Beth-Eden Church." The Rev. Dr. White laid a corner stone, an elegant marble block. The inscription read "Beth-Eden Baptist Church, Organized December 28, 1890, Erected A.D. 18907." The church building was of "fine red brick" and was expected to be "one of the most ornamental and handsome churches in the city." The editor thought, "Rev. Ellis and his congregation have displayed great energy in getting their edifice so far under way and their god work is to be commended by our community."[377] The Rev. Alexander Ellis died June 20, 1900.

The **Rev. Nathaniel McPherson Clarke** was born September 15, 1871, in Jamaica, West Indies. His father, Thomas Clarke, was a Baptist deacon. Clarke attended elementary school then went to Calabar College in Kingston. In 1900, he emigrated to Boston and later studied at Lincoln University from which he graduated in 1906, with a Bachelor in Scared Theology and was ordained at the Twelfth Baptist Church of Boston. For four years, he was pastor of Calvary Baptist Church in Utica, New York. He later served a few years as pastor of the First Baptist Church of Fernandina, Florida. In 1912, Clarke accepted a call to be pastor of Beth Eden Baptist Church. [378] Once in Savannah, he set about the task of advancing his church. At that time conditions in the church were such that would "appall any other than a minister of his stamina. The membership was very small, but among the number were a few loyal ones who were determined to support a proper leader."[379] An indebtedness of $5,000 was soon liquidated and repairs were done on the church.

A *Savannah Tribune* editorial on Clarke's twenty-second pastoral anniversary regarded him as "an exemplary Christian gentleman and a pastor worthy of emulation." The writer claimed, "It is through his untiring efforts and plans that Beth-Eden is one of the few churches in Savannah which has no church debts."[380] The following year Sol Johnson stated in an editorial, entitled, "Years of Unselfish Service," that "No greater tribute was ever paid a minister than that tendered the Rev. N. M. Clarke, B.D., of Beth-Eden Baptist Church." Editor Johnson commented on Clarke's "quiet, unselfish and unassuming manner." He thought the congregation was "a unique church with a set of loyal and faithful members who believe in their church and are ever willing to follow the pastor's leadership."[381] For many years, Rev. Clarke wrote weekly articles in the *Savannah Morning News*, chronicling events in the black churches of Savannah.

The **Rev. William Gray** was born in Allendale, South Carolina, March 20, 1861, the son of Ah and Charlotte Gray. His mother was sold as a twelve-year-old slave to a white family in Barnwell. Gray grew up on a farm and from an early age felt "called by God to preach." He converted at age sixteen and preached to his classmates and conducted the funeral services of his hometown folks. At age twenty, he married Sarah Brooks of South Carolina. They had one daughter. Gray came to Savannah and worked as a coachman and attended night school. Later he attended the Georgia Industrial State College.

According to St. John's Baptist Church History, Father Gray, a member of

First Bryan Baptist Church, accepted a "call" in July 1891, to pastor and helped organize St. John's Baptist Church. The congregation consisted of seven members in "a little four room house with the partitions knocked out." A second building was erected after about a year and this lasted until 1901 when a church was built. [382] St. John's Baptist Church celebrated its anniversary in 1913 with a weeklong schedule of events. The congregation was "one of the largest and best attended churches in the city and has a membership of 2,865. Rev. John Grove was the first pastor of the church and after three years he was succeeded by the Rev. William Gray, the present pastor, who has made it one of the strongest churches in the city."[383] The congregation grew to two thousand by 1920. They rebuilt twice in order to accommodate the growing membership.

Dr. Gray was said to be one of Georgia's "greatest builders, pastors and preachers being very spiritual in his preaching, careful in his pastorate, and visionary in his building." Father Gray, as his church members called him, served as moderator of the Berean Association and seventh vice-president of the State Baptist Convention.[384] He was a Mason and pastored his church from its beginning until his death. Father Gray died at his home 910 Waters Avenue in January 1926. The *Savannah Tribune* stated that the city had "lost an upright citizen and the Baptist denomination a staunch supporter of its principles." His record for pastoring "one church is without equal in Savannah, having been pastor of St. John Baptist Church for thirty-five years. He was one of the most outstanding ministers of the community and during his long years in the ministerial work he has done untold good."[385] His funeral service lasted from 10:00 a.m. to 3:00 p.m. The "church was packed to the gallery and many of the spectators crowded the vestibule stair steps and every conceivable space that could be covered." The attendance was "one of the largest here for a number of years."[386]

Mount Zion Baptist Church was organized May 28, 1876 on West Broad Street near Huntingdon Street. The Rev. A. Neyl, pastor of the Monumental Baptist Church of McIntosh County, the Rev. H. Eaves, evangelist, and the Rev. Andrew Johnson, pastor of the Abercorn Baptist Church assisted in the inauguration of the new congregation. The Rev. A. Neyl preached from the 48th psalm. The congregation was organized with 15 persons from different churches "with letters of recommendation good standing in their churches." A notice in the same issue of the paper however, gave another version of the founding. It stated: "On the 25th of May the Rev. A. Neil, Rev. Hammond Eve and Rev. Andrew Johnson went and organized a disorderly assembly members of the Bethlehem Church who had been expelled from the that church for disorderly conduct, into that so-called church, between West Broad and Gaston Streets. This is to show what kind of ministers of the gospel they are." The notice was signed by F. Lloyd."[387]

Another account states that three ordained ministers and a deacon met in a frame building on Robert Street, in the Frogtown section of Savannah, November

22, 1876 and organized Mount Zion Baptist Church with the Rev. Edward T. Brown as first pastor. In February of 1882 a church building was purchased on West Broad Street, where the former Star Theater was later located. The Rev. W. L. P. Weston, a minister from White Bluff, was called in January 1883 and served until his death in 1908. During the administration of the Rev. M. D. Spencer, formerly from Valdosta, the congregation bought the present church building for $10,000.[388]

In 1912 the congregation bought "two one story stores and two small houses." The lot had measured about ninety feet on West Broad Street and sixty feet on Anderson Street. The plan was "to erect a beautiful brick church edifice on the corner." The original plan was to build a new church on the old site but was changed because "that block is rapidly being given over to business." George H. Bowen, the black real estate agent, handled the purchase.[389]

Messrs. Linton Lyons, Geo. Anderson and William Black, deacons of the Mt. Zion Baptist Church, sued William H. Stillwell and the Rev. McD. Spencer and the trustees of Mt. Zion Church to "enjoin the said pastor and trustees from selling to Mr. Stillwell other property for the church without first getting authority from a majority of the congregation." The complaint alleged that the property was worth about $10,000 but was being sold for $6,500 less than its market value. They accused the pastor of keeping the sale "a secret from the deacons." The pastor was also accused of planning to leave the congregation as soon as the sale was completed. Judge C. B. Conyers signed the injunction.[390] Linton Lyons, Geo Anderson and William Black wrote a long letter to the editor of the *Savannah Tribune*, claiming to have "a large majority of the church with us," and explained their side of the controversy.[391] The Rev. McD. Spencer resigned in 1914 causing a split in the congregation. The Rev. H.D.Butler next served as pastor until 1919. The Rev. John Quincy Adams became pastor of Mount Zion in 1919.

The **Rev. John Q. Adams** (1894-1994), was born March 27, 1894 at 409 West Hall Street in Savannah. The De Renne family owned his grandmother. John W. Davis recruited Adams and two other Savannahians to attend Morehouse College. John Pluckett a wealthy businessman and deacon at the First Baptist Church in Providence, Rhode Island, paid for his tuition to Morehouse College in Atlanta where he did his high school education. He was in Morehouse's first graduation class.[392] He served a tour in the army in 1918 He attended East Broad Street Elementary School and was baptized in 1908. Young and upon graduation from college he taught in Denmark, South Carolina and at Tuskegee Institute, Alabama. In 1919 he returned to Savannah and became pastor of Mt. Zion Baptist Church.[393]

Adams served his church as pastor for almost 60 years and retired in 1978. He was made pastor emeritus of the church. In addition he taught English at Beach for 40 years and retired in 1960. Judge Eugene Gadsden described him as "a good teacher." An ardent supporter of the civil rights movement in Savannah, W. W. Law remembered Adams as one of the few blacks who "paid the $500 life membership from his own funds." Adams also made his church available for meetings of the NAACP. Adams died in 1994.[394]

William J. Claghorn was born in Savannah, around 1822, to Harriet Clark. Later in life, he married Cornelia, a seamstress. They obtained their freedom sometime before 1856. In 1852, the Episcopal Church closed its mission to slaves on the Savannah River,[395] and transferred its ministry to urban blacks in Savannah. The Claghorn family worshiped at the Savannah River mission with the Rev. Sherod Kennerly.[396] The Church's Register of April 15, 1868, lists the Cleghorn family as members living on Bryan Street. He is also listed as number 93 among the communicants of 1869.[397]

Claghorn and the Rev. Kennerly established an Episcopal congregation in the workshop of his bakery on Perry Lane. Kennerly reported that Claghorn "was anxious for the services of the church and took an active interest in the matter."[398] Kennerly wrote: "In the winter of 1855, I procured a place of worship-a large workshop above the longest bakery in the place. The proprietor was a colored man among the most respectable in the city."[399] St. Stephen's was to be "for the exclusive use of the people of color."[400] Thus after a lapse of some 67 years, the Savannah River again produced a black religious leader, though in this case he was a layman. This congregation was the first urban non-slave African American mission in the Diocese of Georgia.

In addition to being a master baker by trade, Claghorn was also a caterer of some renown. Beginning in the early 1850's, Claghorn developed a strong reputation as a caterer and serviced some of the grandest parties in the city. Claghorn catered a repast in the Oglethorpe Hall given by the Chatham Artillery and the Republican Blues, which the local press considered "sumptuous and elegant." He suffered two broken legs as his horse threw him from the wagon while delivering bread on Montgomery Street in July 1856.

The local press reported that: "William J. Claghorn will resume baking on Thursday, the 4th of December."[401] Claghorn was listed in the 1850 census as having a wife and two young children, Mary, six, and Williamina, two years of age. The white press reported: "The supper at Masonic Hall on Monday night was handsomely gotten up, and did credit to the caterer, William Claghorn, an old resident of Savannah and well and favorably known to most, if not all of our citizens...nearly everything on the table was the handiwork either of Claghorn, or some member of his family."[402] The fancy confectionary, the ornamental icing of the cakes, some of which were as beautiful specimens as we ever saw, was made in Savannah, and in the family of the caterer." That year Claghorn was listed as a 38-year-old Master baker with $4,000 in real estate and $2,000 in personal property.[403] Living with him were his wife Cornelia and two children, Mary and Williamina. Wilhelmina died when she was eight years and five months old and was buried May 13, 1856, in Laurel Grove Cemetery South. She was a free person of color.[404] Four white men, presumably the German bakers who worked for him, also lived at the same address.

In 1860, a lot on Harris, Habersham, Macon and Lincoln Streets, was purchased from F. M. Threadcraft for $600 but he generously donated $200 toward the cost.[405] The congregation bought an unused former Unitarian Church, according to one report, put it on rollers, and moved it to Troupe Square. Mrs. Eleanor Pollard claimed that the building was partly demolished and remodeled.[406] Percy Sugden,[407] and William Harden[408] reported that the building was put on rollers and moved to the present site.

The congregation began to worship in its new church April 11, 1860. On March 29, 1860, the city gave St. Stephen's Episcopal Church lot 18, in Troup ward; thereby the congregation was "relieved of ground rent to be used as a site for a place of worship for St. Stephen's Episcopal Church, colored."[409] An advertisement in 1861 stated that a few free pews were reserved for "white and black visitors."[410] A rectory was purchased and Bishop Elliott consecrated the church September 13, 1863. Music was the one missing ingredient for a stable congregation. The Rev. Kennerly decided to solve this problem by obtaining the services of James Porter. As Kennerly wrote, "I became his guardian and carried him to Savannah, to instruct and train a choir for St. Stephen's."[411]

Years later church members William Claghorn, Dr. William Pollard and other black leaders petitioned the Savannah Chatham Board of Education in an attempt to improve the education of black students in the public schools of the city. Claghorn and Pollard were regarded "as thrifty men, respected by the leading whites of the city." William J, Claghorn died at home on March 23, 1878. The Rev. William H. Morris, rector of St. Stephen's Episcopal Church, officiated at his funeral. In 1881, the rector and wardens of Christ Church and Henry L. Giles and Cyrus Campfield, wardens of St. Stephen's Church, formed a committee to raise funds for repairs to St. Stephen's Church. The appeal stated, "Those in whose behalf the plea is made are poor and cannot be expected to provide the funds necessary to enlarge the work as it needs be in order to make it effectual."[412]

James Porter a free mulatto was born in Charleston, South Carolina, in August 1826[413] and was a trained musician. When Bishop Stephen Elliott visited the congregation for confirmation in 1857, he was amazed at the proficiency with which the choir sang the service. He remarked, "They have exemplified a steadfastness and perseverance, as well as capacity for the acquisition, and ability in the execution of musical knowledge, which reflects credit not only upon themselves but their race."[414] He was the first African American Senior Warden in the Diocese, and was in charge of St. Stephen's congregation during the Civil War.[415]

Porter was one of the twenty black leaders who met with Secretary of War William Stanton and General William Sherman, and made a significant contribution to the quality of life in black Savannah.[416] Porter reported to the convention,

"I received my Episcopal appointment as Lay Rector of

> this Church one year ago. Since that time I have endeavored to work faithfully and I am happy to say that notwithstanding we have been and are still, surrounded by many embarrassments, our Church occupies today a better place in the minds of our people than she ever did before. I hold services in this Church regularly twice every Sabbath and in addition to this we have had early morning services on Christmas and also on Wednesday and Friday evenings during lent." (Porter concluded), "This is a very important field and if a good and efficient minister be supplied, one in every way suited to this peculiar work, we think that no fears may be entertained of his raising an abundant harvest unto the Lord.[417]

In 1865, the *Savannah Daily Herald* published an advertisement on the colored churches in the city. The Rev. William Campbell pastored the First African Baptist on Franklin Square. The Rev. John Cox pastored the Second African Baptist Church on Green Square. The Rev. Ulysses Houston pastored the Third African Baptist Church at Bryan and Fahm Street. James Porter, lay reader, was in charge of St. Stephen's Episcopal Church on Calhoun Square and the Rev. William Bentley pastored Wesley Chapel on New Street near Fahm.[418] The church held a fair in February 1865, to raise money to "redeem their beautiful chapel from debt."[419] St. Stephen's Vestry lacked a quorum when it attempted to hold the annual Vestry elections.[420]

Bishop Stephen Elliott's address to the post Civil War convention reported that St. Stephen's "has very wisely resisted all the current nonsense about their superior advantages under the present condition of affairs and has during their want of a white minister, kept themselves together under the lay reading of Mr. James Porter, a very intelligent and well educated colored man, to whom I have given permission to read, without having actually licensed him in that capacity." The Bishop thought: "The events of the war have produced no effect upon this congregation; it continues to carry on its concerns exactly as before and it could only receive mischief by any intermeddling with. It is quiet, orderly, subordinate to Episcopal authority and ready to be guided by those whom it has always recognized as its best and truest friends." He added, "May God watch over them and keep them in the grace of humility and free from all the wild delusions which are now cursing the land."[421]

Porter gave his second report to the convention. He stated: "Our Church continues to grow in importance and it is hoped that our friends will aid us in securing all the means and appliances to present the Church's services in all their beauty and dignity, that we may be able to worship God under our own vine and fig tree, with none to hurt or make us afraid."[422] In 1867, Porter addressed a meeting on the coming election. He admonished blacks not to be afraid because "God was on their side." The local white press reported that both whites and blacks approved of his speech.[423] That same year St. Stephen's members organized the Savannah Mutual Benevolent Association, "to relieve the sick and destitute colored people of the city."[424]

The **Rev. Joseph Robert Love** was born and educated in Nassau, Bahama Islands, in 1839.[425] In 1869 he became the first black to be ordained a deacon in Florida[426] Love did very well in his preordination examination. Unlike many black candidates at that time, he did not request a dispensation from the full requirements demanded by the canons, but "sustained a protracted and searching examination on the full course of study, including the Latin and Greek languages."[427]

The year 1871 represented a sea change for African American Episcopalians in Savannah for on December 26, the Rev. J. Robert Love a black deacon, took charge of St. Stephen's Church.[428] The advent of this tall, heavyset, jet-black West Indian as rector of St. Stephen's caused quite a dither among the mainly high yellow congregants.[429] After only four months at the church, Love made his first report to the convention. He found remarkable vitality in the parish as was evidenced by the "noble exertion put forth by many to help in the work." He had especial praise for the work of the 'Ladies Missionary Society.'

Love established a parochial school, which had an enrollment of 106 students with a daily average attendance of eighty students[430] The Rev. J. Robert Love clashed with the Rev. Timothy Harley, a white Baptist minister, who objected to Bishop Beckwith's signing himself the Bishop of Georgia. Love replied to Hartley's articles and the black press described the exchanges as "the sensation of the hour especially since Mr. Love was a Negro and Mr. Hartley a white man."[431] Despite this verbal victory, Love's tenure at St. Stephen's lasted only eight months.

In 1872, St. Stephen's congregation, following the disastrous example of elder daughter First African Baptist, split into two parts as the Rev. J. Robert Love left with a few members and founded St. Augustine's Episcopal Mission on the west side of Savannah in a rented hall in Yamacraw Village. His successor at St. Stephen's, the Rev. Joseph S. Atwell, another West Indian, commented on the "bad will" Love's leaving caused. Atwell stated that the incident was "more damaging to the harmony and prosperity of the race than all the prejudices whichever before were brought to bear against it from without."[432] Probably the years of white tutelage had left their mark and the congregation was ill prepared for Love's aggressive black leadership.

Several explanations have been given for Love's short stay at St. Stephen's. Roi Ottley in his story of jet-black Chicago Defender publisher Robert Abbott claims that the "color" problem was the main cause of the departure. Ottley claims, without offering any evidence, that Love insisted that black worshippers should enjoy the same rights and privileges as the light-skinned. Ottley also states that eyebrows were arched when Love performed the marriage of a Chinese man to a mulatto woman. Unfortunately, there is no such marriage recorded in the church's register. He also claims that St. Stephen's near-white vestrymen tried to exclude blacks from membership.[433] Ottley adds that Negroes in Savannah placed "a premium" on light skin color.[434]

Ottley claims that Abbott was teased by his own folk because of his dark skin color.[435] Spinster Celia Abbott, matriarch of the Abbotts, a black family with roots going back to the 1780's, bought her own freedom in 1853 and operated a thriving hairdressing salon on South Broad Street with a white clientele.[436] Celia was indignant because Robert's mother was a "field hand." When Celia died, she left an estate worth $5,000.[437] She enjoyed "the patronage of the best families in this city." She died at her residence on Broughton Street in her 52 year. Her remains were taken to St. Simon's Island for burial.[438] Among blacks of that day, social class was almost as highly prized as skin complexion. The social mores of the two Savannahs, white and black, during that period, mandated a high degree of social class-consciousness and clannishness.[439] Savannah born Wanda S. Lloyd, a feature writer of the *Washington Post*, wrote an article after taking the "Black Heritage Trail of Savannah." Lloyd quoted the conductor of the tour as stating that all prospective members of St. Stephen's Episcopal Church had to submit to a "comb test." This comb was supposed to separate "pure mulatto stock" from all other varieties. The acid test was the smooth sailing of the comb through one's hair on the first combing. Failure to sustain the comb's passage resulted in denial of membership[440]

National bestseller novelist John Berendt, in his Midnight in the Garden of Good and Evil,[441] gave his imprimatur to a companion myth about St. Stephen's (now called St. Matthew's) Episcopal Church. Berendt reports that the light skin people use the pews "up front" while the darker members of the congregation sit in the pews "in back." African American Episcopalians have worshipped on West Broad Street, now Martin Luther King, Jr., Blvd., for over 50 years and have never witnessed the events Berendt relates. But it may be that the persistence of this myth says something about race relations in the city.

There is no doubt that a "light skin aristocracy" existed in Savannah. This group obtained its religious sustenance mainly from St. Stephen's Episcopal Church, Second African Baptist and the Congregational Church.[442] Love himself confessed that St. Stephen's congregation, though a small part of black Savannah, exerted "a powerful influence among the people of color"[443] Ottley claims that these "light complexioned blacks" were the accepted "leaders of Negro Society"[444] The somewhat sharp color, caste-like structure of black society in Savannah, mirrored that of Charleston, South Carolina, and later Atlanta, Georgia. In Charleston, the high yellows were concentrated at St. Mark's Episcopal Church[445] and in Atlanta at First Congregational Church[446] Mulattoes as a group, especially those assisted by their white fathers, tended to have more advantages of education and income.[447] Social class rather than 'color' seems to be a more accurate explanation for the attraction of St. Stephen's Church. It was a church of black strivers. A study of black churches in Chicago found that upper class blacks were inclined to prefer the more ritualistic type of church liturgy found in the Episcopal Church.[448]

Energetic as ever, the brilliant but restless J. Robert Love established a parochial day school at St. Augustine's mission, which proved to be a means of "adding to the church daily." He had $1,400 on hand for a church, "the kind gifts of friends from abroad."[449] The Rev. J. Robert Love was listed in the Journal though that year "colored" was not attached to his name. He did not, however, attend the convention. Love began building up the mission. He stated: "The mission enjoys no inconsiderable advantage by being located in the very midst of a large number of colored people within easy reach of all." The rented room was already overcrowded with worshippers. Love felt that the poor state of the mission needed to be improved since doing so "would add to our respectability and influence." He needed school furniture and materials, a schoolroom and above all a chapel, and looked toward the day when the congregation would be "under our own vine and fig tree."

Love thought the Diocese could look to St. Augustine's mission for "happy results for the colored people." Love's membership was composed mainly of persons "hitherto attached to the sects: its Sunday and parish school pupils are taken from the sects." Some years later, while Love was in Buffalo New York, Martha Hollingsworth of Savannah charged him with cruel treatment of a child placed in his care. Love got the child's father, the Rev. William W. Morris, rector of St. Stephen's Episcopal Church, the Rev. Boone, rector of Christ Church to vouch for him. The charge was dropped.[450]

In 1880 the Sunday school and parish in general "had greatly improved and the members had begun to take an active interest in the work." By special exertion, "the debts which have been allowed to accumulate during the past several years have been paid. The people are poor, yet they are striving hard to meet the expenses of the parish, and there is reason to believe that by judicious management they may succeed in their efforts in the course of time."[451] Two white youths were arrested and fined by the mayor for disturbing worship at St. Stephen's Episcopal Church.[452]

Henry L. Giles died in 1885. He was one of the pillars of St. Stephen's Episcopal Church, and had served as senior warden for many years, and "by his devotion and sacrifices to everything that tended to its welfare, had won the love and esteem of the entire congregation."[453] A carpenter by trade, Giles had also worked on the church when the congregation bought it and had worked on many houses in downtown Savannah.[454] St. Stephen's suffered extensive rain damage in August 1887. R. J. Artson, "our well known and experienced carpenter and builder," did the repairs.[455] The following May, the ladies of the congregation sponsored a Japanese Tea party at the home of Mrs. J. P. Jones on Waldburg Street. Admission was 10 cents for adults and 5 cents for children.[456]

The Rev. Henry Hartley, M.D., who ministered at St. Augustine's Episcopal Church, and was the only African American cleric to work and live for a time in Burroughs, left the city for the Diocese of Iowa. Hartley was born and educated in Port-of-Spain, Trinidad. The *Savannah Tribune* regarded him as "one of the most interesting personages that has ever lived in this section." In addition to his religious training Dr. Hartley was "regularly commissioned to practice law and medicine in several of the states. He is intelligently conversant with every religious creed and doctrine and a linguist of no mean order-as fluent with French and Spanish as he is with English, while Greek, Latin and Hebrew are mere toys." Harley was one of the founding members of the South Atlantic Medical Association of black doctors in the city. The writer felt that such a man "of such gigantic parts could have played an important part in our life's drama."[457] On Friday, October 7, 1892, Bishop Quintard of Tennessee ordained the Rev. Dr. Hartley in St. James Episcopal Church in Baltimore. Bishop C. Nelson of Georgia preached the sermon. The Savannah Tribune described Bishop Nelson as "a special favorite among the Afro-American clergy. A grand and noble man he is and we feel that there is no more devoted Diocesan in the House of Bishops respecting Afro-Americans than the Bishop of Georgia. The Bishop came into the colored conference and won our hearts." The paper described the ordination sermon as "grand and inspiring. May God bless him and help him in his work among Afro-Americans in his Diocese."[458]

Shuman, the white man "who raised a disturbance at St. Stephen's Church on Sunday night was fined $25 in police court."[459] Just before the beginning of services members discovered that the roof of St. Augustine's Church and Parish Hall was on fire. The quick action of "Henry C. Holmes who with other members and friends saved much of the valuables in the building. The edifice is partly insured." The fire interfered with the operation of the parochial school. The officers of the Wage Earners Bank offered the Rev. Weston the use of their Hall across the street.[460] In 1913 the congregation announced that the school would close on May 30 and "it will not re-open for another term."[461] The Rev. J. L. Taylor, rector of St. Stephen's organized the Men's Club in 1913. L. M. Campfield was president, Dr. Linton S. Parks vice-president, and W. J. Shaw was secretary, with James R. Davis as treasurer. The club sought "to help the young men of the church and of the city along all lines." Membership was open to members and nonmembers.[462]

Haitian Catholics, who did not participate in the first successful new world slave revolt,[463] came to Savannah in the 1790's as part of the white and black exodus from Haiti.[464] They were the pioneer black Catholics in Savannah. This influx of persons from the West Indies caused quite a commotion in Savannah. Several citizens at a mass meeting in Savannah in 1795, claimed to be "fearful of similar uprisings as a result of the introduction of Negro slaves from the Island," and resolved to prevent "any more French slaves from being landed." Felix, a slave who had taken part in the revolution in Saint-Domingue, was arrested and jailed "until he be shipped out of the United States."[465] Soon however, St. John's Catholic parish began registering the presence of several blacks in its baptism and marriage records.

Sister M. Julian Griffin wrote, "It is notable that the first religious ceremony performed here, after the dedication of the building itself, was the baptism of two black children, slaves of Col. Gordon and Lewis Nicholas Allard."[466] Blacks and whites worshipped together in one congregation from around 1804 when the first church was built. Between 1796 and 1808, over 100 people of color were recorded in the parish registers. [467] In 1816 a newly arrived priest found some "fifteen or twenty" people of color an "edifying part" of the congregation. Over 30 blacks were married in the parish between 1796 and 1816. During the next twenty years sixty-two blacks were married in St. John's.

Bishop John England in 1832, described the black members of St. John's as fond of "entering little sodalities of devotion, and assembling in the afternoon in the church for prayer and singing." They were "exceedingly attentive" to have their own funeral customs observed. He observed that many of the slaves were "extremely well instructed and pious."

Blacks worshipped in the gallery of the church. Years later, the "high yellow" Mirault family became one of the most prominent black Catholic families in Savannah. Aspasia Mirault owned an ice cream parlor, some slaves, and even rented a pew in the church. From 1816 to 1838, about 62 blacks were married in the church.[468] Sister Jane Francis, a white, opened a school for black children in 1855 on Habersham Street near Charlton Street. Another school was opened on the grounds in 1867.[469]

A group of Benedictine Monks arrived in Savannah in May 1874 to evangelize blacks.[470] They organized a parish for blacks in Savannah and a church was built at Harris and East Broad Streets and a school on Perry Street with 75 students.[471] In 1876 they built a chapel on the Isle of Hope. The monks received many candidates seeking the religious life so they bought a small plot of land on the Isle of Hope and planned to build a novitiate and monastery. The yellow fever epidemic of 1876 decimated the group and the work was abandoned.

Months later another group of monks established St. Benedict's Manual Labor School for colored boys on Skidaway Island. The school opened September 30, 1878. The building was dedicated with much fanfare as 600 guests arrived on the Island for the occasion. The monks were quite pleased with the progress of the work and envisioned the possibility of sending "Negro missionaries to Liberia and found an abbey for the colored people of Africa."[472] As it turned out however, blacks had a "horror for farm work," which had been their lot for too many years under slavery and that type of education was not acceptable to the many black families in the area. The parents preferred a "training for their sons which prepared them for jobs as bookkeepers, store clerks or office mangers, anything rather than farm work."[473] The curriculum was adjusted somewhat but the venture was soon abandoned. At that stage of their development, black parents demanded more of those who educated their children. They surely had very high hopes for their children's future. The monks were apparently either unable or unwilling to adapt to the African American mentality in the Savannah area. The Monastery on Skidaway Island was closed in 1889. [474]

Bishop Gross inaugurated St. Benedict's colored Catholic Church January 3, 1875, at the corner of East Broad and Harris Streets. The white and colored societies assembled at the corner of Drayton and South Broad Streets and were accompanied by two bands of musicians. A "large number of colored people, men and women, followed in line." That same evening, Father Smoulder preached the dedication sermon at St. John's Cathedral. The building was "densely packed, one half being occupied by whites and the other by colored people."[475] Two years later, blacks were given the use of the old Cathedral on Drayton Street and McDonough Streets. The building was "thoroughly improved, remodeled and renovated and turned over to the colored Catholics." The Bishop dedicated the building, later known as St. Joseph's, in March 1877.[476] Abram Beasley, husband of Matilda Beasley, later known as Mother Beasley, was buried from this church in September 1877.[477]

In 1881, the monks built a small wooden church on "the Commons," near the border of Savannah, at the corner of Habersham and 32nd Streets. The building was originally "erected for the colored people then changed to a church for whites, when the new church was built on East Broad and Gaston Streets." Father Melchior reportedly "did a work which challenged admiration and labored for the colored people when few others could or would have done so."[478] This white parish was located on 32nd Street near Habersham and in 1902 at was moved to Bull and 33rd. Streets.[479] Mother Beasley contributed financially to this endeavor. In 1902, Sacred Heart moved to Bull and 33rd Streets and in that year the monks built a military high school adjacent to Sacred Heart Church. [480]

Some years later, the monks had gone full circle. Blacks were excluded from the Benedictines' school in Savannah because of segregation. The Poor Clare Nuns arrived on Skidaway in 1885 to run a school for blacks and an orphanage. They apparently were not dignified enough for local Catholics as their begging habits included approaching sailors and ships in the harbor. Bishop Thomas Becker dismissed them in 1886.[481] The Poor Clare Nuns arrived on Skidaway in 1885 to run a school for blacks and an orphanage. They apparently were not dignified enough for local Catholics as their begging habits included approaching sailors and ships in the harbor. Bishop Thomas Becker dismissed them in 1886.[482]

Mother Matilda Beasley founded St. Francis' Colored Orphan Home at East Broad and Gaston Streets, August 15, 1887. She established a community of black Franciscan nuns and financially aided the establishment of Sacred Heart parish for black Catholics. Her religious community was not successful and she ended her days almost as a recluse in a house near Sacred Heart Church until her death in

1903.[483] In 1897 the Institution housed 26 children and was maintained by charitable contributions, but unfortunately, "the little income of laundry work, done within the restricted premises of the Home does not amount to much." The Nuns lamented, "no more work can be undertaken for lack of room, but we look forward to the day when some charitable heart will be inspired to help the good work."

The cornerstone of the new St. Benedict Church at East Broad Street and Gaston Street Lane was laid July 14, 1889. This gothic style church with a seating capacity of 400, "and ample choir facility," was opened on East Broad and Gordon Lane. The basement had five comfortable rooms "which will be used for school purposes, under a corps of good teachers" The Bishop reported that the "entire cost of the church is $10, 655, including the lot, all of which were contributions from the two Bishops and donations outside of Savannah, not one cent having been collected here."[484]

The ceremony drew "a large crowd of people very nearly equally divided between white and colored." The two-story building was for "colored Roman Catholics," who were said to number about 500. Sister Mathilda Beasley, two other sisters and twenty orphans ranging in age from two to sixteen "marched up and formed in line, with two handsome silk banners." A collection was taken up and "quite a handsome sum was netted."[485] The church had two "pretty towers facing East Broad Street. The improvements made later for the purpose of having an Orphan Home for colored girls, spoiled the whole architectural beauty of the Church."

The church was originally dedicated to St. Benedict the Abbot, founder of the Benedictine Order. Years later Bishop Keiley, at the request of the people and pastor, placed the church under the patronage of St. Benedict the Moor.

In 1889, *Savannah Tribune* quoted a report from the Savannah Independent of July 6, on a sermon delivered by Bishop Becker to black Catholics. The Bishop reportedly avowed that he: "had no use for mulattos, that they were a mongrel set of people and that the really black man alone commanded his kind attention and respect." The reporter observed that "the major portion of the colored congregation are mulattos and these words of the Bishop came like a thunder clap upon them, and they have been very irate over the matter ever since."[486] As Gillian Brown wrote, "There have been times in the history of this area when Catholics have been as prejudiced, as avaricious, as narrow-minded as anyone else."[487]

Bishop Benjamin J. Keiley requested the Society For African Missions to take charge of black Catholics. On January 1, 1907 "the Very Rev. I. Lissner Provincial of the Society of African Missions took charge of the work." [488] Bishop Benjamin J. Keiley requested the S.M.A. fathers to take over the black work in the diocese. Father Ignatius Lissner used St. Benedict's parish as the base of his operation. Soon the Savannah Tribune trumpeted these priests had ample experience working with black folks and not surprisingly were more successful than the monks.

In 1908 Lissner founded St. Anthony of Padua in West Savannah. The

Savannah Tribune opined that these priests had,

> "Done glorious work for the welfare of the colored Catholics. The little congregation of St. Benedict's Church in our city has been increased and strengthened; St. Benedict's school with its devoted teaching staff, the good Franciscan Sisters has given a good primary education o children of every denomination."[489]

St. Anthony's school opened in 1909 and within months the three black Catholic schools had nearly 300 students.[490] Bonnie White and J. Miller were the first teachers in the school.

Father Lissner bought a number of lots from the Fellwood tract "on which he intends to establish a school for colored children and a home for old colored and infirm people."[491] Most Pure Heart of Mary was founded in 1911 in the Brownsville section of the city where Charity Hospital and Haven School were located.

In 1916 Father Ignatius Lissner was concerned that the state was making it almost impossible for white nuns to teach in black schools. A chance encounter with Mother Theodore, a nun without an existing religious affiliation, agreed to come to Savannah to organize a religious community called Handmaids of the Most Pure Heart of Mary. The community began in a house on Taylor Street then moved to the top floor of St. Mary's School on 36th. Street. St. Vincent's Sisters of Mercy trained the five sisters. Two of the five nuns taught at the school while the three others "begged door to door for their support and the support of their pupils." This noble endeavor was short lived. Few black women were willing to join the group and the community eventually moved to New York.[492]

The Catholic Mutual Aid Society housed at Gaston and Bolton Streets, was "in a very prosperous condition, both financially and otherwise, having had but three cases of sickness and one death within th past year." The organization presented an Easter Festival in order to raise funds. Tickets were 25 cents each.[493] The object of this Society was "the relief of its members in sickness and death; and development in all that pertains to the best in morals, social and literary acquirements. The members of the society must be communicants of the Catholic Church." The society was organized around 1900. John Scurdy was elected president, James Dowse vice-president and Joseph King secretary/treasurer. [494]

Methodists worshipped with their white co-religionists but "one side of the gallery was appropriated for their use." When Methodist Bishop Capers visited Savannah in 1819, he found "few Negroes who attended Methodist preaching:"[495] The following year the Methodists built a separate meetinghouse for blacks. By 1845, they replaced that building with a splendid new church, Andrew chapel, in Oglethorpe Ward. This chapel was located on Broughton and Jefferson Streets.[496] Trinity Methodist Church supported this chapel over the years and many black preachers were trained and licensed there.

At the end of the Civil War Andrew Chapel was without a regular pastor and was "kept together" by William Bently, C. L. Bradwell, and William Gaines.[497] Seven of the twenty black leaders, who met with Secretary of War Edwin Stanton and Major-General William T. Sherman at the General's headquarters, were members of Andrew Chapel. The Chapel had 360 members and the facility was valued at $20,000. William Bentley, 72 years of age, was born in Savannah and had been a slave for 25 years but was emancipated by his owner's will. He had been in the ministry for about 20 years and was a pastor at Andrew Chapel. Charles Bradwell 40, was born a slave in Liberty County, and remained a slave until 1851 when his owner's will freed him. He had been a minister at Andrew Chapel for 10 years.

William Gaines, 41 years of age, was born in Willis County and was the slave of Senator Robert Toombs until the end of the Civil War. He had been a preacher at Andrew Chapel for 16 years. Glasgon Taylor, aged 72 years, was born a slave in Wilkes County, and remained bound until the end of the war. He had been in the ministry at Andrew Chapel for 35 years. Jacob Godfrey, aged 57 was born in Marion County, South Carolina, and was a slave until the end of the war. He had been a class-leader in Andrew Chapel for 16 years. The Rev. James E. Godfrey a Methodist preacher, who fought in the Confederate Army, owned him. Robert N. Taylor, aged 51, was born a slave in Wilkes County. He was a class-leader at Andrew Chapel for 9 years. John Johnson aged 51, was born a slave in Bryan County. He remained a slave until the end of the Civil War, and had been a class leader and treasurer of Andrew Chapel for 16 years.[498] On January 7, 1858, the city gave lot 10, in Crawford ward east, to the Methodists. This lot was subsequently exchanged for lot No. 4, May 12, 1859, with power to sell and apply proceeds for the church.[499]

Towards the end of the Civil War the Trustees of Trinity Methodist wanted the Andrew Chapel congregation to return the property to them but the chapel refused.[500] Two African Americans, David Deas and J.M. Johnson, held some sort of title to the property. Eventually "The colored people of Andrew Chapel took over that property by paying the claims of the Trustees and changed the name to St. Phillip's Methodist Episcopal Church."[501] . Some years later, apparently another attempt was made to reclaim the property. The matter was finally settled in Superior Court before judge William Schley when the jury "brought a verdict for the plaintiffs, which will have the effect of restoring the trust to the original trustee for the uses and purposes for which it was created."[502]

There are several accounts of the founding of St. Phillip's A.M.E. Church. One narrative maintains that the Rev. Bradwell made "secret arrangements" with the Rev. James Lynch to take Andrew Chapel into the A.M.E. denomination. Lynch, an A.M.E. minister working for the Federal authorities in Savannah was born in Baltimore in 1838. His father, a mulatto merchant, purchased his freedom and that of his wife. Lynch and other agents examined the first teachers for black schools in

Savannah. The Rev. A. L. Stanford "was assigned to Savannah from the original South Carolina Conference."[503] They organized the group as St. Phillip's A.M.E. congregation in Savannah.[504] Jesse Brinson[505] held to the "coup" theory, with the Rev. A. L. Stanford establishing the church June 16, 1865, and being its first pastor. Brinson was chosen as foreman of a city court jury in Novmber 1949. He was reported to have been the first Negro to have "served in this capacity in Savannah."[506] Sanford was the "Worshipful Master of the first Masonic Lodge in Georgia, which is now operating, Eureka."[507]

According to the Rev. R.H. Singleton: "the A. M. E. Church was organized in Savannah June 16, 1865 by the Rev. James Lynch, one of the pioneer missionaries to the freedmen of the South. St. Philip A. M. E. Church was thus organized and became the first congregation of the denomination in Georgia."[508] Rita F. Spitler reported that the Rev. A. L. Stanford founded the Church, which was chartered as St. Phillip's A. M. E. on June 16, 1865.[509] Kermit Smalls quotes a Historical Tablet, formerly at the original St.Phillip's on New Street and now at St. Phillip Monumental on Park Avenue and Jefferson Street, which states,

> "This membership withdrew from the jurisdiction of the M. E. Church South, and in February 1865 under the leadership of Rev. James Lynch and Bro. C. L. Bradwell, a local preacher, formed a separate organization under the government of the A.M.E Church. The storm of 1896 destroyed the old building and scattered the congregation. A few members remained and the Georgia Conference in 1897, at Waycross, Ga., renamed it St. Phillip Monumental Church."[510]

A suitable piece of property could not be purchased for this "Radical Church," as it was then called, "But through the kindness and business sagacity of Mr. Thomas Garnett, one of the trustees of the infant organization, the lot on New Street was purchased by him and deeded to the A.M.E. Church, which became the first piece of property owned by the church in the state."[511] Two and a half months after its founding the Rev. A. L. Stanford established a Sunday school in the church. Thieves broke into St. Phillip's A.M.E. Church under construction on New Street and stole some chairs.[512] When completed the new St. Phillip was "a two story structure with paintings on its ceiling depicting certain scenes of a religious nature."[513]

By July 1872 blacks were apparently acting in accordance with the wishes of the white paper. A correspondent reported: "In the African Church on Bryan Street, there was a large congregation present, which would lead to the inference that the colored folks are more interested in saving their souls than in politics. The majority of the colored people are fast learning that these meetings do not benefit them in the least. Their rights as voters are recognized by the white people, and they will be protected by them in the exercise of the same."[514]

The Rev. Henry McNeal Turner (1834-1915) was born February 1, 1834 on a farm near Newberry in Abbeville County, South Carolina, to Henry and Sarah Greer Turner, free people of color.[515] His mother paid a white woman to teach her son to read and write. Later he worked in a law firm and continued his education.[516] Turner moved to Baltimore and worked in a hospital. At age seventeen he joined the Methodist Episcopal Church South and was licensed as a local preacher in 1853. President Lincoln appointed him army chaplain.[517] and in 1858 he was ordained an A.M.E. minister and worked in Baltimore. In 1865 he was employed by the Freedmen's Bureau in Georgia. Turner was a delegate to the 1866 Georgia black convention and was elected to the Georgia House but was expelled with the other black members. He was reelected in 1870 and served until 1871.

Turner resigned his position as elder to become pastor of St. Phillip's Savannah, in 1872.[518] The white paper welcomed him to Savannah with the comment, "The notorious Negro preacher and radical bummer, has emigrated from Macon to this city, and has been installed as pastor of St. Phillip's African Methodist Church. The Macon Negroes couldn't stand his morals."[519]. Blassingame regarded Turner as the "most influential" black preacher in Savannah at that time.[520] The Rev. Henry M. Turner held a mammoth memorial celebration on the death of Massachusetts's senator Charles Sumner in March 1874 at St. Philip's A.M.E. Church attended by 4000 persons. Elizabeth Greenfield, also known as the "Black Swan" sung during the celebration.[521] The *Savannah Morning News* reported on the "sharp reprimand" Turner gave his people for their lack of support of concert the Black Swan gave to raise money for the building of First Bryan Church.[522]

All the colored churches were draped in mourning for thirty days and colored persons were requested to "place some badge of mourning on the exterior of their respective houses on Wednesday. The bell of St. Philip's Church will be tolled the hour preceding the services."[523] The paper however failed to report on the memorial service or Turner's speech even though it was the largest assemblage of blacks in many years. Turner appeared with others at a political rally in Effingham County before a crowd of three or four hundred persons.[524]

Some months later the paper reacted to a speech of Turner by stating,

> "The malevolence of this Negro is a little surprising. So far as we know he has been treated well by the white people of Georgia. If he has any complaint to make, it should be against the members of his own party and the church in Macon, who drove him from that city some years ago on charges of adultery, or thieving or something of that sort. We have had an idea all along that Turner deserved some consideration but hereafter we shall put hi

> down as a malevolent vagabond. His Radicalism we considered the natural result of his ignorance and color, but when he goes to Chattanooga merely to show his capacity for telling lies about the people among whom he has cast his lot, it is about time to express disgust, if nothing else." [525]

In 1874 the Rev. Henry Turner founded St. James A.M.E. Church "in a blacksmith shop located in the old Jones field."[526] Later a "modern church home, including a parsonage, was erected on the corner of Arnold and Perry Streets at 236 Arnold Street [527] Turner dedicated the church in grand style before "an appreciative audience." The Hon. J. E. Bryant gave an address on Christian Citizenship and the Rev. James Simms offered the "dedicatory prayer." Miss Stella Rowe "presided at the organ."[528]

The Rev. Wesley C. Gaines, pastor of the new Bethel Church being built at the corner of East Broad and Bolton Streets, was having trouble raising needed funds. Work began on the building in May 1874 but by July, the top blew off and later, other parts of the building were blown down. The congregation however was "persevering." Gaines had begun his congregation with "only four members and his congregation now numbers fifty nine regular attendants." The church still owed $400 on the lot and building. The pastor issued an appeal to all in the community to assist him in raising funds to complete the project.

The *Savannah Morning News* vouched for the pastor, asserting: "We can speak knowingly of the Rev. Wesley Gaines. He was formerly a slave of Col. J. R. Sneed, who is well known in our city and always bore a good character, both as a slave and as a freedman and we trust that his appeal for assistance will meet with a generous response."[529] Later, the Rev. J.F.Gillens pastor of Gaines Chapel purchased the lot and building of Morris Missions on Roberts Street. The 1896 Hurricane damaged Bethel A.M.E. Church. It "was blown down and the building will be a total loss. The church contained to organs and book case with a number of volumes."[530]

St. James Tabernacle A.M.E. Church opened a day school at the church for "the accommodation of such as do not attend the Public Schools of the city." School hours ran daily from 9 to 1. John P. Turner was principal, with Oscar Cole, Robert Stewart and Jesse Allen directors.[531] The paper published a letter by Turner concerning the safety of blacks in the nation. Turner, commenting on the recent killings in the country, asked the rhetorical question, "Tell us how long the Negro race can exist at this rate before he will become utterly exterminated."[532] St. James Tabernacle held a Grand Centennial Supper, debate and general exercises in spelling on April 10,[533] and sponsored a picnic at Woodlawn Park in August 1876. The paper described the church as "dedicated to literature and the general elevation of our people as well as religion. Our people who know its value have used it frequently. It is the only place in the city we have open to our people at all times. It is a duty that the colored people owe to themselves to see that it is relieved of the debt which hangs over it."[534] The Masons laid the cornerstone in 1890.[535]

The Rev. Henry M. Turner left Savannah to become general manager of the publishing department of the denomination in Philadelphia. The black paper claimed that "Dr. Turner's name is a household word in Georgia, and on the stump and in the pulpit has but few equals. He will leave our state deep in the affections of all who knew him. He will still be a member of the Georgia Conference, and his family will still reside in Savannah."[536] Gaines Chapel A.M.E. was organized in June 1891 with the Rev. J. F. Gillens as pastor.[537]. The congregation purchased the lot and a building of Morris Mission on Roberts Street. Dedication was set for July 20.[538]. St. Thomas A.M.E. Church was dedicated in August 1892.[539] Bishop Grant assisted in laying the cornerstone of Bethel A.M.E. Church.[540]

Easter Day 1892 was also missionary day at St. Philip's and "quite a collection was raised." The Sunday school presented "a very interesting concert. The little ones showed themselves masters of the occasion." A similar celebration took place at Gaines Chapel, St. James Tabernacle, Bethel and other Methodist churches.[541] Mrs. Mary E. Roberts died that year and her funeral was "the largest attended in some time,"[542] with about twenty-eight carriages were in the procession. The casket was "of the finest ever used with folding cover-lined with satin." It was furnished by Maj. Royal and showed "that he can give as good a funeral as anybody else."[543]

A tremendous hurricane struck Savannah September 29, 1896. It lasted 50 minutes, had winds of up to 75 miles per hour, took 16 lives, damaged 1,000 buildings and destroyed $1,000,000 in property. Every church in the city was damaged.[544] St. Phillip's A. M. E. Church on New Street was almost totally flattened. The *Morning News* printed a sketch of the ruined church. The report stated that St. Philip's on New Street: "suffered more severely than any other church edifice in the city. The steeple of the church was demolished by the storm of 1893 and was restored. The steeple fell yesterday, falling northward across the body of the church and crushing it in. The church appears to be almost a wreck. It will cost several thousand dollars to repair the damage."[545] The church was built around 1869. The parsonage near the church was not damaged.[546] The Rev. L. H. Smith, pastor of the church, appealed to the community for help in the restoring of the church. He reported that the steeple had fallen on the body of the church and had crushed the $1,000 organ to the basement floor. The 1,400 members were faced with an unpaid mortgage of $2,400 and had "not a dollar" of insurance on the church. The estimated cost of rebuilding was put at $40,000.[547]

Much discussion and even more disagreement followed, and the majority of the congregation purchased the property on the corner of West Broad and Charles Streets, from the Epworth Methodist Episcopal South, and worshipped in that building until January 1912, when the building was demolished to make room for the present modern church."[548] At the time the original church was abandoned Brother Jimmie Williams held the mortgage of $1,000. He served the church as secretary for 31 years, secretary of the building fund for 10 years, and as reporter for 21 years. Sam Howard served the church as secretary for more than 20 years. Idella Smith Johnson was organist for more than 44 years.[549]

For a time services were held in the Duffy Street Hall.[550] W.J. Williams, secretary of both the Board of Trustees and the building committee and a "faithful worker in the church for over 30 years, deserves special mention for his untiring efforts in the progressive work of St. Philip's." The new St. Philip's was designed by John Anderson Lankford, of Washington, D.C., and was built by contractor R. F. Pharrow, two well-established blacks.[551] Almost a year after the hurricane Sol Johnson wrote the following editorial:

> "All our readers are aware of the troubles of St. Philip's A.M.E. Church from the destroying of the commodious edifice on New Street, to the selecting of the site on West Broad Street, to the interference of the Bishop, the sending of a minister to take charge of those members who were desirous of remaining at the old site and to the recalling of the pastor Rev. W.H. Harris. His recall by the Bishop; Rev. Harris would not adhere to, having become attached to the people and they to him. They began worshipping independently. In the meantime steps were taken to secure membership into the C. M. E Church.
>
> Bishop R. S. Williams, who resides in Augusta, was written to, the consent was given and he came on Monday to consummate the plan. This body under the leadership of Rev. Harris was received into the C.M.E. connection, and a new edifice for their worship will be erected. Bishop Williams will assist them in this effort. This will be quite an accession to this church. For years St. Paul Church struggled for life and it was only about two years ago during the pastorate of Rev. I. S. Person, and subsequently Rev. W. A. Dinkins that it became known among the masses and its membership increased. At present the church is doing much good work."[552]

Under the leadership of the Rev. Dr. A.A. Whitman a "small but determined band decided to remain at the original spot on New Street and rebuild the walls."[553] He began the work of restoration but his health failed him and the Rev R. H. Singleton who replaced him, completed the $18,700 project and remained as pastor for five years.[554]

St. Philip's on West Broad and Charles Streets celebrated its 50th anniversary in 1915. The festivities were "among the most elaborate ever held by a local church." The new church was regarded as "one of the leading A. M. E. Churches of the country. It is probably the most beautiful church edifice which is owned by the denomination, having been erected a bout two years ago at a cost of approximately $40,000."[555] In typical Savannah fashion, a bit of folk history has it that the, "uppity" members built on West Broad Street while the "regular" folk remained at the original site and rebuilt the church.

The Rev. R. H. Singleton became the pastor of St. Philip's in 1909 and served for seven years. He was the first pastor to serve for more than four years. During his pastorate the building and a rectory costing about $50,000, were completed. In 1916 the Rev. R. V. Branch became pastor and served until 1923.[556] In a single rally he raise $8,000. J. H. Baldwin served as church school superintendent for 14 years. Jesse Brinson followed him and served for 21 years.

The Rev. Charles O. Fisher, a white minister from Baltimore, Maryland, supported by the Northern Methodist Church Conference, founded Asbury Methodist Episcopal Church in November 1871.[557] The ladies of Asbury Methodist Episcopal Church Aid Association presented "a handsome sum of money and other articles, as the proceeds from the fair held in McIntire's Hall in the interest of that church." The principal table holders in the fair were; Mrs. A.L.C. Jones, President of the Association, Mrs. Louisa Hazel, Vice President, Mrs. Mary Hops treasurer, Mrs. M. I. Hardwick secretary.[558] The Rev. Richard Bigham took charge of the congregation around 1885 and "found the church in rather an indifferent condition with a small membership and attendance," but by his energetic work he has "received over two hundred during the year."[559]

Asbury M. E. Church already had a respectable house of worship, but that peculiar love "for the best," led the members to "lay plans for a building that will do credit to the honored name it bears." The pastor felt that "Nearly every church in Savannah is heavily obligated but not too much to pass a little help to us."[560] The church was rebuilt in 1902. Palen Methodist was founded through the "arduous labors of one of Asbury's sons, Rev. P. B. Gibson."[561] It was reported that "some of the members prefer remaining at the old site, several of them being inclined toward the C.M.E. Church."[562] Bishop R. S. Williams, of Augusta gave his consent and they became official members of the Colored Methodist Church. The Methodist Church promised to erect a new edifice for them. For many years St. Paul's C. M. E. Church "struggled for life" and it was only during the pastorate of Rev. I. S. Person, and subsequently Rev. W. A. Dinkins that it became known among the regular folk, and its membership increased."[563]

St. Paul's Colored Methodist Church was established in 1871 for the colored members of Trinity Methodist Church on Telfair Square with the Rev. Lucius H. Holsey as the first pastor. The congregation built a wooden structure on Maple and West Broad Streets.[564] The Rev. I. S. Person, pastor of St. Paul's C.M.E. Church wrote an article in the Savannah Tribune seeking to solicit funds for his church. He stated: "On Sunday July 12, 1896, an effort will be made by the pastor, members and friends of St. Paul C.M.E. Church to raise money to carry on the work of finishing our house of worship at the corner of Maple and Russell Streets." The hurricane of 1896 "had the roof carried away and the sashes broken."[565]

Surveying other black churches in the city, the writer stated, "the Episcopal Church has her cozy home on Habersham, southwest corner of Harris Street." And added, "The Congregational Church, which is greatly noted for its refined taste and intellectual power, worships in one of the neatest churches in the city."[566] Earlier on the church was located at Maple and Cuyler Streets. Later in 1910, the congregation built a church at Maple and West Broad Streets.[567] In February 1897 pastor W. A. Dinkins dedicated the completed church.[568]

In 1884, a group of Sandfly Village residents and the Women's Home Missionary Society of the General Conference of the Methodist Episcopal Church discussed the possibility of organizing a church in the area. Two white missionaries Viola E. Baldwin and Emma M. Lewis were sent to help establish the mission. A Sunday school was started and later Irene Haynes, a community resident, offered "a haven of a log cabin for the school." In September 1884, Viola Baldwin, Cyrus Sams, Thomas Marion Kemp, Cilla Sams, Allen West, Lydia A. Kemp and Jane Hines officially organized Speedwell Methodist Episcopal Church. Thomas Marion Kemp donated land on Skidaway Road for building a church. About $200 was raised and the Women's Home Missionary Society of the General Conference contributed funds to complete the church.[569]

The **First (Alva) Congregational Church** at the Beach Institute was officially organized in April of 1869 when the Rev. M. Sharp was principal, "as an outgrowth of the prayer meetings held by the teachers of the Beach Institute School."[570] According to Frederick Waring, this church has played "an unusually important part in the spiritual and educational life of the Negro community."[571] The city donated lot No. 7, Crawford ward east, to the Congregational Church, colored, January 5, 1870.[572] For several years, the congregation continued to meet at Beach Institute and was reported to be "in a flourishing state" with the addition of 20 new members.[573] The Rev. Rowe served the congregation "acceptably as pastor until he fell a victim to that terrible scourge yellow fever in 1876." He requested to be buried "among the people whom he came south to serve."[574]

In 1878 the Rev. William Markham took charge of the flock and erected "a little chapel on the corner of Taylor and Habersham Streets." Though he served only a short time "on account of failing health," he "did great work among us." This building was opposite St. Joseph's Hospital. By 1893 plans were a foot to erect a new place of worship on Taylor Street. Sunday July 9, 1893, was set aside as the day of "final gathering of means from members only." Contributions from non-members were also received at that time. The Trustees announced that the "entire donation that day exceeded $500." A second day was set aside for fund raising.[575]

The Rev. Leigh B. Maxwell, the first African American minister, to serve First Congregational Church was educated at Atlanta University. When he came to Savannah in 1886, he found the Congregational Mission struggling for existence among a heterogeneous Negro population whose inclination bent toward that which brought forth the Habersham Street front. The *Savannah Tribune* reported that: "Never was a pastor more loved by his own physical and muscular wringing demonstrative Christianity." Under Maxwell the gothic style church became self-supporting and was enlarged in 1894 by the addition of members and the community at large than he was. The storm of 1940 blew down the steeple. Maxwell was "a gifted orator, a polished gentleman and probably the most magnetic character that ever filled a Savannah pulpit" Poor health cut short the tenure of the Rev. Maxwell's tenure. [576] The *Savannah Tribune* reported that "Never was a pastor more loved by his own In 1896 the parents of three white boys who broke the panes of the beautiful front window of First Congregational Church were made to spend nearly one hundred dollars to have the windows repaired.[577]

In 1897 the congregation organized a Young Men's Christian League for young men in the church.[578] First Congregational Church at 421 Habersham Street held a farewell service for their retiring pastor the Rev. Leigh B. Maxwell. Resolutions of the church at the loss of their "much beloved and faithful pastor, with commendations" were read and adopted. The Rev. Alexander Harris spoke "in well-put terms of Rev. Maxwell's character." The church was so crowded that "many people were compelled to stand."

In 1907, a "large and appreciative audience" at First Congregational Church witnessed the "praise and mortgage burning services." The sum of $1,301.54 had been collected. The pastor and trustees then formally presented the mortgages to the church. The officers of the church then formed a semicircle around the table in front of the pulpit. The papers for the $2,000 mortgages were then burned. The women then served some refreshments. The paper reported, "Thus closed one of the most unique, significant and interesting occasion ever witnessed in the history of the church."[579]

In 1914 the First Congregational Church installed a new organ. E.S. Roberts, organist at St. John's Episcopal Church, played for the service one Sunday. The First Congregational Church celebrated its 50th anniversary in April 1919. The anniversary speaker was the Rev. A. L. DeMoore, pastor of Plymouth, South Carolina. The men of the church were expected to have "at least 50 visiting men as their guests and the women a like number of women guests."[580] The congregation operated a kindergarten in the Old Fort district, on Gordon Street. Beginning in the 1890's and for many years, the congregation along with St. Philip's A.M.E and Beth Eden Baptist Church held Sunday afternoon Forums in the old Ford Opera house on Whitaker and St. Julian's Streets.[581]

The Rev. W. L. Cash resigned his position as pastor of First Congregational Church to accept a position in Chattanooga, Tennessee. Sol Johnson regretted the departure "removes from the vanguard of the race in this city one of its worthiest examples of sterling manhood and Christian citizenship." His ministry at the church had,

> "Made a marked and splendid advancement along the lines of constructive Christianity and Christian service. The vital spiritual and educational tone of the church, both and of the city at large have been stimulated and advanced and this city ands this people are deeply sensible of the service and profoundly grateful to the splendid young minister whose light has shown so acceptably amongst us and upon us for so many years."[582]

The **Rev. John H. H. Sengstacke** was born in Savannah in 1848, the son of German sea captain Hermon Sengstacke and a slave woman.[583] Captain Herman Sengstacke, a wealthy German sea captain, on one of his trips from Bremen, Germany, to Savannah, saw a young female slave Tama on an auction block in 1847 and bought her. Sengstacke subsequently married the woman. On Tama's death, their two children were sent to relatives in Germany. In 1869, the son John Herman Sengstacke Jr., returned to Savannah.[584] Sengstacke lost his job as a translator with the Savannah Morning News when the paper discovered that he was colored.[585]

John H. H. Sengstacke Jr., married widow Flora Abbott, the mother of three children, in 1874. Sengstacke organized the Woodville Pilgrim Congregational Church at the three-mile post on Augusta Road, in 1871.[586] The first meeting was at Dundee a half mile from Augusta Road. Later, "the founders bought the present site and one other church united with it." Bro. John H. H. Sengstacke was ordained a Congregational minister in March 1876.[587] Sengstacke reminded the editor of the black paper that his church was not the Louisville Congregational Church but the Pilgrim Congregational Church.[588] He also organized the Sengstacke Band of Hope in 1877, which buried deceased members of the congregation. Pilgrim Congregational Church celebrated its 25th anniversary and the 20th anniversary of their pastor, the Rev. J. H. H. Sengstacke. The pastor gave a history of the congregation.[589] Years later Sengstacke ministry became one of the "longest pastorates of any Congregation minister in the South." For more than 27 years, he worked as a missionary of the American Missionary Association of New York.

The Sengstacke daughters concocted a surprise party for the Rev. J. H. H. Sengstacke. The invited guests included "all the denominations in the community." The Rev. and Mrs Sengstacke had labored in the community "for twenty-six, years, and "their lives were of an exemplary kind; they have reared a family that anyone can boast and feel proud of.[590] The Sengstacke daughters concocted another surprise party for the parents. The occasion was the fifty-third birthday of the pastor and also his wife and his twenty-six years as pastor and schoolteacher. The pastor was also pastor of the Second Congregational Church at 407 Purse Street Savannah.[591]

Flora Abbott Sengstacke was born December 4, 1847, and "during her younger days was very active in the affairs of her community, taking a prominent part in the educational and religious development of the people, her principal role being the work which she did along side of her late husband.[592] The Rev. Sengstacke taught school for the Savannah Chatham School Board and was "one of the first teachers to open school on the western side of the city." The church and school were run together until he "gave up the County school." One congratulatory letter received on his birthday claimed that no person had "done a better and nobler work for our people in Chatham County than you."[593]

In 1903 Miss Rebecca Sengstacke, principal of the Sengstacke Preparatory Academy, was assisted by three teachers. The school consisted of a "kindergarten, grammar, English High School, and music."[594] Miss Mamie Sengstacke married Mr. Thomas H. Thomas in an elegant wedding at her mother's home in Woodville. The "rooms were decorated with vines, evergreen and cut flowers, and a little arch was formed in the doorway between two rooms under which the bridal party stood." The "bride was becomingly attired in a perfect fitting wedding gown of white China silk and carried in her hand a beautiful bouquet of ferns and cut flowers." Miss Mamie M. Knight the maid of honor wore a beautiful gown of white silk. The bride was the eldest daughter of the late Rev. Sengstacke. She was a graduate of Beach Institute and a trained nurse and possessed a "sweet soprano voice." Some nights later another reception was held at the groom's mother's house in Macon.[595]

Robert S. Abbott, son of Flora Abbott Sengstacke, who "cut his press teeth" on his stepfather's Woodville Times, later founded the Chicago Defender, which had a huge impact on black migration to the North. The Sengstacke lived at 257 Augusta Avenue. The other son, the Rev. H. A. Sengstacke, succeeded his father as pastor of Pilgrim Congregational Church. The two daughters were Miss Rebecca Sengstacke, the principal of the Sengstacke Academy and Mrs. Eliza McKay.[596] The congregation called the Rev. Herman Alexander Sengstacke, his son, as assistant pastor in 1901. He pastored the church until his death in 1904.

Ezra Presbyterian Church: The Rev. Claborn founded this church under the auspices of the Presbytery of Savannah in 1871. Services were held in the old grits mill at the corner of Liberty and Habersham Street. The Rev. White succeeded Claborn. The Savannah Presbytery, for "both economic and prudential reasons" turned over the congregation to the Knox Presbytery. The congregation moved to property on West Broad Street facing Alice Street.[597] Spitler claims that the congregation "originated in 1877," and that the 1885 storm completely demolished the building forcing the congregation to move again.[598] Another report states that a fire badly damaged the church and the congregation moved to Oglethorpe and Randolph Streets.[599]

The Knox Presbytery met at Ezra Presbyterian Church in 1896 and a committee was asked to look into the possibility of buying the lot on which Ezra stood. The Presbytery asked the board of Missions for Freedmen for $500 to aid the Ezra congregation in the purchase.[600] The property of Ezra Presbyterian Church on West Broad Street facing Alice Street was sold and the church bought a site on Oglethorpe Avenue and Randolph Street. The church was not rebuilt because "it was impossible at that time to get a good deed to the lot, so a new location was found for the church on Randolph and Oglethorpe Avenue."[601] . This former foundry at 230 East Broad Street was refurbished into "a suitable place of worship."[602]

The **Rev. Samuel Tyler Redd** (1872-1935) was born in Martinsville, Virginia, November 11, 1872, and graduated from Lincoln University in 1899. He became pastor of Ezra Presbyterian Church in 1904. Redd "interested a prominent white citizen in his congregation, who liberally donated to the church and suggested that they that they move to the corner of East Broad and McDonough Streets."[603] In 1910 the congregation bought the brick building and renovated it for church purposes. The congregation then changed its name to Butler Presbyterian Church "in recognition of the great financial assistance given this congregation by R. M. Butler, well known cotton merchant."[604]

Redd served Butler from 1904 until his retirement in 1933. He died at his residence1102 East Broad Street in 1935. He was regarded as "one of the most able ministers in Savannah," and was a leader in fraternal circles, Supreme Commander of the Knights of Moses and a member of the Eastern Star and the Masons. Two sons, Aspinwall Hodge Redd, Samuel Tyler Redd, Jr., two daughters, Eliza Redd Grisby and Veronica Redd Douglas, survived him.[605] In 1954 the congregation moved to Victory Drive.[606]

Editor Sol Johnson in 1892 gave this advice to the church, "The church can do more for the elevation of our people than any other agency. The ministers should go around among the masses of them and endeavor to educate them up to the requirements of the times."[607] Later he also bemoaned the fact that while African Americans in the city would,

> "spend their time, money, influence and yes their lives in building a magnificent church an adorning it with a fine organ while for an institution for the bettering of Negroes at large they will not willingly spend a dime. What we need in Savannah at the present time are less pretentious churches in which to worship God: and place therein as leaders men whose morals are good, whose lives are temperate and who do not identify themselves with churches for selfish worldly aims, or to see and be seen. But men

who go to serve God and to assist in leading others to do the same; much reform is needed this direction." He felt that "many of the better classes withdraw themselves from those who need their work and assistance."[608]

An editorial in 1905 stated: 'this city contains more colored churches, perhaps, than any other city in the United States." The writer surmised that "there are not now over five or six colored churches in this city out of debt and before one debt is liquidated another created. The people are kept at the "grinding stone' from year to year, while pastors are speculating or off on a frolic."[609]

The **Seventh Day Adventists** began their existence in Savannah when Elder R. E. Williams arrived in the city, April 12, 1912, in search of a place to pitch his Beacon Light Gospel Tent in order to "conduct a great religious campaign." A week later Elder J. W. Manns "with a corps of workers" arrived to assist in the work. The first event was held April 25, 1912, with hundreds in attendance and "hundreds of souls" were converted. Twenty-eight persons were baptized in the Thunderbolt River on July 7, 1912. Changing plans because of the positive response, the church bought a lot on 36th Street and began constructing a $5,000 church from money "raised by friends in Savannah."[610] The first church building was constructed on 36th Street in 1920.[611]

Endnotes – Chapter 1

[1] Savannah, Savannah Unit, Federal Writers' Project In Georgia Works Progress Administration, Savannah, 1937, 47.

[2] Jeanine Cook, ed., Columbus and The Land of Ayllon, The Darien News, 1992, 110

[3] Sarah B. Gober Temple & Kenneth Coleman, University of Georgia Press, 1961, 11, 13.

[4] Dorold D. Wax, "Georgia and the Negro Before the American Revolution," Georgia Historical Quarterly, 51(1967): 63-77.): (F.D. Lee and J.L. Agnew, Historical Record of The City of Savannah, J.H. Estill, Morning News Steam-Power Press, 1869, 6.

[5] Allen D. Candler, ed., The Colonial Records of the State of Georgia, 25 vols. (Atlanta 1904-1916), (hereafter cited as CRG). (CRG. 1:56-62.).

[6] Donald Grant, The Way It Was in the South: The Black Experience in Georgia, Carol Publishing Group, 1993, 63.

[7] Harold E. Davis, The Fledging Province, Social and Cultural Life in Colonial Georgia, 1733-176, University of North Carolina Press, 1976, 136.

[8] CRG, 29:1.

[9] CRG, 3: 405: 4:301-303: 20: 336.

[10] CRG, 4, Supplement, 102-103.

[11] Darold D. Wax, 66.

[12] CRG 3: 4:30.

[13] Patrick Tailfer, Hugh Anderson and David Douglas, A True and Historical Narrative off the Colony of Georgia in America, From the First Settlement Thereof Until the Present Period, Charleston, 1741, 218.

[14] William Stevens, "The Origin of Slave Labor in Georgia," The Orion Magazine, (June 1842): 141-153.

[15] CRG 1, 50-52.

[16] Thomas L. Stokes, The Savannah, University of Georgia of Press, 1951, 75.

[17] William Stevens, 143, 148.
[18] Benjamin Martyn, An Account, Showing the Progress of the Colony of Georgia in America, From Its First Establishment, (London, 1741), reprinted in Georgia Historical Quarterly Collections 11, 300.
[19] D. D. Wax, 68.
[20] P. Tailfer, et. Al. vol. 11.
[21] Kathleen Deagan & Darcie MacMahon, Fort Mose Colonial America's Black Fortress Freedom, University Press of Florida, 1995, 16.
[22] Kenneth Coleman, Colonial Georgia: A History, Scribner & Sons, 1976, 139
[23] Stokes, 100.
[24] Mollie C. Davis, "Whitefield's Attempt to Establish a College in Georgia," Georgia Historical Quarterly, 55 (Winter 1971), 460)
[25] CRG. 24, 435-440.
[26] CRG. 5, 422-425.
[27] CRG. 3, 436.
[28] E. Merton Coulter, A Short History of Georgia, The University of North Carolina Press, 1933, 64.
[29] A.E. Sholes, Compiler, Chronological History of Savannah, Morning News Press, 1900, 47-48.
[30] Peter H. Wood, Black Majority, Negroes in Colonial South Carolina from 1670 through the Stone Rebellion, W.W. Norton & Company, 1974, 314-320.
[31] Ruth Scarborough, The Opposition to Slavery in Georgia Prior to 1860, Negro Universities Press, 1968, 27.
[32] Stokes, 118.
[33] CRG, 35, 454
[34]CRG, 1:56-62
[35] Society For The Propagation of The Gospel Journal, B. 18, 197.
[36] C Pascoe, Two Hundred Years of the S.P.G. London, 1970, 28.
[37] (John C. Van Horne, ed., Religious Philanthropy and Colonial Slavery, University of Illinois Press, 1985, 107
[38] J. Marcus, The Colonial Jew, 1492-1776, Detroit 1970, 474.
[39] John C.V. Horne, 104.
[40] James Lawrence, "Religious Education of the Negro in the Colony of Georgia," Georgia Historical Quarterly, (March 1930), 44.
[41] John Van Horne, 129.
[42] John Van Horne, 138.
[43] Van Horne, 130.
[44] Edgar Pennington, "The Reverend Bartholomew Zouberbuhler," Georgia Historical Quarterly HQ, 18(December 1934): 362, 363
[45] CRG. 1, 531-532.
[46] H. Scomp, "Georgia-the Only Free Colony," Magazine of American History, 22(October 1889), 302-303)
[47] A. Leon Higginbotham, Jr., In the Matter of Color, Oxford University Press, 1978, 251.
[48] Betty Wood, The Origins of American Slavery Freedom and Bondage in the English Colonies, New York, 1997, 65-66.
[49] CRG, 18, 144.
[50] CRG. 18, 102-144.
[51] CRG.18: 649-87.
[52] A Digest of The Laws of the State of Georgia, To…1837, Athens, 1837), 777.
[53] Thomas Gamble, History of the City of Savannah, Ga., From 1790-1901, Savannah, 1900, 57.
[54] CRG. 18, 558-666.
[55] Austin D. Washington, "Efforts to Prevent Negro Revolts in Early Savannah," Faculty Research Bulletin of Savannah State College, 21, 2. (1967): 39-41.
[56] Allen D. Candler, Colonial Records of Georgia (1754-1768) Atlanta, 1911, 212.
[57] Thomas Gamble, 59.
[58] Betty Wood, Slavery in Colonial Georgia, 1730-1775, University of Georgia Press, 1984, 169.
[59] Betty Woods, 170.
[60] Georgia Gazette, December 24, 1766.
[61]
[62] William B. Stevens, A History of Georgia From the First Discovery by Europeans to the Adoption of the

Present Constitution in MDCCXCV111, Philadelphia, 1859, vol.11, 376-377.

[63] Georgia Gazette, September 21, 1774.

[64] Betty Wood, "Until He Shall Be Dead, Dead, Dead," The Juridical Treatment of Slaves in Eighteenth-Century Georgia. GHQ 71, (Fall 1987): 377-398.

[65] Gamble, 69.

[66] Gamble, 68.

[67] Charles S. Henry, Ordinance of City of Savannah, Savannah, 1854, 450.

[68] Martha Waring, Charles S.H. Hardee's Recollection of Old Savannah," Georgia Historical Quarterly, 12 (1928), 353.

[69] WPA, 48

[70] CRG 18, 543-552.

[71] CRG. 18, 814-827.

[72] Thomas Gamble, 180.

[73] CRG. 1:58-59; 26 March 1767, in CRG. 18,792. 819-822.

[74] Gray, History of Agriculture, 1, 369.

[75] CRG. 19, part 2, 23-27.

[76] Thomas L. Stokes, 122-123.

[77] CRG, 18:7-47: 19, 1:291-332.

[78] Sylvia R. Frey, "The British and the Black: A new Perspective." The Historian, 38 (February 1976): 235-238.

[79] Carl S. Weeks, Savannah in the Time of Peter Tondee, The Summerhouse Press, 1997, 146.

[80] F.D. Lee and J.L. Agnew, The Historical Record of Savannah, Savannah, 1869, 47.

[81] Richard L. Blanco, editor, The American Revolution 1775-1783, Garland publishing, 1993, 1498.

[82] Gamble, 44.

[83] Thomas L. Stokes, 155.

[84] Thomas Gamble, 44.

[85] Austin D. Washington, "The Dolly's, An Antebellum Black Family of Savannah, Georgia," Faculty Research Edition, The Savannah State College Bulletin, 26 (December, 1972): 101-103.

[86] Mary Sowell, M.A. Thesis, "A Social and Economic History of Savannah, Georgia, During the Revolutionary War," University of Georgia, 1952, 22.

[87] Mary Sowell, M.A. Thesis, "A Social and Economic History of Savannah, Georgia, During the Revolutionary War," University of Georgia, 1952, 22.

[88] Vincent Harding, There Is a River, Vintage Books, 1981, 48),

[89] Gamble, 44.

[90] Harold H. Martin, Georgia A Bicentennial History. W.W. Norton, 1976, 54-55.

[91] Richard L. Blanco, 1501.

[92] Sidney Kaplan, The Black Presence on the Eve of American Revolution, Smithsonian Institute, 1973, 59.

[93] Augusta Daily Constitutionalist, March 30, 1861.

[94] William H. Fleming, Slavery and the Race Problem in the South, Boston, 1906, 13.

[95] Daily Morning News of May 9, 1861.

[96] Daily Morning News, May 25, 1861.

[97] Daily Morning News, June 4, 1861.

[98] Daily Morning News, June 6, 1861.

[99] Daily Morning News, July 3, 1861.

[100] Daily Morning News, May 9, 1862).

[101] Daily Morning News, June 16, 1862.

[102] Daily Morning News, August 14, 1862.
[103] Daily Morning News, October 13, 1862.
[104] Daily Morning News, November 4, 1862.
[105] Daily Morning News, November 30, 1862.
[106] Daily Morning News, December 23, 1862.
[107] Daily Morning News, November 12, 1862.
[108] Daily Morning News, August 26, 1862.
[109] Daily Morning News, October 16, 1862.
[110] Daily Morning News, December 20, 1862.
[111] Daily Morning News, December 20, 1862.
[112] Daily Morning News, April 15, 1863.
[113] Daily Morning News, March 6, 1863.
[114] Daily Morning News, August 14, 1863.
[115] Daily Morning News, September 12, 1863.
[116] Daily Morning News, May 22, 1863.
[117] Daily Morning News, September 9, 1863.
[118] Daily Morning News, October 16, 1863.
[119] Daily Morning News, March 20, 1863.
[120] Daily Morning News, October 19, 1864.
[121] Daily Morning News of March 12, 1863.
[122] Savannah Morning News, June 18, 1863.
[123] Savannah Daily Republican, August 23, 1865.
[124] Savannah Daily Herald, February 22, 1866.
[125] Savannah Daily Herald, February 24, 1866.
[126] Savannah Daily Herald, March 20, 1866.
[127] Whittington Johnson, 157.
[128] W. Johnson, 158.
[129] Margaret Vernon Stiles, Marse George: Memories of Old Savannah, 1878.
[130]
[131] Margaret Vernon Stiles, 2-24).
[132] WPA, Savannah Writers Project. Coll. # 1355, item 121.
[133] Henry J. Kennedy, History of the Savannah Volunteer Guards, Inc. 1802-1992, 1998, 555.
[134] William Starr Basinger, The Savannah Volunteer Guards From 1858-1882, no place of publication, no date, 74.
[135] Henry J. Kennedy, 556.
[136] Henry J. Kennedy, 556.
[137] Henry J. Kennedy, 555.
[138] WPA-Savannah Writers Project, Col. # 1355, item 119.
[139] Charles Elmore, An Historical Guide to Laurel Grove Cemetery South, Savannah, 1998, 4.
[140] Savannah Tribune, December 4, 1920.
[141] Savannah Daily Herald of February 22, 1866.
[142] Savannah Daily Herald, February 24, 1866.
[143] Dudley T. Cornish, The Sable Arm, Black Troops in the Union Army, 1861-1865, University of Kansas Press, 1987, 86.
[144] Luis F. Emilio, A Brave Black Regiment, Ayer Company, 1990, 288.

[145] Savannah Daily Herald, July 19, 1865.

[146] Mills Lane, comp. The New South. Writings and Speeches of Henry Grady, Savannah, 1971, 108-110: William E. B. DuBois, Black Reconstruction in America, An Essay Toward a History of the Part Which Black Folk Played in the Attempt to Reconstruct Democracy in America, 1860-1880, Reprint edition New York, 1969: Benjamin Quarles, Benjamin Quarles, The Negro in the Civil War, Boston, 1953, 42-99: 262-281 and James M. McPherson James M. McPherson, The Negro Civil War, How American Negroes Felt and Acted During the War for Union, New York, 1965, 55-68; 143-159, 241-244)

[147] Ed Jackson, Cornerstones of Black History, 1995.

[148] Savannah Morning News, September 27, 1881.

[149] Savannah Tribune, November 20, 1886.

[150] Savannah Tribune, January 28, 1888.

[151] Savannah Morning News, July 8, 1868.

[152] Savannah Morning News, August 21, 1910.

[153] Savannah Morning News, July 28, 1873.

[154] Savannah Morning News, August 3, 1875.

[155] Savannah Morning News of August 3, 1875

[156] Savannah Morning News, November 23, 1876.

[157] Savannah Tribune, June 15, 1901.

[158] Savannah Morning News, October 2, 1875.

[159] Savannah Morning News, August 7, 1880. In 1885

[160] Savannah Morning News, January 28, 1885.

[161] Savannah Tribune, October 23, 1886.

[162] Savannah Tribune, October 23, 1886.

[163] Savannah Tribune, March 24, 1888.

[164] Savannah Tribune, May 21, 1892.

[165] Savannah Tribune, May 21, 1892.

[166] Savannah Tribune, June 3, 1893.

[167] Savannah Tribune, 1895.

[168] Savannah Tribune, February 15, 1896.

[169] Savannah Tribune, February 22, 1896.

[170] Savannah Tribune, April 10, 1897.

[171] Savannah Tribune, April 30, 1898.

[172] Savannah Tribune, August 20, 1898

[173] Charles Elmore, 27.

[174] Savannah Tribune, October 15, 1897.

[175] Savannah Tribune, August 19, 1905.

[176] Savannah Tribune, August 26, 1905.

[177] Savannah Tribune, January 24, 1914.

[178] Savannah Tribune, January 24, 1914.

[179] Savannah Tribune, December 31, 1953.

[180] Savannah Tribune, August 3, 1918.

[181] Savannah Tribune, October 12, 1918.

[182] Savannah Tribune, October 12, 1918.

[183] Savannah Tribune, April 13, 1918.

[184] Savannah Tribune, April 13, 1918.
Savannah Tribune, May 3, 1918.

[185] Savannah Tribune, January 17, 1920.

[186] Joseph F. Waring, 26.

[187] Albert J. Raboteau, Slave Religion, Oxford University Press, 1978, 92.

[188] Eugene D. Genovese, Roll Jordan Roll, Pantheon Books, 1974, 162-163.

[189] Bob Lee, "Oasis, Something providing relief from the usual; Refuge," Outdoors in Georgia, (January 1976): 19-24.

[190] .P. Franklin, Living Our Stories Telling Our Truths, Scribner, 1995, 331.

[191] Savannah Daily Republican, June 21, 1865.

[192] Savannah Morning News, November 11, 1884.

[193] Sylvia R. Frey and Betty Wood, Come Shouting to Zion, University of North Carolina Press, 1998, 112-114.

[194] Sylvia R. Frey and Betty Wood, Come Shouting to Zion, University of North Carolina Press, 1998, 112-114. Frey and Woods, 113

[195] Frey and Woods, 113.

[196] Letters of the Hon. James Habersham, 1756-1775, Collections of the Georgia Historical Society, 6(1904): 243-244.

[197] Emanuel K. Love, The First African Baptist Church, Savannah, 1888, 143.

[198] Savannah Tribune, January 22, 1898.

[199] "Letters Showing the Rise and Progress of the Early Negro Churches of Georgia and the West Indies," Journal of Negro History, 1(January 1916): 69-92.

[200] John W. Davis, "George Liele and Andrew Bryan Pioneer Negro Baptist Preachers," Journal of Negro History, 3(April 1918): 119-127.

[201] Walter H. Brooks, "The Priority of the Silver Bluff Church and Its Promoters," Journal of Negro History, 7(April 1922): 172-96.

[202] Brooks, 71.

[203] Robert Scott Davis, Georgians in The Revolution: At Kettle Creek (Wilkes Co.) and Burke County, 1986, 109.

[204] Ellen Gibson Wilson, The Loyal Blacks, Capricorn Books, New York, 1976, 12).

[205] Robert Scott Davis, "The Other Side of the Coin: Georgia Baptists Who Fought for the King." Viewpoints, Georgia Baptist History 7(1980): 47-57.

[206] Letter to Rippon, 18, December 1791, The Baptist Annual Register (1792, 1, 333.

[207] David Benedict, General History of the Baptist Denomination in America And Other Parts Of The World, Lewis Colby and Company New York, 1848, 740.

[208] John W. Davis, "George Liele and Andrew Bryan, Pioneer Negro Baptist Preachers."[208].

[209] Davis, 53.

[210] Emanuel K. Love, 34-35.

[211] The Baptist Annual Register, 1790-1793, 334.

[212] Davis, 121.

[213] Davis 121.

[214] Alex Pringle, Prayer For The Revival Of Religion In All Protestant Churches, 1796, 104-105.

[215] Clement Gayle, George Liele Pioneer Missionary to Jamaica, Jamaica Baptist Union, 1982, 3.

[216] Mary Turner, Slaves And Missionaries, The Disintegration of Jamaican Slave Society, 1787-1834, University of Illinois Press, 1982, 17.

[217] Thomas J. Little, "George Liele and the Rise of Independent Black Baptist Churches in the Lower South and Jamaica," Slavery And Abolition, A Journal of Slave and Post Slave Studies, 16(August 1995), 194.

[218] Thomas Little, 195.

[219] Liele to Rippon, 18, December 1791, BAR. Vol. 1, 335-6.

[220] Robert Scott Davis, 49.

[221] Davis, 57.

[222] Bicentennial Celebration Historic First Bryan Baptist Church, 1788-1988, Savannah January, 1988.

[223] Ellen Gibson Wilson, 9-12.

[224] Brooks, 182.

[225] Ellen Gibson Wilson, 11.

[226] Robert G. Gardner et. Al., "A History of the Georgia Baptist Association 1784-1984," Georgia Baptist Historical Society, 1988, 16.

[227] Brooks, 182.

[228] Ellen Gibson Wilson, 29.

[229] Ellen Gibson Wilson, 9.

[230] Brooks, 185.

[231] Brooks, 191.

[232] Brooks, 183.

[233] Liele to Rippon, 18 December 1791, BAR, Vol., 335-6.

[234] Henry Chase, In Their Footsteps, New York, 1994, 544-545.

[235] Whittington B. Johnson, 10.

[236] James M. Simms, The First Colored Baptist Church in North America, Philadelphia, 1888, 235.

[237] Emanuel K. Love, 38.

[238] "Sketch of the Black Baptist Church at Savannah in Georgia, and of their minister, Andrew Bryan, extracted from Several Letters," in Alex Pringle, Prayer for the Revival of Religion in the Protestant Church, 1796, 111-116.

[239] Abraham Marshall to John Rippon, 19 July 1790, The Baptist Annual Review 1, 340.

[240] Donald Grant, "Andrew Bryan," in Dictionary of Georgia Biography, Edited by Kenneth Coleman and Charles S. Gurr, University of Georgia Press, 1983, vol. 1, 128.

[241] Savannah River Plantations, Savannah Writers' Project, 1947, Mary Granger, editor, Reprint, The Oglethorpe Press, 1997, 401.

[242] Georgia Gazette, October 23, 1788.

[243] Reba Carolyn Strickland, Religion and the State in Georgia in the Eighteenth Century, Columbia University Press, 1939, 181.

[244] John H. Davis, "George Liele and Andrew Bryan, Pioneer Negro Baptist preachers," Journal of Negro History, 3(April 1918), 124.

[245] Charles C. Jones, The Religious Instruction of the Negroes In the United States, Negro Universities Press, New York, Reprint, 1969, 51.

[246] Savannah Morning News, January 18, 1888.

[247] Charles C. Jones, 52.

[248] Savannah Morning News, January 18, 1888.

[249] Savannah Morning News, January 18, 1888.

[250] W.W. Law, "Negro Baptists Began Here," Savannah Morning News, July 4, 1976.

[251] Deeds. Vol. G. 1789-90 Chatham County Superior Court (microfilm) Georgia Department of Archives and History, 215-216.

[252] Edgar G. Thomas, The First African Baptist Church of North America, Savannah, 1925, 37-38.

[253] Robert G. Gardener, et al. A History of the Georgia Baptist Association, 1784-1984, Atlanta, Georgia Baptist Society, 1988, 17.

[254] The Baptist Annual Register, 1798-1801, 368: 1790-1793, 339.

[255] James M. Simms, 22-29, 67.

[256] Charles Elmore, 16.

[257] Rev. Edgar Garfield Thomas, The First African Baptist Church of North America, Savannah, 1925, 40.

[258] David Benedict, 739-741.

[259] Charles C. Jones, 51.

[260] E.K. Love, 40.

[261] Savannah Morning News, May 21, 1979.

[262] John Davis, 126.

[263] Savannah Morning News, January 18, 1888.

[264] John Davis, 126.

[265] Love, 2-3.

[266] Savannah Herald, January 13, 1988.

[267] E. K. Love, 57.

[268] Love 57.

[269] Edgar Thomas, 78.

[270] Ira Berlin, Editor, Free At Last, A Documentary History of Slavery, Freedom, And the Civil War, The New Press, New York, 1992, 310.

[271] Whittington Johnson, 180.

[272] Charles Elmore, 25.

[273] Love, 58.

[274] Daily Morning News, July 6, 1859.

[275] Daily Morning News, May 4, 1861.

[276] Edgar Thomas, 78.

[277] Love, 58.

[278] Love, 58.

[279] Love, 58.

[280] Savannah Morning News, May 14, 1888.

[281] E. K. Love, 169.

[282] Eric Foner, Freedom's Lawmakers, A Directory of Black Officeholders during Reconstruction, Revised Edition, Louisiana State University Press, Baton Rouge, 1996, 59.

[283] Eric Foner, 59,

[284] Charles Elmore, 20.

[285] Colored Tribune, March 18, 1876.

[286] Colored Tribune, July 23, 1876.

[287] Savannah Tribune, August 5, 1876.

[288] Eric Foner, 59.

[289] Savannah Tribune, January 8, 1887.

[290] Charles Elmore, 6.

[291] E. K. Love, 85-102.

[292] Edgar Thomas, 56.

[293] Edgar Thomas, 90.

[294] Savannah Tribune, October 21, 1893.

[295] Savannah Morning News, October 4, 1895.

[296] Edgar Thomas, 89.

[297] Savannah Tribune, September 2, 1893.

[298] Savannah Tribune, February 10, 1894.

[299] Edgar Thomas, 111.

[300] Savannah Tribune, January 16, 1915.

[301] Savannah Tribune, September 11, 1897.

[302] Savannah Tribune, October 21, 1893.

[303] Savannah Tribune, May 5, 1894.

[304] Savannah Tribune, May 5, 1894.

[305] Savannah Tribune, January 5, 1895.

[306] Savannah Tribune, December 28, 1895.

[307] Savannah Tribune, September 6, 1897.

[308] Savannah Tribune, September 6, 1897.

[309] Bicentennial Celebration Historic First Bryan Church, 1788-1988, Savannah, First Bryan Baptist Church, 1977.

[310] Love, 163-264.

[311] Bicentennial Celebration Historic First Bryan Church, 1788-1988.

[312] Savannah Morning News, January 1, 1874.

[313] Savannah Morning News, September 23, 1873.

[314] Savannah Tribune, May 7, 1887.

[315] Savannah Morning News, September 27, 1886.

[316] Savannah Morning News, October 7, 1887.

[317] Savannah Morning News, January 21, 1888.

[318] Savannah Morning News, January 21, 1888.

[319] Savannah Tribune, July 7, 1888.

[320] Savannah Morning News, June 3, 1888.

[321] Savannah Morning News, June 3, 1888.

[322] Robert G. Gardner et al, A History Of The Georgia Baptist Association, 1784-1984, Georgia Baptist Historical Society, Atlanta, 1988, 16-17.

[323] Walter H. Brooks, "The Evolution of the Negro Baptist Church," Journal of Negro History 7(January 1922): 11-22).

[324] "The Priority of the Silver Bluff Church and its Promoters," Journal of Negro History, 8(April 1922): 172-196.

[325] Edgar Thomas, 21

[326] Savannah Tribune, April 26, 1928.

[327] Savannah Tribune, July 5, 1928.

[328] Savannah Tribune, July 12, 1928.

[329] Savannah Tribune, August 30, 1928.

[330] Savannah Press, Monday April 28, 1930.

[331] Savannah Tribune, January 27, 1938.

[332] Interview with the Rev. Matthew S. Brown, November 1, 2000.

[333] Savannah Tribune, January 8, 1953.

[334] Savannah Tribune, January 15, 1958.

[335] Savannah Morning News, January 26, 1972.

[336] Henry Holcomb, The First Fruits In A Series of Letters, Philadelphia, 1812, 63-65.

[337] Savannah Morning News, January17, 1976.

[338] Savannah Evening Press, October 3, 1974.

[339] Savannah News-Press, February 8, 1987.
[340] Atlanta Constitution, February 27, 1988.
[341] First African Baptist Church 200th Celebration, Savannah, 1988.
[342] Savannah Morning News, June 5, 1999.
[343] Savannah Tribune, March 10, 1888.
[344] Savannah Tribune, April 23, 1892
[345] Savannah Tribune, May 21, 1892.
[346] Savannah Tribune, June 3, 1893.
[347] Thomas Gamble, 248.
[348] Savannah Tribune, June 3, 1893.
[349] Whittington Johnson, 10.
[350] Savannah Tribune January 1, 1952.
[351] Savannah Evening Press, July 12, 1975.
[352] Charles C. Jones, 56.
[353] Savannah Evening Press, July 12, 1975.
[354] Thomas Gamble, 86.
[355] Will B. Gravely, "The Rise of African Churches in America (1786-1822): Re-examining the Contexts," Journal of Religious Thought, 41(1984), 72.
[356] W. Johnson, 192.
[357] Julia Floyd Smith. "Marching to Zion: The Religion of Black Baptists in Coastal Georgia Prior to 1865," Georgia Baptist History, 65(1978), 50.
[358] Peter P. Hinks, To Awaken My Afflicted Brethren, David Walker and the Problem of Antebellum Slave Resistance, Pennsylvania State University Press, 1997, 118.
[359] Ida M. Martin, "Civil Liberties in Georgia Legislation 1800-1830," (Georgia Historical Quarterly, 45(December 1961), 333.
[360] Act of December 22, 1829, in Acts of the General Assembly, 1829, 170-171.
[361] Charles C. Jones, 56.
[362] Joseph F. Waring, Cerveau's Savannah, Savannah 1973, 60.
[363] Daily Morning News, October 23, 1856.
[364] Savannah Tribune, January 29, 1887.
[365] One Hundred and Sixtieth Anniversary, 1962, Second African Baptist Church, 1962.
[366] Savannah Tribune, March 16, 1889.
[367] Savannah Tribune, May 25, 1889.
[368] Savannah Tribune, August 10, 1889.
[369] Second African Baptist Church History Notes, no date, 2.
[370] Savannah Tribune January 10, 1891.
[371] Savannah Tribune, January 23, 1892.
[372] Savannah Morning News, February 1, 1893.
[373] Savannah Morning News, January 22, 1892.
[374] Savannah Tribune, April 23, 1892.
[375] Savannah Tribune, May 14, 1892.
[376] Savannah Tribune, October 17, 1896.
[377] Savannah Tribune, April 3, 1897.
[378] Savannah Tribune, September 7, 1912.
[379] Savannah Tribune, November 13, 1930.

[380] Savannah Tribune, November 15, 1934.

[381] Savannah Tribune, November 7, 1935

[382] Savannah Morning News, October 27, 1938.

[383] Savannah tribune, July 19, 1913.

[384] A. B. Caldwell, editor, History of the American Negro, Georgia Edition, A. B. Caldwell Publishing, Co., Atlanta, vol. 1. 1917, 379.

[385] Savannah Tribune, January 26, 1926.

[386] Savannah Tribune, January 26, 1926.

[387] Colored Tribune, June 10, 1876.

[388] Historical Sketch of Mt. Zion, Savannah, no date, no pagination.

[389] Savannah Tribune, September 14, 1912.

[390] Savannah Tribune, September 21, 1912.

[391] Savannah Tribune, September 28, 1912.

[392] Evening Press, June 15, 1987.

[393] Georgia Guardian, March 27, 1992.

[394] Evening Press, December 6, 1994.

[395] Joseph S. Atwell, A Brief Historical Sketch of St. Stephen's Parish, Church Book and Job Printing Establishment, 1874, 5,

[396] Interview with Mrs. Eleanor Pollard, November 1977.

[397] St. Stephen's Register, 1868, 10.

[398] Atwell, 5.

[399] Atwell, 35.

[400] Journal of the Diocese of Georgia, 1857, 35.

[401] Daily Morning News December 2, 1856.

[402] Savannah Morning News. January 11, 1860

[403] Sweet, 159.

[404] Laurel Grove Cemetery Savannah, Georgia, Vol. 1, 12 Oct. 1852-30 Nov. 1861, Georgia Historical Society, 327.

[405] Atwell, 7.

[406] Interview with Mrs. Pollard, November 1977.

[407] Savannah Morning News, December 28, 1930.

[408] William Harden, Recollections of a Long and Satisfactory Life, Review printing Company, 1934, 27.

[409] Thomas Gamble, 483.

[410] Savannah Morning News, May 3, 1861.

[411] Atwell, 6.

[412] Savannah Morning News, January 11, 1881.

[413] Frank Bynes, The History of the Mutual Benevolent Society, no date, no pagination.

[414] Journal of the Diocese of Georgia....

[415] Journal of the Diocese of Georgia, 1866, 22.

[416] Savannah Tribune, November 13, 1895.

[417] Journal of the Diocese of Georgia, 1866): 60-61.

[418] Savannah Daily Herald, March 18, 1865.

[419] Daily News Herald, February 24, 1868.

[420] Savannah Daily Herald, April 18, 1865.

[421] Journal of the Diocese of Georgia, 1866, 22.

[422] Journal of the Diocese of Georgia Journal, 1867, 59-9.

[423] Daily News and Herald, May 19, 1867.

[424] Savannah Morning News, October 18, 1869.

[425] W. Roberts, Six Great Jamaicans: Biographical Sketches, The Pioneer Press, 1951, 71-72.

[426] J. Cushman, The Episcopal Church in Florida, 1821-1892, University of Florida, 1965,139.

[427] Journal of the Diocese of Florida, 1870, 38.

[428] Atwell, 21.

[429] Roi Ottley, The Lonely Warrior: The Life and Times of Robert S. Abbott, Chicago, 1855, 35.

[430] Journal of the Diocese of Georgia, 1872, 65.

[431] Savannah Tribune, May 12, 1894.

[432] Atwell, 22.

[433] Roi Ottley, 30.

[434] Ottley, 13.

[435] Ottley, 13.

[436] Ottley, 22.

[437] Ottley, 37.

[438] Savannah Morning News, November 7, 1877.

[439] Ottley, 35.

[440] Wanda S. Lloyd, "Savannah tour traces black heritage" Washington Post, May 27, 1979.

[441] John Berendt, Midnight In The Garden Of Good And Evil, Vintage Books, 1994, 325,

[442] Charles L. Hoskins, Black Episcopalians in Georgia, Strife, Struggle and Salvation, St. Matthew's Episcopal Church, 1980, 63.

[443] Journal of the Diocese of Georgia, 1872, 60.

[444] Ottley, 1955, 35.

[445] Pollard, 1979

[446] Meier, 1959, 139.

[447] Edward B. Reuter, The Mulatto in the United States, reprint, New York, 1969, 180.

[448] V. Daniel, "Negro Classes and Life in the Church," Journal of Negro Education, 13(Winter 1944), 22.

[449] Journal of the Diocese of Georgia, 1873, 76.

[450] Savannah Morning News, May 11, 1878.

[451] Savannah Morning News, August 16, 1880.

[452] Savannah Tribune, September 3, 1887.

[453] Savannah Tribune, November 6, 1886.

[454] Interview with Mrs. Pollard 1977.

[455] Savannah Tribune, August 13, 1887.

[456] Savannah Tribune April 28, 1888.

[457] Savannah Tribune, March 17, 1894.

[458] Savannah Tribune, October 22, 1892.

[459] Savannah Tribune, August 5, 1893.

[460] Savannah Tribune, February 22, 1908.

[461] Savannah Tribune, May 19, 1913.

[462] Savannah Tribune, December 27, 1913.

[463] C. L. R. James, A History of Pan-African Revolt, Drum and Spear Press, 1969, 2.

[464] Savannah Tribune, October 3, 1914.

[465] Gamble, 59.

[466] Sister M. Julian Griffin, Tomorrow Comes The Song, Savannah, 1978, 13.

[467] Cyprian Davis, The History of Black Catholics in the United States, Crossroads, 1991, 80-81.

[468] T. Paul Thigpan, "Aristocracy Of The Heart Catholic Lay Leadership in Savannah 1820-1870," (Ph.D., diss., 1995, Emory University): 567-617.

[469] Gillian Brown, A People of Faith: A brief history of Catholicism in South Georgia, no date of place or publication, 22-23.

[470] Jerome Oetgen, "The Origins of the Benedictine Order in Georgia," Georgia Historical Quarterly, 52(June 1969): 165-183.

[471] Sister Julian 31.

[472] Jerome Oetgen, 174.

[473] Jerome Oetgen, 173.

[474] Oetgen, 180.

[475] Morning News, January 4, 1875.

[476] Savannah Morning News, March 19, 1877.

[477] Savannah Morning News, September 4, 1877.

[478] Savannah Tribune, October 3, 1914.

[479] The Catholic Directory For The Diocese of Savannah-Atlanta, Published and Printed at St. Thomas Vocational School, Savannah, 1940, 81.

[480] Oetgen, 181.

[481] Cyprian Davis, 125.

[482] Cyprian Davis, 125.

[483] Southern Cross, March 18, 1993.

[484] Savannah Tribune, November 30, 1889.

[485] Morning News, July 15, 1889.

[486] Savannah Tribune, July 13, 1889.

[487] Gillian Brown, Introduction.

[488] Savannah Tribune, October 3, 1914.

[489] Savannah Tribune, August 17, 1909.

[490] Savannah Tribune, January 10, 1910.

[491] Savannah Tribune, August 17, 1909.

[492] Southern Cross, May i8, 1967.

[493] Savannah Tribune, March 9, 1907.

[494] Savannah Tribune, January 30, 1909.

[495] Quoted in Sweet, 210.

[496] Jesse Brinson, Authentic History of St. Philip Church, Savannah, 1949, 6.

[497] The 134 Th. Session Georgia Annual Conference, April 14-18, 1999, St. Phillip A.M.E. Church Savannah, GA, 1999, 30.

[498] Savannah Daily Republican, March 1, 1865: Ira Berlin, 310-313.

[499] Thomas Gamble, 483.

[500] Margaret Godley, The Centennial Story of Trinity Methodist Church, Savannah, 1948, 23.

[501] Haygood S. Bowen, History Of Savannah Methodism, Macon, 1929, 141.

[502] Savannah Morning News, July 27, 1870.

[503] Savannah Tribune, May 25, 1977.

[504] The Rev. Wesley J. Gaines, African Methodism in the South: or Twenty-five Years of Freedom, Atlanta, 1890, 5-10.

[505] Jesse Brinson, 6.

[506] Savannah Tribune, November 24, 1949.

[507] Savannah Tribune, March 24, 1938.

[508] Savannah Tribune, October 3, 1914.

[509] Rita F. Spitler, Higher Ground, Historic Churches and Synagogues in Savannah, Savannah, 1995, 52.

[510] Kermit Smalls, Year Book of Colored Savannah, Savannah, 1934, 34.

[511] Savannah Tribune, October 3, 1914.

[512] Daily News Herald, February 4, 1868.

[513] Prof Robert W. Gadsden, Negro Political and Civic Life. no date, 6.

[514] Morning News, July 17, 1872.

[515] Eric Foner, Freedom's Lawmakers, Revised Edition, Louisiana State University Press, 1996, 215.

[516] A Memorial to Bishop Henry McNeal Turner, 1834-1915, Savannah 1985.

[517] W.E.B. Du Bois, Black Reconstruction in America, 1860-1880, Atheneum, New York, 1992, 499.

[518] Stephen W. Angell, Bishop Henry McNeal Turner and African-American Religion in the South, University of Tennessee Press, Knoxville, 1992, 108.

[519] Savannah Morning News, February 23, 1872.

[520] Blassingame, 478.

[521] Blassingame, 428.

[522] Savannah Morning News, March 17, 1874.

[523] Savannah Morning News, March 17, 1874.

[524] Savannah Morning News, November 4, 1874.

[525] Savannah Morning News, October 19, 1874.

[526] The African Methodist Episcopal Church-One-hundred eighty-eight years of Progress, Savannah, 1976.

[527] Kermit Smalls, 33.

[528] Colored Tribune, February 26, 1876.

[529] Savannah Morning News, October 20, 1874.

[530] Morning News, September 30, 1896.

[531] Colored Tribune, March 4, 1876.

[532] Colored Tribune, March 18, 1876.

[533] Colored Tribune, April 8, 1876.

[534] Savannah Tribune, August 19, 1976.

[535] Savannah Tribune, September 6, 1890.

[536] Colored Tribune, May 27, 1876.

[537] Savannah Tribune, June 3, 1891.

[538] Savannah Tribune, July 18, 1891.

[539] Savannah Tribune, July 30, 1892.

[540] Savannah Tribune, September 1, 1894.

[541] Savannah Tribune, April 23, 1892.

[542] Savannah Tribune, September 1, 1894.

[543] Savannah Tribune, June 11, 1892.

[544] A.E. Sholes, 104.

[545] Morning News, September 30, 1896.

[546] Savannah Tribune, October 3, 1896.

[547] Savannah Tribune, October 17, 1896.

[548] Savannah Tribune, October 3, 1914.

[549] Jesse Brinson, 11.

[550] James F. Butler and Frankie N. Golden, Mortgage Burning Celebration, St. Philip A.M.E.,Savannah, June 18, 1944, 5.

[551] Savannah Tribune, September 30, 1911.

[552] Savannah Tribune, September 18, 1897.

[553] Savannah Tribune, October 3, 1914.

[554] Savannah Tribune, October 3, 1914.

[555] Savannah Tribune, June 12, 1915.

[556] Jesse Brinson, 8.

[557] Savannah Tribune, October 3, 1914.

[558] Colored Tribune, May 13, 1876.

[559] Savannah Tribune, November 13, 1886.

[560] Savannah Tribune, July 11, 1896.

[561] Savannah Tribune, October 3, 1914.

[562] Savannah Tribune, September 18, 1897.

[563] Savannah Tribune, September 18, 1897.

[564] Spitler, 58.

[565] Savannah Morning News, September 30, 1896.

[566] Savannah Tribune, July 11, 1896.

[567] Spitler, 58.

[568] Savannah Tribune, February 20, 1897.

[569] Speedwell Anniversary Program, Savannah, 1999.

[570] First Congregational Church, Special Project Committee, Mrs. Mozelle Clemmons, chairman, no date, no pagination.

[571] Savannah Morning News, May 4, 1969.

[572] Thomas Gamble, 485.

[573] Colored Tribune, May 6, 1876.

[574] Savannah Tribune, June 1, 1911.

[575] Savannah Tribune, July 22, 1893.

[576] Savannah Tribune, June 6, 1911.

[577] Savannah Tribune, June 20, 1896.

[578] Savannah Tribune, February 13, 1897.

[579] Savannah Tribune, June 15, 1907.

[580] Savannah Tribune, April 12, 1919.

[581] Savannah Morning News, May 4, 1969.

[582] Savannah Tribune, March 27, 1920.

[583] Charles Elmore, 24.

[584] New York Times, May 30, 1997.

[585] Roi Ottley, 33.

[586] Savannah Tribune, October 3, 1914.

[587] Colored Tribune, March 18, 1876.

[588] Colored Tribune, May 13, 1876.

[589] Savannah Tribune, March 7, 1896.

[590] Savannah Tribune, February 9, 1901.
[591] Savannah Tribune, February 9, 1901.
[592] Savannah Tribune, September 22, 1932.
[593] Savannah Tribune, February 1.1902.
[594] Savannah Tribune, April 18, 1903.
[595] Savannah Tribune, May 5, 1906.
[596] Savannah Tribune, September 22, 1932.
[597] Savannah Tribune, October 3, 1914.
[598] Spitler, 48.
[599] Savannah Tribune, September 22, 1935.
[600] Savannah Tribune, April 18, 1896.
[601] Savannah Tribune, October 3, 1914.
[602] Savannah Tribune, April 3, 1897.
[603] Savannah Tribune, September 22, 1935.
[604] Savannah Tribune, September 22, 1935.
[605] Savannah Tribune, September 22, 1935.
[606] Savannah Tribune, September 22, 1935.
[607] Savannah Tribune, January 16, 1892.
[608] Savannah Tribune, February 10, 1894.
[609] Savannah Tribune, January 1, 1905.
[610] Savannah Tribune, October 3, 1914.
[611] Savannah Morning News, June 5, 1958.

Maafa (unspeakable horror) in Savannah

"Receiving by irresistible power, the work of another man, and not by his consent."

The Reverend Garrison Frazier was born in Granville County, North Carolina. He had been a slave for 59 years and a Baptist minister for 35 years. He bought his and his wife's freedom for $1,000, eight years before emancipation. Frazier was the chosen spokesman for the twenty African American leaders who met with Secretary of War Edwin M. Stanton and Major-General William T. Sherman in the Green mansion, Savannah, on the evening of Thursday January 12, 1865. The question put to the group was, "state what you understand by slavery and the freedom that was to be given by the president's proclamation."

Frazier replied, slavery was: "Receiving by irresistible power, the work of another man, and not by his consent."[1] Even though, as Mills Lane wrote, no one can give a "final and complete" description of the slavery experience,[2] it is also true that Garrison's is one of the missing voices in the telling of Savannah's history. Coming from someone who experienced slavery first hand, his definition of the experience of slavery has much more validity than many of the frottings or theories of hundreds of white historians, visitors, commentators and others, who have pontificated on what the experience must have been like for the slaves.

Eli Whitney, a Yale University graduate, is generally credited with the invention of the cotton gin, almost by accident, or "involuntarily" as he wrote in 1792, while living at the Mulberry Grove Plantation some eight miles from Savannah. Several rudimentary models were already in existence.[3] The introduction of Sea Island cotton from the Bahamas,[4] and the extensive use of this cost-efficient production method of ginning the cotton transformed the region's economy and gave "new life" to slavery,[5] by increasing the value of the slave's labor by ten fold. The invention promised to give labor to thousands of slaves and make the country "grow rich."[6] It also radically altered the economic fortunes of Savannah.[7] These changes inevitably ushered in the reign of King Cotton with the concomitant expansion of slavery and the South's dependence on black labor,[8] and it eroded the rich topsoil of the South. In some ways the cotton gin also facilitated the increase of industrialization and helped to precipitate the Civil War.

Historian Melvin Drimmer held that the gin moved slavery to a higher level, it surely contributed to the South's tenacity in maintaining slavery at all cost.[9] Whitney died "virtually bankrupt" despite the role his invention played in the increase of cotton production.[10] Reflecting on his experience with some businessmen of that period, a visitor to Savannah wrote: "Niggers and cotton-cotton and niggers; these are the law and the prophets to the men of the South."[11] In March 1798 city council and the governor clashed over the seizure of slaves from the West Indies. William Norment, tax Collector of Chatham County, seized "twenty-five Negroes, part of a cargo imported into Savannah on the schooner *Emma*. These Negroes were to be forfeited to the state under the tax act of 1797." The city opposed Norment's seizure, claiming that the Negroes were "brigands from the West Indies and that it would be dangerous to scatter such firebrands among the various plantations to incite plots against the whites." In the end the governor issued a proclamation charging all officers to be alert to prevent the landing of Negroes "accustomed to the horrid scenes of massacre."[12]

Just as in the West Indies sweet King Sugar demanded bitter slavery, likewise in Georgia, white King Cotton had an insatiable appetite for more and ever more black hands. By 1809, an unofficial census of the city listed the population as having 2,311 slaves, 759 or almost one third of whom were under 14 years of age, 1,302 from 15 to 45 years of age and 250 over 45 years of age. The first cotton was shipped from Savannah in 1784 but by 1805 about 27,600 bales of cotton were exported.[13] Cotton production jumped from 1,000 bales in 1790 to 90,000 bales in 1820, to 701,840 bales in 1860, giving birth to what Sieg calls the "halcyon days" in Savannah.[14] In 1771, Savannah had 821 slaves by 1820 that number rose to 3,075, though the percentage of blacks in the population remained constant. The port city by 1819 had developed into a major cotton center and the *Steam Ship Savannah's* crossing of the Atlantic that same year helped to place the town on the map.

An increase in tariffs and a national depression were just around the corner. These two agents subsequently played havoc with the city's future prospects. To make matters even more precarious, in 1820, one of the worst fires to hit the country decimated the town. At least 463 buildings were destroyed. After the disasters, New York's mayor sent a very handsome check for the relief of citizens with the proviso that there was to be no discrimination because of race. The chagrined city fathers sensing an implied charge of racism in the offer declined the proffered help.[15]

However, through it all, slave hands picked the cotton in the interior and other slave hands in Savannah transported it to the ships for export. It was said that in Savannah nothing was heard but, Negroes singing as they were "stowing the cotton." The highly touted, genteel southern graciousness of the "hostess city of the south" was buttressed by the harsh brutality of slavery.[16] Law and social mores excluded African Americans from the "social life of the city" even though many festivities and celebrations were "regularly serviced" by blacks. Slaves and low class whites were compelled to walk on "their side" of Bull Street.[17]

By 1825, Georgia led the world in cotton production. King Cotton's nearly one hundred year reign stimulated the growth of river transportation and the beginning and expansion of rail travel especially the Central of Georgia Railroad and Canal Company. In 1829, another fire broke out but this time the authorities suspected some black arsonists. It was reported that a female slave was convicted, executed, dissected, and exposed, but she died denying the crime. Another female slave was also implicated in the arson.

About one hundred years after some Indians welcomed James Edward Oglethorpe and his followers to Georgia, other Indians were in the throes of the *Trail of Tears* as hundreds of them were driven from their ancestral abodes and pushed further and further into the interior as whites coveted their fertile lands. Competition from Charleston triggered a massive railroad construction.[18] Not surprisingly, this construction depended heavily on slave labor. As Les R.Winn states, the labor of slaves was "used extensively" in the construction of the Central Railroad from Savannah to Macon.[19] The Central of Georgia Railroad and Canal Company, the largest slave owner in Savannah, owning over 120 slaves during the period, used Irish immigrant labor but was forced to fall back on slave labor to construct its 190 mile line from Savannah to Macon.[20] Once again, it was a case of Africa to the rescue. The Irish had freedom of choice and many chose not to submit themselves to the rigors of laying tracks. Slaves had no alternative because they were the property of their owners.

The 1830's also witnessed the return of Savannah's prosperity. Charles Hardee recalled that slaves and some poor whites hauled cotton in drays pulled by horses or mules, from a railroad depot or from a wharf on the river, to a warehouse for storage until sold, and when sold it was hauled to the compress, and from the compress to the side of the ship. The drays were heavy and had two low wheels, with wide tires and a heavy axle. A large part of the weight of the load was thrown on the backs of the animals. Some carried as much as five bales of cotton, weighing not less than twenty-two hundred pounds, made the load too heavy for two horses or mules to pull through the thick sand. This method of transportation was very labor intensive. Three compresses were located on the riverbank. Slaves loaded ships with the help of a contraption operated from on shipboard. They hauled the cotton bale by bale on an inclined landing stage, and lowered it into the hold of the ship.

Amelia M. Murray gave her assessment of the slave: "he is lazy and improvident; slavery makes him work and ensures him a home, food and clothing; it provides for sickness, infancy and old age; allows no tramping or sulking and knows no pauperism."[21] William Harden observed: "almost all slaves would steal if they thought they would not be detected." In many cases according to Harden they "felt they had a right to" the property.[22]

Historian William A. Burns claims slaves in Savannah formed a "significant part"[23] of the city's work force. All male slaves 16 to 60 years of age were obliged to "clean the streets and commons, the trash being thrown in a galley in the bluff at the foot of Whitaker Street and burnt."[24] They were laborers, skilled workers, and artisans. Slaves worked in the planting and exportation of rice, on the waterfront, in the cotton industry, and in the preparation and exportation of lumber. The city changed from a major rice exporter, to the largest cotton port and the lumber capital of the Atlantic coast. The city's entrepreneurs seemed to be affected with the "cotton madness virus," as the population doubled between 1840 and 1860. The construction of Fort Pulaski was meant to safeguard this prosperity.

Lumber was floated on rafts down the Savannah and Ogeechee Rivers. Later it was taken from the river, scrubbed clean of mud and stacked up eight or nine feet high, with proper ventilation to facilitate drying and seasoning. Two Savannah Rice Mills owned a large number of slaves, as did the Savannah Steam Saw Mill and the Royal Vale Mill. Legal restrictions guaranteed that African Americans slaves would never share the bounty, but provide a reliable source of labor that their owners could exploit to advantage. Despite these strictures, there were many black carpenters, coopers, and bricklayers in the town.

Before the Civil War, black labor was holding its own in Savannah and slavery was far from a "dying economic system." The white press informed its "mechanic friends" that it had not approved the policy of their movement as regards the "exclusion by law, of the blacks from mechanical employments." The reporter thought the action would be unfair to the interest of slave owners or be an encouraging sign of "the decline of slavery." made its position as regards the relationship between slaves and whites perfectly clear. It stated: "Here the white man, whatever his condition or calling, is the acknowledged superior of the black and this superiority is felt and conceded by the black himself, whether in the field or workmanship, working with and under the direction of his masters?"[25] Between 1810 and 1860, the city's slave population jumped by 325 percent from 2,725 to 8,417.[26]

The cost of slaves at least tripled between 1800 and 1859. Often times slave owners tended to make a higher profit when they hired out their slaves, sometimes resulting in more freedom for the slave. In January 1853, several slaves were offered for sale "A man 35 years old, his wife 32, a woman 23 years with her boy child of 3: A woman 28 years, one 26 years, two girls 18 years. A girl 17 years and a boy 15 years and one 12 years."[27] By February a "gang of ninety-eight prime Negroes," were sold for $483 each and it was "deemed a very good price."[28]

In July, a boy of about fourteen years, "very smart and intelligent, accustomed to wait in the house and capable of tending a horse," was advertised for sale.[29] As was "a prime likely young fellow, a first rate cook for steamboat or hotel." Later that month a "mulatto woman, 28 years old, a house servant, washer and ironer, with her two children, a girl 13 and a boy 10," were also offered for sale.[30] William Wright advertised for sale "a mulatto man, 30 years old-first rate carpenter, also a man, 22 years old-a first rate bricklayer."[31] During February, the Georgia

House of Representatives passed a law to prevent the separation of Negro mothers from children under five years of age.

In March that year, the city Marshall arrested Edward Bertram for "inducing a Negro woman to run away from her owner."[32] William Everett was arrested "on a charge of Negro stealing."[33] In the 1850's, slavery was a profitable business in Savannah, supporting several slave brokers and auctioneers. Many slaves were sold on the steps of the courthouse though there were slave marts at Habersham and Bryan Streets and Bryan Street opposite the city market. W. H. Wright offered for sale "A mulatto woman, 28 years of old, a house servant, washer and ironer, with two children, a girl 13 and a boy 10. Apply to W.H.Wright." The Pulaski House had a pen in the basement, which housed slaves belonging to their guests. William Wright advertised for sale, "a Mulatto Man, 30 years old-first rate carpenter, also a man, 22 years old- a first rate Bricklayer."[34] A man 32 years (a house servant) was sold for $1,355, and a woman 22 years old (a field hand) with a child was sold for $1,205. The 35 slaves were sold for an averaged over $830 each. As the paper stated: "These sales indicate not only that Negroes are commanding good prices, but also that there is money in our community seeking investment in that species of property."[35]

Slaver William Wright was doing a brisk business in his chosen profession. In March, he sold at the Courthouse, "a Negro man 32 years of age, (a house servant), for $1,355 and a woman 22 years old (a field hand) with child for $1,205." He also sold an additional 35 Negroes for an average price of $830 each. The *Daily Morning News* commented, "These sales indicate not only that Negroes are commanding good prices, but also that there is money in our community seeking investment in that species of property."[36] Wright had another big sale in May. He offered "a valuable family of Negroes: a brown skin man, 21 years old, good house servant and hostler. A brown skin woman, 25 years old, house servant with her three children, likely and hearty-a brown skin woman, 22 years old, house servant, a brown skin girl, 18 years, good seamstress-a brown skin girl 17 years, house servant-a brown skin girl, 16 years, house servant and nurse." The slaves were reported to be "all of good characters." By August one of Wright's slaves, Isaac, found himself in Magistrate's Court "charged with harboring and concealing Rachel, a slave." The jury recommended and the Magistrate ordered Isaac to receive 25 lashes. [37]

King Cotton and the concomitant, "cotton insanity," transformed Savannah from a "sickly hole in the woods," as British soldiers regarded it, to a town that "traded in wealth and did not produce wealth of her own."[38] In 1858, the State Comptroller reported that the state had 432,124 slaves in 1858 and 443, 364 in the following year or an increase of 11, 240 slaves. The average value of slaves in 1858 was put at $526.39 and in 1859, $612.63, an increase of $ 86.24. Chatham County with 11, 997 slaves in 1858 had the second largest slave community in the state. One year later Chatham County led the state with 12, 235, an increase of 238 slaves.[39]

The state was in a phase of progress that would have important consequences later on.

French aristocrat John Montalet, from Haiti, migrated to Georgia and in 1798 bought the Hermitage plantation. It seems certain that he brought many slaves with him to the plantation. The architect, brick maker and industrious native of Scotland, Henry McAlpin who had lost his family's fortune before age 21 and had migrated to America in an attempt to regain his fortune, owned the property from 1818 until his death in 1851. In 1820, Henry McAlpin and his slaves built and operated one of the first railroads in America. This railroad transported a fifty-one by forty-five feet large frame building covered with a pitched roof between the kilns. Each kiln was filled with green unburned brick and was removed between kilns when the kiln was fired. A huge four-wheeled truck on an iron railroad pulled the unit.

The iron rails were also made on the plantation. Since McAlpin also bred and trained racehorses on the property, it is likely that these animals were used to pull his train. Over the years between 186 and 400 slaves worked at Hermitage Plantation. In 1824, the Steam Saw-Mill and Cast Iron Foundry operated on the plantation. Its advertisements claimed that its iron products were executed in a style equal to that of "any factory in the United States." Many of English architect William Jay's Savannah houses may have had ornate iron castings from the Hermitage Plantation. In 1833 McAlpin had completed building Chatham County's Courthouse of "good and substantial brick." The culverts of the Central of Georgia Railroad, where McAlpin was a director, were also built by slave labor.

Slave labor at the Hermitage Plantation is perhaps more celebrated for the famous *Savannah Grays* manufactured there over a period of half a century. Slaves made thousands of bricks from the usually thick strata of an iron carbonate clay found in the area, at one time said to be 44 feet deep. Ralston Lattimore estimated that two thirds of the bricks used to build Fort Pulaski were purchased in Savannah between 1833 and 1842. In 1934 however, the acting superintendent of the Fort claimed that over the years the salt and carbon dioxide in the air caused a chemical reaction that made the bricks crumble. The bricks were said to be both durable and porous. About 200,000 bricks were acquired from building wreckers to make the necessary repairs to the Fort. This unusual demand ignited a new interest in the venerable Savannah made bricks. An architect working on the repair of the Fort is credited with coining the term "grays" to describe the brownish chocolate purplish colored bricks.

Brick making in the Savannah area began in the 1730's in ovens on the banks of the Savannah River under the Trustees Garden bluff. Some of the later types were made, among other places, at the Lovell Brick Company on a yard on Louisville Road near Pooler, which was active from 1785 to 1910. Mark Kreuzwieser reported in 1984 that while modern bricks were selling for about 16 cents each, the

Savannah grays were selling for 80 cents to a dollar each. It was then reported that more than 1,000 buildings in the Historic District were constructed of Savannah grays.

In one sense the existence of so many thousands of these *Savannah Grays* today, in the former Central Georgia Railroad buildings, Fort Pulaski and many homes in the historic district, bear stark but silent witness to the resilience of the hundreds of slaves who made them. In like manner, in keeping with the "two-ness" of Southern history, the stately mansions that adorn the historic district also attest to the opulence of the white owners who reaped huge profits from exploiting black slave labor while keeping the slaves "under due order and subjection."

In addition to the obligatory "Big House," McAlpin built on his plantation: a two-story kitchen, smokehouses, a storage house, a laundry, brick slave houses and a two-story hospital with separate rooms for men and women. McAlpin maximized the capital invested in his slave property by using then as co-lateral as he traded, borrowed, or bought more slaves.[40] When he died in 1851, the Hermitage Plantation was reported to be one of the best equipped and most efficiently run plantations in the country. An appraisal done in 1853 indicated that there were 172 slaves valued at $63,890.06 living on the premises, 42 horses, 21 mules, 32 hogs and 32 colts. The plantation had 80,000 bricks valued at $640, about 300,000 unburnt bricks, 250,000 feet of sawed lumber and 32 hogs.

Savannah in 1820 had a population of 3,866 whites, 582 free coloreds and 3,075 slaves, for a total population of 7,523 persons, 48.6% of who were nonwhite. By 1840, the total population reached 11,214 of whom 5,888 were white, 632 free coloreds and 4,694 slaves. Poor white men, mainly Irish immigrants, competed and clashed with slaves and free coloreds for jobs on the wharves, railroad yards, in the cotton industry and warehouses. Carpenters, masons, and those in the mechanical trades also faced stiff competition from blacks. White and black women competed as seamstresses, laundresses and domestic servants. As one Savannahian said "what respectable parent wishes to place his son at a trade alongside an apprentice who is a slave."

Up to the time of emancipation, blacks were scattered throughout Savannah, even though from 1790 slaves were required to live with their owners as a control strategy.[41] Owners rented out their slaves at will. Blacks made up from one quarter to one half of every ward in the city. Blacks and whites were "pretty equally divided in most wards."[42] The edge of the Fort, Yamacraw and Springhill were regarded as black areas. Bancroft's 1848 census showed that Oglethorpe ward in West Savannah had 1,327 blacks and 999 whites. Currytown in the southeast had a black majority population and poor quality housing. Women domestics formed a large cohort of black workers. The lumber concerns owned 77 slaves, cotton 11, brick makers 25, and the largest single business, Central of Georgia owned more than 120 slaves. By 1820, more than half of the Savannah's households owed slaves.

Over the next 40 years Irish immigration reduced the percentage of slaves in the population to 35%. One third of all white families in the city owned slaves and by 1860 about half of the white families owned slaves.

About 193 slaves operated steamers, plying the Florida and Augusta trade routes. The famous Pulaski Hotel owned 60 slaves and the city hospital had its own slaves. Many slave owners hired out their property and in a few cases obtained a higher return on their merchandise than any other form of business transaction. The Federal Government hired slaves to do repairs on Fort Jackson and build Fort Pulaski, advertising in the local press for workers. The city of Savannah used hired slaves in its scavenger department. Many slaves worked as draymen, transporting cotton to ships on the waterfront. The Central of Georgia Railroad on the west side and the Savannah, Florida and Western Railroad on the east side all had tracks which brought cotton to the riverfront for export.

Slaves hiring themselves out had to purchase a badge from the city before they could ply their trade. The price of the badge depended on the job to be performed and the sex of the slave. Failure to wear this badge exposed the slave to the possibility of receiving 39 lashes or the owner could be fined three dollars. Whites who hired slaves without badges could also be fined but the slave was to be jailed until the fine was paid. This badge stipulation began with a law passed in 1774. The law was further amended in 1815. Slaves were not allowed to sell to other slaves though some Savannah slaves received an exemption from this law. There were also slave carpenters, masons, and several other craftsmen. In 1848, some 83 slaves worked at skilled trades.

The urban milieu of Savannah offered many distractions from the drudgery of slavery. The slaves' amusement, however, was always dependent on the fickle whim of whites. Blacks engaged in fishing, and an occasional circus. They rowed the boats for the popular water sports on the Savannah River. Two unusual blacks, a Major Small and a Captain Qua, even engaged in a duel. As it happened, one participant failed to show up. Drinking and carousing were frowned on. In fact, not more than seven blacks were allowed to gather by themselves without the consent of the authorities. In a word, they could not enjoy the simple pleasures of the day.

Blacks throughout slavery were known for their love of clothes and color. They sometimes decked themselves out in their best finery and promenaded on the sidewalks, or drove around in carriages, much to the chagrin of some whites. Others used the holiday seasons to maintain, as best they could, the ancestral customs and dances with or without the permission of their owners. Whenever they felt like it, blacks enjoyed themselves regardless of the consequences. An area east of Habersham Street was notorious for its wild lifestyle. It contained many boarding houses for sailors, liquor shops, and brothels. The population was said to be "very mixed."

South Carolina Governor Adams, in a message to the Legislature, claimed that the South believed that: "A mysterious providence has brought the two races together on this continent for a wise purpose, and that the existing relation has been mutually beneficial." The Governor considered Southern slavery to have "elevated the African to a degree of civilization which the black race has never obtained in any other age or country." Finally, he thought slavery had "civilized the African. It has exalted the white race itself to higher hopes and purposes and we should press it forward to a perpetuity of progress."[43] This Southern self-serving "religio-politi-cal-economic pseudo theology," reached its zenith. Slavery was now proclaimed a "bonum commune," a common good, for both the slaves and their owners.

Meanwhile on the ledger side of affairs the paper announced that: "The annual profits derived from the slave trade is estimated at about $17,000.00 for each vessel-after two voyages."[44] In December 1858 the city was "filled with rumors to the effect that the yacht *Wanderer* had landed a cargo of Africans on some of the Islands on our coast and that they had been conveyed into the interior."[45]

On March 2, and 3, 1859, Joseph Bryan, the leading local slaver, offered about 436 slaves from the Butler Plantation for sale. This grand sale took place at the Tenbroeck Race Track about three miles from the city.[46] The event was widely advertised and almost all the hotel rooms in Savannah were filled for the occasion. The slaves were brought to the grounds and housed in stables. A few days prior to the sale, several buyers arrived to inspect the merchandise. These slaves were from a rice plantation south of Darien and a cotton plantation on St. Simon's Island, Georgia. Many were competent in the crafts required to cultivate their crops. They were all full-blooded Africans and had been born and reared on Butler's Estate. None had been previously sold. To cope with this new experience, they decked themselves, as best they could, with the women in turbans and the children in their caps.

One reporter commented that some slaves showed "heavy grief" in their faces, while others seemed to accept their fate with indifference. Others still tried to curry favor with buyers who seemed to be humane in appearance. The youngest was 15 months old. An effort was made to keep families together, though for the occasion, a family was defined as a man and his wife. The sale brought in a total of $303,850. [47]

A *Newark Advertiser* reporter saw at a racetrack near Savannah, "hundreds of well dressed Negroes with purse in hand ready to bet various sums on their favorite nags. Certainly, a happier, careless set of beings is seldom found. I could not help contrasting them with the almost naked and starving blacks we sometimes meet at home."[48] Meanwhile Captain John Bryan was making a brisk profit selling and buying slaves at his Johnson Square location and at the La Roche's Brick Yard. In 1860,[49] Bryan advertised the sale at his place on Johnson Square, of "a gang of 138 Negroes." He also offered a "likely country raised girl, 17 years old and a capable servant, also several men and women and children." In addition, he had "a number one cook, and a prime woman with three children." Finally Bryan advertised "140 rice field Negroes."[50]

Confederate Vice-President Alexander Stephens gave a memorable speech at the Athenaeum in Savannah March 21, 1861. He stated:

> "Our new government is founded upon exactly the opposite idea; its foundations are laid, its corner-stone rests upon the great truth, that the Negro is not equal to the white man; that slavery-subordination to the superior race-is his natural and normal condition. (Applause) This, our new government, is the first, in the history of the world, based upon this great physical, philosophical and moral truth." Stephens concluded, "With us, all of the white race, however high or low, rich or poor, are equal in the eye of the law. Not so with the Negro. Subordination is his place. He, by nature, or by the curse against Canaan, is fitted for that condition which he occupies in our system."[51]

In September 1861 Joseph Bryan advertised that he had "A likely Girl, 15 years of age; good cook, washer ironer and seamstress and a good woman, 27 years old, washer and ironer. A No.1 carpenter aged 30 years. It was signed, Joseph Bryan, Johnson Square, next to Merchants' & Planters' Bank."[52] Gen. W. Wylly, Esq., sold at the courthouse "ninety Negroes of all ages and sizes, belonging to the estate of Randolph Spalding deceased. The total amount of the sales was $114,930. The average price was $1,277."[53] By 1864 Captain Bryan had died and A. H. Sadler and James M. Hines leased his place of business near Monument Square and announced that they would "buy and sell Negroes and other property on commission."[54] Towards the end of the year J.G. Kesterson, an agent, advertised the sale of a "lot of prime Negroes for sale at J. A. Stevenson's, No. 108 Bryan Street."[55]

Cotton production suffered during the Civil War as plantations were leveled, the railroad system was destroyed and millions of dollars invested in slaves were lost. The British have a saying, as their monarchs succeed one another, "the king is dead, long live the king." By 1867, King Cotton had regained his throne. The Savannah Exchange was formed in 1872 and business on Factor's Walk boomed again. Eventually the dollar value of cotton decreased and finally the boll weevil after World War 1, forced the economy to shift to naval stores.

Free Persons Of Color

From the beginning, blacks and whites in the Savannah have been locked in a macabre bond. Whites could deal with blacks as long as they accepted the whites' definition of them. Blacks have always refused to accept this definition. To many whites, the black slave was essentially an inferior variety of being, shiftless, lazy, and incapable of improvement but a source of profit. The slave had his locus in the society, which according to some, was set by God, or at least by the Bible. Neither white nor black slave, a new individual soon appeared on the scene, the free person of color. These free African Americans appeared in Georgia during colonial times. Their numbers increased by immigration, escaped slaves from other states, purchased freedom, or manumission.[56] Jack Gibbons bought his wife for $400 in 1799 and paid $275 for his children in 1801.[57] A few got their freedom by simply running away.

By 1792, the Haitian slave revolt sent thousands of whites and their slaves and some free blacks, seeking refuge on mainland America. Some blacks landed in Savannah and injected new life into the local black community. In 1795, the city fathers prohibited the landing of any ship that had docked in Saint-Dominique or Haiti.[58] Though always few in number, free blacks in Georgia registered a 753% increase from 398 in 1790 to 3,000 in 1860. In the decade 1820 to 1830, they increased by 40% but dropped by 10% between 1840 and 1850. This small number of people attracted an extraordinary amount of attention on the part of the white authorities.

As historian Ruth Scarborough stated, the number of laws passed to control these free blacks showed that, the society regarded them as "undesirable members."[59] In 1800, there were 181 free persons of color or 3.5% of the population. Ten years later the number jumped to 530 or 10.3% of the population.[60] Savannah had 29.4% of the state's free persons of color.[61] Free coloreds were subjected to the same controls as slaves. In 1768 the first tax was imposed on coloreds as a separate class.[62] In 1793 state law required all free Negroes, mulattoes, and mustizoes entering the state to register within thirty days of their arrival. The free person of color had to list his occupation, place of birth, residence and prior residence and purpose for coming into the state. A suitable fine or imprisonment was attached to this law. By 1818 this registration had to be done annually. This law also imposed a fine of $100 on all free persons of color entering the state. By 1859 they could be sold into slavery for entering the state. They could not acquire real estate or slaves or hold an interest in either. This law was repealed for Savannah in 1819. Free people of color could receive credit only with the written permission of their white guardians. They could not keep houses of entertainment or sell goods, spirituous liquors. They were subject to taxation and an additional poll or head tax.[63]

By 1822, the city required all free men of color to labor 20 days on public works, while the women could perform their obligation by working in the city hospital. On October 22, 1829, the city passed an ordinance, which required all free persons of color living within the city to register with the Clerk of Council listing his residence and occupation. A fine of $100 was imposed on all those who failed to register.[64] All free persons of color between 15 to 60 years, registered in Chatham County had to do public work or face a whipping. Henry Clay described the status of the free Negro as "the most corrupt, depraved and abandoned...they are not slaves and yet they are not free."

The laws, proclaimed them free; but "prejudices" trumped all laws that entitled them to the rights "of freemen."[65] They could not associate with slaves nor engage in any kind of business transaction.[66] Black sea men disembarking at the port faced many restrictions.[67] Between 1850 and 1860, Savannah had the highest number of free blacks in the state. In 1850 about 70% of Savannah's free blacks were mulattos. A free colored vagrant was liable to be sold into slavery for two years on the first offense and be sold into slavery for life on the second offense.

The 616 free blacks in Savannah in 1820 were prohibited from owning or working in liquor stores, as masons, or mechanics, and if they worked as bricklayers, blacksmiths, cabinet makers, house shop carpenters, tailors, bakers, or butchers, they had to obtain a special badge. While most barely subsisted in 1840, about 34 were mechanics, two butchers, five barbers, two engineers, and two pilots. The total free colored population was put at 632, 262 men and 370 women.[68] By 1850, Chatham County's 435 free people of color had real estate valued at $28,850.[69] In 1857, free blacks coming into Savannah had to pay the city a tax of $100.[70]

A few lucky ones enjoyed privileges above their station. However, even these had to "know their place," as one false step often meant swift and sure retribution. The successful individual was one who knew how to navigate the edges of the strict class and race parameters, while studiously cultivating a few sympathetic whites. In 1833, about 187 blacks paid taxes, all paid poll taxes and 86 defaulted on their taxes. The criminal code tended not to distinguish between a free person of color and a slave, though such a distinction was introduced in 1811. Free people of color had to carry certificates or testimonials of their freedom. A typical one read, "To whomsoever this may come. These are to certify that the Bearer, who calls himself Harry, is and ought to be considered, a free man, until sufficient appears in a legal way, to the contrary. Given under my hand at Savannah the 23 rd. day of May 1758. Henry Ellis.[71]

In Savannah blacks had to obtain an $8 badge in order to sell in the city. Failure to comply could entail a fine of $20 or a whipping.[72] Free Negroes could be whipped or fined five dollars for owning dogs. Whereas free coloreds accounted for 15.9% of the black community in 1820 by, 1840, they had dropped to 11.9% of the black community. In 1840 free persons of color had 34 mechanics, 2 butchers, 5 barbers, 2 engineers add pilots.[73] In 1830, of the 124 free coloreds who were heads of families, 74 were female.[74] By 1850, the majority or 480 of the free persons of color were mulattoes and by 1860, 410 of the 705 free coloreds were mulattoes.[75] The city of Savannah had a population in 1860 of 13, 875 whites, 705 free coloreds, and 7,712 slaves, or a total population of 22,291 persons. The free coloreds fell even further as a percentage of the black community. It was 9.1% of the black population. Blacks were 37.8% of the population down from 48.6% in 1820. Thus while the total population tripled in forty years the total black population only doubled.

Affirmative action laws to give whites the edge were passed in 1845. Free people of color were prohibited from being mechanics.[76] Savannah's free blacks never reached the social and economic levels of their fellow blacks in Charleston, South Carolina, who in 1790 had established the Brown Fellowship Society, to look after their needs, but were better off than free people of color in Petersburg or Richmond.[77] However, by 1850, some 435 of Chatham County's blacks owned real estate valued at $28,000.00 while in 1860 the 725 free persons of color had real estate worth $23,000.00 and personal property in the amount of $47,190.00. The ruling white elite did everything it could to stifle the chances of survival for these few hundred free coloreds.[78] In 1859, the law stipulated that vagrancy could be punished by resale into slavery on the second conviction.[79]

Through it all, there were some remarkable survivors. In spite of legislation, which hindered them, a few through luck, mother wit and hard work, did fairly well. Tailors from Haiti were very successful businessmen. Loius Mirault made clothes for some of the leading personalities of Savannah. When he died in 1828 he owned six slaves and had $1000 in real estate. Andrew Morel, a tailor, owned two slaves who worked in his shop. He owned $1,600 in real estate in 1850.[80] In that same year McPherson Bowman, a 24-year-old mulatto farmer, had property worth $12,000.00, and was probably the richest black in the county.

Many free women worked as vendors of small wares, hairdressers, washerwomen and shopkeepers. Pastry workers and seamstresses did a brisk and very profitable trade. Aspasia Mirault, a popular pastry cook, operated a business at the northeast corner of Bull and Broughton Streets, while her husband's business place was located at Broughton and Whitaker Streets. She was "highly respected," and her business was "well patronized by the white people."[81] Susan Jackson was born in 1786, and became a pastry cook who owned her shop and had rental property on Broughton Street, which in 1860 gave her $80.00 per month. Her estate was valued at $15,000. She owned three lots valued at $2,200 and owned four slaves.[82]

Maria Cohen born in St. Augustine, Florida, came to Savannah in 1827 and worked as a washerwoman. When she died in 1855, she left three slaves to be held in trust for her daughter, Hannah and her son Abraham. Cohen owned slaves since

1833,[83] and her daughter a seamstress, had personal property worth $1,000 and one slave in 1869. Anna Gibbons in 1860, had real estate worth $9,200.00 and personal property valued at $1,000.00 and owned two slaves. Free women owned most of the black slaves owned by blacks. In 1855 ten blacks owned a total of 32 slaves.[84]

Little Warsaw

In the early 1800's, one got to little Warsaw after a long and torturous day's sailing from Thunderbolt, through the Marsh Creek. On arriving ashore, one entered a unique Southern community. Charles Odingsells, a white man, lived there in almost complete isolation with his 73 slaves on three plantations. In 1809, Odingsells left instructions in his will to manumit a black woman and her children. The will stated, "It is my will the Negro wench Hannah and her children and her mother old Lucy be liberated by petitioning to the Legislature to have an act passed for that purpose. I desire (Hannah) to be liberated for her faithfulness to me in sickness and taking care of my property for years... I give and bequeath to the mulatto boy Anthony, son of Hannah, in trust to Executors this Island known as Little Wassaw...to maintain him and give him an education and said Negroes are to be given up to him when he comes of the age of twenty-one years, together with little Wassaw Island, to be disposed of as her might think proper."[85]

In all probability, Anthony was his son.[86] Anthony was born on Skidaway Island in 1796.[87] Some nine slaves and little Warsaw were to be held in trust for the boy, to maintain and educate him until he reached the age of 21 years. By 1854 individual manumission was prohibited.[88]

Odingsell's first guardian, C.O.Screven, eventually had to give up this responsibility because of failing health. On attaining maturity, Anthony was to come into possession of his inheritance including nine slaves. With this wealth, young Anthony lived the life of a country squire. Some 50 acres were under cultivation of cotton and 100 acres were full of pine trees. He paid poll tax for himself and his wife. By 1834, he set about building an 18 by 40-foot house on Little Warsaw. His only child, Lucy Ann, was born in 1835, and later married and settled on the Island. Anthony Odingsells owned 15 slaves and 200 acres of land.[89] He sold a slave for $385 in 1833.[90] The industrious Anthony Odingsells in 1860 had some 2,000 acres valued at $3,000.and owned 35 milk cows, 50 sheep, and 75 swine valued at $550.00. He maintained his unique status as the richest black in the area. The Odingsells River perpetuates his name. He was a black gentleman farmer, fisherman, well educated, and well off. He died January 15, 1878 in his ninety-fourth year.[91]

Protectors Of the City

"Stout fellows, the pick of the colored population,

Devoted to the protection of the city."

A fire in 1738 and another three years later destroyed several buildings including the filature.[92] At that time Savannah had twelve streets and six squares with Yamacraw and the Trustees Garden forming the outer suburbs. The western and eastern outer limits were Jefferson and Lincoln Streets and South Broad now Oglethorpe Avenue formed the southern boundary. The first fire ordinance was promulgated in 1758.[93] About fifteen men organized themselves into Savannah's first fire department.[94] On Saturday, November 26, 1796, one of the great fires to plague Savannah in its early history destroyed 229 of the 400 buildings in the city, including Christ Episcopal Church and the Independent Presbyterian Church. Hundreds were made homeless. Fighting fires was then an unorganized activity. In January 1820, another devastating fire consumed 463 tenements and covered an area from the river to Broughton Street and from Jefferson Street to Drayton Street. Something had to be done.

During the fall of 1821, city council formed about seventy-five free men of color into the Franklin Fire Engine and Hose Company and the Union Axe and Fire Company.[95] Savannah was divided into four fire districts and a watchman was located in the steeple of the City Exchange. Alarms were sounded according to the ward numbers. In time some engine houses were located in public squares, along with water cisterns. In 1824, the General Assembly authorized the city to organize the Savannah Fire Company headed by a chief. The actual work of putting out fires was to be done by free men of color and hired slaves.[96] White officers, called "Masters of Engines" were to be in charge and they were empowered to administer prompt and immediate correction, to any slave who disobeyed or otherwise offended any rule. Each slave was provided with a badge that conferred on him all the "immunities and privileges of a fireman." Blacks pulled the first fire engines.[97]

On March 11, 1825, city council passed an ordinance requesting the city marshal to immediately "take an account of the Negro firemen between the ages of sixteen and sixty and to make a return of the same to the chief fireman." Any slave or free man of color enrolled in the fire department who failed to answer an alarm would be subject to a fine not exceeding ten dollars, or jailed for not less than five days nor more than fifteen days. Free men of color were exempt from poll tax. Once each month they were obliged to practice their fire drills, "cleaning and keeping in good condition the ropes, buckets, hose, ladders and engines." Each slave was paid fifty cents for demonstration. Slaves were also "subject to fire duty in the same way" and "were required to drill at least once a month."[98] They were to receive 12 ° cents an hour. The first slave or person of color at the scene of a fire was to receive a reward.[99] City council appropriated thirty dollars for each fire "for the encouragement of free persons of color, free Negroes and hired slaves, who may be active in carrying engines etc., to extinguish fires."[100] By 1828 there were 178 slaves and 96 free men of color fighting fires in Savannah.[101]

In 1828, a report to Council stated that 178 slaves and 96 free Negroes worked in the fire department. There was also a white company of 17 men.[102]. Each fireman was required to obtain, at his expense, a cap or hat on which shall be put the initials F.C., to be worn whenever he was on duty. Once a month the black firemen were ordered out for the purpose of playing off the engines and drilling in the use of them, cleaning and keeping in good condition the ropes, buckets, hose, ladders and engines. Council passed an ordinance providing that "every male slave between 16 and 60 years of age, who received a badge from the city, should be registered and enrolled under the Fire Company and be subject to drills and regular duty."[103]

When Charles S. Hardee came to Savannah in 1835, he found the fire department equipped with combination suction and propelling engines hose and hose carts, fire buckets, a hook and ladder and an axe company. The firehouses were located in the squares, public wells (or pumps) in the squares, and at the intersection of the streets, and cisterns,[104] in the squares near the engine houses. The hand engines had long bars on either side and when they were moved briskly up and down produced a suction and propelling power a pressure strong enough to reach the top of a building. Fire buckets were constructed of heavy black leather and were about two feet long, round, and with a handle across. Fire buckets held about three gallons of water. Engines had to be dragged by firemen through the thick sand of the street by a rope attached to the tongue of the machine, a very slow and laborious process.

The law required each homeowner to keep a number of fire buckets equal to the number of fireplaces in the house. The custom of furnishing the black and white firemen with liquor during and after the fighting of a fire was discontinued in 1839.[105] Some whites began to take an interest in fighting fires and in 1846, formed the Oglethorpe Fire Company. The Washington Fire Company was formed in 1848; the Young America Fire Company also came into being. This group, composed of "the rough element of whites," attacked the slaves while they were on fire duty.[106] They soon engaged in fights with the black firemen of the Savannah Fire Company. The council was forced to disband a group of white firemen. The local press also began complaining that paying slaves to fight fires could cause them to become "impertinent" and that the custom was decidedly "injurious of slavery itself."

As it happened though, the slaves and free blacks took as much pride in their fire companies,[107] as whites did in their connection with the military companies of the city. African Americans had at last found an outlet for their wounded humanity. The black Fire Companies were very popular within the black community and their annual parades were well attended. Despite all this positive activity on behalf of the city, black firemen were never given the social respect or recognition that their contribution to the city's safety warranted. They remained firmly kept at the bottom of the social pyramid. In 1849 there was much commotion when the Savannah Fire Company adopted a resolution to allow the black firemen to wear uniforms.

Two white companies, the Oglethorpe and Washington, protested this move as "degrading to the white firemen" and council rescinded the decision. The white fire chief resigned when the council failed to take action after some white firemen had again abused some black firemen. In May 1850, the Fire Company adopted a resolution allowing the black firemen to wear uniforms. Two white companies objected to this move as degrading to white firemen. The council forbade the mayor from permitting this move. Later the council rescinded this motion, and the black firemen were allowed to wear uniforms. At that time the city was divided into five fire districts.[108] In May 1851, black firemen celebrated their annual parade. The black firemen in their gray uniforms used these parades to display their prowess in throwing water at great distances. Rivalry between the companies was "something to be admired." The twelve companies included the axe and bucket companies. The fire engines were "tastefully decorated with flowers." There were about "four hundred stout, strong, happy faced fellows-the elite of the colored population of Savannah." The engines were decorated with floral wreaths, and all the men were in high spirits. They marched to Bay Street where the mayor inspected them. The men then gave three cheers for the mayor, the fire chief and finally for themselves.[109]

In 1852 black firemen sang their familiar refrains as they marched away, "much exhausted by their long and severe exertions," from twelve hours of labor fighting a particularly vicious fire. They sang the popular "I bet my money on the bobtail nag." They brought their engines up the Bay, "marching to the well kept tune of their accustomed refrains." The editor reported that it occurred to him, as they passed his office, "cheerfully singing in chorus, their smiling faces beaming through the smoke and the sweat of their late encounter with the devouring element that the sight would have done a Northern wooly-head philanthropist much good. There had been no riotous demonstration of brute instincts-no conflict of company with company-but all had labored voluntarily and with a spirit of generous emulation, and now they were returning from the scene of their exertions, cheerful and gratified with the reflection that they had borne a part in the strife against the common enemy, and had done good service in a common cause. We think Philosopher Greeley's theories would have been greatly disturbed if he could have heard he happy fellows sing: Bet my money on de bobtail nag; someday bet on de bat."[110]

A report on the parade of May 1853 stated that the turn out was "an inspiring display of real stamina and solid worth," as some 400 men, the elite of the Colored population, showed their mettle. Engines, lanterns, and torches were gaily and most tastefully arrayed in fresh flowers and ribbons. In the parade, the men wore white pants and loose white blouse shirts, gathered in at the waist with broad patent leather belts, giving them, it was said, "a very handsome and imposing appearance." After being reviewed by the mayor, they returned to their quarters.[111] The Fire Department remained plagued by problems and was reorganized. At the same time, another dispute broke out between black and white firemen. In June 1853, white firemen of the Oglethorpe Company were accused of having beaten and maltreated black firemen during the process of putting out fires. City council committee on fire reported the disorganization of the department. The following year another dispute occurred during which time the fire department was disbanded.[112] *The Sandersville Georgian* reported on the 1854 parade. The correspondent stated, "we witnessed a part of the display made by the black fire companies on Friday. We could not help thinking them happier, even in their servitude, than thousands whose sympathies are excited for the poor Southern slave."

In 1855, four uniformed companies of black firemen took part in the funeral precession of a deacon of the Third African Baptist Church. That same year the firemen's parade "presented a most formidable array of our colored fire preventive force." The Mayor and Aldermen reviewed the companies, which extended from Whitaker Street on the right, near Abercorn and "presented a very handsome and imposing appearance." The Axe Hook and Ladder companies numbered 60 men dressed in white. The Hose Cart A had 40 men dressed in white shirts and cloth pants. The Hose Cart B had 30 men dressed in blue coats trimmed with red, and white pants.

Anthony Wall, 67 years old and "the oldest colored fireman in the city," served with his company for over thirty years. His company, Engine No. 1, Warren had about 50 men dressed in grey coats trimmed with red and white pants. Engine No. 2, Pulaski, had 62 men dressed in white shirts and black pants. Engine No. 3, Franklin, had 87 men dressed in blue shirts trimmed with red and white pants. Engine No. 4, Neptune with 50 men were dressed in white shirts trimmed with blue, and white pants. Engine No. 7, Tomochichi had 70 men dressed in yellow coats trimmed with black and white pants. Engine No. 8, Wild Cat, had 94 men dressed in blue shirts with white trimming and white pants. Engine No. 11, Niagara with about 90 men wore green coats trimmed with black, and white pants. All the companies had at least two white officers each. At the end of the inspection the companies marched to South Broad and Bull Streets where they competed for a silver goblet, and one assumes, "bragging rights." As it happened Engine No. 8, Wild Cat "whose stream was thrown 177 feet," won that day.[113]

The next year's parade was even more extravagant. A Savannah paper regarded it as the "most formidable array of the black fire preventative force." The parade participants displayed "perfect order and discipline as they passed in review before city officials." The Axe, Hook and Ladder companies had a contingent of 60 men. The Hose Cart A with 40 men, Hose Cart B with 30 men, Engine No. 1 Warren with 50 men, Engine No. 2.Pulaski, 62 men. Then there was Engine No. 3 Franklin with 87 men. Engine No. 4 Neptune had 50 men, Engine No. 7, Tomochichi with 70 men, Engine No. 8 Wild Cat with 94 men. In addition, Engine No. 11, Niagara with 90 men. After the inspection, the men competed at the corner of Bull and South Broad streets for a silver goblet. Engine No. 8, Wild Cat with a thrown stream of 177 feet won the silver goblet. Franklin No. 3 won the competition for throwing the longest stream of water. Some 668 black firemen paraded and competed. This was 35 more than the previous year.[114]

Toney, the well-known colored fireman died in 1856. His funeral was "the largest ever seen in this city." An estimated 1,000 African Americans of all age groups attended including 400 colored firemen. He belonged to Fire Company No.1. The chief fireman's 1857 report to the council listed the black companies as follows: Axe, Hook and Ladder company with a Truck of two folding ladders and manned by 53 free blacks. Engine No. 1 located in Reynolds Square with 80 slaves. Engine No. 2 was located in Pulaski Square with 79 slaves and Engine No.3 in Franklin Square with 60 slaves. Engine No. 4 in Wright Square with 65 free blacks, Engine No. 7 at the corner of Fahm and Indian Streets with 73 slaves. Engine No. 8 at Fireman's Hall operated by 78 slaves. The engine No. 11 in Johnson Square had 96 slaves, Hose Carriage No. 1. In Columbia Square manned by 21 slaves, for a grand more than 600 black firemen.[115] The Hose Carriage No. 2 was housed at Firemen's Hall with 25 men of color.[116]

In 1857 there were nine black companies in the fire department. The Axe, Hook and Ladder Company, Fireman's Hall, truck for ladders, 26 axes and belts, two white officers and 50 free men of color. Engine No 1, Reynolds Square, engine with hose carriage attached, 400 feet hose, had two white officers and 80 slaves. Engine No. 2, Pulaski Square, engine with hose carriage, 450 feet two white officers and 79 slaves. Hose Carriage No. 1, Columbia Square, hose carriage 400 feet hose, one white officer and 21 slaves. Hose Carriage No 2, Fireman's Hall, hose carriage, 300 feet hose one white officer and 25 free men of color. Engine No. 3, Franklin Square, was composed of an engine, a 400-foot hose two white officers and 60 slaves. Engine No. 4, Wright Square had an engine with 300-foot hose, two white officers and 65 free men of color. Engine No. 8, Fireman's Hall had an engine, a 600-foot hose, two white officers and 78 slaves. Engine No 11, had and engine with a 650-foot hose two white officers and 96 slaves.[117] City Council seized the equipment of the Young Armenia Fire Company because of insubordination. Some whites again expressed fear of this extensive black organization.

On May 27, 1859, the black firemen were again on a parade with the mayor, aldermen and a large crowd in attendance. At 2:00 p.m., some 155 free blacks and 608 slaves paraded in full regalia with their highly decorated engines, followed by an immense crowd of black supporters. As they were about to be inspected in front of the Firemen's Hall, the Exchange bell gave out a fire alarm, and in an instant all the men, while dressed in their parade uniforms, began dashing away with terrific speed: "While the air filled with their shouts, ran to put out a fire at Alice and Montgomery Streets." After the fire was extinguished they resumed the inspection.

The parade finally marched down Bay Street and disbanded. The men sang their merry refrains followed by "hundreds of well-dressed and orderly Negroes who made the air vocal with their good-natured clamor." The newspaper article ended on a somber note. We thought, "Such a sight might almost cure a Northern abolitionist of his insanity."[118] Although these stalwart sons of Mother Africa left no diaries, it is not difficult to imagine their pride as they made the best of the only opportunity opened to them to affirm their manhood in a social and legal and political system dedicated to its annihilation.

By 1860, the department had four white and 10 black companies of which seven were hand engines, two horses and one axe. The Warren Hand Engine No. 1 was located in Reynolds Square, Pulaski Hand Engine No. 2, in Pulaski Square, Franklin Hand Engine No. 3 in Franklin Square, Neptune Hand Engine No. 4, in Wright Square, Tomo-Chi-Chi Hand Engine No. 7 at Fahm and Indian Streets. Niagara Hand Engine No. 11 was located in Johnson Square. Wild Cat Hand Engine No. 8, located at Fireman's Hall. Columbia Hose Company No. 1 was located in Columbia Square. Hose Company No. 2 was located at the Fireman's Hall and the Axe Company No. 1, was also located at the Fireman's Hall.[119] On June 17, the pay of blacks working on the engines increased to 20 cents an hour.[120]

John Butler, "a colored man, a member of Pulaski Fire Company No. 2 was struck by a fragment of shell in St. Julian Street, while engaged in removing his engine into a position assigned them in Franklin square." He was removed to a private residence and died in about two hours after receiving his injuries. The paper reported that the fire was set by Union troops.[121]

The Firemen's parade of July 5, 1865, was one of the largest of the period. The blacks assembled on South Broad Street and were joined by the Colored Union League of Savannah, composed of about 250 men. Word around town had it that these Union Leagues, quasi-military organizations, engaged in military drills with muskets and pistols. The procession marched to the Third Baptist Church where the Declaration of Independence and President Lincoln's proclamation were read. In the afternoon, various fire companies gave a thrilling display. Among the groups were Warren dressed in blue shirts, with red breast, white pants and glazed hats, 82 men. Next was Franklin in white shirts, red tops, white pants, and glazed hats, 104 men. Niagara wore blue jackets, glazed hats, with the officers in green coats, some 90 men and 22 boys. Several other groups, also, each neatly dressed, passed in review by an ecstatic black community, some 655 of Savannah's finest blacks. Some white soldiers and firemen overturned a black fire engine and played football with the glazed caps of the black firemen.[122]

The firemen's parade of 1865 witnessed a shift in white attitudes toward black firemen. About four years later white units were paid $6,000 while blacks were paid only $ 190. This money was to be used for equipment and fees. The press preserved for posterity "the words of the peculiar songs and choruses with which our Negro firemen enliven the tiresome homeward pull from a fire." One person sang the single line and the whole company, sometimes as many as one hundred men, joined "with full strength of lungs in the choruses."

Capt. Bob-We's going down de river to New Orleans
Chorus-Ho Susyanna, ho
When we git dar we'll tell 'em yous a comin
Ho Susyanna, ho.
As we go I'll tell you of a wonder,
Ho. Susyanna, ho.
One day, in lightnin' rain and thunder,
Ho Susyanna, ho.
I went down to Hell town, and seed de devil chained down.
Ho. Susyanna, ho.
Devil says to dis nigga, "What are you arter?
Ho Susyanna, ho.
"I'se fireman, " says I, on the Champion of the Water.
Ho Susyanna, ho.
"She's de fastest boat from de mountain to de sea.
Ho Susyanna, ho.
"For she's got wings where de wheels ought to be.
Ho Susyanna, ho.
"But de whiskys give out, and I thought I'd come down.
Ho Susyanna, ho.
"To see if you wanted a fireman in Hell town."
Ho Susyanna, ho.
De devil he grinned till he scared dis nigga,
Ho, Susyanna, ho.
And his eyes kept a shinin' out bigger and bigger,
Ho Susyanna, ho.
Nigga wants to go, but de devil wants to keep him.
Ho Susyanna, ho.
So, de nigga start to run like a painter a leapin'
Ho Susyanna, ho.

De devil called and I bawled-oh. How I did run man.
Ho Susyanna, ho.
De devil damned and I ran, and I fooled him out of one man.
Ho. Susyanna, ho.
(*Savannah Daily Herald,* February 11, 1865.)

The local press reported on another parade of the colored fire companies. The Warren Fire Company No. 1 and Hose Cart, with 105 men, decked in white pants, blue shirts trimmed in red, headed the parade. Pulaski No. 2, 85 men strong, and the Hose carriage were dressed in white shirts with black trimmings. The Franklin Fire Company No. 3, had 113 men, the Tomochichi No. 7 had 80 men. The parade lined up at the Firemen's Hall then paraded down South Broad Street to East Broad through East Broad to Bay, up Bay to the Exchange, where they were dismissed.[123] The *Savannah Republican* reported on the "conduct of those soldiers, citizens, and vicious little rascals that interfered with the colored firemen on the 4th of July." The paper concluded: "We saw a crowd of people gathered around a lot of boys who were using the firemen's hats as footballs in one of the squares, while others satisfied their fun by jumping on the hats. These firemen's hats cost something like eight or ten dollars apiece, and no man but a coward would be guilty of committing such a contemptible act."[124]

Black companies paraded on New Year's Day 1866. The event was reported to have been "in a very orderly manner and the deportment of the firemen was highly commendable."[125] In April the fire chief disbanded Engine No. 2 because of "insubordination on the part of the colored members."[126] A colored band from Charleston arrived in the city to take part in the firemen's parade.[127] The firemen's parade that year did not have fewer engines in parade. Mayor Anderson inspected them. The paper took "pleasure in bearing testimony to the generally excellent deportment of our colored firemen yesterday. Their conduct and bearing, while evinced a commendable self-respect on their part, and a just pride in their organization as firemen, was orderly, peaceable and respectful. We observed no evidence of any kind, other than an amicable and confiding spirit, which in times past, pervaded the entire body."[128]

Later in the year, the press reported that the "various colored fire companies and other colored societies were out in full blast yesterday, for the purpose of attending a picnic at Bradley's place across the canal.[129] Several bands of field music and with colors and banners flying led the procession. The banners were inscribed with the names of the different societies, such as "Independent Elect Cherry Bean Society." In April the black Company Engine 2, was disbanded, because of "insubordination" on the part of some members. A colored band played for the white Oglethorpe Fire Company No. 1, as they paraded "through the principal streets."[130]

By January 1867, the Savannah Fire Company resigned as a body. There were only 7 black companies by then. Under the reorganization the colored companies were continued and one colored Axe company was formed.[131] In 1868, the black fire companies were Hand Engine No. 3 in Pulaski Square, Hand engine No. 4 in Franklin Square, Hand engine No.5 in Columbia Square and the Hand Engine No. 7 Tomochichi. During the 1868 firemen parade "the line was stopped in front of a bar room on Fahm Street and a squad went in and called for drinks. They drank and then seized the decanters to carry liquor to those in line." When the bar tender intervened "they turned upon him and beat him. A police man came up and attempted to arrest the disorderly ones when he was also beaten."[132]

The following month Captain Edward Taylor head of Axe Company No. 8, wrote a letter to the paper disclaiming any responsibility on the part of his company and objecting to any call for disbandment of the Axe Company.[133] By the end of 1868, there were fewer black companies. The hand engine No. 3, (Pulaski) with jumper: hand engine No. 4 (Franklin) with jumper; hand engine No. 5, (Columbia) with hose carriage; hand engine No 7, (Tomochichi) with jumper.[134] Black firemen had a successful annual parade and inspection in 1869. They were complimented on "their orderly appearance and the neatness and good condition of their apparatus, and promised to see that they received sundry little repairs and supplies of which they stand in need." The groups then marched to the Court House Square for the annual competition. Suddenly an alarm was sounded and all the companies "were off with a rush, leaving the procession to the care of the musicians, color and banner bearers."

On their return after putting out the fire the reporter wrote "We notice the fact to the credit of our colored firemen, that their bright uniforms did not prevent them from rendering effective service at the fire. They pitched into their work with a will, regardless of the damage to their uniforms, many of which were sadly soiled and injured."[135] In 1869 the local press complained that the *Macon Messenger* was "rather heavy on our Savannah Negroes, of the Axe companies. Who recently visited Macon."? The Macon paper had insinuated that the Savannah folk had stolen chickens, geese, pot rabbits, etc.[136] As the Reconstruction era progressed, some reorganization of the fire companies occurred because of "the freeing of Negroes."[137]

Black firemen began to use their parades as political statements. Parades were now held on May Day, July 4, Liberian Independence day and additional ones on the anniversary of the passing of the fifteenth Amendment. They all followed a regular pattern of a brass band at the head, the fire companies, fraternal organizations and clubs. In 1871 the last three Hand Engine Companies of blacks was disbanded and the engine house in Washington Square was torn down and the firemen disbanded. By 1875, there were no African American firemen. Thus ended a glorious period of fighting fires, 1821-1871,[138] by the sons of Mother Africa, in the city of Savannah. After a lapse of nearly a century, their descendents resumed the task of protecting the city.

Isaac Butler was born in Savannah in 1830 and lived in Yamacraw. In 1856, he joined First African Baptist under the Rev. Garrison Frazier and was a choir member during the pastorate of the Rev. U. L. Houston. Butler was a "conspicuous figure on the streets when the iron hand pumps were the only means of supplying water." He was a pump-maker and at the same time head wheelwright for a firm at West Broad between Pine and Bryan. Butler worked there for more than 50 years. During his days as a fireman, he was foreman of the Tomochichi Hand Engine No. 7 and "rendered the city much service." Butler was "in good circumstances and was a highly respected citizen."[139] Isaac Butler's will was probated in Judge McAlpin's Court. The will directed that the $12, 000 in cash and $32,000 in real estate be left to his children and grand children.[140]

Staying Power

Rev. Andrew Cox Marshall

"There never has lived a Negro in Savannah who was the equal of Reverend Andrew C. Marshall."

Andrew Cox Marshall (1755-1856) was born in South Carolina in 1755. His mother was a pure blooded Negress and his father an English plantation overseer. The father died shortly after he returned to England and it was Marshall's belief that his father had arranged for his manumission, but his father's untimely death left the child a slave.[141] Young Marshall came to Savannah in 1766. He was sold in 1778 to John Houston, the Revolutionary Governor of Georgia. By age sixteen, he had already married a wife, but was soon separated from her by sale after Houston's death. Marshall believed that Houston had decided on his freedom in 1796 as a reward for having once saved the Governor's life. The heirs, however, refused to implement the will as written and Marshall ran away in order to avoid being sold. He was captured and sold to Judge Clay.

His new owner was a congressman and as his coachman, Marshall visited the north on several occasions meeting, among others, General George Washington. A Mr. Bolton subsequently bought Marshall. It was said that as family coachman Marshall would drive Mrs. Bolton to Christ Church (Episcopal) in Savannah and hurry off to his own church. Richard Richardson advanced him $200 and with the money he had saved, Marshall was able to purchase his own freedom, that of his wife, four children, his wife's father and his stepfather. Marshall operated a successful drayage business until about fifty years of age.

Marshall joined the Baptist Church around 1785 and was eventually licensed to preach. He taught himself to read,[142] became a good reader by much practice, but never learned to write. In 1806 he became an assistant pastor to his mother's brother, the sainted pastor of the First Colored Church, Father Andrew Bryan,[143] whom he succeeded in 1815.[144] In 1824, he owned property valued at some $8,400, the highest valued property of any black in the area.[145] He also owned a slave who worked in his drayage concern. Marshall continued his secular work and did not receive a regular salary from his mainly slave congregation. He did however, receive certain sums at set times. In 1826, he owned a gig[146] Marshall owned a lot in Yamacraw, a large two-story brick house, a four-wheeled carriage and horses and shares in the Marine and Fire Insurance Bank.[147]

Despite all his accomplishments however, between 1819 and 1821 Marshall became unpopular with whites and the Baptist denomination.[148] His former esteem did not save him from the humiliation of his subjugated status as a person of color. He was accused of violating the law prohibiting purchases from blacks that did not have permits to trade.[149] This contraband was common practice and many whites had amassed fortunes from this endeavor.

His white friends never deserted him. Richard Richardson, his onetime owner and several other whites came to his aid. The constable was reminded that he was not to "scratch his (Marshall's) skin or to draw blood." Richard Richardson stood by his side to guarantee that the law was obeyed to the letter.[150] This was Marshall's second encounter with the law. Earlier on, he had preached without a license and prosecuted for the offence. By 1830, church membership increased to more than about 2,000. This increase triggered discussion about the need to have a larger facility for worship. At that time the white Baptists were in the process of moving from their church on Franklin Square to a new location.

The two groups had agreed on an acceptable price,[151] and money to buy the white Baptist church had been put aside before the break.[152] Around November 1, 1832, "the First African Baptist Church took charge of the building at Franklin Square."[153] During his pastorate, Marshall had been influenced by the theology of the Reverend Dr. Alexander Campbell, an ardent follower of the Disciples of Christ. As it happened, the doctrine of the brotherhood of all men was a key component of Campbell's new doctrine. Marshall apparently invited Campbell to preach at his church. To no one's surprise this invitation triggered a fierce controversy among the white Baptists and in Marshall's congregation with almost every member taking sides for or against Marshall.[154] Deacon Adam Arguile Johnson, who had won the respect of many in the congregation, led the opposition. Marshall and about 2,640 occupied the formerly white Baptist Church on Franklin Square.[155] A council of white Baptists formally accused Marshall of doctrinal deviation in adhering to the doctrines of Alexander Campbell. This finding was later endorsed by the Sunbury Association, which declared Marshall's church dissolved and began to arrange to constitute a new black congregation under the aegis of the white Baptist church. Copies of the resolution were sent to the Mayor of Savannah, the Legislature and the white trustees of the colored church. After some five years of controversy, Marshall had not yet been deposed.

This mainly slave congregation was well aware that they had to "succumb to their white brethren in everything else," but in the matter of Baptist polity, both the congregation and Marshall were adamant in their refusal to relinquish this tenet of Baptist congregational autonomy. The congregation persistently refused to dismiss Marshall. The white Baptists, maintaining the white obsession with keeping blacks "under due order and subjection," were equally resolute in their attempt to dissolve the congregation. Once again religion, that two-edged sword, showed its sides. The very faith, which enabled blacks to survive the restrictions slavery imposed, also emboldened them to challenge white authority, this time camouflaged with a patina of Baptist theological rhetoric. The white Baptists appealed to the mayor and church trustees to pressure the black congregation but both parties refused to intervene.[156] After five years, the conflict was somehow resolved peacefully.

By 1840, the membership increased to 2, 016 and First African Baptist became the largest Baptist congregation, black or white, in the city. After a few years, the Reverend Andrew Marshall was eventually restored to his former place of prominence in Savannah's religious milieu. The secret of his staying power was perhaps found in his personality, which as one biographer claimed had he not been black would "have made him a leading character anywhere." He could penetrate the disguises of any charlatan and "few men, white or black surpassed him in reading human character."[157] This inner strength of character gave him invincible perseverance in all his ordeals. Though he loved to feign ignorance by stating that he had "never had a day's learning in his life," all who encountered him recognized that he possessed a superior mind.

In addition to his mental acuity,[158] Andrew Marshall had a commanding appearance. His stature was "neither stout or tall," with a snow white "Afro hairstyle." Marshall's church attracted many visitors. It was said: "every intelligent stranger who came to Savannah went to hear him preach." Sir Charles Lyell, the geologist, regarded Marshall's sermons as "scarcely, if at all, below the average standard of the composition of white ministers."[159]

Fredriker Bremer, the Swedish traveler, worshiped at Marshall's church in 1850 and wept as he expounded the scriptures. The Reverend John Overton Choules of Newport, Rhode Island, marveled at the "great sweetness and power of Marshall's voice" and wrote that he knew of no Northern doctor "who could read (aloud) as well." The Reverend Dr. John M. Krebs, pastor of Rutgers Presbyterian Church in New York City, wrote a long description of a worship service, which he and some twenty-four other whites attended. One May morning in 1855, Krebs attended services at the Independent Presbyterian Church in Savannah and in the afternoon visited Marshall's church. Krebs found the black church "a neat substantial structure that accommodated about 1000 persons." Whites on entering the church were led to pews in the middle tier, immediately in front of the pulpit. The venerable Marshall appeared "hale and robust." He used a walking cane to steady himself as he rose to offer prayer in a "clear articulation and with a strong voice."

Marshall's sermon was delivered in a conversational tone of voice that reached the farthest corner of the huge building. He spiced his sermons with incidents from his life's experience. He never used notes. The large library of books Marshall owned surely served him well. Before distributing the Holy Communion, Marshall announced that his was not a Baptist table but Christ's table, and that all who loved him were welcome there. Both black and white received the sacrament. The Reverend Andrew C. Marshall did not travel much during his long ministry. It is said that he visited Macon, Augusta, where he converted some 350 souls, Milledgeville, Charleston and even New Orleans. He is reported to have preached to the Georgia legislature.

The church on Montgomery Street had been built of wood and a city ordinance prohibited any replacement of a wooden building by another one. Marshall ardently desired to build a new church so he conceived the idea of making a trip to the north in search of funds. He decided to accept the standing invitation of the Rev. Dr. Krebs to visit his church in the North. The *Daily Morning News* commented on a report in the *Savannah Republican* which suggested that the Rev. Andrew Marshall should be sent North on a "missionary tour" in order to "enlighten the minds of Northerners on the slavery issue." The paper regarded the article as "a very high compliment to Uncle Andrew," but felt that approach depended "too much on the persuasive power of the old Negro preacher's eloquence when he supposes that he could convince the antislavery fanatics of the North of truths which for a quarter of a century have been vainly urged not only by the best intellects of the South, but by many of the best and purest men of the North itself."

The article further stated: "We have too much respect for Uncle Andrew, to see him, in his old age, subjected to the annoyance and exposure to evil associations which he would encounter in such a fruitless service." And claimed that the "worthy old man has too much good sense, and too strong an attachment to his 'old Savannah home' to allow him to expatriate himself on so chimerical a mission."[160] In 1850, Marshall was listed as a 94-year-old drayman with $5,000 worth of real estate and was the second wealthiest Negro in the County. He owned 8 slaves.[161]

In 1856, the Reverend Marshall and his wife set out by boat for the North. The *New York Times* in an article entitled "A Preacher a Century Old," reported on a service in the Oliver Street Baptist Church. The reporter found Marshall preaching to a "large concourse of people." This "robust and hearty colored preacher" with "a full-toned voice and a manner far from disagreeable," with a "sonorous and deep voice." The reporter found Marshall's "style of pulpit oratory" and Geechee accent, "peculiar." Marshall used no notes, as was his custom, and even boasted that like the apostles, he had not had a "day's learning in his life." Marshall's hair was "white as driven snow" and his skin was a "dark mulatto hue, and his form stout, and weighed probably about 200 pounds." his features were "unmistakably African." Marshall's sermon, which included an account of his life and the trials of his uncle, the sainted Andrew Bryan, was judged a "very fair doctrinal sermon, which was heard with attention."[162].

Soon, however, Marshall's health grew worse and the doctors advised his wife to return to Savannah. They departed by land and got as far as Richmond where they were forced to spend the last month of his life. In December 1856, the local press carried a solemn announcement: "Andrew Marshall, the old celebrated preacher, so well and so proudly known to our citizens, died in Richmond, Va. On Tuesday last, aged 100 years." Marshal was regarded as "one of the most gifted of his race and his many excellent traits of character had won him the respect and esteem of all who knew him."[163] The venerable Andrew Marshall died December 8, 1856.

His congregation paid to bring his remains to Savannah. Marshall's funeral was conducted on December 14, 1856. The former pastor of the First Baptist (white) Church, the Reverend Thomas Ronbeau, who happened to be in the city, preached the eulogy. At the conclusion of the funeral rite, "the immense congregation formed in procession, the deacons and other church officers of the various churches came first: next, the remains of the deceased, followed by the Colored Benevolent and Temperance Societies, and after them a long line of carriages some fifty in number, and a multitude of pedestrians." The funeral procession moved up West Broad Street to Laurel Grove Cemetery South where the body was placed in a family vault.[164]

During his over 40 years as pastor of the church, Marshall converted 4,000, baptized 3,776, married 2,400 and buried 2,040. He owned a lot in Yamacraw, a two-story brick building, and another lot in the village of St. Gall; 4 wheeled carriages and horses; 4 shares of stock in the Marine and Fire Insurance Bank of Georgia. His wealth and position however never saved him from the humiliation of the brutal slave system. He still bore the burden of his color. During his long life, he survived two depressions in 1819 and 1837. But the greatest and most lasting achievement of Marshall's life was his obvious ability to effectively minister to his brethren still in servitude.

The staying power modeled by his uncle, Father Andrew Bryan, remained with him throughout his life. Marshall strongly opposed drinking and kept "a strict salutary discipline in all his church activities." Mutual Benefit Societies existed in his congregation. Through these, the poor and infirm, especially the free coloreds who had no owner to care for them, were looked after. He was jealous of "mere animal excitements during his services and abhorred the protracted church meeting." Marshall was greatly respected by all citizens. The minutes of the Sunbury Baptist Association of November 1857 claimed that for many years Marshall "was the leading religious spirit among his colored brethren and maintained what he so well deserved the respect and confidence of the whole community." William Harden thought that the Reverend Marshall was, "literally worshipped by his congregation and had the confidence and respect of all the white people of Savannah."[165] According to Simms, Marshall had a "commanding appearance"[166]

Like David Margate almost a century earlier, Marshall was able to "transpose" white theology to meet the needs of his slave congregation and yet phrase it in such a way that whites could not readily grasp his message. A classic example of this art form is the sermon Marshall preached which Dr. Krebs reported. Marshall stated: "our skins are dark, but our souls are washed white in the blood of the lamb. Nor is he (Christ) the propitiation for our sins only. My brethren the time was in this city and through this southern country, when you would scarcely ever see the face of our white master in a (black) house of prayer; but how is it now?" And he added, "How many of those to whom we are subject in the flesh, have recognized our common master in Heaven, and they are our masters no longer. They are fellow-heirs with us of the grace of life. They sit with us at the same table of our common Lord. They are our friends, our brothers, our guardians, our fathers; and we are traveling together to that blessed land where we shall dwell together in the presence of Jesus Christ, their Lord and ours."[167]

Marshall was greatly respected by all citizens, and "an idol among his own color."[168] Love's assessment of Marshall was the most accurate, "never has lived a Negro in Savannah who was the equal of Reverend Andrew C. Marshall.[169] Marshall was "unvarying in his deference to white people and was never distrusted for any disloyalty to the public peace."[170] Over a century later, Savannah historian J. Fed Waring stated: "Mr Marshall was one of the greatest people we've had in Savannah"[171] Thus ended the life of the Rev. Andrew Cox Marshall; erstwhile slave turned businessman then preacher of the gospel. His funeral was one of the largest in the history of Savannah.[172] After more than one hundred years of "making bricks without straw," the Venerable Andrew C. Marshall had prevailed against the wind of oppression with unusual fortitude.

Rev. Alexander Harris

"Negro Veteran Goes To Reward"

Alexander Harris (1818-1909) was born free, the child of free parents, in Savannah, July 9, 1818.[173] He and his mother moved to Augusta and while there he learned the blacksmith trade. He returned to Savannah after his mother's death. Harris was "chief musician" for the Republican Blues and when that company entered the Civil War, the "faithful drummer cast his lot with them and performed valuable and gallant service for the cause he claimed as his own." In battle with his company he "displayed courage and fortitude." While on duty at Fort Pulaski, Harris had charge of the reconstruction of the old moat, performing this task "with great zeal and energy." Later he supervised black laborers constructing fortifications in the vicinity of Savannah and acquitted himself "with great credit."[174]

Harris was most likely educated in one of the underground schools in black Savannah during slavery. He "possessed a good education" and "did much toward the establishment of the Georgia State Industrial College For Colored Youth," (now Savannah State University), and "always befriended the cause of education among Negroes," especially the Baptist Sunday School movement. For many years he was one of the city's black fireman, and was one of the black leaders who met with Secretary Edwin Stanton and General William T. Sherman in January 1865.[175]

Harris was a licensed minister of First Bryan Baptist Church in December 1864. For many years he headed the "poor fund," which during the yellow fever epidemic of 1876, dispersed several hundred dollars to the needy. He was one of the founding members of Eureka Lodge No 1, on February 4, 1866 and assisted in the formation of the Grand Lodge, which he later served as Grand Master. Harris was regarded as "a high type of a Mason, and was a jurisdiction within himself. He was loved by Masons all over the state."[176] It was "largely due to his efforts" that the colored Masonic Widows and Orphans Home of Georgia was established.

Early in 1871, the Rev. Ulysses L. Houston, pastor of First Bryan Baptist Church, apparently resigned from the church in order to pursue political office in Bryan County. Houston took up residence in Bryan County and became a candidate for the legislature.[177] It may well be that he intended to return to the pastorate following the election. It is also possible that some of his "troops" planned to "save" the position for him. Historian Robert Perdue saw the political interference of white Democrats as one of the factors pushing the issue.[178] As it happened, the Rev. Alexander Harris desired the position of pastor and maneuvered to secure his own selection to the office. Sometime in May 1871, a heated debate engrossed a large percentage of the congregation as to who should be the pastor of the church.

During the regular morning service on February 11, 1872, the Rev. James M. Simms "a violent Negro politician, and antebellum ex-fiddler," and the Rev. Ulysses H. Houston "the ex-pastor," interrupted the service.[179] That same evening Harris was again interrupted and "while the contestants were wrangling as to who should pray, someone in the gallery fired a pistol shot at the pastor." This created much excitement and the worshippers tumbled "Pell mell" out of the church. Soon a detachment of about twenty policemen from the Barracks appeared on the scene. The two divines "who have obtained some notoriety as Radicals since the termination of the war," and Abram Eddy were arrested but soon bonded out to the tune of $400. [180] The matter that came before Recorder's Court attracted "the attention of hundreds of colored people in the city, who gathered about the police Barracks and crowded the Recorder's Court."

Harris' friends obtained a warrant from Justice Isaac Russell for the arrest of those discharged by Recorder's Court and they appeared in the Magistrate's Court.[181] The case of James M. Simms, Ulysses H. Houston and Abram Eddy concluded in the Superior Court on June 28, 1872. The prosecution "made a very powerful speech, in which he reviewed in the most scathing manner the career of "Simms, the fiddler, so-called Representative and would-be-judge, showing conclusively that he was an evil, disorderly, turbulent character." Simms retained "an air of insolent nonchalance and apparently appreciated, as a compliment, this unveiling of his character." The jury in the end "returned a verdict of guilty as to Simms and Houston and not guilty as to Eddy."[182]

The *Savannah Morning News,* always on the look-out for an occasion to hold up blacks to ridicule, claimed that though blacks imitated whites "in the worship of the ever living God," they did not seem "to understand the principles of Christianity, and unite with the forms of the church, the habits of their little less heathen brethren in the wilds of Africa." The paper further stated that: "The millions of money contributed towards Christianizing these people by the philanthropists of Europe and America have been wasted, as the conduct of the so-called Negroes of the South has amply illustrated since the close of the war."[183]

The upshot of all this mayhem was that the Rev. Alexander Harris and forty-five followers left First Bryan Baptist Church on Bryan Street, and constituted and built the First Bryan Baptist Church on West Broad near Waldburg Streets in 1872. Harris remained pastor of the church until his death. He assisted in the formation of many Baptist Associations, was moderator of the Mt. Olive Association and was one of the organizers of the State Baptist Convention. Harris also served as pastor of Nicolsonboro Baptist Church on White Bluff Road about nine miles from Savannah. He dedicated that church in October 1892.[184] A large crowd witnessed the laying of the cornerstone in 1890. The Revs. Harris, Love and Durham conducted the services. The three hundred seat church cost about $1,000 and showed "the energy and push possessed by the people of this little settlement."[185]

Prof. William H. Harris, son of the Rev. and Mrs. Alexander Harris died January 14, 1888. He graduated from Atlanta University in 1878, with "high honors" and taught school in Thomasville from 1878 to 1884. He also taught in Louisiana and Florida for many years, and was a "most fluent and eloquent speaker." Harris had a "fair knowledge of Hebrew and a very good knowledge Greek and Latin." Prof. Harris was "passionately fond of music and had few equals among our people as an organist."[186] Prof. S. B. Morse, James H. C. Butler, John McIntosh, A. B. Tolbert and P. A. Denegal, classmates of the deceased, provided music for the funeral service. The Revs. L. B. Maxwell, Ulysses H. Houston and Emanuel K. Love delivered remarks during the services held at First Bryan Baptist Church on West Broad near Walburg Streets.[187]

In 1896, Harris and his wife Frances celebrated their 50th wedding anniversary with a banquet at First African Baptist Church. The couple was married January 3, 1846.[188] Mrs. Frances Alexander died in February 1900. She was regarded as "one of the oldest and best known of the colored residents, and was held in high esteem by both white and colored citizens. She was a remarkable woman in many respects and was noted for her gentleness and good deeds."[189] First Bryan Baptist Church of West Broad and Waldburg Streets celebrated its 22nd anniversary with a sermon delivered by the Rev. W. G. Johnson of Augusta, while Prof. Sam B. Morse and Dr. Davis furnished the music. The Masons attended the service in full regalia.[190]

The Rev. Alexander Harris died at his home, 525 West Oglethorpe Avenue, October 9, 1909. He was "one of the leading Negro citizens of the state." The *Savannah Morning News* reported: "Though his skin was black, his heart, his soul and his life were as staunch for the right, as clean and as upright as those of any man who ever claimed the divine right of citizenship in the community." He had won the respect of "white and black alike."[191]

The Rev. Geo. H. Dwelle of Augusta, "an old friend in church and Masonry," spoke "very feelingly over the bier of his deceased friend."[192] Free blacks, Harris and Dwelle were childhood friends in Savannah and were "above their fellows in intellect, in training and education." Neither "had ever felt the yoke of slavery, nor the weight of bondage had not stamped out their individuality." They were "closer than brothers" and realizing the "long uphill fight before them, they formed a compact. If either should die, the other was to provide for his friend's burial, with all the rites and solemnities." Dwelle also served the Confederate forces during the Civil War. [193]

Though 92 years of age, the Rev. Geo H. Dwelle journeyed to Savannah and conducted the services for his life-long friend.[194] Many surviving members of the Republican Blues attended his funeral and paid their "last tribute to the memory of the dead."[195] Harris was referred to as "almost the last of the old time Negroes who were so interwoven with the sacred history of the old South."[196] His funeral was "simple yet dignified," in keeping with his request. The Daughters of the Confederacy sent a wreath and the Republican Blues an elevated star. The Southern Cross of the Confederate States of America was placed on his grave in black Laurel Grove Cemetery South. The Rev. Alexander Harris had indeed lived "a strenuous life of uplift." He served the church with distinction, becoming one of "the most prominent ministers of his day." The *Savannah Morning News* report on his death was entitled, Negro Veteran Goes To Reward.[197] The ritual of the Order of the Eastern Star was "faultlessly conducted, followed by the Masonic rites."[198]

Rev. Ulysses H. Houston

"The last of the Old School of Fathers."

Ulysses L. Houston (1825-1889) was born a slave in Beaufort County, South Carolina, February 1825 and came to Savannah when he was five years of age.[199] James B Hogg, a white "thorough Baptist and a deacon of the Savannah Baptist Church until his old age," owned Houston and raised him in his home "with much care and piety."[200] Houston joined First Bryan Baptist Church at age 16.[201] The pastor, the Rev. John B. Deveaux, baptized him and Houston became a member of Deveaux's musical group, the *Old One Hundreds.* He married in 1848, and on November 3, 1851 was ordained a deacon.

Although a slave, his owner allowed him to hire out his time in exchange for the set fee of $50 per month. Eventually Houston made enough money to buy his freedom. He also worked for a time as a nurse in the Federal Naval Hospital in Savannah, where sailors taught him to read. A butcher by trade with his own stall in the market, he traveled widely buying cattle.[202] Through it all he kept up his study of the Bible.

During the Southern Baptist Convention held in the city, and since "no ordination of Negro preachers being possible without the presence and sanction of the white brethren," the congregation requested that they ordain Houston. A panel of white ministers examined him and ordained him May 12, 1861.[203] On October 20, 1861 the congregation of First Bryan Baptist Church called Houston as pastor. At that time they numbered about 106 souls. Houston was among the twenty African Americans who met with Secretary Stanton and General Sherman. In 1865 he served as treasurer of the Savannah Educational Association.

In April 1865,[204] the Reverend Ulysses L. Houston led about 1,000 African Americans to Skidaway Island to stake out a new promised land. The settlers laid out the area, selected plots by casting lots and organized themselves into a self-governing community. About 362 of the settlers were in families headed by 96 men and three women, to till 2,875 acres. Each head of family was to receive forty acres of land.[205] They were to keep and work the land for three years and they could purchase the land and receive such title as the United States could convey. Blacks who enlisted in the army could relocate their families on the settlements. Garrison Frazier was the first elected governor and a sheriff and three inspectors were elected. By June 1865, Skidaway Island had several hundred acres under cultivation and the Reverend Houston was quite satisfied. As he stated: "We shall build our cabins and organize our own government for the maintenance of order and the settlement of all difficulties." A new black Oglethorpe had laid out his town. The *Savannah Republican* carried a long article on the progress of the black Skidaway settlement. It reported "quite a large party of ladies and gentlemen paid a visit yesterday afternoon to the above island in response to an invitation from the Governor, Frazier, who is now in charge of the prosperous infant colony settled on Skidaway." The reporter stated that as the group approached the settlement they "heard the soft strains of sacred songs soaring over the silent waters."

Several hundred acres were "in an advanced state of cultivation on which there is a large quantity of fine corn, a small lot of cotton, an abundance of snap beans, potatoes, cucumbers, watermelons and cantelopes." There was a "Governor, Sheriff and three inspectors on duty on the island, elected by the people and perfect harmony prevails." The colonists were building a chapel for divine worship. The reporter concluded the article with the words "Our visit firmly convinced us of one thing and that is that with proper encouragement the Freedmen can be made not only self sustaining but a valuable auxiliary to our agricultural interests."[206]

President Andrew Johnson's pardons issued May 29, 1865, returned all the lands to the former owners and blacks again had to look elsewhere for the Promised Land. The traumatic failure of this experiment in black land ownership must have been a crushing blow to Governor Ulysses Houston, but he continued serving his people. In January 1867, some blacks on the Back River Sea Island Plantation claimed that they had paid taxes to the government and that the land was theirs.[207]

In 1848, Lord Harris the Governor of Trinidad, commenting on the societal consequences that followed the emancipation of slaves in the colony, in which instance the owners were compensated for their loss of property, while the slaves got nothing, stated: "A race has been freed, but a society has not been formed."[208] Lord Harris bemoaned the fact that though freedom was important, the absence of a solid economic base to sustain that freedom would inevitably make that freedom almost meaningless. In Savannah, black folks were freed but they were denied and lacked the economic resources to support themselves. In addition the authorities were already concocting new laws, and putting in place economic controls that would safeguard white supremacy and again guarantee that African Americans would remain "under due order and subjection."

The Rev. Ulysses L. Houston was elected to the Georgia legislature from Bryan County in 1869.[209] The pastor, assisted by three deacons, baptized 138 persons in the Ogeechee canal at the foot of River Street. About 5,000 to 8,000 persons gathered on the banks to witness the event. Houston and one of his deacons dipped the candidates under the water and handed them over to two deacons.[210] One month later the pastor baptized another ninety-nine persons, for a total of "two hundred and fifty-four since the earthquake, and the revival still continues."[211]

Houston was regarded as a "man of the people highly popular with the several societies of his race in this city and is one of the oldest Masons in the state." He served several terms as Vice-President of the Georgia Baptist State Convention and was moderator of the Zion Baptist Association for 17 years. He was "greatly beloved by his people to whom he ministered and had the confidence of all who knew him."[212] The pastor and congregation built a new church that "will ever stand as a monument to his energy and love for the cause of Christ and his church." Houston dedicated the new church building June 10, 1888. The church was "crowded to its utmost capacity with an attentive audience. The Rev. James Merilus Simms, his boyhood companion, presented him with "a fine communion service." The singing was "excellent."[213] Houston was truly the last of the "old School of the fathers" that labored in this part of the vineyard. A "forcible preacher," he baptized "a greater number of persons than under any other in the State excepting that of the Revs. Andrew Bryan and Andrew Marshall." Foner reports that Houston owned $500 in real estate in 1870 and had personal property worth $125.00.[214]

Houston and his congregation celebrated the church's one-hundredth anniversary in 1888. They sponsored a special anniversary concert featuring Madame Selika, "the great prima Donna accompanied by Mr. S. W. Williams the celebrated Hawaiian baritone soloist and Miss Q. Brown elocutionist," in the Savannah Theatre. Tickets were 35 cents, reserved 50 cents and gallery was 25 cents. The Rev. Geo W. Griffin, assistant pastor, preached a special anniversary sermon and in the afternoon the Rev. Alexander Ellis of Second Baptist preached some "words of encouragement" to the children. At night the church "was crowded to its utmost capacity. The Rev. E. R. Carter of Atlanta preached the annual anniversary sermon from the text: "Lord, who shall abide in the tabernacle; who shall dwell in thy Holy hill." The church was "crowded to its utmost capacity by members and friends." The congregation was "in a prosperous condition, having been newly furnished up, and finished is one of the neatest in the city."[215]

The Reverend Ulysses L. Houston died Wednesday, October 3, 1889, having served his church as pastor for 28 years. He lived at 254 Bryan Street.[216] At the request of the longshoremen and a number of societies, the body was "embalmed and preserved until Sunday, when the greater number of laboring people may attend the funeral."[217] On the day of the funeral the body of the deceased "rested in a glass-top casket in front of the pulpit." Every space in the nave and the aisles was packed. The columns and chandeliers were draped in black. The pulpit was clothed in mourning. A black banner was suspended over the coffin with the inscription in white letters: "Behold the bridegroom cometh; go ye out to meet him."[218]

Before his funeral service began, a large crowd gathered near the line of the procession "to show their last mark of respect." The Reverend S. C. Roberts, moderator of Zion Baptist Association, presided at the service and the Reverend E. K. Love pastor of the First African Baptist church offered a prayer. The church was "heavily draped in mourning and with the casket in front of the pulpit presented a sad scene."[219] After the funeral service the Chatham Light Infantry in uniform, the Forest City Light Infantry in citizens dress with white badges, both of which the deceased served as an honorary member, the Bryan Mutual Aid Association and Eureka Lodge No. 1. A. F. & A. M received the body with the customary honors. The funeral cortege proceeded east on Bryan Street to West Broad Street. Over "sixty vehicles were in the procession."[220] The clergy occupied twelve carriages. Houston's lifelong friend the Rev. James M. Simms, preceded Houston's mother, followed by relatives and friends. Those unable to enter the church marched alongside the cortege as it proceeded to the cemetery.[221]

The Central, Charleston and Savannah, and Savannah, Florida and Western trains, brought large numbers of people to attend the funeral. The local press estimated that about 7,000 to 8,000 persons attended the funeral. About 1,000 to 1,200 came from Bryan County. This attendance made his funeral the "largest that probably ever took place in Savannah." The deceased was said to be "one of the oldest and one of the most notable of the Southern colored ministry."[222]

The family remained in mourning until the drapery was "removed from the First Bryan Baptist Church where the deceased was pastor."[223] In 1892 a monument was placed over the grave.[224] The Rev. James M. Simms, executor of Houston's will, sold "all those certain seven lots, in the eastern section of Savannah, belonging to the estate of Ulysses L. Houston, deceased, for payment of debts."[225] Thus ended the odyssey of the Reverend Ulysses L. Houston: born a slave, sometime governor, and legislator. He was a truly remarkable black Savannahian.

Rev. James M. Simms

"To work for the Uplift of his Race."

James Merilus Simms (1823-1909) was born December 27, 1823, in Liberty County, Georgia. He, his brother Thomas and his mother Minda Campbell, were slaves of the Potters family. According to one report, his mother bought his freedom for $300, and this act of his mother "did much to inspire him to work for the uplift of his race."[226] The Reverend Emanuel K. Love claimed that Simms bought his own freedom for $740 in 1857.[227] In 1841 Simms was converted and baptized by the Reverend Andrew Marshall, but was later expelled from the church because of "continual neglect of his Christian duties," and also because he indulged in "fiddling and numerous other sins." It was said that: "few were the social events of either race, that he was not present with his band."[228] Simms rejoined the church on October 31, 1858.

A carpenter by trade, Simms was part of the black workforce, which built the First African Church. At one time, he also worked as a waiter in one of Savannah's hotels. While serving tables, he would listen to the conversations of the guests and with a dictionary in hand would teach himself the meaning of words.[229] Simms could both read and write. He served as clerk of the church and it was said: "His push and pluck made him prominent rather than the wish of the people to have him an officer."[230]

James Simms was ordained a deacon January 29, 1860 and licensed to preach in March 1863. In 1860, he was caught teaching "a room full of children and severely punished,"[231] the only black known black punished because he had the temerity to teach other blacks to read and write. His school was located on Berien Street near Jefferson Street.[232] He was also fined $50.[233] When Simms saw his fellow blacks being forced to work for the Confederate cause by repairing buildings and Forts, he found the activity so repugnant that he left the city and went to Boston, Massachusetts.

This Boston sojourn was destined to change the direction of Simm's life in many ways. He joined the Union army,[234] and was also inducted into the Masonic order of the Grand lodge of the State of Massachusetts. In 1765, Prince Hall, a 17-year-old black from Barbados, West Indies, migrated to Massachusetts and eventually became a Methodist minister. On March 6, 1776, a regular English Army lodge received Prince Hall and 14 others into the Masonic order. Prince Hall petitioned the Grand Lodge of England for a charter. The Grand Lodge of England issued a charter September 29, 1784, setting up the African Lodge #459, F. & A. M. at Boston, Massachusetts, with Prince Hall as Worshipful Master. This lodge later became the "mother lodge" of black Masonry in America. This Lodge commissioned Simms to establish the order in the South. The Twelfth Baptist Church of Boston ordained Simms a Baptist minister on April 17, 1864, and the American Baptist Home Mission Society charged him with the evangelizing blacks in Georgia and Florida.[235]

Simms returned to Savannah February 2, 1865,[236] and soon became the agent of the laborers at Rice Hope Plantation. Simms was one of sixteen black ministers who signed a petition protesting the treatment of blacks by the Union army,[237] and demanded the right to vote. The pastor of the First African Baptist

Church, the Reverend William Campbell, refused to recognize Simms' ordination. However the Rev. Ulysses Houston, pastor of First Bryan accepted Simms' ordination so he moved his membership back to his old church, "whose roof sheltered him when Mr. Marshall was its pastor, and in whose Sunday school he received his earliest religious teachings."

This irrepressible young man soon joined the Union Leagues and helped to organize several chapters of them around the city. These quasi-military groups drilled on the neighboring Plantations, to the consternation of several whites. On July 26, 1865, Simms led a procession of Union Leagues in celebration of Liberia's independence. Simms encouraged young blacks to join the federal troops and became an army chaplain with the rank of captain. He was to collect a pension from this activity. At a meeting in Savannah attended by some 7,000, James M. Simms was said to be "the man of the hour." A reporter stated: "it is impossible to describe the intense enthusiasm exhibited by the speaker." The crowd applauded Simms' every word, "roused as it was by his clear musical voice, distinct enunciation and elegant style of delivery." Though "small in stature, he allowed nothing to daunt him in his purposes. Nothing fired him more than his great burden to lead his people in their quest for freedom." Simms claimed that whites knew nothing about blacks because during slavery blacks had to "use dissimulation towards their master." Now he said, as free men, blacks could "tell the truth."

Simms called for black officials at all levels of the government. He wanted offices filled by both white and colored men who were capable of serving with honor. He stated: "I would have white and colored aldermen, and white and colored policemen, and the sooner people know it the better." He also expressed the hope that his children, then at school in Massachusetts, would one day represent this area in Congress.[238] White Republicans were quite impressed with Simms and urged him to help organize the party in Savannah. He became secretary in October 1867, and became a member of the executive committee in 1867.[239] He was elected delegate-at-large to the Republican Party national convention in 1872.[240] In 1867 the local white press announced his forthcoming paper the *Southern Radical and Freedmen's Journal*, which was later, changed to the *Freemen's Standard* in 1868.[241] Simms, along with James Porter, won the election for house seats from Chatham County. He had seriously taken "an active part in seeking to secure the political rights of his people."

James Simms began to pressure the Republicans to give blacks half of the appointments and even when the blacks were expelled and later returned to the House, he insisted that blacks should have their fair share of offices. During his service in the House, he proposed many radical bills, including one on education. In a New Year's Day speech in 1868, Simms, and others of "our city notables of dark color and origin," reminded the audience of the need to obtain a good education. A year later Simms was back in Boston complaining about the "savage persecutions" which blacks were subject to in the South. Since the expulsion of blacks from the Georgia legislature, Simms asserted that about three hundred blacks had been killed in Georgia and that no individual had been brought to justice for these offenses. The local press changed his given name to "The Little Mulatto Jim Sims," and stated that though Simms "pretends to be a preacher of the gospel of truth," he had "become terribly demoralized by his carpet-bag and scalawag associations."[242]

Simms was fully aware of the need for black businesses in Savannah but also recognized the almost insurmountable handicap a lack of capital represented. He tried to formalize the establishment of the black Chatham Mercantile, Loan and Trust Company but failed in this effort. When the Ku Klux Klan began terrorizing blacks, Simms wrote that blacks would not "tamely submit to be attacked and murdered." By 1871, the governor had appointed James M. Simms a judge on the Chatham County District Court. The Savannah Bar Association met in the City Court room to receive the report of a committee: "appointed at the previous meeting to consider the insult offered to the people of this District in the appointment of a judge of the District Court, and to suggest suitable action to be taken by the Bar in reference to the outrage." The committee reported that Simms had "no right to exercise, the functions or discharge the duties of judge of said District Court."[243]

The white press reported: "The newly appointed nigger Judge James M. Simms," had declared that if the Bar of Chatham County refused to recognize him officially, he had made up his mind to forward his commission to General Alfred Terry, and "have him indorse it."[244] As it turned out, this judgeship was abandoned soon after its establishment. Simms then worked as a custom official and was active in the 1872 bus boycott.[245] Democratic rule was restored and white Georgians entrenched their position. Within some five years, Republican endorsement of the 1877 compromise showed that white Republicans were not going to enforce the rights of blacks. They failed to prevent disfranchisement and in 1883, the U.S. Supreme Court declared the Civil Rights Act of 1875 unconstitutional.

In 1861, Congress gave public land to states to provide funds for the operation of land-grant agricultural and mechanical colleges. The money was part of the Morrill Land Grant Act. By 1890, this act was amended and required that some money must go to educating blacks. The legislature gave $4,000 to Atlanta University but discovered that a few whites were actually attending that school. When the new bill was enacted, the Georgia legislature decided to establish a separate black school rather than have blacks and whites attend the same school. A strong effort was made to have this new college, The Georgia Industrial College for Colored Youth, located in Savannah. A group of blacks along with Simms offered a sum of money and land in Savannah. About 150 blacks held a meeting at First African Baptist Church in March 1891. Simms informed the group that Augusta and Macon were bidding for the school. When the school was established in Savannah, the *Savannah Tribune* stated "the most important event in the history of the colored people in Georgia since their emancipation, is the establishment of the above-named college."

The Reverend Emanuel Love wrote that Simms was "among the ablest men the church has ever produced." He was endowed with an "iron will,"[246] His work for the "upliftment" of blacks was truly remarkable. In the end he failed not because he lacked the intelligence, or stamina but because the intimidation, violence and racism of that day doomed his efforts to failure. Savannah never had as large a number of educated blacks as Charleston, South Carolina. The swift but "splendid failure" of Reconstruction in Georgia was but a harbinger of what was to follow in the other states of the South.

Simms married Priscilla Holmes. They had four sons, James Jr., born December 1890, Wendall born 1891, David born 1893, and Plutarch born 1895.[247] In 1888 Simms published *The First Colored Church in North America.* His wife Priscilla died February 8, 1895.[248] The Reverend James Merilus Simms, born a slave, became, through perseverance and an indomitable will to succeed, a model leader of black Savannah. He carried out his mother's admonition to "uplift his race." The Rev. James M. Simms died Tuesday, July 9, 1912, at the ripe age of 89 years.[249]

Thomas Simms, like his brother James, was also a "freedom fighter," in the days when "hope unborn had died."[250] Though born a slave, he became a brick mason and hired himself out. Thomas Simms made several attempts to escape slavery. On February 21, 1851, he disappeared from Colerain plantation outside Savannah and the next day boarded a boat and ended up in Boston.[251] Once in Boston Simms lodged at a colored seaman's house and got a job at a local hotel. Thomas' wife divulged his location and his owner dispatched an agent to capture him.[252] Fugitive Simms was captured in April even as he "made strong efforts to evade the officers and cried murder and other violent ejaculations." A famous court case ensued. The *Boston Bee* described Simms as "23 years old, has a wife and several children in Savannah and is said to be a very bright, intelligent looking Negro-one who from his manners and general appearance would not be taken for a slave."[253] In the end the judge ordered him to be sent back to Savannah and at 5: 00 A.M. one morning a posse of hundreds of armed policemen led Simms to a boat bound for Savannah.[254]

The Boston Abolitionists had apparently planned to free Simms.[255] The *Morning News* regretted that: "his manners have not been at all improved we are told by his late associations; and what we hear of his insolent bearing be true, a little wholesome chastisement would do him no harm: while it would have a salutary effect upon those of his class who are likely to be influenced by his example and the notoriety he has acquired."[256] Thomas Simms was jailed and whipped for being a "runner, a problem slave who ran away."[257] After being bought and sold a few times he ended up in Vicksburg, Virginia. With his owner, Simms traveled to Tennessee but escaped again and finally reached Boston. Later in life he worked as a messenger at the Department of Justice and as a brick mason.

Col. John H. Deveaux

"A strenuous life from boyhood even to the finality."

An article entitled "Savannah's First Citizen" says of Deveaux, his was "a strenuous life, from boyhood even to the finality. His application to duty and performance of the same had much to do with the termination of his life."[258] Even with the paucity of information about his life, it is clear that Deveaux must be numbered among that quintet of extraordinary sons of Mother Africa who, "yet with a steady beat," refused to succumb to the horrors of life behind Savannah's Moss Curtain.

John H. Deveaux (c. 1848-1909) was born in Savannah in around 1848, to Isaac and Rosa Deveaux. His grand father was the Reverend John B. Deveaux, one time pastor of First Bryan Baptist Church. The family lived on Oglethorpe Avenue near Habersham Street. The original family came to Savannah from Haiti in the late 18th century. Isaac Deveaux is listed in the 1850 census returns as 30 years of age and a carpenter. Rosa 26, James 6, John 4, and Charles 10 months, all were listed as mulattos. However, in the 1860 census returns, Isaac Deveaux is listed as 48 years old, Anna 26, James 14, John 12, Charles 2, Laura 8 and all were listed as white. Isaac Deveaux died on November 6, 1895 at age 76. His survivors were Col. John H. Deveaux, Charles C., the Honorable James Deveaux and two daughters, Mrs. Anna Deveaux Tucker, and Mrs. Laura Deveaux Taylor. The Honorable James Deveaux was Macon's state senator during Reconstruction, and a delegate to the National Republican convention on two occasions.

Since the education of slaves and free blacks was illegal up to the Civil War, Deveaux was most likely educated in one of the underground colored schools in Savannah. When John Deveaux was 13 years of age, Georgia seceded from the Union. An article in the *Savannah Tribune* claims that he was conscripted to serve the Confederate cause. What is certain is that Deveaux served in the Confederate "Mosquito fleet." This fleet plied the inner harbor in an attempt to harass the Federal forces. According to Jacob Gardner, in a letter to the *Savannah Morning News,* claims that Deveaux was a "mess boy for Lieutenant J. F. Pelot."[259]

Lieutenant J. F. Pelot, Deveaux, black pilot Moses Dallas, and others set out in the gunboat, *Savannah*, on an expedition down to Green Island to attack the *Water Witch*, a Federal gunboat anchored in the Green Island sound. As they were about to board the *Water Witch*, Pelot ordered Deveaux to get out of the boat while Pelot and a black pilot boarded the *Water Witch*. Both were killed. Deveaux secured the body of Pelot and delivered it to his family. Deveaux also worked on the *Samson* under the command of Commodore Tattnall, and on the *Resolute*. An officer once described Deveaux as a "reliable and respectful boy." Deveaux was a lad of 16 years when General Sherman captured Savannah and doubtless was captivated by the sight of black troops in the city. Most likely, he followed closely what African Americans were doing immediately after freedom.

In January 1870, at age 22, Deveaux received an appointment as a clerk in the customs house of Savannah. Two years later, on January 2, 1872, he married Fannie Moore at St. Stephens's Episcopal Church. Her parents were John Moore and Sarah De Lamotta Moore. The rector, the Reverend J. Robert Love, performed the ceremony with Richard W. White and Thaddeus Nurrell as witnesses. Young Deveaux served in every position in the custom house and became "an expert in each department of the service and his rulings were never turned down." In 1876, a yellow fever epidemic devastated Savannah. Deveaux and two other clerks were the only ones still on duty. One died of the fever and later Deveaux was the only official on duty at the port. For more than two weeks, he ran the custom house by himself, "thus keeping the commerce of the port unbroken." Deveaux himself contracted the dread disease. He and other African Americans who worked at the custom house became very active politically even getting involved in the 1872 Streetcar boycott. This did not sit too well with some blacks.

A joint meeting of the Chatham Light Infantry, the Delmonico Guards and the Union Lincoln Guards was held to consider "the political welfare of the colored man." After much discussion on the politics of the day, including the governor's race, a resolution "denouncing John H. Deveaux, Negro Custom House employee and John E. Bryant the late Deputy Collector," was adopted and most of those present resolved "to have nothing to do with them in future." The *Savannah Morning News* stated: "This action speaks well for our Negro population. It is convincing proof that they are beginning to realize that the people among whom they are born and reared and whose sole and only interest are in this state, have more at stake in the securing of good, honest government and a just enforcement of the laws."[260]

When the black troops were reorganized in 1899, Deveaux was demoted to major but later was made a life colonel by the Georgia legislature. In 1898, when Deveaux offered his services and that of his troops in the Spanish-American war he was rebuffed. An ardent Mason, he served as Grand Master for 12 years and was Grand Secretary. He was a member of the Hilton Lodge No. 2, one of the founders of the Odd fellows, and charter member of Myrtle Lodge 1683 and the Household of Ruth 118.

In 1889, President Benjamin Harrison appointed the 41-year-old Deveaux collector of customs for the port of Brunswick. On November 30, he appeared before notary public S. Barchardt and took the oath of office. The *Morning News* opposed his appointment and called for his removal. A Brunswick delegation composed of Goodyear, Downing, Bule and Collins went to Washington, D.C. but failed to dislodge Deveaux. When a yellow fever epidemic broke out in 1893, Deveaux again remained at his post and faithfully disbursed the $40,000.00 the Treasury Department sent for the sufferers. Deveaux's youngest son died in February and a daughter died in September 1895.[261] In 1896 a letter the editor signed "An Admirer," stated that Deveaux went into politics during a difficult time but he "was always loyal to his party and race; held many responsible position and came out with a clear record."[262] Deveaux was "one of the original McKinley men at the long-ago conference at Thomasville."[263] Deveaux's work was "personally known to President McKinley. As secretary of the Republican state executive committee and is hand in glove with Boss Buck."[264] President William F. McKinley appointed John Deveaux as collector of customs at the port of Savannah in 1897. Deveaux was the unanimous choice of black Republicans.

The Cotton Exchange and the Board of Trade protested the appointment of Deveaux and tried to get the mayor and aldermen to support their position. They refused. The only reason for this opposition was the fact that Deveaux was African American. In his four years at Brunswick he had done a "very creditable job and had been in the customs service for 26 years." The Savannah post was considered the biggest plum in the state and carried much honor. A group of Black Republicans in Brunswick held a meeting May 8, 1897, at the Odd fellows hall and endorsed Deveaux for the position in Savannah. They stated: "No Republican in Georgia has labored longer or with greater zeal than Col. Deveaux for the Republican Party." None had brought more ability or wise experience to its councils or proven himself in every sense true or more sagacious leader." Black Savannah also sprung to Deveaux's side. A meeting was held on December 22, 1897 and two days later, some 1,000 Blacks met under the chairmanship of the Reverend L. B. Maxwell with Dr. Cornelius McKane as secretary and passed several resolutions of support. Among them was one, deploring the action of the Board on December 19, 1897.

The action, the group felt, discriminated "against a large class of citizens which is unjust." The participants also passed another resolution, which showed their awareness of the delicate racial situation in Savannah. It said in part: "We recognize and appreciate the good will and harmony existing between the two races, and have confidence in our white friends with whom we have lived so long, with whom we expect longer to live, that the mere matter of a competent colored man as collector of customs for the post will not in any way disturb the friendly relations that now exist."

While serving as collector of customs at Savannah another yellow fever epidemic occurred and again Deveaux was one of the few to survive it. All but seven of the thirty clerks were stricken but Deveaux remained on duty. Three of the seven were eventually affected by the fever and after running the customs for some weeks Deveaux himself also almost succumbed. By any standard Deveaux was a truly extraordinary individual and possessed a "mindset" that served him well. As the scion of one of "the best families" of Savannah's high yellow "aristocracy," he felt comfortable dealing with both black and white Savannahians.

In the late 1890's some blacks criticized him for not being militant enough, especially when there was a sharp divide in the Republican ranks with blacks who favored Thomas B. Reed and the largely white faction supporting Alfred E. Buck for state party chairmanship. Deveaux, a McKinley man, supported Buck, also a McKinley protégée. Those who worked with him regarded Deveaux as "guarded in his manner." However, his ability and efficiency were highly praised by all. Whites regarded Deveaux as a "High type of his race and a credit to himself and his people." They felt that a less prudent individual would have disrupted the established social customs of his day. African Americans regarded him as a man of plain speech. Deveaux impressed all with whom he came into contact as a substantial citizen, possessing strong conviction. He was said to be "fearless in the exercise of his civil prerogatives, true to the principles he conceived to be right and compromising advocated of human dignity."

Whites were also impressed by the service Deveaux rendered to the Confederate cause. It was said that each year he would lay a wreath on the tomb of Lieutenant Pelot and above all because "when he was in a position to do so, he saw that old (Confederates) were provided for in either employment or otherwise." As Jacob Gardner wrote "his life as a man is an example others could follow with profit." Deveaux was, above all, a very astute politician and had mastered the game of patronage. His middle-class background served him well. His temperate ideas and goals enabled him to maintain a "dignified tone and circumspection." His long dealings with the Republican elite formed him into a shrewd operator who could work with Republicans and Democrats. This enabled him to hold on to his position as secretary of the Republican State Central Committee from 1892 until his death, during many intra-party squabbles.[265] In 1870, and again in 1874, he ran for clerk of the Superior Court, once held by another black, Richard White. He never won. Party politics was his forte. Deveaux was a delegate to most local and state gatherings and 6 times to Republican National Conventions.[266] In 1900, the Rev. Emmanuel Love and Richard Wright challenged Deveaux for the leadership of the Savannah Republican Party.

Col. Deveaux appointed Captain L.M.Pleasant inspector of customs.[267] That same year Deveaux was appointed Lieutenant Colonel for life of all the Negro troops in the state. To the end of his life, Deveaux remained one of the foremost African American Republicans in the state. Senator Cann of Savannah introduced a bill at the beginning of session to restore the rank of lieutenant Col. to Deveaux and make it permanent to his successors but the military committee killed the clause "making it permanent to his successors."[268] In 1902, President Theodore Roosevelt reappointed Deveaux the collector of the port of Savannah. It was said that he "absented himself whenever foreign war ships or a national officer came calling." On such occasions, he sent his white deputy to represent him. As the *Morning News* reported "He never obtruded his rank or presumed upon his privilege as collector of port." Eric Foner claimed that Deveaux "held the highest patronage positions awarded to any black Georgian in the late nineteenth century." He also reports that Deveaux was worth between $20,000.00 and $50,000.00.[269]

As a moderate realist, Deveaux did what was necessary to survive and maintain some level of dignity in his day. One June 9, 1909, Deveaux died at his home, 514 East Taylor Street. The rector of St. Stephens Episcopal Church, the Reverend Richard Bright, conducted his funeral. Many blacks and whites attended it. The *Savannah Morning News* carried an article entitled, "Why Colonel Deveaux Could Not Be Removed," which claimed that Deveaux had "rendered Savannah conspicuous service."[270] The paper thought that he "stood as a sentinel" in times of the outbreak of yellow fever.

The *Savannah Tribune* of June 19, 1909, reported "The esteem in which he was held at his own home was attested by the large concourse of friends and citizens who followed the remains to its final resting place." The paper also reported: "many were the tears shed by men and women as they stood to pay tribute to this most remarkable man." A report quoting the *American Baptist,* stated, "He was one of the few race leaders who held the confidence and esteem of the rank and file of the people both young from the time he entered public life until the day of his death."

The *Savannah Morning News* commented that his death "practically eliminates the Negro from politics in Georgia." In this way ended the life of one of the most remarkable African American Savannahians of all times.

Endnotes – Chapter 2

[1] Ira Berlin, ed., *Free At Last: A Documentary History of Slavery, Freedom, And The Civil War,* The New Press, 1992, 314.

[2] Mills Lane, *The People of Georgia, An Illustrated History,* Beehive Press, 1992, 107.

[3] Daniel H. Thomas, "Pre-Whitney Cotton Gins in French Louisiana," *Journal of Southern History,* 31(May 1965): 135-148.

[4] Edwin L. Jackson et al. *The Georgia Studies Book,* University of Georgia, 1992, 163.

[5] Constance McL. Green, *Eli Whitney and the Birth of American Technology, Little Brown and Company,* 1956, 191.

[6] Green, 61.

[7] Betsy Fancher, *Savannah: A Renaissance of the Heart*, Doubleday, 1976, 46.

[8] Green, 93.

[9] Melvin Drimmer, ed., *Black History A Reappraisal,* Doubleday, 1968, 115.

[10] Edward Chan Sieg, *Eden on the Marsh, Savannah*, Windsor Publications, 1985, 54.

[11] Quoted in, Preston and Barbara Hines, *Savannah, A History of Her People Since 1733,* Frederic C. Beil, 1992, 82.

[12] Gamble, 78.

[13] Thomas L. Stokes, 217.

[14] Sieg, 61.

[15] Sieg, 57.

[16] Thomas L. Stokes, 265.

[17] Sieg, 65.

[18] Thomas L. Stokes, 235.

[19] Les R. Winn, *Ghost Trains & Depots of Georgia, 1833-1933*, Big Shanty Publishing, 1995, 11.

[20] *Savannah Republican,* November 20, 1851.

[21] Amelia M. Murray, *Letters from the United States, Cuba and Canada,* New York, 1856, 206-207.

[22] William Harden, 46.

[23] Burns, 181.

[24] Gamble, 57.

[25] Daily Morning News, July 29, 1851.

[26] U.S. Census, Washington D.C., 1811: US. Census, 1860, Washington, D. C., 1864.

[27] *Daily Morning News,* January 15, 1853.

[28] *Daily Morning News,* February 3, 1853.

[29] *Daily Morning News,* July 16, 1853.

[30] *Daily Morning News*, July 26, 1853.

[31] *Daily Morning News,* January 4, 1854.

[32] *Daily Morning News,* March 29, 1854.

[33] *Daily Morning News,* April 30, 1855.

[34] *Daily Morning News,* January 4, 1854.

[35] *Daily Morning News,* May 15, 1856.

[36] *Daily Morning News*, March 5, 1856.

[37] *Daily Morning News,* August 30, 1856.

[38] Savannah Revisited......

[39] *Daily Morning News,* October 25, 1859.

[40] *Connect Savannah,* May 26-June 1, 2000.

[41] Joseph F. Waring, 28.

[42] Joseph F. Waring, 28.

[43] *Daily Morning News,* November 27, 1856.

[44] *Daily Morning News,* February 9, 1857.

[45] *Daily Morning News,* December 14, 1858.

[46] Albert B. Hart, ed., *American History told by Contemporaries*, vol. 1V, Welding of the Nation 1845-1900, 75.

[47] *Daily Morning News* February 9, 1859.

[48] *Daily Morning News,* March 6, 1860.

[49] Frederick Bancroft, *Slave Trading in the Old South*, New York, Frederick Unger Publishing, 1931, 233, 378.

[50] *Savannah Morning News,* January 2, 1860.

[51] Henry Cleveland, *Alexander H. Stephens, in Public and Private: With letters and Speeches, Before, During and Since the War,* Philadelphia, 1886, 717-729).: *Augusta Daily Constitutionalist,* March 30, 1861.

[52] *Daily Morning News* September 29, 1861.

[53] *Daily Morning News,* June 18, 1863.

[54] *Daily Morning News,* July 2, 1864.

[55] Daily Morning News, October 17, 1864.

[56] Austin D. Washington, "Some Aspects Of Emancipation In Eighteenth Century Savannah, Georgia," *Faculty Research Edition of the Savannah State College Bulletin,* 26(December 1972), 104.

[57] Deed Book 1-R, 164-166; book 1-S, 303.

[58] Records of Savannah, *Minutes of the Council*, 1794-1796, 310.

[59] Ruth Scarborough, *The Opposition to Slavery in Georgia Prior to 1860*, Negro Universities Press, 1968, 192.

[60] Edward F. Sweet, "The Free Negro in Ante-Bellum Georgia," (Ph.D. diss., Indiana University, 1957): 13-15.

[61] Sweet, 27.

[62] Ralph B. Flanders, "The Free Negro in Ante-bellum Georgia," *The North Carolina Historical Review,* 9(July 1932):250-272.

[63] W. McDowell Rogers, "Free Negro Legislation In Georgia Before 1865," *Georgia Historical Quarterly* 16(March 1932): 27-37.

[64] *Savannah Ordinances,* (1829), *Minute Book* #2, 30.

[65] Scarborough, 192.

[66] Edward G. Wilson, *A Digest of all the Ordinances of the City of Savannah,* John M. Cooper and Company, 1858, 36.

[67] *Acts of the General Assembly,* 1808-1860, 30.

[68] Ralph B. Flanders, *Plantation Slavery in Georgia,* Chapel Hill, 1933, 204.

[69] Sweet, 154.

[70] Edward G. Wilson ed., A Digest of All the Ordinances of the City of Savannah, 1858, 174-175.

[71] Scarborough, 143.

[72] Edward G. Wilson, comp. 173.

[73] Bancroft, Census, 13, 42.

[74] Sweet, 201.

[75] Sweet, 200.

[76] Sweet, 139.

[77] Whittington B. Johnson, 418, 426.

[78] W. McDowell Rogers, "Free Negro Legislation in Georgia Before 1965." *Georgia Historical Quarterly,* 16(March 1932): 27-37.

[79] Rogers, 34.

[80] W. B. Johnson, "Free blacks in Antebellum Savannah: An Economic Profile, *Georgia Historical Quarterly,* 64(Winter 1980), 422.

[81] William Harden, 48-49.

[82] Whittington B. Johnson, 423.

[83] Sweet, 173.

(Whittington B. Johnson, 428).

[85] *Chatham County Will Book*, 1800-1817, 157.

[86] Edward F. Sweet, "Social Status of the Free Negro in Antebellum Georgia, *The Negro History Bulletin*, XX1, (March 1958), 130).

[87] U.S. Census, 1860, 1025.

[88] Thomas R.R.Cobb (ed.), A Digest of the Statute Laws of the State of Georgia, Kelsen & Burke, 1858, 983.

[89] Coulter, Georgia: *A Short History*, 277.

[90] Phillips, American Negro Slavery, Appleton-Century, 1919, 435.

[91] Whittington B. Johnson, 425.

[92] A.E. Sholes, 46-47.

[93] Stanley Levine, "Fire, How Early Savannah Was Lost And A History Of Its Fire Department A Guide For Historic Preservationists," (MA thesis, 1993, Savannah College of Art and Design), 7.

[94] *Savannah Evening Press,* November 19, 1941.

[95] Thomas Gamble, 150.

[96] William Harden, *Recollections of a Long and Satisfactory Life,* Savannah, 1934, 19-20.

[97] Paschal N. Strong, "Glimpses of Savannah, 1780-1825," *Georgia Historical Quarterly,* 33(March, 1949): 28.

[98] Gamble, 151.

[99] Gamble, 152.

[99] Quoted in John E. Maguire, Historical Souvenir Savannah Fire Department. Savannah, 1906, 20.

[101] Thomas Gamble, 153.

[102] Thomas Gamble, 152.

[103] Gamble, 152.

[104] Gamble, 162.

[105] Gamble, 196.

[106] Gamble, 196.

[107] William Harden, 19.

[108] Thomas Gamble, 197.

[109] *Savannah Republican,* May 31, 1851.

[110] Savannah Morning News, April 12, 1852.

[111] Daily Morning News, May 28, 1853.

[112] Thomas Gamble, 237.

[113] *Daily Morning News,* May 26, 1855.

[114] Daily Morning News, May 31, 1856.

[115] Thomas Gamble, 238.

[116] *Daily Morning News* of September 22, 1856.

[117] Thomas Gamble, 238.

[118] *Daily Morning News,* May 28, 1859.

[119] John Maguire, 27.

[120] Thomas Gamble, 239.

[121] *Savannah Republican,* January 29, 1865.

[122] Savannah Republican, July 6, 1865.

[123] *Savannah Daily Herald,* July 6, 1866.

[124] Savannah Republican, July 7, 1865.

[125] *Savannah Daily Herald,* January 3, 1866.

[126] *Daily News Herald,* April 27, 1866.

[127] *Daily News Herald,* April 30, 1866.

[128] *Daily News Herald,* May 26, 1866.

[129] *Daily News Herald,* July 27, 1866.

[130] Savannah Daily Herald, October 31, 1866.

[131] Thomas Gamble, 277.

[132] *Savannah Morning News,* July 28, 1868.

[134] Thomas Gamble, 278.

[135] *Morning News,* May 12, 1869.

[136] Savannah Morning News, August 17, 1869.

[137] Thomas Gamble, 275.

[138] James E. Chase, *Savannah Fire Department,* Savannah, 1898, 61.

[139] *Savannah Tribune,* June 10, 1916.

[140] Savannah Tribune, June 17, 1916.

[141] J. P. Tustin, "Andrew Marshall-1786-1856," *Annals of the American Pulpit or Commemorative Notices of Distinguished American Clergymen of Various Denominations,* ed., William B. Sprague, New York, Robert Carter and Brothers, 1860, 6:253.

[142] James Simms, 80.

[143] Simms, 240.

[144] William B. Sprague, 251-64: James Simms, 46-78.

[145] *Digest of Savannah City Taxes for* 1824.

[146] Sweet, 203.

[147] (Whittington B. Johnson, "Free Blacks in Antebellum Savannah: An Economic Profile," *Georgia Historical Quarterly* 64(Winter 1980):424.).

[148] James Simms, 238.

[149] James Simms, 240.

[150] Carter G. Woodson, *The History of the Negro Church,* The Associated Publishers, 1972, 99.

[151] Special meeting April 4, 1832, Mabel Freeman La Far, The Baptist Church of Savannah Georgia, Savannah, Georgia, 722-23; Love, 31.

[152] Emanuel K. Love, 31.

[153] Emanuel .K. Love, 32.

[154] Atlanta Constitution, February 27, 1988.

[155] Love, 163.

[156] Kenneth K. Bailey, "Protestant and Afro-Americans in the Old South: Another look," *Journal of Southern History*, 12(November 1975), 468.

[157] J. P. Tustin, "Andrew Marshall," in *Annals of the American Pulpit,* ed., William Sprague, New York, 1859, 258-59.

[158] Charles C. Jones, Jr., *History of Savannah,* Syracuse, 1890, 511,

[159] (Citation ???).

[160] *Savannah Republican,* May 25, 1855.

[161] Sweet, 171.

[162] *The New York Times,* July 8, 1856.

[163] *Savannah Morning News,* December 11, 1856.

[164] Savannah Republican, December 5, 1856.

[165] William Harden, *Recollections of A Long and Satisfactory Life,* Savannah, 1934, 32.

[166] James Simms, 242.

[167] James Simms, 247.

[168] *Daily Morning News*, December 6, 1856.

[169] Love, 44.

[170] E.K. Love, 53.

[171] *Savannah Morning News,* January 17, 1976.

[172] *Savannah Republican,* December 15, 1856.

[173] *Savannah Tribune,* October 16, 1909.

[174] Savannah Morning News, October 10, 1909.

[175] Charles Elmore, 26.

[176] *Savannah Tribune,* October 16, 1909.

[177] *Savannah Morning News,* February 12, 1872.

[178] Robert Perdue, 40.

[179] *Savannah Morning News,* February 12, 1872.

[180] *Savannah Morning News,* February 13, 1872.

[181] Savannah Morning News, February 13, 1872.

[182] Savannah Morning News, June 29, 1872.

[183] *Savannah Morning News,* February 12, 1872.

[184] *Savannah Tribune,* October 15, 1892.

[185] *Savannah Tribune,* November 12, 1892.

[186] *Savannah Tribune,* March 3, 1888.

[187] *Savannah Tribune,* January 21, 1888.

[188] *Savannah Tribune,* January 11, 1896.

[189] Savannah Morning News, February 12, 1900.

[190] *Savannah Tribune,* February 15, 1896.

[191] Savannah Morning News, October 10, 1909.

[192] *Savannah Tribune,* October 16, 1909.

[193] *Savannah Morning News,* October 11, 1909.

[194] *Savannah Tribune,* October 16, 1909.

[195] *Savannah Morning News,* October 11, 1909.

[196] *Savannah Morning News,* October 10, 1909.

[197] *Savannah Morning News,* October 11, 1909.

[198] *Savannah Tribune,* October 16, 1909.

[199] *Savannah Morning News,* October 7, 1889.

[200] Love, 131.

[201] *Savannah Tribune,* October 5, 1889.

[202] Dorothy Sterling, editor, *The Trouble They See,* Doubleday & Company, Inc., 1976, 31.

[203] Love, 132.

[204] Eric Foner, *Freedom's Lawmakers*, Louisiana State University Press, 1996, 110.

[205] Josef C. James, "Sherman at Savannah," *Journal of Negro History,* 39 (April 1954): 128-135.

[206] Savannah Republican, June 19, 1865.

[207] *Daily News Herald,* January 21, 1867.

[208] Eric Williams, *History of the People of Trinidad and Tobago,* Andre Deutsch, 1962, 96.

[209] *Savannah Tribune,* October 5, 1889.

[210] *Savannah Morning News,* September 27, 1886.

[211] *Savannah Tribune,* October 30, 1886.

[212] *Savannah Tribune,* October 5, 1889.

[213] *Savannah Tribune,* June 23, 1888.

[214] Foner, 109-110.

[215] *Savannah Tribune,* January 26, 1889.

[216] *Savannah Tribune,* November 23, 1889.

[217] *Savannah Morning News,* October 4, 1889.

[218] Savannah Morning News, October 7, 1889.

[219] *Savannah Tribune,* October 12, 1889.

[220] *Savannah Morning News,* October 7, 1889.

[221] *Savannah Tribune,* October 12, 1889.

[222] *Savannah Morning News,* October 7, 1889.

[223] *Savannah Morning News,* November 21, 1889.

[224] *Savannah Tribune,* February 13, 1892.

[225] *Savannah Morning New,* December 24, 1889.

[226] *Savannah Tribune,* July 13, 1912.

[227] Emanuel K. Love, *A History of the First African Baptist Church,* 1888, 165.

[228] *Savannah Tribune,* July 13, 1912.

[229] Dorothy Sterling, ed., *The Trouble They Seen,* Da Capo Press, 1994, 107-108.

[230] Edgar Thomas, The First African Baptist Church of North America, Savannah, 1925, 134.

[231] *Savannah Tribune,* June 9, 1906.

[232] Kermit Smalls, 23.

[233] Love, 166.

[234] Thomas, 135.

[235] Love, 166.

[236] Thomas, 166.

[237] Eric Foner, 1996, 196.

[238] Dorothy Sterling, 108.

[239] *Daily News and Herald,* May 20, 1867.

[240] Perdue, 41.

[241] Eric Foner, 196.

[242] Savannah Morning News, January 3, 1868.

[243] *Savannah Morning News* of January 27, 1871.

[244] *Savannah Morning News,* February 3, 1868.

[245] *Savannah Morning News,* November 145, 1872.

[246] Love, 165-167.

[247] U.S. Census, 1900, Georgia vol. 11, sheet 23.

[248] *Savannah Tribune,* February 16, 1895.

[249] Savannah Tribune, July 13, 1912.

[250] James Weldon Johnson, *Lift Every Voice and Sing.*

[251] *Savannah Morning News,* April 9, 1851.

[252] Edward H. Savage, A Chronological History of the Boston Watch and Police, from 1631-1865, Boston, the author, 1865, 378.

[253] *Savannah Morning News,* April 9, 1851.

[254] *Savannah Morning News,* April 21, 1851.

[255] *Savannah Morning News,* April 21, 1851.

[256] *Savannah Morning News,* April 21, 1851.

[257] Theodore Parker, *The Boston Kidnapping,* Boston, Cosby, Nichols and Company, 1852, 43.

[258] *Savannah Tribune* of June 7, 1934.

[259] *Savannah Morning News,* June 11, 1909.

[260] *Savannah Morning News,* August 3, 1876.

[261] *Savannah Tribune,* February 16, 1895.

[262] *Savannah Tribune,* April 25, 1896.

[263] *Savannah Tribune,* March 20, 1897.

[264] *Savannah Tribune,* March 20, 1897.

[265] John M. Mathews, "Black Newspapermen and the Black Community in Georgia, 1890-1930," *Georgia Historical Quarterly,* 64(Fall 1984): 360.

[266] *Savannah Morning News,* November 11, 1870.

[267] *Savannah Morning News,* February 21, 1901.

[268] *Savannah Tribune,* December 28, 1901.

[269] Eric Foner, 63.

[270] *Savannah Morning News,* June 10, 1909.

figure 1

figure 2

figure 3

figure 4

figure 5

figure 6

figure 7

figure 8

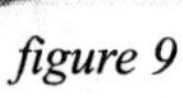

figure 9

figure 10

figure 11

figure 12

A part of the Congregation in Morning Worship

figure 13

figure 14

figure 15

figure 16

NATHAN ROBERTS, chairman of the trustee board, president of the B. Y. P. U., treasurer of Sunday school, Sec.-Treas., State Baptist Convention and proprietor of Roberts' Funeral Home.

JACKIE JOHNSON, Chorister of choir, Sunday School and B. Y. P. U.

HENRY McCULLOUGH, chairman of deacon board and secretary of trustee board

MRS. VICTORIA B. ROBERTS, secretary of the Missionary Society, group captain and director of the young people of Georgia

14

figure 17

figure 18

figure 19

figure 20

figure 22

figure 23

figure 24

figure 26

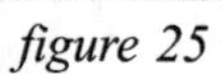

figure 25

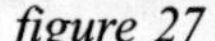

figure 27

figure 28

figure 29

figure 30

figure 31

figure 32

figure 33

FREE PERSONS OF COLOR.

Anderson, Claudia
Anderson, Sarah
Anderson, Margaret
Bond, Henry
Butler, Rachel
Burke, Elizabeth
Brown, Henry
Brown, Martha
Boyd, Aurian
Boyd, Jeremiah
Boyd, Caroline
Benjernine, Molsne
Burke, Joshua
Baker, Louisa
Brown, Henrietta
Barnwell, Louisa
Bogans, Samuel
Borquin, Francis
Baptiste, John
Burke, Charles
Bong, Ann
Bell, Ann Jane
Burke, Charles
Baker, William
Bisbee, William
Brown, Maria
Brister, Cyrus
Bisbee, Louisa
Chevers, Rebecca
Carlay, Alexander
Clay, Rose
Cox, John
Culloten, Mary
Cohen, Hannah
Color, Ellen
Carrier, Henry
Campbell, Jane
Carter, Elizabeth
Carter, Mary
Denslow, Buckey
DeVillers, Virginia
DeVillers, George
Dunning, Priscilla
Dupont, Anna
Davidson, Rose
Desvergers, Francis
Davis, Letitia C
Doing, Caroline
Dolly, Petro
Debrois, Patsey
Dorsey, Jared
Devaux, Isaac
Edy, Diana
Evans, Harriot
Endy, James
Erwin, William
Edmund, Mary
Formelle, Charlotte
Gibbons, Harriet
Gordon, Mary Ann
Hunt, William J
Hassett, Sarah
James, Mary
Johnston, Sarah
Jalineau, Mary
Jalineau, Rose
Jones, George
Jones, Polly
Irwin, Mary
Jackson, Cornelia
Johnston, Mary
Kelly, Julia
Kimball, Thomas
Kirk, Isabella
Kelly, Jeremiah
Morehead, John
Mayer, Susan
Morehead, John
Marshall, Lewis
Marshall, Mary
Marshall, George
Marshall, Rachel
Miller, Sallie
Morel, Anne
Moultrie, Mary
May, Thomas
McQueen, Stephen
Moore, Mary
Motta, Sandy
McHardy, Francis
Myers, Sarah Ann
Moore, Levi
Miraltet, Simon
Mirault, Josephine B
Miller, William
Myers, Rebecca
Mirault, Laura
Neyle, Cecelia
Odingsell, Venus
Odingsell, Mary Ann
Oliver, Caroline
Pollard, William
Pindar, William
Page, Judy
Piles, Susan
Reid, John
Richards, Josiah
Roberts, Obadiah
Robin, Scott
Reed, Margaret
Sheftall, Derby
Sims, Margaret
Sheftall, Jackson
Sheftall, Mary
Sallins, Sarah N
Sweet, Rachel
Sevally, John
Stone, John
Symons, Hannah
Thomas, Louisa
Turnbull, Maria
Taylor, Hannah
Verdier, Maria
Wilson, John
Wilson, Mary Ann
Ware, Ann
Ward, Elsey
Williams, James
Weston, Tyler
Whitfield, Sampson
Willis, Caroline
Wade, Edward
Walls, Thomas
Walls, Rebecca
Williams, Rose
White, Matthew
Young, Mary
Young, Cloida

By order of the Court.

WM H. BULLOCH,
Clerk I. C. C. C.

figure 34

figure 35

figure 36

figure 37

figure 38

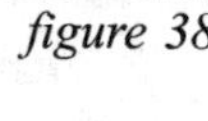

figure 39

figure 40

figure 41

figure 42

figure 43

figure 44

figure 45

The Struggle Begins

Stanton & Sherman Meet Black leaders

Major-General William Tecumseh Sherman's capture of Savannah was a mixed blessing. Blacks had generally framed the Civil War in theological concepts. To them the general's victory was but an instrument of God's providence and the fruit of their efforts in resisting slavery. The God of their "weary years, the God of their silent tears" had indeed performed his wonders. It was a day of jubilee. For whites the trauma centered on their loss of property, the loss of an assured sense of white superiority and the possible loss of their obsessive desire to keep blacks "under due order and subjection." This double vision of one objective reality, the South's loss of the war, was a harbinger of the future inability of both sides to deal with the experience. As that son of the South William Faulkner once said: "In the South the past is not dead, it is not even past."

As early as 1861 when Federal forces threatened the Sea Islands, several slaves escaped to freedom. On May 9, 1862, General David Hunter, the Commander of the Department of the South, issued his own emancipation proclamation for Georgia, Florida and South Carolina. President Lincoln canceled this order.[1] Sherman seemed to have been somewhat unconcerned about the condition of the slaves. Sherman used a black corps of pioneers to fell trees, and build roads and bridges on his path to Savannah. However, his problem was what to do with these thousands of blacks who had followed him to the city.

Federal troops in Georgia captured Tybee Island in November 26-27, 1861, and Fort Pulaski fell to General Quincy A. Gillmore, April 10, 1862[2] Sherman's famous "march to the sea" began November 15, 1864 with a contingent of about 70,000 men. His path covered a swath 40 by 300 miles. Historian Benjamin Quarles considered the assistance blacks gave Sherman's foraging army "incalculable."[3] Months later Sherman confronted Confederate General William Hardee who defended Savannah with 10,000 troops. By December General Sherman's demand that the city surrender, was refused. General Hardee laid out pontoons from River Street to Hutchinson Island and placed obstructions in the Savannah River. Days later his troops abandoned the city.

General John Geary entered the city with his Federal troops on December 21, 1864, and took control as Savannah's leadership surrendered without a whimper. Mayor Dr. Richard Arnold left us a clear appreciation of the role African Americans played in the city prior to emancipation. He stated: "Our domestic institutions which made us dependent on organized slave labor renders our situation unique.

That sudden cut away and no props or stays supplied, our whole social fabric has fallen in and entirety from one end of the South to the other." William Gordon, writing to his mother, expressed anguish that was more personal: "I really don't see... how you are to live if you come down here. Your servants will all expect wages when you return and will not work for you unless you pay them."

General Sherman arrived December 25, 1864,[4] and sent President Lincoln his famous telegram from the city: "I beg to present to you, as a Christmas gift, the city of Savannah, with 150 heavy guns and plenty of ammunition and also about 25,000 bales of cotton." Savannah was spared the destruction that occurred in Atlanta but there was general chaos. Food, money and commerce were in short supply. The safety of persons and property was threatened. Sherman had been loath to use blacks in his army, now he had to deal with them and Savannah's whites faced the daunting reality of armed black troops garrisoned in the city. While in Savannah, the general headquartered in the Green home on Macon Street, and received several visitors, both black and white. Among the visitors was Edwin Stanton, Secretary of War, who had come to Savannah on January 11, because the administration was concerned about the number of refugees, and reports about Sherman's treatment of blacks.[5] Stanton also wanted to learn the views of blacks about their new position in the society and their plans for the future.

On the evening of Thursday January 12, 1865, twenty African American leaders met with Secretary Stanton and General Sherman at the General's headquarters.[6] The delegation was made up of Garrison Frazier, William Campbell, John Cox, Ulysses Houston, William Bentley, Charles Bradwell, William Gaines, James Hill, Glasgon Taylor, James Mills, Abraham Burke, Arthur Wardell, Alexander Harris, Andrew Neal, John Johnson, Adolphus De La Motta, Jacob Godfrey, Robert Taylor, James Porter, and James Lynch. Their ages ranged from 26 to 72 years; six had been free before emancipation, two had bought their own freedom; five were born free and nine were slaves before. In terms of religious affiliation, eight were Baptists, one Episcopalian, and three of unknown religious persuasion. Seven of them were born in Savannah. One was born in Baltimore. The others were born in other parts of Georgia, or other states. James Lynch at 26, the youngest of the group and an elder of the African Methodist Episcopal Church, had only recently come to the city. They chose Garrison Frazier as their leader and spokesman.

Frazier had been a Baptist minister for 35 years and was endowed with "fair natural gifts, a commanding presence and a good voice." The dialogue was conducted in written question and answer form. When asked to define slavery, Frazier described the experience of slavery as "receiving by irresistible power the work of another man, and not by his consent." Freedom he replied was "taking us from under the yoke of bondage and placing us where we could reap the fruit of our own labor, take care of ourselves, and assist the government in maintaining our freedom." Frazier reiterated that being responsible for their well being meant "to have land, and turn it and till it by our own labor."[7]

His desire was perfectly clear. He said: "We want to be placed on land we are able to buy and make it on our own." Frazier saw the future of his people balancing on the tripod of land, suffrage and education. They wanted the government to assist them to attain these goals. Stanton then asked the black leaders in what manner they would like to live. Frazier replied: "I would prefer to live by ourselves, for there is a prejudice against us in the South that will take years to get over: but I do not know that I can answer for my brethren." [8] The subsequent experience of African Americans proved that Frazier's judgment was unusually prophetic.

When polled, the others agreed with the opinion expressed by Frazier, except James Lynch, who felt that blacks and whites should live together. Though we have no written diaries or books by these men, it is obvious that they had discussed these points before the meeting and that there was some difference of opinion on the matter of living with whites. When asked whether they had enough intelligence to look after themselves Frazier replied, that he had no doubt that "there is sufficient intelligence among us to do so." Frazier obviously knew about the underground schools in existence in the city for many years. Stanton was amazed at the precision of the replies and stated that he doubted whether any member of the President's cabinet could have given "a better analysis of the situation." Several consequences followed this meeting.

Bound for the Promised Land

General Sherman issued Field Order #15, January 16, 1865, four days after he met with the city's African American leaders.[9] It was a document intended to answer a very practical problem. Local blacks were anxious to begin enjoying the benefit of their newfound freedom and satisfy their hunger for land. The order stated that certain lands were: "Set apart for the settlement of Negroes now made free by acts of war and the proclamation of the President of the United States."[10] It reserved abandoned fields and plantations from Charleston south, the abandoned rice field along the rivers for 30 miles back from the sea, and the country bordering the St. John's River, Florida, are reserved and set apart for the settlement of the Negroes. The Confiscation Act of 1862, providing for the seizing of property from certain classes of Confederates, formed the basis of this order.

On Thursday evening February 2, 1865, hundreds of African Americans from Savannah and vicinity attended a meeting at Second African Baptist Church. The local press reported "The pews in the body of the house were filled. The galleries presented a "sable cloud of faces." Seats were placed in the aisles and every seat in the house was occupied and there was still a crowd at the door anxious to obtain an entrance."[11] The choir sang *America* and at the request of General Saxton From Greenland's Icy Mountains, from India's Coral Strands. According to Dr. John Duncan, Lowell Mason of the Independent Presbyterian Church in Savannah first set these words to music. The Rev. Ulysses Houston, the pastor of the Third African Baptist Church, then offered prayers.

General Rufus Saxton explained that because of the war and the providence of God "they were free men, that all their relations of life had been suddenly changed; that now they would no longer be provided for, but must provide for themselves; that the government which had made them free had set apart the islands of the coast for their occupation, and that the head of each family was entitled to forty acres of land." The general finally reminded them that it was their duty "to support the government which had set them free." In addition, he encouraged their able-bodied young men to enlist in the armed forces. General Saxon "was listened to with profound attention."[12]

The Rev. Mansfield French reminded the blacks that "their freedom was a gift of God, the President had only proclaimed it, and General Sherman had brought it to them." The enthusiastic congregation responded with hearty "Amen," and "Bless the Lord," and in addition, "Yes, Yes." The time had come he said, when "their old habits must be changed. Their old masters were not bound to help them, they must help themselves." There were "many tearful eyes in the congregation while the Reverend gentleman was speaking and a responsive "Amen" frequently broke forth from those who listened for the first time to "an able exposition of the changes which the war had wrought in the life and prospects of the slave."

He encouraged their young men to enlist in the armed forces, "but all others should at once go to the islands and commence operations, living in huts till they could get houses. They must take their hoes, spades and shovels and lay out their gardens and raise vegetables for the market and chickens and corn and cotton. They must begin at once and not sit idly upon the docks." The firmly held story of the promise of "forty acres and a mule," that is the unused mules of the Federal forces, among African Americans nation wide, had its genesis at Second African Baptist Church.[13]

Meanwhile Federal authorities advertised for colored laborers who would be given "good pay and rations."[14] The Superintendent of the Freedmen Bureau for Georgia, J. E. Bryant, encouraged blacks to make contracts with anyone willing to employ them.[15] African Americans mourned the death of President Lincoln. One Savannah paper reported "Passing through the western portion of our city yesterday afternoon one of our reporters noticed that the lintels of the doors of all the houses of the colored people were draped in mourning as a token of sadness of the occupants at the loss of President Lincoln."[16] Some six months after Lincoln's death,

President Andrew Johnson canceled the order that confiscated lands. Whites were in the process of changing their attitude to labor. The time when any white tried to avoid labor because the black man was supposed to do that had ceased. The "time has arrived when honest labor is about to be appreciated."[17] Henry Dittmer, a white man, purchased land on Middleground road between White Bluff and Ogeechee Roads, and laid out the areas into lots. Blacks bought the lots and Dittmersville village, two miles south of Savannah "suddenly come to life."[18]

The paper ran a headline "Trouble on Skidaway Island: The Negroes Firing on Fishing Boats." The article stated that: "Negroes have taken possession of an old Fort, erected there during the War; and from this point they fired musket shots at all fishing boats which passed the Island, which were manned by white men."[19] There was a heavy concentration of blacks in Yamacraw. More than half the black churches and businesses were located in predominantly white areas and blacks lived in almost every street in Savannah. Though race relations had been relatively mild, the increase of the black population seems to have heightened tensions. Whites sought to keep blacks "in their place." Blacks were barred from jury duty and faced stiff competition for certain jobs. In addition, some 3,000 black children were without school places. African Americans had come out of slavery with a large pool of skilled former free and slave craftsmen.

Soon however, land values became depressed and a series of crop failures steadily reduced the value of their holdings. Even then, they still had preponderance in certain trades. Some 50% of the porters, bricklayers and cotton workers were black. Black Savannah, as well as white Savannah, was a class-structured community. The free blacks had enjoyed a few advantages during slavery, in terms of education and property. With the coming of emancipation, these former free blacks exerted an influence on black Savannah that was well beyond what their numbers would suggest. The 46 most prominent black families held 234 of the offices in the approximately 19 clubs and mutual aid societies that came into being. At the apex of the social structure was the black 'aristocracy', mainly though not all, "high yellows."

About 84 of the black elite families had per capita holdings of $783. Social life swirled among balls, picnics, military parades, literary events and the like, with music being supplied by the Skidamore Club String Band, the Braham Band and others. The churches provided a very convenient vehicle for African Americans to assert their personhood which even slavery could not obliterate. Between 1865 and 1880, they organized 10 new churches.[20]

In July 1868, a riot broke out in Yamacraw and several persons were arrested, but the leader, Charles Thompson, escaped. He was later apprehended and fined $75. By November the authorities had to station patrols on Louisville Road to quell another riot by heavily armed Negroes. A large force of armed white citizens was sent to guard the Ogeechee and Louisville roads. A large wagonload of muskets was taken out to the Ogeechee Road for distribution to blacks.

Later on March 11, 1880, a debate was held at the hall of the Lone Star Cadets on the subject, "Was the Negro Slavery in the U.S., a Curse in Its Character?" A.P. Clark and Alan N. Collier argued the negative, while M. Gibson, and R.N. Rutledge argued the affirmative. The affirmative prevailed. Yet another group held a mass meeting at McIntire Hall chaired by C.L. Brown. This body was said to be opposed to the mulatto clique who for 15 years had considered full blooded blacks entitled to nothing but the vote.

Congress passed the Civil Rights Act in April, 1866, and in June the 14th Amendment was sent to the states for ratification. Blacks met in Augusta and organized the Equal Rights Association. In November, the Georgia legislature rejected the 14th Amendment. A constitutional convention met in Atlanta in March 1868. A subsequent election placed three local blacks in the house and one in the senate. In July the legislature approved the 14th Amendment and the state was restored to the union.

Within a short time political chicanery reached its apogee. In August, 1870, Savannah opened its new $28, 500 police barracks. Savannah at that time had 11 houses of ill fame, 50 streetwalkers, 150 kept women and 265 prostitutes. By 1872 much work had been done on the streets and sewers. In 1870 military rule was removed and the Democrats regained political control. Six years later the city experienced severe financial difficulties and about 1,000 people died from a yellow fever epidemic. To make a bad situation even worse there was a series of spectacular fires. The Presidential election of 1876 brought about the "compromise" entered into by the Republicans that resulted in the abandonment of black interests. By 1880 King Cotton had regained his throne and over one million bales of cotton were shipped from Savannah. The 1886 earthquake caused havoc among the populace and three years later an Easter fire destroyed about $1,000,000 in property. Savannah then went into the "Gay 90's."

The Hunger for Education

Federal authorities, who came to Savannah in the wake of General Sherman's rout of the Confederate troops, were amazed at the "hunger" blacks had for education.[21] The local press reported that it was "as refreshing as wonderful to see with what earnestness and eager avidity these liberated people seek for information. All manifest a great desire to learn."[22] This hankering after education had a very long gestation beginning in 1751, when the rector of Christ Church operated a school for slave children.[23] This hunger later drove many "bearers of the flame," that extraordinary phalanx of black teachers, slaves and free persons of color; many of whom, though enjoying few advantages themselves, nevertheless devoted an extraordinary amount of energy and endured incredible sacrifices to guarantee their fellow blacks an education. From the beginning the authorities used education as a means of keeping blacks "under due order and subjection."

By May of 1770 slave codes increased the fine for teaching blacks to $500 and opined: "having slaves taught to write or suffering them to be employed in writing may be attended with great inconveniences."[24] Blacks however also remained steadfast in their "hunger " for education. The nub of the problem was how to benefit from slave labor, while simultaneously keeping the slaves totally submissive to white control.[25] As Waring wrote, "who could tell really what was going on behind those 'happy' black masks?"[26]

Julien Fromantin, a free colored and a native of Saint Domingue, or present day Haiti, immigrated to Savannah via Charleston, around 1818 and in 1819 established an "underground school" for blacks. A member of St. John's Catholic parish, he was the first known "bearer of the flame."[27] Fromantin advertised himself as a carpenter in order to conceal his teaching activities.[28] From 1819 to 1829, he openly operated his school, but as the authorities passed more stringent laws in the wake of black revolts or suspected revolts, Fromantin took his school further behind Savannah's Moss Curtain. He continued teaching until about 1844.[29]

White Savannah's reaction to the discovery of David Walker's anti-slavery "incendiary" *Appeal* in the city in December, 1829, demonstrated that they were aware that many blacks in the city were quite capable of reading "the inflammatory document."[30] At that time, several fires had been discovered in many cities including Savannah, Augusta and Macon.[31] Not surprisingly, the Georgia Assembly passed another law, which toughened the prohibition against teaching slaves or coloreds to read or write.[32] The authorities were also concerned that the free people of color might plant "strange ideas of freedom" in the minds of the slaves. Denmark Vesey's conspiracy in the neighboring city of Charleston in 1822 greatly increased this fear in Savannah that literate blacks might prove to be a menace to civil tranquility.

The mayor of Savannah issued a proclamation March 20, 1830, warning that captains of vessels "having free persons of color on board, are required to bring their vessels to anchor opposite the city."[33] An 1833 law gave the city fathers greater security. It stated, in part, that any person who will "teach or cause to be taught" any slave or free person of color to read or write within the city or will keep a school for that purpose will be fined a sum not exceeding $100 for each and every such offense. If the offender happened to be a slave or free person of color, he received up to thirty-nine lashes of a whip.[34] This law also affected black preachers, as they could no longer preach without a license.[35]

Catherine and Jane Deveaux. This pioneer mother and daughter team made a unique contribution to black education in Savannah. Catherine Deveaux a free woman of color, and a well-known seamstress, was born in Antigua, the West Indies.[36] She was the wife of the Rev. John B. Deveaux who was born a slave in Savannah October 15, 1774.[37] The family was very active in Second African Baptist Church. Mother and daughter taught the children in their home;[38] while the father was a deacon at the church, and a pioneer in black music, as the first president of the "Old Hundred Society of Sacred Music," founded in 1817 and reputed to be the first black singing group in the city.[39] John Deveaux became the patriarch of one of the "most distinguished colored families in the city,"[40] Susan Waters, daughter of Lachlan and Eleanor "Nellie" Pollard, informed the author that Jane Deveaux was educated in Boston. Longtime principal Robert W. Gadsden, in a 1952 lecture, claimed that Deveaux's father sent her abroad for further education.[41]

When Jane Deveaux returned home she continued helping her mother in their underground school.[42] Jane Deveaux began teaching blacks to read and write during a hazardous period when the authorities initiated a crack down on black education. She used "a variety of subterfuges" to elude the "lynx-eyed vigilance of the slave-holder," during the more than 30 years she conducted her school in a "story and a half house at the corner of Price and York streets."[43] Professor Gadsden thought "Somebody 'inched her' and she had the children go upstairs and stay up there until the inspectors left, who came in and found nothing." This task demanded a considerable degree of commitment to alleviating the "hunger" of her people for education since one false step courted disaster. Federal official J. W. Alvord, secretary of the Boston Tract Society, reported that though quite advanced in age in the 1860's, she was still "teaching with great eagerness and zeal." Jane Deveaux owned real property worth more than two thousand dollars in 1860.[44] The census of 1860 reported that seven free blacks attended school in 1860.[45] It is not known whether the census taker was aware of the few underground schools in the city.

Public sentiment regarding the education of blacks began to change by the 1850's. A white, F. C. Adams, wrote a series of articles in the local press advocating the education of blacks as a means of increasing their economic value and their fidelity to their masters. The Agricultural Convention of Georgia adopted this view, and petitioned the state legislature to repeal the 1829 law. The proposal passed in the house in 1852, but was defeated in the senate. Catholic Sister Jane Frances, a white Sister of Mercy, also operated a school for blacks in 1855.[46]

James Porter's parents wanted him to be a missionary but an injury during his youth made that dream impossible to achieve. Porter and his wife were brought to Savannah in 1856,[47] to teach music at newly established black urban congregation, St. Stephen's Episcopal Church, now called St. Matthew's Episcopal Church.[48]

Porter soon established yet another underground school for blacks and used his trade as a tailor to cover up his school activities.[49] Frank Bynes reported that Porter's tailor shop was located at 177 West Bryan Street. According to Professor Morse, Porter's school "had a trap door where, when about to be surprised or apprehended his pupils might save themselves." He also reported that Porter was a "lover of his race," who devoted his whole life "to improve and ameliorate their condition." While serving as organist of St. Stephen's Episcopal Church, Porter also taught music to most of the black church musicians in the city, and was regarded by Prof Morse as, "the father of the present leaders of music in this city."[50]

When Secretary of War William Stanton met with some twenty black leaders of Savannah January 12, 1865, James Porter was among them.[51] He was the senior warden of St. Stephen's Episcopal Church and functioned as a lay reader. Porter had charge of the church during the Civil War. Though Bishop Elliott reported to his Convention that he regarded Porter as a "very intelligent and well educated colored man" yet the Bishop stated that he had given Porter "permission to read, without having actually licensed him in that capacity."[52] Edwin Cooley, agent of the A.M.A., thought Porter was "well-educated for a colored person here," but he also found him "somewhat opinionated."[53] A Quaker abolitionist instructor in the city around the same time had a more kind evaluation of Porter. She found him "admirably qualified."[54] Porter was elected president of the political Association, which met in Augusta to secure the rights of blacks. He addressed a meeting in Chippewa Square March 18, 1867, and urged blacks to vote. They had nothing to fear he said, because "God was on their side."[55]

Years later, Porter served twice as an assemblyman from Chatham County in the Georgia Legislature.[56] As a legislator Porter sought to provide free education for all children and chaplains for the House and he wanted to know whether the $1,400 collected from blacks in Savannah in 1869, had been used for their education. Assemblyman Porter declared that poor blacks in Savannah were liable to be shot for exercising their political rights and that colored schools "had been allowed to perish for want of encouragement."[57] Porter was elected a delegate to the Republican Convention in Atlanta in 1867, and a justice of the peace. He was later appointed an inspector of customs.

Porter became the first president of the Mutual Benevolent Association when it was founded in 1876.[58] Porter served as principal of West Broad Street School from 1872 to 1878.[59] While serving as principal of West Broad Street School, Porter applied for the position of U.S. Minister to Liberia but was unsuccessful.[60] Porter owned $3,000 in real estate in 1870 and $400 in real property.[61] In 1879, and as an A.M.E. minister, he was transferred to Thomasville where he taught, preached and wrote the book, *English Grammar for Beginners*. He later served churches in Florida, Mississippi, Alabama, Bermuda and finally, Canada. In 1882, the Rev. Alexander W. Wayman found Porter "a man of extensive information."[62]

Mary Woodhouse, a free woman of color, and a seamstress by trade, was a member of St. Stephen's Episcopal church,[63] and operated a school for some 25 to 30 slave and free children, in her home on Bay Lane between Habersham and Price Streets.[64] Her daughter, Mary Jane, assisted her in this endeavor. Classes began about nine in the morning and the students concealed their books with paper to give the impression that they were learning a trade. The kitchen doubled as a classroom.[65] Her husband was a cooper by trade and owned two slaves in 1830.[66] Mary Woodhouse was delinquent on taxes on her $60 home in 1847.[67]

Louis B. Toomer, a free mulatto, was born in Charleston, South Carolina: the exact date is unknown. His death certificate gives 1830 as the year of birth, but the census of 1900 lists him as being born in April 1840. What is certain is that he came to Savannah "in early manhood," and got involved in local affairs. He was a blacksmith by trade and attorney Thomas E. Lloyds was his guardian. Prof Gadsden stated that Toomer taught school during slavery days. In 1861 Toomer married Elizabeth Claghorn who owned a slave. Toomer was the first principal of the second school blacks established in Savannah after the Civil War.[68] He later served as principal of an A.M.A. school, and "was one of the early instructors in the public school system."[69]

In 1872 Toomer volunteered his services as president of the Educational Association of the First District. He was described as "a law-abiding, worthy colored man in every respect."[70] Between 1869 and 1883 Toomer worked for the U. S. post office and in 1872 was promoted to Superintendent of general delivery. He "was well read and at a time, quite a student of Shakespeare."[71] He was secretary of the Savannah Benevolent Society[72]

In 1883 Toomer was arrested and accused of tampering with the mail and stealing $198. Fellow church member Albert Jackson paid his bond and he was released. This act shocked many blacks since Toomer had "occupied a prominent position among the colored people." He had been in that position for the past fourteen years and was the Adjutant in the Georgia Battalion, colored, and a leading member of the St. Stephen's colored Episcopal Church. He was regarded by all as an influential colored politician, and held high positions in several colored secret organizations."[73]

On April 20, 1884, Toomer was found guilty and fined $25 plus costs. Active in politics from 1870, he served as a registrar of Chatham County and was prominent in local Republican politics and was one of the memorable "three hundred and six," of the Grant campaign for the Presidency in 1880. Toomer, Turner, and Isaac Seeley led a march of some 400 blacks in Liberty County, demanding the right to vote. He had been involved in the struggle for freedom and was an "earnest and untiring worker in behalf of our people."[74]

Toomer sponsored the arrival of Edwin Belcher who assisted in the establishment of the Mutual Benevolent Society as he had similar groups in Augusta and Macon. He lived at the corner of Bryan and Ann Streets. He was a founder and one of the publishers of *Colored Tribune,*[75] and was editor of the *Savannah Echo* for a few years. In 1890 Toomer became a notary public. Judge Louis B. Toomer and his little son were "knocked down by a loose trolly wire at West Broad and Bolton

Streets while returning from the circus."[76]

Louis B. Toomer was "one of the founders of the St. Stephen's Episcopal Church and aided much in its early struggles." He also helped establish the Republican Party in Savannah. Toomer was buried from St. Augustine's Episcopal Church with the Rev. J. C. Dennis officiating. A wife, a daughter and several sons survived him.[77] His grandson Louis B. Toomer, a banker, politician and realtor, became register of the U. S. Treasury. The register boasted that the whites who attempted to deprive him of a local political appointment, actually booted him up to a higher national position. The job paid $10,200, while the custom house job paid only $6,000 a year."[78]

Matilda Taylor (Mother Beasley) was born in New Orleans in 1834 of mixed African and Indian parentage. She came to Savannah and eventually opened a school.[79] It was reported that she remembered "the kindnesses that had been done for her in her childhood by Negroes." And she "devoted her fortune to the founding and maintenance of St. Francis Home an Institution for Negro orphans."[80] In 1869 she married a wealthy mulatto widower, Abraham Beasley. He was a grocer, saloon owner, and restaurateur, and had been probably the only black slaver in the city's history. Beasley had amassed a substantial amount of property in the city, on Skidaway Island and on the Isle of Hope. When he died in September 1877, he left all his property to his wife, who subsequently entered the religious life and reportedly donated most of the property to the Catholic Church.

Matilda Beasley attempted to found an order of Catholic nuns called the Sisters of the Third Order of Saint Francis. It remains unclear whether she was an officially professed Franciscan sister after her one-year novitiate spent in England. Beasley returned to Savannah and she and two other black sisters established a religious lifestyle according to the Franciscan Rule. This nucleus increased to five nuns by 1896, however she failed to obtain official sanction from the Franciscans. This community of black nuns was suppressed in 1898. The Missionary Franciscan Sisters of the Immaculate Conception took over the operation of the orphanage and Mother Beasley retired.[81]

Late in the 1890's, the orphan home, which was established on August 15, 1887, was moved to East Broad Street when St. Benedict's Church was built. That location supported both a church and a school for the benefit of black Catholics. The goal of the home was to "afford a shelter for orphan and destitute children (girls only) of the Diocese of Savannah, regardless of creed." The girls were given a "thorough Christian training," and taught such industrial work as would "enable them to earn an honest livelihood in the future." Some twenty-six children were kept in the school, which was maintained chiefly by charitable gifts.[82] A day school was added in 1907 and the orphan home continued to the 1940's.

Enfeebled by age and ill health, Mother Beasley gave up the work in 1897. In 1901 she occupied a cottage near Sacred Heart Church at 1511 Price Street.

Mother Beasley died in 1903. Having given away "all her property, she has been cared for by the people of Sacred Heart Church. She occupied a cottage near the church and all her needs were supplied by the people of the Diocese." Father Gregory of St. Benedict's "paid a high tribute to her pious life and charitable work."[83] In March 1982, almost 80 years after her death, the city of Savannah dedicated Mother Beasley's park in her honor. The $110,000 project included basketball courts, football and baseball fields and playgrounds.[84]

Susie King Taylor was born a slave on the Isle of Wright in Liberty County August 6, 1848. At the age of seven, she was sent to her grandmother in Savannah. Her great-grandmother had been a midwife in the city and her grandmother sold chickens and eggs in the city market. She was a washerwoman, and operated a boarding house for bachelors, from which she "made a good living." The grandmother sent this precocious child to Mary Woodhouse's school on Bay Lane. After Mary Woodhouse had "taught her all, she knew," she suggested to the grandmother that the girl be sent to another school[85] Taylor next went to a school taught by another outstanding black teacher, Mathilda Taylor (Mother Beasley.).

Taylor, who wrote an account of her ordeals in obtaining an education in Savannah, was one of Woodhouse's most famous students. During the war, Taylor was sent to St. Simon's Island to operate a school for blacks[86] Taylor later also opened her own school and operated it for some years until the students started going to the Beach Institute. Taylor then closed her school. Throughout the agony of the last decades of slavery, black teachers remained steadfast in their determination to educate their people, yet historian Richard Haunton, states that, apart from Sunday schools, Savannah had no educational facilities for blacks, "slave or free."[87]

The Savannah Educational Association, sometimes called the "Colored Educational Association," played a decisive role in channeling the hunger blacks had for education. Cotton shipper Abraham Burke called a meeting of fellow blacks at the First African Baptist Church and organized the Association within weeks after the fall of Savannah to Sherman's forces. The Savannah Educational Association was composed exclusively of colored persons of this city, and the "Teachers are all colored persons, residents of Savannah,"[88] Its purpose was to "establish schools for the improvement of its people, and to raise money to support them." The Rev. Alexander W. Wayman reported that he and the Rev. James Lynch and Elisha Weaver attended this meeting. [89]

The Reverend John Cox, chairman of the Association was born in Savannah in 1807 and had bought his freedom in 1849 for $1,100.00.[90] Cox had been a preacher for about 15 years and in 1865 he was the pastor of the Second African Baptist Church. James Porter of St. Stephen's church was secretary of the Association and the Rev. Ulysses L. Houston; pastor of First Bryan Baptist Church was treasurer. [91] Prof Richard R. Wright, in a talk on the development of black education in Savannah, claimed that this action of the Savannah Educational Association "greatly encouraged" the black populace who "assisted in their efforts to establish these first schools," to the tune of about $900.[92] John Alvord, James Lynch and John French administered an examination and certified ten blacks as teachers. The government gave the blacks two buildings, which they rehabilitated into free schools in January 1865.[93] Blacks had to contend with white indifference to educating blacks and very limited economic resources.

The Bryan Free School was the first school opened by the Savannah Educational Association. It was a large and "commodious building, corner of St. Julian and Barnard Streets, west of the Market."[94] Another source located the building at 418 West Bryan Street. Prof. Gadsden reported the building as located "just across the street from the First African Baptist church, a building that became latterly a fish house."[95] John S. Montmollin, a slave trader, constructed this building about 1850.

The property was bought by prominent Savannah slaver Alexander Bryan, who previously used the premises as a holding pen for slaves.[96] It reportedly still contained "handcuffs, whips" and other artifacts "all giving a faithful description of the hellish business." This building was renamed "Bryan Free School" and had a student body of 450, with James Porter as principal. The Rev. Alexander W. Wayman visited this school and saw a draw full of bills of sale for slaves.[97] James Porter was said to have had "much training (as a teacher) in spite of the penalties threatened under the old regime,"[98] and to have "an excellent education, and is well fitted to fill the trust confided to his care."[99]

The Savannah Educational Association held a mass meeting at the Second African Baptist Church on Green Square, with "at least one thousand persons" in attendance. The aim of the meeting was to raise "an educational fund to be appropriated to the education the colored children of Savannah." The black schools were well represented "which are now in successful operation, numbering about eleven hundred pupils." Charles Bradwell was president, James Porter secretary, and Ulysses Houston was the treasurer. Several distinguished divines addressed the audience as well as black soldiers attached to the Union Army, such as Chaplain Waring of the 102 Massachusetts Volunteers and Sergeants Jones and Burket of the 54 th. Massachusetts Volunteers.[100] An examination was held at the school, on July 12, 1865, "in grammar, ancient and modern history, orthography, geography, arithmetic, elocution, singing and declamation."[101]

There was a very orderly assemblage of some 350 children between the ages of 7 and 17 years, all very neatly dressed. Every student paid strict attention to the teacher. The event opened with a brief religious exercise after which principal, James Porter, conducted the examination. The correspondent was astonished at the great proficiency manifested in the various branches of high school studies. Prizes of books were awarded to the scholars exhibiting the highest proficiency. The first prize was awarded to master James Butler.[102] Some months later the paper expressed the hope that the building "will never again be used for a slave trader's office, but it should be kept for the purpose of educating the black race, and not to sell them." Within weeks the school outgrew its space and the student body was transferred to the Massie School.

The **Oglethorpe Free School** was the second school established by the Savannah Educational Association January 15, 1865.[103] It was located in the "Stiles House" on Fahm Street "near the corner of Joachim and Farm Streets." Another source listed its location as 18 Farm Street. The building bad been formerly used as a Medical College and later as a Confederate Hospital. The paper reported that the building was "through the instrumentality of Divine Providence dedicated to teaching the children of bondage the inestimable blessing of a proper use of liberty and how to act in their new condition of life." Louis B. Toomer was the principal and there was a student-body of 450 students. A. DeLamotta, a Macon native, was his assistant principal.

The *Savannah Republican* regarded Toomer as an "indefatigable principal." The paper reported that during an examination the students behaved in a most orderly manner, giving their undivided attention. Book prizes were awarded to the scholars exhibiting the greatest proficiency and social deportment. The first prize was given to William Marshall and the second went to Elizabeth Hill.[104] The Oglethorpe school was considered by the *Loyal Guardian* to be "the best organized of any we visited in Savannah,"[105] and the principal Louis B. Toomer, was considered to have much ability in the management of the school.

Toomer and his teachers were individuals who, "despite all the obstacles, bitter prejudice, and opposition that has beset them, have continued in the good work of educating and elevating this despised race of people, until their progress is most flattering."[106] Savannah's black leaders, at that juncture, knew exactly what they wanted, political and economic freedom and above all the vehicle for obtaining that goal, an education. The black public also strongly supported the schools. A local paper reported that the work of educating the colored people of the city was progressing "with good results." The paper hoped that "the government will continue to sustain these schools now that they have proved so complete a success."[107] By October the press reported that "upwards of seven hundred colored children have been attending schools conducted by the Savannah Educational Association, under the Superintendence of Messrs. James Porter and L. B. Toomer."[108]

The white Northern teachers of the American Missionary Association were quite amazed that local blacks wanted to maintain full control over their schools and, in fact, felt they could run them better than the whites. Some blacks did not even want whites to teach their young.

General Saxon appointed the Reverend S. W. Magill of the A. M. A., as the Superintendent of Schools for the Freedmen.[109] Magill reported that he had charge of some 700 students, 200 women and 500 children and eight white young female teachers from the North. In March, 1865, Congress approved a bill setting up the Freedmen's Bureau designed to manage all affairs for the welfare of ex-slaves. A second bill of Congress empowered the Bureau to sell or lend any property, which had belonged to Confederates, and to use the proceeds for the schooling of blacks.

The Savannah Educational Association paid monthly salaries of from $15 to $35 to some 38 teachers in 1865. The monthly tuition was one to two dollars. Blacks contributed more than $1,000 to maintain their schools.[110] The *Loyal Georgian* reported that the Association "had failed to pay the teachers for several months" and that without pay, they "have continued their labor for the welfare of their people."[111] The Savannah Educational Association depended very heavily on black support to make up the difference between what the Bureau and religious groups donated to the Association and the actual cost of running its schools.

The seven colored schools closed for the winter of 1866 after conducting examinations. The Yonkers school was located in the basement of the First African Baptist church. The Hospital school located east of the park. The Lamar and Andrew schools at Andrew's chapel on New Street, the Bethlehem High school also on New Street, the Bryan school west of the market and the Oglethorpe school at the old Oglethorpe College building.[112] The depressed economic condition of the city's blacks, caused in part by the huge influx of black migrants into the city, white racism, a high mortality rate for blacks, and general economic dislocation caused by the recent war, were destined to thwart this herculean effort on blacks' part to educate their own children. In April 1866, E.A.Godey, the Superintendent of schools, announced that the new "mission school" at the corner of Price and Harris Streets was to be dedicated.[113] It was to be "used as a school for colored children." A large number of blacks attended the dedication ceremony.[114]

By 1867, the A.M.A. had become more involved in the running of schools in the city. This Association was founded in 1846, as an out-growth of earlier groups, among which was the Amistad Committee, which had engaged in African missions and antislavery activity. Originally non-sectarian, it came to be dominated by the Congregational Church but it worked closely with the Federal authorities. The Bureau, the American Tract Society, the Freedmen's Aid Society, and the A.M.A. at first assisted with the operation of seven colored schools. However, the A.M.A. apparently had a hidden agenda and was biding its time. The "Yankee School marms," sacrificing themselves in what W.E.B.DuBois called the "Ninth Crusade,"[115] were perhaps unwitting pawns in a nefarious scheme to take over all the black schools in the city.

The Reverend James M. Simms gave a lecture at the Third African Baptist Church for the benefit of the Savannah Educational Association. The title of his talk was "The Dealings of God vs. The Dealings of the Nation upon the Negro Question."[116] The Belton Minstrels also invited James Porter to give an address for the benefit of the Association. The Georgia Legislature passed the Savannah School act, which established the permanent Board for the education of white children.

Meanwhile, the black pride embodied in the S.E.A. and the white paternalism of the A.M.A. now pitted against each other, forced a showdown. The opportunity presented itself when the Savannah Education Association was unable to raise the necessary funds to maintain its schools and had to appeal to the A.M.A. for financial aid. Colored schools were short of books, there were insufficient funds to pay the teachers, and the $1.00 to $2.50 per month tuition put a heavy burden on poor parents.[117] Once again, blacks behind Savannah's "Moss Curtain," were destined to face yet another whirlwind, this time the political and economic clout of the American Missionary Association. Though the S.E.A. met all the criteria required for help from the A.M.A., that organization adopted a policy whereby it would help the S.E.A. only on condition that it control the spending of funds and take the major role in running the schools. Jacqueline Jones has demonstrated[118] how the stage was set to gain control of black schools.

Two glorious years of a valiant, though doomed, effort to rid the black community of illiteracy came to naught. Blacks had the will and stamina, but lacked the economic base for such a venture. Nevertheless, the sense of being able "to do something to improve their lot," remained with that generation of blacks for many years and would manifest itself again in subsequent decades. In the end, the American Missionary Association gobbled up the Savannah Educational Association.

A letter to the *Daily News Herald* claimed that there were 3,000 white children of school age in the city and that over 2,000 of them were in school. There were about 1,000 blacks in the colored schools taught by white northerners. The schools for whites were said to be "two grammar schools, two intermediate, and one primary school, with buildings well adapted to purposes of instruction."[119] During August of 1867, the paper asserted: "The people of Savannah, though crippled in resources, have recognized the claims of the colored people and co-operated to improve their condition." Declaring Beach had been a "marked success," the paper commented on the "vast improvements" being done to Beach Institute. The "low one-story school house has been demolished and a spacious edifice is being erected." The building was scheduled to be dedicated the following October.[120]

Beach Institute (1867-1919) was the name given to the newly built school opened in 1867 by the "merged" A.M.A and the gobbled up Savannah Education Association.[121] The Freedman's Bureau constructed the $13,000 building at the corner of Price and Harris Streets. Its namesake, Alfred E. Beach, editor of the Scientific American, had donated funds for purchasing the lot on which the building stood. The school was a neat and substantial frame structure, *55* feet by 60 feet. The first floor contained four large rooms with sliding doors and windows. Four other classrooms and an anteroom were on the second floor. The rooms were well lit and furnished with standard desks and black boards. The whole establishment was said to be "in style, with every convenience that a modern school could have need for."

To the east of the Institute was a teacher's house built in part from black contributions, at the cost of $3,000. The A. M. A. agent in charge of the Savannah District reported at the beginning of 1868 that there were 711 black students, 59 of whom had been free before the war. There were 8 white teachers and 1 black teacher in the school. Some 28 white northerners were teaching in the area at that time. The school had an elementary and normal department. Students were taught the Bible and were well disciplined. They were not allowed to drink, smoke, use profane language or arrive late for school. There was a tuition fee of one to two dollars per month. Some local whites resented these "Yankee teachers" who were trying to "elevate" blacks by teaching them to read and write.

Beach Institute was a public school from October 1874 to February 20, 1878 when it was partially destroyed by a mysterious fire February 21, 1878.[122] Repairs amounted to $7,775.[123] The A.M.A regained control of Beach and the school opened with four teachers and 183 students. Two additional teachers were later employed. The six teachers were Laura Lowell, Sarah Lamotte, Stella Lowe, the principal of the school and Isabelle Beachum. James H. C. Butler and Alice Miller were the only black teachers at Beach at that time. That same year the Chatham Superior Court amended the Board's charter to include "the direction, management, and superintendence of public education of all children, including colored children, or children of African descent, between the ages of six and eighteen years."[124] White children numbered 2,082 in 7 schools while blacks accounted for 1,019 children in two schools.[125] The A.M.A. reclaimed control of the school on March 4, 1878. In response to this move by the A.M.A., the Board of Education transferred the student body to the Fairlawn House at East Broad and Gaston streets.

Prof. George B. Hurd, principal of Beach Institute, wrote an article on the Institute for the *American Missionary* in which he reported the school as founded in 1867 with six hundred students. In 1904 he estimated that "nearly 3, 000 colored children here are without school privileges." He claimed "many of the teachers of the public schools are among its graduates and also a number of well known residents of both sexes." He added, "Beach has a peculiar hold on this community. It has done great work for the uplifting of our people and is destined to do greater work, especially if the services of the present principal are continued and he is given encouragement in the plans he has to further it."[126]

Principal Flora F. Lowe had 312 students and began the school day with devotional exercises and singing. The rest of the time was taken up in the study of "the various branches taught in his school in which students show themselves so proficient as to call forth expressions of surprise and commendation from several gentlemen present, including the examining committee." Miss Flora F. Lowe and James Butler taught the grammar grades. The students excelled "in grammar and arithmetic, early analyzing and preparing difficult sentences." Miss Helen La Motte taught the girls. B. N. Zetter Superintendent of Public Schools in Macon, commented that as regards Butler's grammar class, "there was nothing equal to it in Macon."[127]

In 1886 Beach Institute had a daily attendance of 250 students, but many potential students were turned away for lack of space. A new room was fitted up for the sewing department. The school sought to "impress its pupils with those things which will be of use to them in every day life. The neatness and good discipline of the students was remarkable. This state of affairs was said to "speak volumes for the noble old American Missionary Association, under whose auspices the Beach is run."[128] Prof. Richard Wright, of Augusta, gave a lecture at the Beach Institute Chapel on the topic, "The Progress of the Negro for the Past Twenty Years." Wright claimed that the progress had "been remarkable." Our people "are rising" he said, and "the day will come when this Southland will be theirs."[129]

Sol Johnson praised Beach because "the great good that this institution has done for this community is untold. Hundreds of men and women have received their uplift in life from Beach and all of us of an appreciative turn can do naught but sing the praises of the American Missionary Association and the many teachers who have left their homes to work among us." He also complimented "Prof. Weld and his corps of teachers for the work that they are doing."[130] Beach opened in October 1912 with a new school curriculum comprised of a college preparatory course, a domestic science for girls and mechanics for boys, commercial course and a teachers' course.

The teachers' course was designed "to prepare students not only to pass teachers' examinations but to drill them in methods of teaching and to give them some actual experience in the school room." Printed copies of the new courses were available at the *Savannah Tribune* office, Mrs. Mary E. Harper, 2310 Harden Street, or Beach Institute, 512 Harris Street East.[131] In 1913 Beach's interior was "thoroughly renovated." The ceiling was refurbished and the [132] side repaired and necessary painting done. The building was "as good as new." These repairs were done through the generosity of G. H. Henry of Lincoln, New Hampshire, who gave the school $1,000 for improvements.[133] In May 1912, Beach held its commencement exercises for a class of twenty-three, the largest in its history.

Towards the end of the 1914-1915 school year, a rumor "was widespread" that Beach Institute would be closed. Principal L. M. Rowland wrote a letter to the *Savannah Tribune* in which he explained that the A.M.A. "will be slow to close a school of the standing of Beach, the need of which is so evident, that this a matter that has never come up for consideration and the friends of the school may feel assured that the school will continue." The principal concluded that the "work at Beach is on a higher plane than ever before."[134] In 1917 principal L. M. Rowland described Beach as "the only high school for colored people in the city of Savannah." The school had 92 children in the elementary division, 62 in the secondary, for a total of 154 students. There were 5 white teachers and 1 colored. The school facility and an adjacent the principal's residence was valued at $17,000. The income and expenditure for 1913-1914 was $3, 763.[135] The Congregational Church Brotherhood opened a free kindergarten in the annex of the church with Lucie B. Spencer, a trained kindergarten teacher who graduated from Atlanta University and had worked, as principal at the Haines Institute in Augusta.

In May 1919, word was received that the American Missionary Association intended to close Beach Institute, the oldest black private school in the city having been established in 1867. The school had 125 pupils and went up to the twelfth grade. A few people met at the Tribune office to plan strategy for saving the school. Editor Sol Johnson considered the news:

> "A terrible shock to the community-much like the first news of the untimely death of a life long friend. And it is: for Beach has stood like a sturdy oak for half a century to shelter those who sought her ministrations. Like a mighty lighthouse to save and succor those who struggled to find their way Like the light house Beach has turned the steps of many a wavering soul into the path of definiteness and certain goal; and like the mighty oak, Beach has shed its countless acorns, its myriad unnamable influence all over the land. There, many a humble spirit came to do penance, to find succor, to feel inspiration.
>
> There many a choice spirit, which might have "wasted its sweetness on the desert air," found a new zeal had its fires kindled, and saw its first gleam of the upper air and light. Beach harks back to the darker days, when hope was most all a hopeless people possessed; when those first pioneers braved the unfriendly atmosphere of a clime when hate and revenge and contempt still hung like a miasma, everywhere; when there were few churches, few schools and opportunity was but a guess. Beach came like the flame of a match into a dark cellar loathsome, unkept and hopeless.
>
> The very positive influences of those earlier saints planted in the hearts and minds of those who first at their feet, still live in the sweet lives of the "remnant" that remains, and in the lives of children of those whose lives took direction there. The sacred and holy spirit of the first workers rose high above convention and denomination, and invaded the homes and institutions of all the people of this community.
>
> From Beach went teachers, preachers, Sunday school workers and all who sought to help and to raise a people enslaved to poverty and ignorance and superstition and sin...School conditions for Negroes in Georgia are unsettled and inadequate in most places

> and chaotic and purposeless in many Belabored by systems and regimes unfriendly to Negro cultural advancement, few public institutions are little more than processes which control the mental latitudes of our children, circumscribe their visions and ambition and stifle their aims..."[136]

The Congregational Church gained control of Beach Institute and reopened it as a Continuation School. The A. M. A. officials met with a group of about 80 local blacks to look into the possibility of opining Beach Institute. Architect Holmes stated that the Beach property was "very badly run down and that it would require about $3,000 to put it in proper condition." More than half of those present "subscribed $1050 a year for the support of the work of the A.M.A League. Frank Callen headed the group of fundraisers.[137]

The long search for an education seemed further beyond reach of blacks. They were quite concerned about the shortage of school accommodation available to their children. It was also evident that their erstwhile Northern friends were not as helpful as had been expected. In addition, rumor had it that Beach Institute was about to become a high school.

In July 1872, a group of blacks petitioned City Council "in regards to the education of Negro children."[138] City Council referred the matter to the Board of Education. Blacks decided to pressure the local School Board to provide school accommodation for their children. Blacks petitioned the Board of Education, claiming that, "The Beach Institute will be converted into a High school or College thereby curtailing the use of those facilities which have been offered for the past six years. It will be readily seen that unless more schools are established, hundreds of children will of necessity grow up in ignorance. Your petitioners would, therefore, pray that such measures be taken to prevent the threatened evil."[139]

The black elite was involved in this move. Among them were Dr. William Pollard, Albert Jackson, Charles Middleton, the Rev. Alexander Harris, C.L. DeLamotta, William Campbell, Louis Toomer, John Deveaux, J.Horace McCarthy and Thaddeus MorreL, Bishop Henry M. Turner, James Porter, A. K. DesVerney, the Rev. Ulysses Houston, Simon Mirault, Duncan Scott, William Woodhouse, Simon Mirault Jr., James Simms, Charles Hernandez, J. Lowe, E.D. Butts, John Savage, J.M. Johnson and L. Moore. The Board advised the petitioners to recommend to the A.M.A. to turn Beach Institute over to the Board. A smaller group, made up of Albert Jackson, Dr. William Pollard, the Rev. Alexander Harris, Robert Carter and Charles Middleton met with the A. M. A. to urge the group to transfer Beach to the control of the Board of Education, to be operated as a free public school for blacks.

After much discussion, the Board and the A.M.A. could not agree. The A.M.A. claimed that the Board demanded too much control over its teachers. Schools for blacks in Chatham County had dwindled from 13 in 1865 to five by 1870. It is possible that the Board of Education wanted more control over the education Beach was delivering to black students. Catholic schools were at that time under Board supervision with a somewhat similar arrangement as the A.M.A. demanded. The legislature meanwhile updated its law establishing a statewide public school system in Georgia. The amendment laid the groundwork for an eventual dual system of education under the guise of "separate but equal" facilities for black and white children. Two years later this provision was modified to read, "so far as practical." The sources of income for this state tax for education based on the poll tax, taxes on liquor, shows, and exhibitions. It was to be distributed on a formula that favored white children.

The Board of Education argued that it had made several fruitless attempts to gain control of Negro schools. It claimed that it had "always been willing to educate Negro children and it is hoped the Negroes have come to see that it is to their interest to trust the education of their children to men they have always known rather than to parties who do not understand the wants and character of the race they seek to serve."[140]

About 300 hundred blacks and 100 whites attended a discussion in September 1872 on the best means to obtain an education for black children.[141] About two-thirds of the white children were in publicly financed schools while less than one-third of black children, were in such schools. President Arnold reported: "The subject of schools for colored children in the city has long excited the interest and attention of the Board. As the state has as yet contributed no funds to the county for educational purposes, it has been entirely out of the power of the Board to take any steps in the premises heretofore the Board claimed.[142]

Savannah's blacks were powerless to directly make the Board do their bidding. However, life behind the city's "Moss Curtain" observed certain almost mutually accepted mores. Blacks, therefore, put their faith in petitions and perseverance. They could merely object or try to "shame" whites into "doing the right thing." Some whites prided themselves on their "old South" paternalism in dealing with blacks. Whites had the edge in this power play since they had the ability to set and carry out policy, make and enforce laws. As they did in 1755, whites in the 1800's were using education as a tool for keeping blacks in "due order and subjection." They probably agreed with the *Columbus Daily Sun,* of 1866, which regarded an educated Negro as "a danger threatening our social fabric."[143]

St. Stephen's Episcopal Church School became the first school the Board of Education operated for African Americans. Partly as a response to pressure from blacks, the Board of Education decided to act. As it happened at that time, the church operated a private school with more than 130 children. Several members of this education committee were members of St. Stephen's and could have suggested that the Board take over the operation of their school as a public facility. The Rev. J. Robert Love, the first black cleric to work in the Diocese, reported to the Diocesan

Convention of 1871: "There is also a parish school now in operation, under the direction of an efficient and pious teacher, superintended and aided by myself. The school numbers one hundred and six, with a daily average attendance of eighty."[144] The "pious teacher" was, undoubtedly, James Porter. On November 13, 1872, an examination for teachers was held, and Julia Maynard and Elias Yulee were chosen as teachers for the girls and the Rev. Samuel Sims and Eliza Pollard for the boys. Men were paid a salary of $750 and women $450 per year.

The Board of Education rented the building from St. Stephen's Episcopal Church,[145] and took over the operation of this already existing church school located in the unused parsonage of the church,[146] and made it the first free public school for blacks in the city.[147] The building, located near the corner of Macon and Lincoln streets, was remodeled into four classrooms, with 4 teachers and 178 students.[148] This was six years after the Board was established for the education of white students. Within months the new principal, the Reverend Samuel Sims, died and the Board appointed James Porter in his place.[149]

Mayor Screven thought that the "wise and just efforts of the Board of Education" had encountered some opposition from certain blacks but that the Board had always "aided by intelligent and worthy colored citizens, who, appreciating the benefits of well-directed instruction, contributed their own earnest efforts." The mayor stated, "There are now 220 colored children in regular attendance at the public school at the corner of Macon and Lincoln streets under the instruction of four teachers, employed by the Board of Education, and it is gratifying to be able to state, on the authority of the Superintendent of education, that the behavior of the children is good and their progress is promising." The city ceased directly appropriating money for education in 1881.[150]

A letter to the editor, signed "Truth," found it necessary to make three points which, "should be well known and duly appreciated." These schools were "free, i.e., open to all classes, creeds, and conditions of colored children, without exception and without distinction." The teachers were "not bound to yield to any other authority than those of the Board of Education."

The letter finally reminded its readers "no clique of colored men are establishing these schools; (as some would make us believe) but that the Board of Education (white men) are taking this necessary step to ameliorate the condition of their colored fellow-citizens, and that therefore they (the Board of Education) are the true benefactors."[151] The public school housed in the two-story building at the rear of St. Stephen's Episcopal Church was mysteriously damaged by fire November 22, 1873.[152] The 178 students were transferred to the O'Byrne Building (Scarbrough House) at the corner of West Broad and Pine streets.[153]

The Rev. Richard Bright, West Indian born and a graduate of the General Theological Seminary in New York, was the first African American ordained an Episcopal priest in Georgia. Georgia's Bishop, The Rt. Rev. Cleland K. Nelson ordained Bright at St. Stephens's June 2, 1892.[154] The *Savannah Tribune* regarded the event as, "a fitting tribute to Mr. Bright's ability and a credit to the church and an honor to the race.[155] Bishop H. C. Potter had ordained him a deacon May 24, 1891.[156] Bright, the third West Indian born leader of the congregation eagerly took up the baton of his predecessors. He was but the latest "bearer of the flame" from that remarkable congregation, keeper of that hunger for education that his predecessors in the parish, Mary Woodhouse, James Porter, and Louis B. Toomer all manifested during the hazardous days of slavery.

Within months Bright organized the first black operated kindergarten and primary school in Savannah. He wrote a catechism for his Sunday school, abolished pew rents and made the parish financially independent. A report in the black press stated: "The schoolrooms are ample and spacious-there is no overcrowding; the desks etc., are first class; the rooms are well lighted and ventilated; it is well provided with globes, maps and black boards; a stove in each room keeps the little ones comfortable in cold weather." Students are taken up to the third grade. As a primary school St. Stephen's "is second to none."[157] The *Savannah Tribune* reported that Bright's school was "fully equipped in every way." It added, "Some of Savannah's best families, have patronized the school from the start." The school was established "for the public, for all sorts and conditions." The reporter stated "no child in Savannah ought to be sent to school without having passed through St. Stephen's Kindergarten." There was accommodation for 100 students and the rooms were kept in good condition.[158]

The young rector unexpectedly found himself in the vortex of Savannah's colored schools problem. Bright had solicited funds for his private church school from friends in the North. An article in the *Savannah Morning News* accused Bright of falsely using the plight of the colored public school children to promote the advancement of his own private school at 57 Harris Street. Bright was portrayed as "trying to obtain money under false pretenses." The rector responded to this malicious attack with a letter to the *Savannah Morning News*, which was subsequently published in the *Savannah Tribune.*[159] In his letter, Bright took pains to answer, point by point, all the accusations. He quoted school Superintendent Baker as reporting a year earlier that "The accommodations for the colored children are still very restricted. The rooms in the two school buildings now used are very much crowded, and there were perhaps 800 applicants turned away from the school last year."[160]

Some weeks after the raucous erupted, Bishop Nelson paid his annual visit to St. Stephen's congregation and in his sermon commented on the school controversy. He strongly defended Bright against all his attackers, including school Superintendent Baker. The black paper later reported that "Rev. Bright came out of the school controversy unscorched and his falsifiers have all taken the back track."[161] In 1894 Bright received a call to a church in Florida. St. Stephen's members urged the community to pressure Bright to stay put. He did.[162]

Two years later, the ladies of the congregation prepared a sumptuous feast at the Harris Street Hall in celebration of the rector's anniversary. Lachlan M. Pollard gave the rector a watch. The Rev. Alexander Harris and the Rev. J.J. Durham made speeches.[163] Bright celebrated his tenth anniversary as rector with three special services at 7:30 a.m. 11:00 a.m. and 8:00 p.m. on November 3, 1901. At the 8:00 p.m. service, his sermon dealt with the history of the congregation. The school on Harris Street had "an enrollment of more than a hundred pupils." A sewing school was also in operation. The Rev. Richard Bright preached the Baccalaureate sermon at Beach Institute. Among other things the rector said, "The very first thing, my friends, that God would have you do, is to be industrious." He added, "Render the same service to your own race that you do to the dominant race."[164]

A bazaar, at the Labor Hall at Abercorn and Bryan Streets, was set for the first week in December in order to raise funds to buy some "badly needed pews."[165] In 1906 when Bright celebrated his fifteenth anniversary in the parish, Lachlan Pollard wrote an article in the *Savannah Tribune* praising Bright for having established "the first Kindergarten in Georgia for Negro children and made many sacrifices to carry on this work successfully. The children from his school have made their mark wherever they have gone. While the membership of this parish is not large owing to the many removals to other cities, the spiritual and financial condition is in a most healthy state."[166]

Three years later the Rev. Bright celebrated his eighteenth anniversary as rector. He was complimented for having:

> "Rendered effective service at St. Stephen's since his rectorship and has raised a standard of Church work that many others could profitably imitate. He has made St. Stephen's an independent or self-supporting parish and is building up a loyal parish. Rev. Bright is well liked by the citizens. His interest in the unfortunate ones is well known by those who are very near to him.
>
> Unostentatiously he works and possibly he does more good in this respect than many others. Rev. Bright was the first person in the city some years ago to have printed and distributed circulars on the tuberculosis question. Some time ago he was honored by being appointed Archdeacon of the Diocese of Georgia, a position never before held in the state by one of our race. The *Tribune* commends Rev. Bright for his earnest and effective work and congratulate him on his eighteenth anniversary as rector."[167]

E.B.Beckwith wrote a long article on the school, with the somewhat strange title, "A Practical Step In The Race Problem." Beckwith found Bright to be an individual "possessing rare intellectuality and being powerful of expression, the efforts of Rev. Bright put forth in his sermonic talks and lectures were always literary gems of the first water." Beckwith observed that Bright "has for nearly twenty years devoted himself, his time and his energy to the splendid up building of his own people."[168] The school located at 57 East Harris street, had eighty children divided into kindergarten and primary sections. For a time the children used the large public square in front of the church for recreational purposes, but had to end this practice when they were "subjected to both insults and indignities from the rough element of white children who used to play in the square." Beckwith regarded the school as "one of the noblest struggles for elevation of[169] a race, in the city."[170]

The Rev. Richard Bright resigned in 1913 and moved to Philadelphia. In a letter published by the *Savannah Tribune,* Bright thanked the public for its support over twenty-two years of his ministry in the city, and added that he was not running away from duty, "but rather going in pursuit of a wider sphere of duty and service." The paper also included some letters from white friends who expressed regret that Bright was leaving the city.[171] Editor Sol Johnson described the Rev. Richard Bright as one of Savannah's "most constructive and prominent citizens." He stated, "Seldom, if ever before, has there been a greater universality of regrets expressed over the departure of one of our citizens than there has been over the departure of Rev. Bright." Shortly after his arrival in the city Bright, in 1892, "organized in connection with his church work, the St. Stephen's Kindergarten, the value of which can be measured by the excellence of the boys and girls who received their first literary impressions within its walls." He "was a great organizer and as such succeeded in making St. Stephen's Church one of the strongest Negro Episcopal Churches in the country."[172]

The new rector of St. Stephen's Episcopal Church, the Rev. Dr. Junius L.Taylor, organized a Men's Club towards the end of October, 1913. Its purpose was "to help the young men of the church and the city along all lines. Membership was open to all youth in the city members and non-members." St. Stephen's Episcopal Church's Kindergarten and primary school celebrated its twenty-third year of existence with the rector's wife, Mrs. Lucy Taylor, a graduate of Hampton Institute, as the lead teacher.[173]

Mrs. Eliza Pollard Deveaux, (1855-1952) Miss Sis, as most people called her, was born in Savannah February 15, 1855.[174] She was the daughter of Dr. William Pollard and related by marriage to Jane Deveaux who taught school for some thirty years during slavery. Miss Sis was most likely educated in one of the underground black schools during slavery days. She began her teaching career in the school St. Stephen's Episcopal Church operated in its unused rectory. In 1872, the Board of Education took over this school and not surprisingly some of the teachers, among them Miss Sis and James Porter, who taught in the church operated school, were among the first teachers to be employed by the Board to run the school.

Miss Sis taught for one year in this free school, and then at West Broad Street School from 1873-1898.[175] The *Savannah Tribune* summarized her twenty-six years in the teaching profession by stating: "There are but few teachers in the state with the experience of Mrs. Deveaux, and her place among the corps of teachers will be hard to be filled." She was a strict disciplinarian "of the best kind," and in her class "law and order" always prevailed.

While regretting the resignation of Mrs. Deveaux, the paper remarked that Miss Sis "can rest assured that her labors have been attended with excellent result and that she has the unstinted good will of her colleagues and the hundreds of scholars whom she has taught."[176] She resigned from the teaching profession in 1898 and died at her home, 306 East Park Street, at the age of 97, in 1952. [177] Sol Johnson in an editorial stated:

> "In the passing of Mrs. Eliza (Sis) DeVeaux, Savannah has lost a citizen whose family has influenced the business, social, civic and educational life of this city for more than one hundred years. She was prominent in the affairs of this community before many of those who affectionately knew her as "Miss Sis" were born. She was a teacher in one of the first public schools opened in this county for Negro children, and she remained a teacher in the West Broad Street School for many years, where by both precept and example she as one of a triumvirate of women, did so much to make good and useful citizens of the city's boys and girls. The few of her former students who survive-she outlived most of them-remember her as a sympathetic but firm disciplinarian whose advice and intention were direct and beyond misunderstanding. Mrs.. DeVeaux's devotion to her church was attested by her regular attendance upon its activities up to within the few years. Our community has lost a highly respected citizen; her friends an unswerving champion."[178]

Mrs. Lula E. LaFayette, wife of Albert S. LaFayette, a mail carrier, died in August 1896. She taught at East Broad Street School for several years and was an accomplished dressmaker. Her husband, two young sons and a sister, Mrs. Minnie Walton, survived her. Her funeral from St. Stephen's Episcopal Church "was largely attended."[179]

Sol Johnson in an editorial on the anniversary of St. Stephen's Episcopal Church had this to say:

> "The membership has always been among the more prominent of our citizens. They had much to do with the well being of the city, and the progress of the race. After the inauguration of

educational work for our people at Beach Institute, the property of this church was first used for the public school purposes, which was removed to the Scarbrough Mansion, West Broad and Pine Streets. St. Stephen's is doing a distinctive type of religious work in the city; its ministers being men, well fitted to lead. Its line of colored ministers beginning with Rev. Bright, then Rev. J. L. Taylor, Rev. J. S. Braithwaite, added to the worth of the church.

This reputation is being sustained by the present priest, Rev. Gustave Caution, a young man well prepared to carry forward the work. He has entered heartily in the affairs of the city and increasing friends for the church. Its distinctive membership never refrains from taking an active part in civic affairs and lending leadership to same. In the true history of the city, St. Stephen's will hold a most prominent place."[180]

Catholics had a long and proud tradition of educating blacks in Savannah. Catholic layman Julien Fromantin ran the first known black underground school in Savannah. Sister Jane Francis, white, and Matilda Taylor (Mother Beasley), operated underground schools during slavery. Bishop Verot assisted by the sisters of St. Joseph founded a school for blacks in 1867. In 1874 Benedictine monks from Europe established St. Benedict's parish and a school on Perry Street for urban blacks. The establishment of a school and monastery followed this attempt on the Isle of Hope, which the last terrible yellow fever scourge in 1876 decimated.[181]

The monastic community and school on Skidaway grew to about seven members with two blacks, brother Sirius Palmer from Skidaway Island and brother Rhaban Canonge originally from New Orleans.[182] This endeavor also failed. A community of Poor Clare nuns arrived on the Island with the intention of establishing a school and orphan home for blacks. This petered out in 1879.

Sacred Heart school on Habersham south of Anderson was opened on April 18,1881, as a Catholic free school for coloreds. The Sisters of Mercy took charge of the school in October 1882.[183] Later the *Savannah Morning News* reported, "there are few institutions, founded in Savannah since the war, that have brought more benefits to the Negroes than the church of the Sacred Heart and the school on Lincoln Street, established by the Catholic church of St. James. This building later became a white school in 1883."[184]

In 1885 the Franciscan School on Skidaway opened with great fanfare. The nuns were to operate a day school that "would be free to all colored children in the neighborhood who cannot afford to pay tuition." Bishop Gross believed that "the best way to elevate the Negro is to elevate their women by teaching them virtue and refinement."[185] In 1907 the SMA Fathers took over St. Benedict's parish and the school. The *Savannah Tribune* expressed the view that the "school needs no recommendation. The efficient work accomplished in the past especially in the last year has won the praise and the admiration of all those who have sent their children." The school not only gave "a thorough elementary education, which by no means is inferior to that of any of any public school, but it also imparts to the children solid moral teaching." The paper estimated that "the very presence of the brown robbed Franciscan Nuns has a salutary influence on the children."[186]

The Rev. Ignatius Lissner bought several tracts of land from the owners of the Fellwood tract where "he intends to establish a school for colored children and a home for old and infirm people,"[187] and in 1910 established St. Anthony's in Springfield Terrace.[188] Within months they added a night school headed by Hampton Institute graduate Robert Gibson.[189] The Catholics were in the process of building St. Mary's School at 36th and Bulloch Streets. The two stories and a basement building of durable pressed brick was to be forty-three by seventy-three feet. The paper regarded the school to be "a fitting monument to the Catholics in their untiring efforts to better the advancement of our people in this city." Other Catholic schools were in West Savannah, in Springfield, at Chatham Hall and at St. Benedict's Mission on East Broad Street. [190]

Many "substantial improvements "were made to the four black Catholic schools for the new term beginning September 29, 1913. St. Benedict's at Gaston and East Broad Streets had four Franciscan nuns on staff with the Rev. G. Obrecht as manager. Miss Percy May Tweedy taught St. Augustine's School in Springfield Terrace. St. Anthony's in West Savannah had two teachers, Miss Eliza Rankin and Miss Lucille Brown."[191] On Monday morning, September 30, 1912, four black Catholic schools opened their doors. St. Benedict's at East Broad and Gordon Streets had 8 grades taught by 4 Franciscan sisters. St. Mary's on 36th and Harden Streets "a splendid school building with all modern equipments, "had 5 grades taught by 3 teachers, Miss Gertrude Davis, Miss Coletta Greene and Miss Carrie Elliott." The Rev. J. A. Dahent was the manager of the Most Pure Heart of Mary School on Harden and 36th Streets.

The Rev. J. B. Thuet was in charge of St. Augustine's School with Freddie Campbell "a young and intelligent lady, a graduate of St Benedict's and Beach school will be the only teacher.[192] Many substantial improvements had been made to St. Benedict's school on Gaston and East Broad where the Rev. G. Obrecht was manager. Four Franciscan Sisters taught at the school the school of the Pure Heart of Mary on Harden and 36th• Streets had a change in management as the Rev. E. Peter replaced the Rev. J.A.Dahlent.

By 1920 St. Benedict's School had an enrollment of 400 students and 7 teachers. Several pupils were turned away "because of lack of accommodation." St. Mary's had 130 students and 2 teachers, St. Anthony 90 students and 2 teachers. Catholic school accounted for more than half of all black students in private schools.[193] About 420 blacks registered for the ex-Servicemen evening school at St.

Benedict's School.[194]

Private Schools opened the first week in October 1912, with "a large attendance and the present enrollment surpassing that of last year." The school "known for the past three years as Forest City High School changed its name to the Forest City Industrial School." Among the larger private schools Beach Institute had 141 students and 6 teachers, Berean Baptist Academy 212 pupils and 4 teachers; Swangin School had 120 students and 5 teachers. E. R. Dennis School had 100 students and 3 teachers, the Forest City Industrial School had 91 students and 3 teachers while the Woodruff School had 65 pupils and 2 teachers. In the Catholic schools, St. Benedict's had 160 students, St. Mary's 130, St. Augustine's 40 and St. Anthony's 80 students.[195]

Several private schools expanded their facilities. Among the larger private schools, Beach Institute was thoroughly renovated to the tune of one thousand dollars and its enrollment increased by twenty new students over the previous year. Berean Baptist had ninety-one students fewer and Forest City lost 41. Butler Presbyterian increased by fifteen, while Catholic schools added forty students.[196]

The members of the Savannah area African Methodist Episcopal Churches met at the new St. Philip's A.M.E. church to review plans for the establishment of Central Park High School on White Bluff Road, some three miles from the city.[197] Blacks owned all the lots around the area. The school was intended to accommodate the "large overflow of students, which occurs at Morris Brown every year." George H. Bowen, a prominent local African American real estate agent, and an agent for the Central Park Land Corporation facilitated the purchase.[198] The building costing about $10,000 was opened in 1914. The plant consisted of two buildings, a large three-story brick building and a frame structure. John Maxwell was Principal: there were 6 teachers, and workers, 105 students, of whom 80 were elementary, 25 secondary, and 40 boarders. The school's income was $2,815, with the African Methodist Episcopal Church supplying $2,000 of that amount. Tuition and fees amounted to $250 while other sources were listed as $300. School expenditures were $1,675 and there was an indebtedness of $5,000, which was part of the cost of the recently completed building. The plant was valued at $20,300.

Among the larger private schools, Beach Institute had 241 students and 6 teachers, Berean Baptist Academy had 212 pupils and 4 teachers, and Butler Parochial School had 205 pupils and 4 teachers. Swangin School had 120 students and 5 teachers; the E.R Dennis School had 100 students and 3 teachers. Forest City Industrial School had 91 students and 3 teachers while the Woodruff school had 65 students and 2 teachers. The Congregational Church Brotherhood opened a free kindergarten in the annex of the church with Lucie B. Spencer, a trained kindergarten teacher, as principal. She graduated from Atlanta University and had worked at the Haines Institute in Augusta.[199]

The Swangin School was the largest private school in the city with 208 students, followed by St. Benedict's with 180, the Presbyterian school with 165, Berean Baptist 150, St. Mary's Catholic 145, Beach Institute 98, Dennis School 75, St. Stephen's Episcopal 50, St. Augustine's Episcopal 50, Woodruff 45, First Congregational Free Kindergarten 29, Seventh Day Adventist 20, Glover 14, Foster school 20 and the smaller private schools about 71. The total number of children in colored schools was listed as 4,524.[200]

Mrs. Emma Swangin was principal of the Swangin School. The large two-story building located in the Duffy Street School, was located at West Broad and Duffy streets. It was a two-teacher public school, which was used for about thirteen years and then became the Adelphia Hall. Later Miss Emma Swangin conducted her school in the building.

She began a night school on Tuesday, Wednesday and Thursday nights. There were thirty-two students, most of whom were adults. The method of instruction was "such that it is not at all embarrassing to adults who wish to improve themselves." A parent's auxiliary of the school was recently organized "in order to aid in the advancement of its work." The school applied to a Superior Court judge for incorporation of the school and a board of trustees had been selected.[201]

The Swangin School, the largest black private school in the city, "imbued with the idea of larger service" and with the "advice and support of several prominent citizens," decided to become an independent corporation. The trustees of the Swangin Normal and Industrial Institute purchased a ten-acre tract of land on Augusta Road, four miles from the city, with a frontage of several hundred feet. They planned to relocate the school from its Duffy Street location to a new school on Augusta Road as soon as funds became available.[202]

As the 1920 school year opened, some private schools registered the "largest enrollment most of them ever had." The Seventh Day Adventist School had 100 students and three teachers: Congregational Kindergarten 25 pupils and two teachers, the Yamacraw Kindergarten 33 students and 1 teacher, Mrs. Hulett, 25 students and 1 teacher, and Central Park 16 students and 2 teachers.[203] The Swangin School housed in the Duffy Street Hall, had 208 students. St. Benedict's with 180, the Presbyterian school with 165, Berean Baptist 150, St. Mary's Catholic 145, Beach Institute 98, Dennis School 75, St. Stephen's Episcopal 50, St. Augustine's Episcopal 50, Woodruff 45, First Congregational Free Kindergarten 29, Seventh Day Adventist 20, Glover 14, Foster School 20 and the smaller private schools had a total of about 71 students. The total number of children in colored schools was listed as 4,524.

Haven Industrial Home School (1882-1941) was a school for the education of Negro girls. It was named for Methodist Bishop Gilbert Haven who was born in 1821 and died in 1880. The Women's Division of Christian Service of the Methodist Episcopal Church established the school. Mrs. G. E. Palen of Philadelphia secured funds from her millionaire brother, Jay Gould, and started a small school in the parsonage of Asbury Church. The Methodist women bought a building at the corner of Burroughs and Henry Streets; formerly the suburban residence of Dr. Reppard built in 1886, and transferred the school to that building. In 1896, Miss S. M. Lewis, matron of Haven Industrial School, celebrated her 50th birthday "with a pleasant parlor entertainment consisting of appropriate songs and recitations." The young ladies of the school planned the surprise party and presented her "with a very beautiful gold watch as a token of their love and gratitude."[204]

The Women's Home Missionary Society opened the Mary Haven Home at the Speedwell Mission in 1880. Money from the 1912 sale of the Cuyler Street Haven Home[205] was used by the Methodists to add an annex to Speedwell Mission, a few miles from Savannah. The building was to be a two-story brick structure. The Missionary Society acquired a lot at Sandfly on which Speedwell School for Girls was started. Miss Alexander and Miss Georgia A. Hurd organized the school. As the students increased a larger building was constructed and Miss Hurd was appointed principal.

The new Haven School had two white and two black teachers, with a student body of 65 in an eight-grade elementary school. The school's income was $3,220 for the 1913-14 school year. All of it came from the Women Home Missionary Society and the expenditures were almost entirely for salaries.

Mary Templeton Alexander, born in Yonkers, New York, June 6, 1871, was sent to Savannah to teach at Haven School and she organized one of "the first kindergartens for Negro children in Savannah."[206] A new Haven School costing $75,000 was built on the site later occupied by Bartlett Middle School 207 Montgomery Cross Roads.[207]

In 1920, Haven Home Industrial School on Montgomery Crossroads, five miles from Savannah, and about a mile from Sandfly had an enrollment of 90 students, 80 of them boarders. The school was regarded as "one of the best equipped Negro schools in the state. Its plant is thoroughly modern in every respect and has every convenience for the pupils and teachers."[208] The school had eight grades and the first two years of high school work together with domestic science, arts, and music. A special teacher for chorus and piano music and a domestic science department was enlarged.[209] Laura Mae Allen, Marie Alpharetta Brown, Phyllis Esther Bryan, Carrie Bell Brown, Lula Louise Green, Ruby Euretha Hoover, Nellie Mae Jones, Georgia Evelyn Rock, Gertrude Geraldine Roberts and Dora Lee Smith graduated in 1920.

The school closed in 1932 and the missionaries were assigned to Florida where they taught until retirement. Chatham County School Board bought the building and used it as a school. Miss Alexander retired to the north but returned in 1945, when Miss Hurd retired, and lived with Miss Alexander until she died in 1958. Sol Johnson commented: "Miss Alexander will always be remembered for her quiet devotion to her Christian convictions which influenced the lives of many young women toward better living."[210]

In 1895, the Reverend Joseph Roberts opened a school at Ezra Presbyterian Church, 117 West Broad Street. From 1897 to 1910, the school was conducted at Randolph Street and Oglethorpe Avenue. Later in 1910, the school was operated in the basement of the church at 230 East Broad Street then called Butler Presbyterian church. The Reverend Samuel Redd and his wife, Martha Redd, Mann Williams, Rosa McDonald, Ludile Cooper and Evelyn Grant were the teachers.

Martin J. Crawford's Academy started in 1883 and lasted for more than 20 years. The Reverend J.H. Sengstache established the African Union School in 1871. The Reverend J. Robert Love, the founder of St. Augustine's Episcopal Mission in Yamacraw, opened a school in 1872, [211] and St. James Tabernacle started a school in 1876.

The Baptist Academy began in 1907 in the Longshoreman's Hall at the corner of East Broad and Anderson streets with Alice Brown as principal. From 1911 to 1915 it used the school at the Mechanics Hall. The Seventh Day Adventists opened the Bethel Mission School at 610 West 36 th Street.

Springfield Terrace School (1915-1941) had its beginning in a little church called Hannah's Chapel in 1915, with a few pupils and one teacher, Mrs. Melissa Lewis, organizer and founder. The school then changed to a pay school for a fee of ten cents a week. Seeing the possibilities of a growing community and the need for a public school, the Rev. Grant, then the pastor of Hannah's Chapel assisted the parents in getting up a petition to ask the Board of Education for a teacher. The petition was granted and Mrs. Lewis was appointed to the position. Under her efficient administration, the school continued to grow. She organized a Mother's Club. After several terms of successful teaching, Mrs. Lewis was appointed elsewhere. Mr. Du Henri Brown succeeded her. A valuable asset to the cause of the school was lost when Rev. Grant's term expired as pastor of the church.

The members became dissatisfied with having the school in the church, and charged for its use. However, the people were determined to have a school. They taxed each parent and the Mother's Club gave entertainments to raise money for the rent. This condition existed for a while and finally they decided to move to another place. A dilapidated building on Gwinnett Street was secured. The parents purchased boards, posts and everything essential to make the building comfortable. Mr. Brown organized a night school for the benefit of the grown folks, which he taught without compensation. The work of the Mother's Club had grown so large that Mr. Brown changed the name to "The Parent-Teachers' Association," and joined the State Association. In 1925 a four-room brick veneer school was built facing Johnson Street in the Springfield Terrace plantation for $14, 973 on land donated by the city.[212] Miss O. H. Lee McIver was became principal after Miss Emma Quinney left to go to Florence Street School in 1930.

West Broad Street School was the second school for blacks operated by the Board of Education. James Porter was the first principal of the school in the Scarbrough House. The number of teachers doubled. They included Eliza Pollard, Emma Simpson, Laura Porter (the principal's daughter) Elias Yulee, Emma Higgins, Mary Ingliss and Cornelia Atwell, wife of the new rector of St. Stephen's Episcopal Church. Dr. Arnold, president of the Board of Education, expressed the opinion the new West Broad Street school gave evidence that the "colored people are becoming more and more impressed with the importance of educating their children."[213] A correspondent for the *Savannah Morning News* reported on a visit to West Broad Street School in July 1875. He witnessed some closing exercises, which he found "very creditable indeed."

Some of the copies of the papers were finely executed, especially those of "Porter, Blake, Robinson, Mackey, Ingliss, Lord, Butler and a few others." In sum, the reporter felt that quality of the students' work "argued well for a class of children, many of whom but a few years ago were ignorant of the English alphabet." Two hundred and thirty-one boys were enrolled. Eliza A. Pollard, Laura F. Porter, assisted Principal James Porter and Mattie A. Upshaw.[214] The Scarbrough House was rented for $300 a year. The lease of the building was coming due when the property was put up for sale. George W. De Renne bought the building [215] and on April 30, 1878, donated it to the Board of Education for the education of "persons of African descent."

A codicil in the deed stipulated that no "religious instruction" should be given in the building, and the document further mandated that the building could be used for the education of whites, if the time ever came that there were no blacks in the city.[216] There were 2,070 black students in the system. Porter resigned as principal in 1878 and J.H.C. Butler was appointed as the second principal of West Broad Street School. A four-room annex was built by the Board of Education in 1889 at the cost of $2,000.[217]

Abraham Burke wrote a letter to the editor of the white press appealing to his fellow blacks, claiming that the time had come respond to the "great danger of the lives of our dear children who attend the West Broad Street Free School." He envisioned a drive to raise about $5,000 within a twelve-month period to do the necessary repairs to the building. The editor described Burke as a "well known representative colored man in Savannah." He thought Burke's "fears altogether groundless as to the condition of the West Broad Street Colored School building. It has stood the storms of many a year, and is one of staunchest buildings in the city." He suggested that the money raised should be spent on "the modification and modernization of the building."[218]

A grand jury's report of 1896 stated: "The West Broad Street School we found in a great part entirely unfitted for school purposes. The building erected in the rear of lot is good and well lighted with proper ventilation but the majority of the rooms in the Old Homestead lack light and ventilation. Some of these rooms with 45 to 50 scholars, with one and two windows in them. The building should be replaced with a new and modern one, or else the present building have more windows and doors cut where it is possible to have them so changed."[219] In 1914 the school had 14 classrooms with 750 children who "come mostly from the section of the city known as Yamacraw." The principal, Prof James H. C. Butler, supervised 14 teachers.[220]

East Broad Street School (1878-1941) was the "old Fairlawn Plantation residence," then the Fairlawn Hospital, which served as a school until it was partially destroyed by fire in 1893. Miss Lowe was the first principal.[221] It was originally an eight-room wooden structure located in a small block between Bowen and East Broad Streets and Gaston and Hartridge Streets. Major Bowen owned it, and it became a school in 1878 to accommodate the children displaced by the fire at Beach Institute.[222] The building was raised in 1883,[223] and in April the new Colored School opened with an address by Col. W. H. Woodhouse. Principal H. C. Floyd presided. Captain Mercer president of the Board also addressed the students. A school bell was presented which one of the students rang for the first time. The *Savannah Morning News* described the building as a "handsome edifice and the improvements and conveniences which it enjoys." [224]

In 1892 six more rooms were added at the cost of $5,035. On March 22, 1893 the building was partially destroyed by fire. It was repaired October 1893 with $4,750 from the Federal Emergency Relief Association. This school accommodated children on the eastside of the city. The DeRenne family also donated this building to the School Board to be used "solely for the education of colored children in appreciation of services rendered by their ancestors."[225] Later a four-room annex was added. Soon the school was said to "burst at the seams," with some 100 students in each class room [226]

Blacks were still expressing their concern about the lack of schools for their people. This led the 275 black members of the "Grant and Wilson First District Club" to re-organize themselves into the "Educational Association of the First District." The Board purchased a site on Henry Street for an additional schoolhouse for whites. The black paper hoped "the colored children will not be forgotten in this matter."[227] During the hurricane of September 1896, "All three of the colored school buildings were more or less damaged, the East Broad Street building most. A portion of the roof was blown off and the windows on the east and south sides were blown in."[228] In 1914 the school housed 800 students coming from east of Price Street. The school had a principal and 15 teachers. Lucy Laney was the first principal of East Broad Street School.[229] The building was later brick veneered.[230]

Anderson Street School (1894-1903) at 1312 East Broad Street,[231] was once the Longshoremen's Hall. It was intended to alleviate the overcrowding at East Broad Street School. Superintendent Ashmore stated that the "The building now rented buy the Board for Anderson Street colored school must sooner or later be abandoned. The building is poorly constructed, and badly arranged for school work." Prof. John McIntosh was principal.[232] The board later opened a school in the former St. Paul C.M.E. Church, at the corner of Russell and Maple Streets. Prof Gadsden described the school as having four 20x20 rooms housing at one time 105 children.[233]

Maple Street School was located on the corner of West Maple Street near Russell Street. In 1903, the Board of Education bought this former C. M. E. Church, for $2,250 and remodeled it into a ten-room school. There were four rooms upstairs and four downstairs. The "toilet arrangements for both boys and girls were very poor." The Board later added two rooms. As Prof. Gadsden observed "Somehow or other the Board got the money to build schools for white children. I don't know how they got the money, but these schools were built."[234] Prof John McIntosh was principal of this school that catered to 500 students from the Western section of the city. This school replaced the seven-room Anderson Street School. [235]

Cuyler Street School, a colored public school, was in the planning stages in 1913. It was the first black public school the Board of Education built. The school was expected to cost $40,000, and to be "one of the finest public schools in the south for Negroes and will accommodate about 1,000 children." It was a two-story 21-room structure with a basement, erected at a cost of $ 52,500 on a plot of land 230 by 300 feet at 2201 on Anderson Street between Cuyler Street and Ogeechee Road. The lot was the old ground of the Haven Home School.[236] It was reported to be "the first grammar school of the city to have the industrial and domestic science departments."[237]

The school opened in 1914, with John Wesley Hubert A.M., as Principal. Prof. Hubert of White Plains, Georgia, graduated from Morehouse College, Atlanta, and later did post-graduate work at the University of Chicago. He had been head of the Natural Science Department of Tuskegee Institute, Alabama and head of the Farm School at White Plains, Ga. Prof. Hubert remained the principal of Cuyler School for twenty-five years.

The principal came from a truly illustrious black family. His father, Zack Hubert, was born a slave in Warren County, Georgia. Later he married Camilla Hilman, the daughter of "one of the most prominent Negro families of that County." They had twelve children. John Wesley was the first-born. While serving as principal, he was "active in almost every movement of interest among Negroes in Savannah and Southern Georgia."[238]

The Board announced in August that the two higher grades in the three Negro schools, the seventh and eight would be transferred to the new Cuyler Street school, that ninety minutes would be taken from the academic work and applied on industrial features and that in order to accomplish this some of the less important subjects would be eliminated. Sol Johnson thought, "The Negroes need rightly be exercised over these complicated changes,"[239] He felt that "to force all eight, and seventh grade Negro children to come to the new Cuyler school will unquestionably work hardship on the greater number of them, as the majority of them will be forced to walk long distances, twice a day through all conditions of weather, if they hope to do the work assigned them"[240] The distance the children had to travel was very much an issue.

The Search for more and better schools: The long quest for adequate school accommodation seemed beyond the reach of blacks. James S. Brantley presided and Cyrus Campfield was secretary at a meeting called to investigate the education available to black youths. A committee of four was appointed to prepare a suitable petition to the Board of Education of Chatham County, asking for the establishment of a public school and the creation of a suitable building. About 331 children between the ages of 6 and 16 were not attending school.[241]

Yet another meeting of blacks was held in October, at McIntyre Hall, for hearing an address on education. The *Morning News* considered the address "a skewed political scheme to ensnare the colored people. His references to the Public Schools were false and malicious."[242] The local daily added:

> "It is time for the colored people to become sensible of the truth that the adventurers in our community who pretend to be so anxious to have educational privileges extended to the colored children, are actuated solely by selfish considerations. It is the votes, and not advancement of the colored people that they want.
>
> Having accomplished their corrupt ends, they will turn their dupes adrift to get along the best way they can. If the colored people are really in earnest in the matter of educating their children, they will heartily support, and cheerfully co-operate with the Board in their efforts to establish schools for their children."[243]

John H. Mulligan, "the colored lawyer from the Hub, who, for short we have dubbed "Boston," called on the press to complain against the false accusation that he had been imprisoned in Boston. He was scheduled to deliver an address to blacks in McIntyre's Hall. The *Savannah Morning News,* recommended to blacks that it was "far better for them to follow the teachings of a sensible, conservative, earnest man of their own race than to follow the teachings of a sensible, conservative, earnest man of their own race than to remain forever the dupes of thieving carpet-baggers."[244]

Some conservative blacks gathered in McIntire Hall to hear an address on education from Boston Mulligan. At the beginning there was "not a dozen persons present...however...subsequently there was quite a large crowd." At the end of the meeting the following resolutions were unanimously adopted:

"Whereas, It has been said that the colored people of Savannah, in the county of Chatham, in the State of Georgia, in the United States of America, are ignorant and not fit to enjoy the rights of manhood, and that unless their taxes are paid colored children cannot receive the benefit of free instruction in the public schools.

Resolved, that be it so or not, we will pledge ourselves to our own homes, because we were born here; and further, be it *Resolved*, that we will not go against any of our white brethren who are trying to elevate our race. *Resolved,* that we as a people will live in harmony with all mankind and will obey the laws of the State in which we live, and of the Government of the United States.

Resolved, that we as a people, do put our confidence in said Board, knowing that we were born among them, and that we can tell them of our grievances better than a carpet-bagger, or than any of our race who are trying to sell us, to foster their own selfish ends.

Resolved, that we will live in union with our people, and all measures of the Board of Education, believing firmly that their object is the accomplishment of the best interest of our race."[245]

Harper's Monthly of 1874 reported a "Good deal of absurd prejudice in Savannah against the colored man yet, and although the Board seems inclined to do its duty, the citizens do not urge any elaborate effort to raise Sambo out of ignorance," [246] The Monthly thought blacks needed "good teachers, raised from its own ranks."[247]

Superintendent Baker, in his report for the 1873-74 school year, gave his own interpretation of the pressure blacks were applying to the School Board. He claimed that blacks, "if left alone, they would soon learn to appreciate the honest efforts made in their behalf. Notwithstanding the innuendoes of pretended friends, thrown out for the purpose of exciting prejudice against them, these schools are constantly growing in popularity and usefulness." The Superintendent obviously fancied himself as an expert on blacks. He added that much misrepresentation had been made by designing men as to the action of the board in relation to colored schools. The Board, he claimed, had abundant reason to believe that its action had gained the approval of the "old and settled portion of the colored citizens of Savannah."

Meanwhile, blacks in March, 1880, were involved in a heated debate in the Lone Star Cadets Hall on the question, "Was the Negro Slavery of the U. S., a curse in its character?' It was decided in the affirmative. A.P.Clark and Allen N. Collier argued the affirmative while M. Gibson and R.N.Rutlledge took the negative.[248] The Superintendent of schools reported that there were two colored schools in the city with 24 colored teachers and 1,443 students. The cost per capita per annum was $9.[249] The white press grappled with the direction Negro education should take; finally, it croaked: "the greatest need of the race is moral culture. The mental improvement of the Negro will require a long time before the average of intelligence attains any considerable height."[250]

In 1884, the Board declared that it had information that many blacks were concerned that because of the results of the presidential election of that year; they would not be treated fairly. The Board passed two resolutions stating that it assured the colored people of this city and county that "they may promptly dismiss all such fears as utterly destitute of foundation," and that the colored people "may put implicit faith in the abiding intention of the school authorities of this city and county to do full and entire justice to the educational interests of their children." The Board claimed that the well-informed colored people understand that they have nothing to fear from the Democrats.[251]

Colonel Blanton Duncan of Huntington, Mississippi, wrote an article entitled, "The Future of the Negro Race," in which he expressed the view that the only way to improve the Negro was to make sure that he should "not be educated above his station, but should be educated to fit it. If he is to be the peasant of the South, he should be educated to understand that his happiness and welfare depend upon his being honest, thrifty and reliable."[252] The *Savannah Tribune* reported that "hundreds of children were turned away from the colored schools this year for want of room." The economic hard times due to crop failures also exacerbated the plight of the black community.[253] When school opened for 1886 about 500 colored children could not find accommodation.[254] An "Observer" wrote the *Savannah Tribune* concerning his surveillance of the colored school situation in the city. He appealed to the paper to keep up its pressure on the Board to "have ample school facilities for our children." He claimed that about 500 to 600 children were denied accommodation in the colored schools.[255]

By 1890, a committee of blacks was asked to locate a suitable spot for another school. The Board found the chosen lot was too small. The committee was sent out to find a larger lot but nothing happened. A letter writer to the *Savannah Tribune* observed that it was reported that the colored schools were "filled to their utmost capacity." The previous year it was also stated that those schools were "filled to their utmost capacity." This year, "mirabile dictu," the writer reported, they must be filled beyond their "utmost capacity" because there was no increase in school places. Feigning to be "no metaphysician," the writer suggested that this problem perhaps could be on the next teachers' examination.[256]

In 1892 the *Savannah Tribune* published a letter from "Homo," headed, "Hundreds Turned Away, Sent to the Streets For Their Education." The lack of accommodation for public school children in the city was described as "simply appalling." There were over 3,000 colored school age children but only 1, 388 were in school. In 1889 the Board of Education knew that more than 500 children were turned away and "sent back to the streets to get their diplomas." Moreover, a committee of "three of our most prominent colored men" brought the matter to the attention of the Board but to no avail.

An article in the *Savannah Tribune* entitled "The School Fund," "criticized whites for claiming that they paid half of the school tax used to educate blacks. The author thought that there were "hundreds of the colored population who pay an enormous tax on their property" then there were black convicts "leased out and the money received from that source is devoted to the school fund, thus it is seen that the colored people of the state are not being educated from the pockets of our white friends, but to the contrary they are reaping a part of the fund that is gained by the labor of our people."[257] The Alumni of West Broad Street School organized themselves into a body at the home of the principal, James H.C.Butler.[258]

A letter to the *Savannah Tribune* signed "Tax Payer," asked: "did it ever occur to you, in your tirade about the insufficiency of colored schools, that the colored people get (10) times the more school money than their proportion according to the amount of taxes they pay?"[259] The paper thought "at least the colored citizens especially those who have the prosperity of the city at heart, have always been faithful to their white friends and for it deserves really more at their hands than they are receiving."[260] A Teachers' Aid Society was permanently organized at West Broad Street School with Prof. J.C.Rose as chairman. Miss Anna B. Hooker at No. 7, Fahm Street organized a summer school for boys and girls at 50 cents per month. Music was to be taught at an additional cost of one dollar per month. In 1893, the Emersonian Literary and Social Circle was organized at the residence of Miss Florence Lewis. The objective of the group was to "promote the literary, moral and social growth of its members."

Following another report by Superintendent Baker that some 800 colored children were turned away from schools due to lack of space, the *Savannah Tribune* advanced the proposal that "much good can be accomplished by our large churches" for the mass of our children, "if they would open kindergartens and "take up a collection of about ten cents a month from each member for its maintenance."[261] Perhaps as a consequence of the Superintendent's reports, the Rev. L.B.Maxwell, Attorney A. L. Tucker and a correspondent from the *Savannah Tribune,* visited several colored schools in the city.

The group felt that Beach Institute was "keeping its well-earned reputation as an excellent institution of learning." The team next went to St. Stephen's Episcopal Kindergarten and Primary School and reported that the rector's wife was in charge of the Kindergarten and that she was "doing well in molding the minds of these little ones for future usefulness. Too much praise cannot be given this effort." At East Broad Street School, they found that "some teachers have to contend with sixty and seventy-five scholars, many as three occupying one desk." The ventilation in many rooms was very poor notably in the primary grades.[262] Haven Home School was another school visited. The survey group found the staff "self sacrificing consecrated Christian white women who have left their homes and friends, devoting their lives to the upbringing of our people. A more devoted set of Christian women I have never met." The students were said to be "a happy contented lot of children whose actions showed that they were under the best moral, religious and intellectual training."[263]

In September the paper complained, "Our public school buildings are badly in need of repairs but so far the Board of Education has taken no steps to have this attended to, yet only a few days will elapse before the term commences. Will they attend to this?"[264] By the end of the year, there was a report that the School Board had "resolved to erect another public school building for the colored children and a committee was appointed to select a site for the same."[265] The paper reminded its readers that some years earlier the Board made the same recommendation and it was "loudly commended for the step by the colored citizens," but nothing was done.[266] In 1896, Mrs. Henry Hodge, a white benefactor of several causes among blacks, funded a black kindergarten on Bay Street. The school was named for her husband Henry Wilson Hodge. Mothers were able to leave their children at the center in the morning and fetch them in the afternoon after work.[267]

Colonel Mercer was appointed to the Board in 1888 and served as president from 1894 to 1908. He was clearly a strong advocate of keeping blacks "under due order and subjection," and obviously regarded their lack of education as a very effective tool to achieve that goal. Board president Mercer pointed out that out of 27, 700 tax returns less than 700 were from colored people and the poll tax "of many of them are paid by white men." Sol Johnson expressed shock that "a man of Col. Mercer's standing and ability make such an uncalled for attack upon th colored citizens and their ability in providing for the education of their children." Editor Johnson went on to show that blacks strongly supported merchants who pay the taxes and therefore indirectly paid part of the taxes.[268]

In 1896, Otis Ashmore became the Superintendent of Schools. At the end of his first year he reported, "The colored schools were crowded to their utmost limits," and students would not be accommodated. Sol Johnson did not miss the opportunity to chide his own folks. He stated: "Our boys and girls will continue to be hewers of wood and drawers of water, with few exceptions, until more of our men with means branch out in business so that they can be employed."[269] And: "We are aware of the fact that the school facilities of this city are very much curtailed, yet many parents are too careless about their children getting an education. Parents should stint themselves so as to allow their children this privilege."[270] Governor Candler suggested that increasing education for blacks had the effect of increasing their crime rate, and that education would "ruin" blacks.[271] Blacks who were 47% of the population of Georgia received 25% of the money spent on education. In 1900 the Board opened a school with 169 students at the Old Odd Fellows Hall at 624 West Duffy Street. In another report Ashmore stated, "a serious problem now confronts the Board in providing for the large number of colored children who are unable to find school accommodation at all."

The Evening Press carried a report entitled "The Education of the Negro," in which the author claimed that education "unfits" the Negro "for usefulness."[272] He thought that the schoolhouse at Anderson Street was poorly constructed and not fit to be a school. The *Savannah Tribune* considered the most pressing needs of blacks were "more school facilities for their children." It claimed that there were about 5,000 colored school age children, of whom about 2,199 were in the public school system. Some 3,000 then were unable to secure a school accommodation.[273] About two years later, black citizens organized to open a two-grade school at Duffy Street Hall. Superintendent Ashmore reported in 1902, that "our present school accommodations are not sufficient to meet the demand for colored children, and quite a number have not been able to find room in the schools. The establishment of the Duffy Street School relieved the pressure to some extent, but still there is much need for further accommodation."[274] The Superintendent paid tribute to the "ability and hard worked and poorly paid teachers."

In many grades, the black teachers "have a sufficient number of children for two teachers, yet they have to bend all their energies and might to give all of these children the proper instruction and at the same time maintain discipline." The *Savannah Tribune* chided Ashmore for pointing out the lack of school seats for the colored children but failing to recommend that the Board increase the availability of the school seats. Johnson pointed to the $23,700 spent on Negro education, which was far below "their fair share."[275] In 1902, the Auxiliary Educational Board of Chatham County appointed a committee composed of the Rev. J.J.Durham, Rev. T.B.Lillard and a Tribune representative. This committee presented a petition to the Board on the conditions of the colored schools in the city. The report stated that the four colored schools were "in very crowded condition, some of them having more pupils than seating capacity."

About 1,300 of the students who made application for admittance into the school had been turned away because there was no room for them. The committee found that many of the children had to walk long distances to get to school. Some pupils in Fair Lawn school and East Broad had to walk from Brownsville and the extreme southwestern part of the city. Others who attended West Broad Street School had to walk from the extreme southern and southeastern part of the city.[276] Later this committee's report was referred to the committee on school houses. John Mc Intosh was appointed principal of Maple Street School. Three grades were soon added.[277] In 1914 the building housed 500 students from the westside of the city.

Sol Johnson observed that Maple Street School was intended to:

> "Accommodate the children of the Anderson Street School and those in the two grades in the Duffy Street School. Other than this there will be little room for an increase of the number of children who attended last year, and the thousands of children will be without accommodation. The crying need of these children should

put every race loving man and woman to thinking and only cause a redoubling of efforts to secure facilities for them."[278]

Judge Thomas Norwood gave "An Address on the Negro," in Savannah in 1907, in which he proposed a unique solution to the race problem. The judge advised that all those who married across their race should be expelled from the state or brought to court.[279]

In 1904, Johnson claimed, "Fortunate indeed is the child who was able to be admitted. Each year very many students "are turned away for lack of accommodation and nothing is being done in a tangible way." Johnson thought that both Duffy Street School and Maple Street School, where rooms were added, were "but a drop in a bucket." He regretted that hundreds of children "are growing up in ignorance." Sol Johnson took Col. Mercer to task for trying to keep blacks as "hewers of wood and drawers of water," and strictly subservient to the white race.

He felt that the Board president was "not satisfied with compelling the colored children to study histories and readers containing articles derogatory to the race, he has, it is stated, ordered the pupils of the public schools to sing "Going back to Dixie." Johnson did not object to "the air of Dixie with the proper words but added, "when Col. Mercer paraphrased it with reflective words,"= then it is time for our objections to be raised, and it should be raised in the way that would be telling." Johnson did not want to encourage teachers to "rebel against the Colonel's orders, but they would not be helping the race and would be stultifying themselves in using the words as prepared."[280]

Months later, the Col. Mercer suggested that the core content of the studies conducted in the black school should be reduced by eliminating "superfluous, essentially useless" subjects and recommended that the Board "erect comfortable and substantial, but not expensive" buildings as black schools.[281] The Board adopted the suggestion and referred the matter to a committee of the board. Sol Johnson commented that Mercer "was in a class by himself' and even suggested that the president was "of a good age with much experience, but his age and experience have been affected by years of invalidism, which no doubt is the main cause of his attitude toward us as a race."[282] Johnson felt that Mercer's opinions ran "counter to some of the leading minds of this state and country."[283]

The president also told his Board, "We have been reproached, and with some justice, by many of our best colored citizens for not providing school facilities for a larger proportion of their children as compared with the advantages offered the white children."[284] He then went on to justify his stance. He pleaded limited funds precluded an equal distribution of resources to both races, but added that, since whites "will perpetually fill all offices of trust and responsibility in our city and furnish its capitalists, organizers and rulers, paramount and obvious reasons force a discrimination."

The law, however, entitled the coloreds to equal facilities, "as far as practical." Mercer added, "For the life of me I cannot see how a child destined to pass from the school into domestic service, and to fill during the future the role of a cook, washerwoman, or house servitor, or to spend all the years in the forms of manual labor, or in hoeing cotton or corn, can possibly derive any larger happiness or practical betterment in life by ability critically to construe a sentence in works they have neither time nor chance to read, to name a list of royal plunderers and destroyers, or locate divisions or multiples of earth's surface as much of a terra incognita to them as the mystic and incomprehensible life that trembles in the stars."[285]

Editor Sol Johnson chided Mayor Tiedman for his rather derogatory remarks about blacks, in the matter of blacks and the pool rooms on West Broad Street. Johnson wrote:

> "Of course this may have been an oversight on the part of our esteemed Mayor, or perhaps he is unaware of the fact that there are between three and four thousand Negro children who have been crowded out of the city schools and are crying for an opportunity to find school accommodation somewhere. But whether an oversight or a matter of ignorance, the fact remains only too clearly that there is a sad lack of school facilities for our Negro boys and girls, and on account of not being able to get places in the city schools, they are for the most part running wild in the streets, while their parents are out laboring hard to make ends meet....
>
> It is a shame, a disgrace and immeasurably unfair for us to have to pack our children, like sardines in a box, into the three and a fraction schools which we have while ten beautiful structures adorn the streets of the city for the education of little white boys and girls whose numerical strengths is proportionately the same as that of Negro children. It is a very poor comparison of the distribution of educational funds and it might be made to look a little better by the addition of one new school building to the dilapidated and unsanitary ones we now possess." [286]

In September 1912, Judge Samuel Adams, President of the Board of Education, claimed to have always been in favor of giving the Negro children better advantages of education than "we have given them." He cited the "lack of means, as the reason for the Board's failure to improve the level of black education." He said: "I appreciate the fact that relatively speaking much less has been done for the Negroes than for white children. We are all very much pleased by the purchase of the property on Anderson Street, which has heretofore been used for educational purposes." This purchase will enable the Board of Education to enlarge its usefulness to the colored children." Judge Adams added, "I recognize that the best education for them is that which will fit them for life's duties and work, and therefore that the vocational features should be stressed as far as possible."

Teachers' salaries were raised in 1913, with white principals being raised from $2,000 to $2,180 while colored principals' salaries were raised from $1,200 to $1,380 a year. Most other black teachers received a $45 salary increase.[287] As schools opened for the year some 2,835 Negro children enrolled in the public schools. It was hoped that the opening of the three grades at Haven Home School, two of which were conducted at the Duffy Street Hall, would relieve the usual rush for seats at other public schools. When schools opened however, the three large black schools were "literally besieged by hundreds of parents who got no further than the front doors" and the Haven Home school had its full quota of new pupils long before the hour set for closing. As the *Savannah Tribune* stated "It was pathetic to see the disappointed parents leading their little ones as they departed from the schools."

In 1915, the black paper carried a headline, "Hundreds Not Admitted." The four black schools in Savannah had a total student body of 2,786. West Broad Street had 836, East Broad Street had 700, and Cuyler Street 688 and Maple Street School had 512 students. The paper felt that the "utter lack of adequate accommodation for colored children was never more plainly shown than last Thursday morning during the hours of issuance of admission cards at the schools when hundreds of parents besieged the entrances to the various schools, only to be told that there was no more room."[288] The following week the *Savannah Tribune* reported, "1,500 Negro Children Unable To Get Seats In Public Schools." Most private schools increased their attendance.

By October of the following year, the *Savannah Tribune* carried another startling headline, "Over Seven Hundred Unaccommodated." Cuyler Street School had an enrolment of 1,038 students, East Broad Street School 832, West Broad Street School 820 and Maple Street School had 615 students for a total of 3,305 students. The private schools had 1,055 students.[289] That same year the relatively "laid back" style of black Savannah was jolted as thousands of blacks left by train for Northern cities in search of jobs.[290] Meanwhile, it seemed on the school front the situation was apparently getting worse.

Superintendent Gibson introduced his Plan for Reorganizing the Colored Schools in order to accommodate more students.[291] The plan called for some schools begin double sessions at least in certain grades. The Board authorized this practice, which lasted for the next some 20 years. The new plan "was expected to affect principally the first and second grades at all the schools and the third and sixth grades at Cuyler Street School, the third, fourth and fifth grade at East Broad Street School." Twenty minutes was cut from the fourth, fifth and sixth grades and ten minutes from the third grade. The first and second grades were unaffected. Students in double session began classes at 8 o'clock instead of 9 o'clock. And remained until noon. The afternoon session began at 12:30 until 4:00 o'clock. Compensation for teachers with double sessions was set at time and a half. The principals at the four schools selected which teachers taught double sessions. [292]

Black parents continued their efforts to obtain an education for their children. Mrs. M.L.Ayers was president of the Parent-Teachers Association of Cuyler Street School. At the November meeting of the group the First Aid Committee "with their enthusiastic zeal" supplied the school with many useful remedies for the medicine chest. Many parents were sending plants for the windows. Miss Saffie C. Houston, the Seventh grade teacher, purchased a bookcase for the convenience of the children, "saving them the trouble of taking so many books to and from school." Parents and friends were asked to assist "in paying for the pianos."[293]

Sam Amaca, a black, was arrested for having in his possession a 20-verse poem entitled "Bound for the Promised Land." The poem dealt with the "hardships the Negro has to stand in Georgia under the Crackers' law." J. N. Chisholm and A. P. Walker were judged to have been the main "instigators" scattering the poetry around the city. Five Negroes were arraigned in police court before judge John E. Schwarz in May 1917 on "charges of disorderly conduct by handling written matter which may incite a riot among the colored people of the city, as well as over Georgia." Two men were sentenced to 30 days at the Brown farm and the other three had their cases dismissed.[294]

In June 1919, the *Savannah Tribune* lamented the fact that "every citizen and taxpayer of Chatham realizes the dire need of a Negro high school in Savannah." It hoped that the coming school bond issue would bring about the closing of West Broad Street and Maple street grammar schools replaced by modern sanitary ones. The paper thought "all progressive Savannah, including the Board of Education, will agree that Savannah Negroes need and are entitled to a high school to provide for the further training of those who leave the grammar schools."[295]

Johnson hoped that in the upcoming bond issue "the colored people will get two long-promised, modern schools which are to take the places of Maple Street Church and the ancient, archaic and antique old manse on West Broad Street, called West Broad Street School. East Broad Street School is badly in need of remodeling and renovating and a whole lot could be done for its yards and its sanitation. At least another grammar school is badly needed to accommodate the increasing school population." He though that a "a just distribution of the public funds would dictate that a Negro high school be provided now."[296]

When classes began in October 1919, three of the four black schools were "compelled to resort to the double session system in several of the grades in order to accommodate the overflow. Cuyler Street and East Broad Street had each had "eight double sessions grades while West Broad Street School had four grades in double session, while Maple Street School had one session each day. The Cuyler Street School P.T.A. operated a kindergarten. Cuyler Street School had 1,405 students, East Broad Street 1,041, West Broad 730 and Maple Street School had 537 students.[297]

Sol C. Johnson wrote one of his most reflective and painful editorials titled, "Board and Negro Schools," shortly after the 1919-1920 school bond issue. Johnson stated:

> "It would appear from the little information which filters from the meetings of the Board of Education that little or no consideration is being given the matter of the Negro public school. It is taken by inference that the plans, so far matured, contemplate the erection of a pretentious and thoroughly constructed school building in Chatham Crescent, and a modern up-to-date and spacious building for the Junior High School on the site recently purchased from the Georgia Infirmary.
>
> It may be these two great modern structures will consume the whole issue of the bond for schools amounting to $500,000. In matters of this kind where the public are being expended for the public service, the custodians always look fully to meeting and satisfying the needs and wishes of the whites.
>
> There is no disposition to prorate the expenditures of the public funds, as amongst and for the benefit of blacks and whites on the basis of their relative needs, nay even on the basis of their just dues. This ignoring and neglecting of the Negro element of the community is due to the fact that the Negro does not vote, has no voice in the government under which he lives, has no say in the direction of his public officials and hence is in no position to demand fair consideration, or any consideration for that matter. The Negro is the ward of his community, the suppliant, who gets the crumbs that fall from the rich man's table. Only this and nothing more.
>
> Who can dispute these assertions when he witnesses this manner of handling and apportioning the public funds in every avenue of public funds in every avenue of public benefits and service? Haven't we an excellent array of school buildings for whites in this community as it is? They may not be adequate for the needs but they are magnificent as compared to the archaic old structures provided for Negroes. And there are nearly if not quite as many Negro children of school age in Savannah as white and the reason why no more Negro school children apply for admission is to be

found in the chaotic condition obtaining in the schools themselves.

Negroes are liable for all the taxes or other charges levied by the government for which white men are liable; but Negroes are not being given their just apportionment of the benefits for which their taxes are levied. As we have said before, the Negro's elimination from the politics of his community renders him powerless to secure his just share of the public benefits.

We do not know what the Board of Education has in mind to do about the West Broad Street Negro School and Maple Street School. Surely these tragic spots must flash across their minds as they discuss school improvements. There are no words, which can exaggerate the pathetic and awful aspect of Negro school conditions at these two places. Both impossible of sanitation, particularly well fitted to promote disease and ill health, and veritable death traps from the standpoint of fire or foul weather.

We wonder if the Negro children are being forgotten? We wonder if anybody cares?

There has been lots of talk about the new school to take the place of the West Broad Street School, in the past; but as we have come down nearer to the actual point of spending the bond money, the powers that be have become strangely and ominously silent about this.

Why cannot the Negro children needing so much more, being entitled to their equitable share and capable of furnishing full forty per cent or more of the children of school age in Chatham County, be awarded, say one-fifth of that $500,000?

If Savannah wants to do a real big thing, and then only simple justice, it will build two Negro schools, at once, to replace the old manse on lower West Broad and the old church on Maple Street.

At least, it cannot be out of place to touch the gentlemen of the Board on the shoulders to ask whether they have forgotten us. There certainly can be no harm in knowing our fate if we have been. We helped carry the bonds for the schools as well as those for good roads…."[298]

In February 1920, a group of Morehouse College students performed in the Auditorium. Johnson used the occasion to remind his readers:

"Our people have placed too little emphasis on higher education. They have allowed wild theorists to preach trade and indus-

> trial training so much that we have had very little higher training, and that if we are to have leaders to take the places of those who are now before us, we must train them in such schools as Morehouse and others in that class. There is little danger of our having too many college men. We have entirely too few."[299]

In March Johnson returned to the school situation with an editorial entitled "Negro in Public Education." He recorded the fact that when the bond issue was broached "every Negro preacher appealed from his pulpit to have his congregation register every vote in the church for schools." Black societies and the two black newspapers supported the bond. Blacks were powerless to make the white power structure do its bidding. [300]

The two ministerial alliances representing the black churches in the city and some businessmen, wrote the Board of Education trying to ascertain whether the reports in the white press to the effect that all the bond money would be spent on white schools, was in fact true. The group pointed out that "while at least seven white schools were being built in the city during the past twenty years only one was built for them. The other three buildings now used as school houses were converted into such and two of these are in such poor and dilapidated condition that they are not only a disgrace to the city but a menace to the health of the children attending them."[301]

It was subsequently reported that only a white junior high school would be built.[302] The lack of school accommodation caused an increase in the number of double sessions in the system. There was a total of twenty-six double sessions, six more than the previous year. Cuyler Street School and East Broad Street School had eleven sessions each, West Broad Street School four. Maple Street School did not hold double sessions.[303]

Meanwhile School Superintendent Otis Ashmore, who held that position for more than twenty years, expressed the opinion that he observed blacks to be "undoubtedly deficient in the reasoning faculty. This is not an accident, but is apparently constitutional. The Negro children under my observation display considerable ability in matters, which involve only perception and memory . . . He shows himself unquestionably deficient in logic. He is unable to argue from cause to effect." Ashmore thought the education of blacks beyond secondary level, "entirely useless." [304]

The Rev. L.B.Maxwell, pastor of the First Congregational Church, preached a sermon, printed in the *Savannah Tribune*, in which he referred to the need for more colored schools. He stated, "If any people anywhere at any time ever had any strong grounds upon which to make a plea, we have. The future of our children like Able's blood cries to those in authority for permission to live." He claimed, "Our plea is not based on the fact that almost the same number of white children as colored in our city have more than two times the number of schools we have. We do not care whether the whites have six or sixty. We make our request because we have a direful need. Two public school buildings are not sufficient to accommodate our children."

Prof. J. C. Ross came to Savannah from Windsor, Ontario, Canada, in the latter part of the 1870's and taught in the private schools of the city. In the mid 1880's he was appointed principal of East Broad Street School and remained in that position until his health failed him. He was one of the leading Knights of Pythians in the country, and Supreme Chancellor of the order. He greatly advanced the work of the order in this city.[305]

Ross "was given a leave of absence with part payment on account of his health." Many past students attested to "his ability as a teacher and the deep interest he manifested in their welfare even after they left the school room." It was said that there was "nothing narrow or selfish about Prof. Ross. He was distinctly a man of the people," and "had not a scintilla of selfishness, neither in words nor action," was ever ready and willing to help all "worthy causes and enterprises of the race, especially in encouraging his students after school life in their avocations." and was "among the oldest members of Crescent Lodge of this city." Prof Ross died in 1904 and his remains were buried at Windsor, Ontario. His wife, mother and sister survived him.[306]

Prof. & Mrs. John McIntosh. John McIntosh (1863-1916) was born in Savannah in 1863. He graduated from Atlanta University and after teaching in several rural schools he helped found the Dorchester Academy in Liberty County. In 1880, he was elected to the state legislature from Liberty County. He later returned to Savannah and taught at East Broad Street School from 1894 to 1903. While teaching at East Broad Street School, Prof McIntosh operated a private school in the building during the summer for the benefit of children "who want to catch up in their studies with their classes or keep up with their grades till school re-opens in the fall."[307]

Prof. and Mrs. McIntosh celebrated the birth of a child on October 26, 1893.[308] He served as principal of Anderson Street School for eight years. In 1894, that school was later called Maple Street School, where he served as principal until 1918. The Prof. was "one of the most widely known schoolmen in this section of the state."[309] Prof McIntosh was "prominently connected with the large fraternal organizations of the city," being a member of J. W. Simms Lodge, Masons; Protection Lodge, Odd Fellows; and Crescent Lodge, Knights of Pythias, being one of the founders of the latter.

An editorial following his death declared "The passing of Prof. John McIntosh removes from the ranks of good citizens and from the field of education a most worthy and distinguished character." His teaching career was said to have "touched and influenced many students." He was said to have been "essentially a school man-a school master of yester-years, when innovations and fad and fanciful methods were unknown: he was of the old line type, those who believed that thoroughness and close application to the fundamentals and essentials in education were of prime and imperative importance."

Prof. Mc Intosh was a prominent member of First Congregational Church. Jessie Mae McIntosh, his wife, one son, Sergt. John McIntosh, serving in France, and three daughters, Etta M. Judkins of Washington, D.C; Mabel G. Wright and Jeannie O. McIntosh, survived him.[310] His will left to his wife, a "life interest" in the property at 614 and 618 East Gwinnett Street, with "a reversion to the children." He left half of his interest in the house at 312 East Duffy Street, along with the property at 616 East Gwinnett Street.[311]

Mrs. Ophelia McIntosh was born in Liberty County but came to Savannah at an early age and attended Beach Institute. After completing her studies at Beach she returned to Liberty County and taught in a country school for many years. She married John McIntosh and both of them taught for four years in Liberty County. The couple then moved to Savannah. Ophelia McIntosh was "a woman of a very quiet disposition." Mrs. McIntosh died in 1915. She was a member of First Congregational Church and the Rev. W. L. Cash, the pastor, officiated at her funeral. Many schools sent condolences. Her husband, one son and three daughters survived to cherish her memory.[312]

Prof. James Henry Coy Butler (1852-1921) was born in Savannah April 14, 1852.[313] He probably studied in one of the colored underground schools in the city before going on to Atlanta University. We know almost nothing about his early life and how he managed to attend Atlanta University from which he graduated in 1873. On returning to Savannah, he entered the teaching profession. He, his wife Sarah Butler, and Alice Miller formed a remarkable troika ever pulling their people forward. These unique Atlanta University graduates and West Broad Street School bearers of the flame, who lived together, perhaps established a record.

Principal James H. C. Butler stayed at his post from 1878 to 1921; his wife taught at West Broad Street School from 1875 to 1926, and their friend, Alice Miller, taught at Beach Institute in 1876 then at West Broad Street School from 1877 until 1921, for a total of 143 years from one household. James H. Butler Jr., their son, in a sense extended the tradition of education in that for many years he was the manager of the *Savannah Tribune*.

Butler, the pace setter of the trio, first taught in a one-room school in Dittmersville, then at Beach Institute and finally in 1878, he followed James Porter as principal of West Broad Street School. According to Frank Bynes,[314] Butler joined the Mutual Benevolent Association in 1877, one year after its founding.

The students of Prof Butler's class treated him "to a little surprise party," in his classroom. The paper described Butler as "the indefatigable Principal of West Broad Street School."[315] In 1894 at a joint meeting of the Alumni of both East and

West Broad Streets Schools, held at the Duffy Street Hall, Viola Norwood presented him with a beautiful "silver service" on behalf of the graduates of the class of 1894.[316] During the early part of 1921, some students of West Broad Street school presented principal Butler a "handsome armchair" and a letter which stated in part, "And now that the courses of the sun are rounding out full fifty years of service spent by you in training the young of this community into useful citizenship, we of those who have loved you through all these years feel it a real pleasure to express such an affection as we feel." Prof Butler replied in kind.

His reply of thanks for the students' gift stated, "As I recline in this comfortable chair, I shall think of you, every one of you, and rejoice that it has been my pleasure and privilege to have entered into your lives and to have, in some measure, at least, encouraged you in the way of success. And so your words and deeds of abiding affection are a source of great solace to me in my declining years."[317]

Prof. James H. C. Butler died at his home at 511 Henry Street, October 14, 1921. The *Savannah Tribune* wrote an editorial on Butler's life entitled, "Fifty Years of Service for Others." The *Savannah Morning News* ran an unusually long article on Prof. Butler describing him as "a model public school teacher thorough in the work, he sought to perform, patient with those of little opportunity, and possessing a rare ability in disciplining his school and those who came under his tuteledge."[318] The *Savannah Tribune* also reported that as a "mark of respect for the splendid service which his life has been to this community, several of the banks and business houses closed the afternoon of his funeral."

Five years after his death, the graduates of West Broad Street School commissioned an excellent oil painting of Principal Butler, done by renowned artist Harleston of Charleston, South Carolina. Prof. Robert W. Gadsden, Principal of East Broad Street and Paulsen Street Schools, and a former student of Prof. Butler, presided over the festivities. Gadsden was described as "a product of West Broad Street School."

Mrs. Sarah Flemister Butler retired in 1926. Sol Johnson in an editorial entitled, Service Unsurpassed, regarded her as,

> "Among the pioneers who laid the foundation and built upon it the splendid system of public learning that we are now enjoying. She is the last one of those who begun with her the service, and now she has decided to retire from active work.... Undoubtedly, the life and labor of Mrs. Butler, will be an incentive to others in the system as well as her influence has been to those whom she tutored. All of her former scholars, her co-laborers and friends join in the hearty wish that hers will be a long life of improved health, reflective of the immense good she has unconsciously and unselfishly rendered."[319]

She was utterly faithful in supporting her husband throughout all of his professional life. In recognition of her long years of faithful service, the Board of Education granted her retirement with full pay. The paper reported that, "This is an act never before tendered one of our teachers, and to our knowledge, but to one white teacher."

In January, 1935, the *Savannah Tribune* carried a solemn front page headline, "Beloved Teacher Enters Rest."[320] Mrs. Sarah J. Flemister Butler was dead. The paper declared that her life "was centered in her school work and her interest in the children never waned. This continued to the time of her passing." The writer claimed,

> "No teacher was more beloved than Mrs. Butler, and not any of them surpassed her in encouraging higher education. The trio consisting of herself, Miss Alice B. Miller and Mr. Butler were the cause of scores of boys and girls attending college, even giving of their means in assisting the worthy ones whose parents were not able to do fully their part." life was centered in her school work and her interest in the children never waned." The writer went on to say: "No teacher was more beloved than Mrs. Butler, and not any of them surpassed her in encouraging higher education.... Mrs. Butler was an outstanding character. Positive, but kindly in her manner, frowning upon the frivolous, but ever ready to lend encouragement.[321]

John Wesley Dobbs, grandfather of Atlanta Mayor Albert Maynard Jackson, and prominent Mason in the state, attended West Broad Street School as a youth. He recalled Miss Sarah, as the children called her, as "positive, direct and almost dramatic in the manner in which she unfolded the truths as laid down in the text books." Dobbs was a classmate of the Butlers' only son, James, and recalled that as an adult in later years, he would stop off at the school when in the city, to see his former teacher and reminisce on the good old days. He thought, "It would be impossible to even attempt to estimate the worth of such a life as hers."[1]
The Butlers and Alice Miller were active members of First Congregational Church. As with her husband, the funeral was held at her home. The Rev. A. D. Pinckney, pastor of First Congregational Church, conducted the service with the assistance of the Rev. Gustave H. Caution, rector of St. Stephen's Episcopal Church. Madeline R. Shivery, Nettie A. Gordon, Prof. Gadsden and Romeo M. Smith, with Lucile B. Johnson at the piano provided the music for the occasion.

The quartet also sang at the gravesite. Her former students, Prof. Robert W. Gadsden, funeral director Lachlan Pollard, Romeo M. Smith and *Savannah Tribune* owner and publisher Sol C. Johnson were the pallbearers. The paper reported: "The quietness of the service at the home and grave reflected her life in its simplicity and impressiveness. There were no outbursts of feeling, but inwardly, all mourned the passing of Savannah's noble character, whose memory will be ever retained by those who knew of her worth." A son James H. Butler, a daughter-in-law, and a grand daughter survived her, Louise Butler Walker, a senior at the University of Wisconsin, survived her.[2]

Miss Alice Miller was born in Rome, Georgia, and came to the city after graduating from Atlanta University in October 1876. She joined the faculty of West Broad Street School. The Board's record differs somewhat from the *Savannah Tribune's* story. Miss Alice B. Miller died May 25, 1921. The *Savannah Tribune* reported that on the day of her death "as usual, she conducted her class room work and retired that night." The paper stated that Miller's death represented the "Passing of another of the strongest forces for education and uplift among the colored people in this city." She was regarded as "one of the pioneers of education among our people in this city and section. She had served through those sterner years when there was little or no interest in Negro education."

Sol Johnson's editorial entitled "Dying in Harness," proclaimed her "a most excellent example of the true teacher, possessing all the qualities of manner, character and splendid fitness for her worthy work." She was intensely interested in the public civic and charitable affairs of the community. She was said to have been a woman of "strong and independent conviction." Miller had served as a teacher in West Broad Street School for forty-three years.[3] She was a member of First Congregational Church and her funeral service was held at her home.

Robert Washington Gadsden (1874-1979) was born May 1, 1874, in Sandersville, Washington County, Georgia, to Isaac James and Lucy Noble Gadsden. His father was born in Charleston, South Carolina, and his mother in Edgefield, South Carolina. In his unpublished seventy-eight-page autobiography, *A Story of my life,* Gadsden referred to the time of his birth by stating, "This was an awful time in which to be born."[4] His father, a coach painter, had hoped to move to a larger city in order to improve his work prospects. His aunt, Judy McKnight, was the town's midwife. The final "encouragement" to leave Sandersville came from an unexpected source.

The Ku Klux Klan knocked at the family's door one night, in search of his father's friend, Bob Allen. During their search of the premises, the mob discovered his father's shotgun and taking it outside, smashed it against a tree, breaking it into small pieces. Shortly after this incident, the family went to Savannah to attend a weeklong festival and were so charmed by the city that his father finally decided to relocate there. In October 1879, the family took up temporary residence at the home of the De Lyons family, at the corner of Wayne and Montgomery streets. His mother's sister, Aunt Maria Brown, later procured a place for them to stay at the southwest corner of Jones and Bull Streets.

Young Robert was sent to Mrs. Matilda M. Monroe's private school. Carol Trotty, her sister Norma, and Katie Benjamin, Rose Ann Drayton and Willie Jefferson were his classmates at this school. There he learned to read from the green primer and the blue back spelling book. Completing the third grade, Robert was sent to West Broad Street School and was admitted to the fourth grade. James H. C. Butler was Principal of the school. Singing rehearsals were held each Friday. Gadsden regarded these exercises as a "most enjoyable experience." The leader "had no instrument for guidance or accompaniment except a tuning fork."[5]

Usually the Principal and four teachers stood in front of the class and sang the complete song. Then the children sang a bar or two after the teachers had done so. Teachers Lydia Cary, Alice Miller and George S. Williams sang soprano, alto, and bass, respectively, while the Principal sang the tenor parts and conducted. Jim Coffee, Dick Bryan, Lou Hines, Josephine Anderson, Anna Pappy, Henry Johnson, and his brother Jack were the outstanding singers. Gadsden thought his public school curriculum was "probably as good as that of any other city in the state." He studied from Monteith's *Geographies,* Robinson's *Series of Arithmetic*, Barnes' *Readers and Histories*, Swinton's *History*, Reed's *Spellers* and Harvey's *Grammars.* He also learned about famous African Americans such as Crispus Attucks, Peter Salem, Solomon Poor, the 54th Massachusetts Regiment (Negro) under the command of Col. Robert Shaw, Harriet Tubman, Sojourner Truth, Helen Craft, Denmark Vessey, Nat Turner, and other Negro heroes. Gadsden, in his *Autobiography* added, "The Negro student in High school today knows very little about the Negro's contribution to American history, because books containing such information are taboo." Gadsden graduated from West Broad Street School in 1890.

A long quote from Gadsden's *Autobiography* is perhaps necessary in order to try to re-capture a decisive moment in his life. He wrote:

> "I wanted very much to go to Atlanta University, because I knew most of my elementary teachers went there. I knew that Albert Ashton, John Taylor, James Coffee and Alonzo Baker went there, too, but I did not dream that I would ever get there. And I cannot express the feeling that came over me when my mother informed me that I was to go there also."[327]

As he would recall later, "going to Atlanta was one of the most significant events in my life."

At Atlanta University, Gadsden observed that many young men were unable to cope with the rather strict rules of the day. Smoking on or off campus, drinking, or "slipping out at night," were sternly forbidden. At that time the school authorities emphasized that they were acting "in loco parentis," and demanded the same respect and obedience. Many students needed to work during the summer.

Many city boys became hotel bellhops, waiters and porters, and then found jobs as Pullman porters. As he wrote: "None of the Savannah boys who entered college when I did were able to remain in college." They were too young and inexperienced to get county schools to teach during the summer months. During the first three years, Gadsden himself almost dropped out. The presiding A.M.E. elder of an Effingham County School expressed great interest in him. Gadsden packed his canvas telescope bag and set out for the area. The trip however, proved fruitless, as no teachers were in fact needed.

Alice Miller, one of his teachers in elementary school, was a great encouragement and insisted that he persevere. The summer of 1892 was about the "toughest of all so far as getting something to do, was concerned." Gadsden got a job to take a cow to a pasture in the morning and bring her back in the afternoon. He was soon joined by other youths and they spent their time "singing-harmonizing." They eventually formed a quartet, calling themselves the Southern Stars.

Back home for the summer of 1893, Gadsden got a job as a bar-boy at $4.50 per week at Irishman John J. Sullivan's Café. This relieved the pressure on his washerwoman mother who suffered from asthma attacks. He wrote, "I saved my earnings as bar-boy and was able to buy all the clothes I would need during my freshman year. This helped my morale beyond my ability to put into words all this meant to me." Gadsden participated in the all campus activities at Atlanta University. In the fall of 1896, Gadsden participated in what may have been the first Negro intercollegiate football game.[328] At the time, he was a fullback who weighed less than 140 pounds and played the game between Atlanta University and Tuskegee Institute.[329]

He also toured many northern cities with the original Atlanta University Quartet, which included, at one time, James Weldon Johnson, composer of the Negro anthem *Lift Every Voice and Sing,* his brother Rosamond Johnson and George Towns. The quartet sang to raise money for the University. Gadsden graduated from Atlanta University in 1897. He taught at Delaware State College and at Knox Institute, in Athens, Georgia, and worked for several summers on the instructional staff at Albany State College and Georgia State College.[330]

In the fall of 1902, Gadsden began his teaching career in the Savannah/ Chatham school system. When a local branch of the Young Men's Christian Association was organized at Morse's Hall in 1902, Prof. Gadsden was elected temporary chairman.[331] He was appointed Principal of East Broad Street School in 1904,[332] and remained in that position until he retired in 1947. In addition he served as Principal of Maple Street School for six years and Principal of Paulsen Street School for twenty-four years. Gadsden's father, Isaac Gadsden, died in 1907 and was buried from St. Phillip's A. M. E. Monumental Church.[333] His mother died in 1912 and was also buried from St. Philip Monumental on Hull Street.

In 1913, James Weldon Johnson visited Savannah and was invited to address a civic gathering. At that time his "famous National Anthem was little known and its music difficult to secure." His friends wanted to surprise him by having it sung. A few copies of the music were obtained from Atlanta University and Prof. Robert W. Gadsden trained and directed a small chorus and "on the night of the gathering Lift Every Voice And Sing, was rendered for the first time in Savannah, proving quite a pleasing surprise to him. It touched him keenly as can be remembered by those who had the pleasure of being present." [334]

In 1929 a group of students, teachers and the general public, honored Gadsden for his twenty-five years as principal of East Broad Street School. Sol Johnson editorialized that Prof. Gadsden had led "an administration of efficiency and progress. Those best acquainted with the school system credit Prof. Gadsden as being one of its valuable assets. He keeps in the vanguard of school ideas, compelling preparation on the part of teachers, who loyally join in turning out children with records unsurpassed. The two schools presided over by Prof. Gadsden are ideal ones, and of much credit to the system." Johnson concluded, Prof. Gadsden "in his unassuming way is doing so much to put the stamp of worth upon our children."[335]

Gadsden fulfilled the resident requirement and was a candidate for the M. A. degree but never completed his thesis.[336] In 1940 a few leading citizens celebrated Prof. Gadsden's some thirty-eight years in the teaching profession. Prof. Gadsden was praised for the many years he served the public in "a most generous in a most acceptable manner and given generously of his wide knowledge and able assistance to those to those community efforts which tended to advance the educational, religious and cultural life of the city. Unaffected by the success that has attended his long Principalship over Savannah's second oldest Negro public school. Robert W. Gadsden, suave, modest, thoroughly capable, aggressive and ever conversant with the modern trends in his profession, has been a fitting example to the youth who have come under him and a credit to his fellow citizens who join his workers in felicitating him upon the milestone he has just passed."[337]

The Board of Education recognized his 45-year contribution to the education of the city's black children by naming a school in his honor.[338] Gadsden School is located at 919 May Street in the Currytown section of West Savannah. In his youth, Gadsden was a member of St. Philip Monumental A.M.E. Church in Yamacraw. Sometime after he returned from Atlanta, he joined the Congregational Church, and, aside from his family, it would be safe to say that his church held a greater place in his life than many of his other interests. His dedication expressed itself in the many and varied activities in which he participated and in the offices he held.

An ardent churchman, Prof. Gadsden was the superintendent of the Sunday school, supervisor of the church kindergarten, the organist, choir director, and clerk, a member of the memorial committee, chairman of the deacons for twenty-five years, and director of Every Member Canvass. He served as chairman of a survey committee, which developed a very well received report, entitled, "We Look at Ourselves." He was a member of the pulpit supply committee, and chairman of a committee to revise the constitution of the church. He also held the position of Deacon Emeritus.

Gadsden joined the Prince Hall Masons in 1904 and during his many years of service held many important positions in the Grand Lodge. He was a past Master of Pythagoras Lodge No. 11. He served a long tenure as a Grand Lodge officer and the late Grand Master John Wesley Dobbs appointed him chairman of the influential committee on Foreign Correspondence. Because of his work in the field of free Masons, Gadsden was made a thirty-third degree Mason in 1957. He also held membership in Omega Psi Phi Fraternity.

Prof. Gadsden married Laura Louise Maxwell Hutchinson at Lucy A. Lucas's residence on Hartridge Street with the Rev. W. L. Cash officiating, and "only the more intimate friends were present."[339] Laura Gadsden was born April 6, 1876 and was a teacher at East Broad Street School,[340] and a Sunday school teacher at Beth-Eden Baptist Church.[341] She was a member of the Frances E. Harper Literary and Social Circle founded in 1900. The couple had four children, Lucy, Margaret, Robert, and Eugene. Mrs. Laura Gadsden died October 1919.

Prof. Gadsden was president of the Teachers' Culture Club; charter member of the re-organized GTEA and was Chatham County's delegate to the Conference on Negro Education, Washington, D.C., in 1934. He was director of the Music Lovers Club of the Urban League, and a charter member of the Hub. Gadsden was a charter member of the local Negro Boy Scouts of America, and served for more than twenty years as chairman of Advancement and was second oldest Silver Beaver man. Gadsden was chairman of the Associate Board of the Chatham-Savannah T. B. Association, and a member of the Board of Trustees of Charity Hospital.

His second wife, Mrs. Geneva L. Stiles-Gadsden, was born in Savannah June 27, 1892, the child of Charles Stiles and Annie Smith Stiles. She attended the local public schools and then graduated from the Georgia State Industrial College for Colored Youth. Geneva Stiles taught at Antioch School from 1905 to 1912, then from 1912 to 1930 at East Broad Street School, and finally from 1930 to 1940 she taught at Florence Street School. She taught school for about 45 years. She died in 1957.[342] One of the Gadsden children, Margaret Caution, stated: "Mrs. Geneva Stiles Gadsden was a great influence on the lives of the four Gadsden children, as far as social graces, church membership and family cohesiveness. She was a strict Episcopalian and passed on her love of the church to the girls. The boys went to their father's church."[343]

During January and February of 1967, Professor Gadsden gave a series of Friday night lectures on black life in Savannah. Sponsored by the local branch of the National Association for the Advancement of Colored People, these talks in the

Public Library were titled, *The Negro's Political and Civic Life, The Education of the Negro, Negro Churches, Businesses and Fraternal Organizations,* and *Old Savannah, A Typical Day in the Life of a Savannahian, 80 Years Ago.* Some of the talks were later published by the Association and are located in the Public Library. Governor Busbee in a message to Prof. Gadsden on his 102nd birthday stated: "reaching 102 years of age is a rare and enviable accomplishment and I am proud of you."[344] The *Savannah Evening Press* of June 23, 1979, reported that Gadsden's "recollections of early days in Savannah are preserved on tape in the NAACP Historical Library."

These wide ranging topics depict Gadsden's interest in the unfolding fate of African Americans in the city. Not surprisingly, his civic affiliations also made him very influential in the social milieu of black Savannah. When Boy Scouting came to Jim Crow Savannah, blacks were not allowed to join the movement. Later Gadsden was one of the leaders propagating the Boy Scout movement among blacks.

He served as chairman of advancement for the Negro Scout District, on the Divisional Committee of the Boy Scouts, as chairman of the Savannah Inter-Racial Committee, chairman of the Citizens' Committee and a member of the Mayor's Advisory Committee. Gadsden was secretary of the Board of Directors of the Y.M.C.A., a member of the Associate Board of the Chatham-Savannah Tuberculosis Association, member of Mu Phi Chapter of Omega Psi Phi Fraternity and Illustrious Potentate of the Mystic Shrine.

In the October 3, 1914, special edition of the *Savannah Tribune* Prof. Gadsden wrote an article entitled "Public Schools of Savannah," which gave the history of black schools in the city. In February 1930, in his column "Something to Think About," Gadsden wrote about the development of black education in Savannah.[345] Then in 1934, when Prof. Kermit O. Smalls published the *Year Book of Colored Savannah,* Prof. Gadsden contributed an article entitled *Education,* on the education of blacks. Shortly after this publication, and for several years, Prof. Gadsden wrote a weekly article in the *Savannah Tribune* entitled, "Something to Think About." When in 1952, School Superintendent William Early decided to celebrate the 80th anniversary of the first public school for blacks, operated by the Board of Education, Prof. Gadsden was commissioned to tell the story. Gadsden's paper was entitled *Eightieth Anniversary of the First Negro Public School in Chatham County.*

The Rev. Dr. Ralph Mark Gilbert, president of the Savannah Branch of the National Association for the Advancement of Colored People, led other community leaders in honoring Prof. Gadsden with a city-wide banquet following his retirement. In April 1974, the 27th year of his retirement, Gadsden's children and their spouses, Mr. and Mrs. Robert W. Gadsden Jr. of Washington, D. C., Mrs. Lucy G. Solomon, and the Rev. and Mrs. Gustave H. Caution and Attorney and Mrs. Eugene H. Gadsden, hosted a gala reception for their father's 100th birthday.[346]

In 1968 a reporter asked Prof Gadsden how long he would like to live. Gadsden replied: "As long as I am useful and no handicap or problem to anyone."[347] The record shows that he also had a prophetic streak in him. Prof. Robert W. Gadsden died June 22, 1979, at age 105.[348] He died as he had lived, of use to many people and an inspiration to not a few. Almost to the end of his life, he visited the school named for him.[349] Prof. Gadsden was the oldest retiree in the Savannah/Chatham school system and the oldest in the state. Due to a vacancy in the pastorate at First Congregation Church at that time, and at the request of his children, the author, then rector of St. Matthew's Episcopal Church had the distinct honor to conduct Prof. Gadsden's funeral at the Congregational Church.

Lucy Lucas Gadsden was born in Savannah, March 24, 1907, in a small duplex house on 32nd Street, between Martin L. King Jr., Blvd., and Montgomery Street. She was educated at Haven Home Kindergarten, then attended first grade in Haven School. Later Prof. Burksteiner privately educated her. She then went to Atlanta University. Her sister, Margaret Gadsden, Nona Mitchell (Hopkins), and Edith Jackson (Jones), were a few of the Savannah students attending Atlanta University. Lucy graduated in 1926 and became a kindergarten teacher in Birmingham, Alabama. She next taught in Hamlet, North Carolina, for one year and then returned to Savannah and taught in several elementary schools.

Lucy Lucas Gadsden married Henry Anthony Solomon June 14, 1934, at St. Stephen's Episcopal Church. He was born October 15, 1906, and was educated in the local public schools. He worked as a letter carrier for over twenty years. They had three children. A son died in infancy. Laura Geneva Solomon married William Vault. Laura Vault graduated from Talladega University and taught in Washington for many years and retiring there in 1998. They had two children, Brooks and Robert Vault. The second daughter, Margaret Louise Solomon, also a graduate of Talladega University, married Judge George H. Brown. They had two children, Laurita and George H. Brown, Jr. Margaret taught for some years and died in 1994.

Lucy Solomon continued her education at Savannah State College, the University of Georgia, and South Carolina State University at Orangeburg, South Carolina. She retired in 1972, after forty-six years in the teaching profession, as the librarian of Gadsden Elementary School. Henry A. Solomon died February 7, 1960.

Margaret Gadsden was born in Savannah April 24, 1908. She attended Haven Home Kindergarten and did her first grade in Haven Home School. She and her sister Lucy joined St. Stephen's Episcopal Church in their teen years. She "fell totally in love with the church. The order of the service, the sophistication of the priest, the history and use of the physical properties of the church, the vestments, the acolytes and the choir al combined."[350]

Since there was no high school for blacks in Savannah, the Rev. Gregory, pastor of the Congregational Church conducted high school classes at Beach Institute for mid-term graduates. Margaret completed high school, and two years of normal training as a kindergarten teacher graduating with honors from Atlanta University in 1927. She taught for several years in Hamlet, North Carolina, returning to Savannah in 1931. Most of her teaching years were spent at Haven Home School.

In 1945 Margaret joined the WAAC and was stationed at Fort Devons, Massachusetts, Fort Des Moines in Iowa and Fort Leonard Wood in Missouri. Shortly after demobilization, she married the Rev. Gustave Caution, rector of St. Matthew's Episcopal Church, June 7, 1947. Father Caution died in 1980. She found the rector's life "somewhat lonely." Margie Caution served as organist of both St. Stephen's and St. Matthew's Churches for many, many years.[351] She received her B.A. from Georgia State College in 1947. Encouraged by Georgia's offer pay for the graduate education of blacks who left the state, since local mores precluded blacks from obtaining such degrees in the state, Margaret Caution obtained her M.A. in Education, from Colombia University in New York in 1959. In 1957, Mrs. Caution was elected teacher of the year for Haven Home School. She served as secretary of the C.C.T.A., and was chairman of the sixth grade countywide group. She taught school for 44 years and retired in 1972. Thus Prof. Gadsden and his two daughters, Lucy and Margaret, taught school for a total of 135 years. In 1988 Margie Caution married Raymond Snype. He died in 1993.

Robert Washington Gadsden Jr., was born March 6, 1910, in Savannah and received his early education in Savannah's public schools then attended the Georgia State Industrial College for Colored Youths, now Savannah State University, graduating with a Bachelor of Science and later obtained a Master's in Social Work from Atlanta University. He taught school for a few years and later worked as a social worker in Chicago and New York. Gadsden served with the rank of sergeant in the United States Army during World War 11 in India. Robert W. Gadsden Jr., worked for the Federal Government in Washington D.C, from the 1950's until his retirement in 1973. He was married to Dr. Marie Davis Gadsden of Washington, D. C. He died in 1993.

Eugene H. Gadsden was born February 4, 1912, in Savannah. He attended the local public schools, and graduated from Cuyler High School. The graduation exercises were unique that year as both the junior and senior graduations were held together. He was the valedictorian of the senior high class, Elbert Kelson was salutatorian and Wilhelmina Girardeau took third honors.[352] Gadsden next did his pre-college work at the Georgia State College for Colored Youths, then went to Lincoln University and graduated in 1937. Unable, for financial reasons, to attempt his first love, the study of medicine, Gadsden decided to pursue a legal education at North Carolina Central University.

Prior to studying law he was connected with Yamacraw Village, serving as a management aide. While a law student he helped integrate nurses in a federal hospital in Durham. He obtained his law degree in 1953 and on passing the North Carolina bar, Attorney Gadsden was co-counsel in two civil rights lawsuits, one of which resulted in the admission of black students to the University of North Carolina.[353] He passed the Georgia Bar examination in 1955.[354] He opened his law office at 458 ° West Broad Street.[355] In May, 1962, was admitted to practice before the Federal District Court.

In 1965 he became the first African American lawyer to be admitted to the Savannah Bar Association and was named assistant Chatham County attorney. Gadsden was in the vortex of the civil rights struggle in Savannah and defended many arrested protestors. The *Nathaniel Wright et al. vs. The State of Georgia,* was taken to the Supreme Court of the United States and established the right of black citizens to use all public recreational facilities of Savannah and Chatham County. He was local counsel from 1962-1967 in the school desegregation suit with the Board of Education. Wesley W. Law, longtime civil rights activist and former president of the local NAACP branch, stated: "as a trained lawyer and a member of a well-known family, Gadsden earned the respect of blacks and whites alike." Former city mayor Rousakis commented: "He was a pillar of strength in this community when we needed him the most. He wasn't afraid to lead."[356] *Savannah Morning News,* August 10, 2000.

Eugene Gadsden was, however, very successful as an attorney for the local branch of the NAACP and a "smooth" political operative. He served as chairman of the Political Advisory Council. In 1970 he was appointed a recorder pro tem, and one year later, April 1971 he presided over Recorder's Court. Governor George Busbee appointed Gadsden a Chatham Superior Court judge. Later. A century earlier another Georgia Governor appointed James M. Simms to a Savannah judgeship, but he never took office because the legislature later abolished the office. In 1984 Gadsden received the R.A. "Papa" Dent Award from the Georgia Association of Black Elected Officials.

Judge Eugene Gadsden won all subsequent elections for his judgeship. The local branch of the NAACP presented judge Gadsden with the Freedom Award for his thirty years of public service. Gadsden retired from the bench to senior judge status, in 1992. The Georgia Legislature had to pass a special law in order to make him eligible for state retirement benefits. The Savannah Area Chamber of Commerce presented Gadsden with its Oglethorpe Award in 1992 and in 1999 he received the Arthur M. Gignilliat Jr., Award. Judge Eugene Gadsden died in August 2000. Perhaps the greatest accolade came from his wife of 60 years, Dr. Ida J. Gadsden. She said, "He was a very loving person. He was always there for us."

Some Other African American Teachers, bearers of the flame, who taught school in Savannah beginning before 1920 need to be remembered. **Alice M. Ellis** was the daughter of West Indian born the Rev. Alexander Ellis and Mrs. Helen Smith Ellis. The Rev. Ellis was born in Jamaica in 1838 the year slavery was abolished in the West Indies. Ellis emigrated to the United Sates in 1864 and settled in Boston. In 1881, he came to Savannah to be the pastor of Second African Baptist

Church. Some years later, he left Second African Baptist and founded Beth-Eden Baptist Church.

Minnie Ellis Steele and her sister Alice M. Ellis, also a teacher, spent their early youth in Boston where their father was pastor of the Old Joy Street and Day Star Baptist Churches. They were educated at Boston Teachers' College. Alice Ellis taught school in Savannah for 51 years. She taught for 25 years at West Broad Street School, 20 at Cuyler Street School and 17 years at Cuyler Junior High School. She was an accomplished organist and was organist at St. Stephen's Episcopal Church.

Helen M. Ellis Steele taught at West Broad Street School. She married Alexander Steele. She taught school for 42 years. Mrs. Steele returned to Boston, "in order that her children might have the excellent educational advantages which she had enjoyed." Their children, Joseph Alexander Steele graduated from the New England Conservatory of Music; Gertrude Steele Lombard graduated from Teachers College; Julian Steele graduated from Harvard University, Etta M. Steele graduated from Simmons College Boston and Ruth Steele graduated from Hunter College, New York City.[357] Mrs. Louisa A. Quarterman-Woodard taught school for over 50 years. Sallie C. Houstoun taught for 47 years, Rosa Ashton for 47 years, and Lizzie E. Hendrickson taught school for 47 years.

Emma Quinney taught school for 47 years. In 1930 when Florence Street School was opened she became its principal and remained at that post until she retired in 1948. She was a member of Beth Eden Baptist Church. Principal Quinney died on Christmas day 1951 and was buried from Beth Eden Baptist Church. Ezra Johnson, Gus Hayes, J. J. Martin, John Law, Sr., and Samuel Kelson were her pall bearers. Editor Sol Johnson had this to say about principal Quinney:

> "The entire community was saddened during the Christmas week by the passing of one who was greatly loved and esteemed as a person and as a teacher who touched the lives of many of Savannah's citizens over a period of years. Miss Emma Quinney possessed an engaging personality and was a born teacher of children. The same quality which endeared her to children won for her many friends among adults.
>
> She began her teaching career when a young woman in the West Broad Street School moved through the grades up to the Principalship after having served in the Maple and East Broad Street Schools. Her first Principalship was at Springfield Terrace from which she was promoted to the Florence Street School where she served with her usual efficiency and understanding until her retirement three years ago. She had and merited the confidence of the school authorities just as she had the love and esteem of the children and teachers over which she presided, and of the many friends

who sustain the irreparable loss her passing brings." [358]

Virginia Boxx taught for 47 years, Mattie J. Reynolds for 44 years, Henrietta C. Houston for 44 years, and Carrie B. Hendrickson taught school for 44 years. Rosalie Brown taught for 42 years and Mrs. Nettie A. Houstoun-Gordon taught school for 42 years.

Mrs. **Mabel R. Alford** was born in Savannah. She completed her schooling at West Broad Street School, the attended the High School section of Atlanta University and finished the normal course at the University in 1915. She received her B. S. degree from Savannah State College and did graduate work at the University of Pennsylvania and Columbia University in New York. Elementary schooling in the city public schools then went on to and Rebecca G. Houstoun for 41 years. Mrs. Helen E. Spencer taught for 40 years and Samuel S. Kelson for 40 years. About 23 other teachers taught school for 30 or more years.

The **Teachers' Culture Club,** "for the improvement of their teaching ability," was started in 1913.[359] The club celebrated its fifth anniversary at the home of Miss Madeline Shivery at 518 Henry Street. The club was described as "though modest in spirit, this club has undertaken to accomplish real progressive work. The genius of things educational in this community were, in a measure anticipated by the Teachers' Culture Club." The club provided "inspiration for professional study." In reference to the recent teachers' examination, it was reported that "much of the subject matter of the examination had in various ways, been discussed at the meetings of the club." There were more than twenty teacher members of the club.[360] The Rev. S.T. Redd gave the invocation at the club's January 1918 meeting. Prof. Gadsden addressed the gathering and Miss Florence Callen reviewed the year's work. In 1918 the group decided on a summer school for teachers first at Cuyler Street School. The Board of Education contributed $400 to augment the $10 each teacher paid to participate in the summer school. Experts from other states were brought in to lecture the teachers on the latest teaching techniques.

Prof. John W. Hubert and others organized the Chatham County Teachers' Association. A publication entitled, The Chatham County Teachers Association, 1913-1965, stated: "Among some notable efforts of the early organization were an attempt to have the history of the Negro placed in the Negro Schools; another was to establish a Credit Union under the chairmanship of W. S. Mann. The time may not have been ripe for these efforts, because the teachers did not cooperate."[361]

CHAPTER 3: THE STRUGGLE BEGINS

Endnotes – Chapter 3

[1] *The War of Rebellion: A Compilation of the Official Records of the Union and Confederate Armies,* Washington, D.C., 188.

[2] *The War of the Rebellion: A Compilation of the Official Records of the Union and Confederate Armies* (Washington, D.C. 1880-1891), Ser.1, Vol.14, 341. Ser. 111, vol.11, and 42-43.

[3] Benjamin Quarles, *The Negro in the Civil War,* Da Capo Paperback 1989, 318: Thomas L. Stokes, 287.

[4] A.E. Sholes, 79.

[5] *Savannah Daily Herald*, January 26, 1865.

[6] Ira Berlin et al., 310.

[7] Savannah Daily Republican, March 1, 1865.

[8] Josef C. James, "Sherman At Savannah" *Journal of Negro History,* 39(April 1954): 127-137.

[9] *Savannah Daily Herald,* January 28, 1865.

[10] *Savannah Daily Herald,* January 28, 1865.

[11] *Savannah Daily Herald,* February 3, 1865.

[12] *Savannah Daily Herald*, February 3, 1865.

[13] Savannah Daily Republican, February 3, 1865.

[14] *Savannah Morning News,* February 4, 1865.

[15] *Savannah Morning News,* July 1, 1865.

[16] Savannah *Daily Herald,* April 25, 1865.

[17] *Savannah Daily Herald,* October 7, 1865.

[18] Daily Morning News, July 3, 1867.

[19] *Savannah Morning News, December 18, 1868.*

[20] Blassingame…..

[21] A. D. Mayo, "Common Schools in the South," U.S. Commission of Education, *Reports*, 1895-1901, 1,419.

[22] *Savannah Republican,* March 25, 1865.

[23] James B. Lawrence, 41-57.

[24] quoted in Joseph F. Waring, 66.

[25] John P. Cony, "Education in Colonial Georgia," *Georgia Historical Quarterly,* 15(June 1932), 45.

[26] Joseph F. Waring, *Cerveau's Savannah*, Georgia Historical Society, Savannah, 1973, 29.

[27] Whittington Johnson, 128.

[28] Julia Floyd Smith, *Slavery and Rice Culture in Low Country Georgia: 1750-1860*, University of Tennessee Press, Knoxville, 1985, 16.

[29] Joseph F. Waring, *Cerveau's Savannah,* Savannah, 1973, 66-67.

[30] Cary Howard, "The Georgia Reaction to David Walker's Appeal," (Cary Howard, "The Georgia Reaction to David Walker's Appeal,"[30]

[31] Cary Howard, 34.

[32] Thomas R.R.Cobb, *A Digest of the Statute Laws of the State of Georgia in Force Prior to the Session of the General Assembly of 1851,* Athens 1851, 981.

[33] *Savannah Georgian,* March 22, 1830.

[34] Georgia Acts, 1829: William Dawson, *A Compilation of the Laws of Georgia to 1831,* Milledgeville, 1831,

413): *Digest of the Ordinances of the City of Savannah,* Savannah, Georgia, 1854, 184.

[35] Waring, 30.

[36] Whittington Johnson, 12.

[37] James M. Simms, 256.

[38] Whittington B. Johnson, "Free African-American Women in Savannah, 1800-1860:Afluence and Autonomy Amid Adversity," *Georgia Historical Quarterly,* 76(Summer 1992): 277-278.

[39] *Savannah Tribune*, December 4, 1915.

[40] James M. Simms, 57.

[41] Robert W. Gadsden, *Negro History,* NAACP Lecture, 1968, 2.

[42] Robert W. Gadsden *Negro History,* Savannah 1952, 2.

[43] Gadsden, 2.

[44] W. Johnson, 161.

[45] 8th Census of the United States, 1860, 507.

[46] Sister M. Julian Griffin, V.S.C. *Tomorrow Comes the Song,* 1978, 17.

[47] Atwell, 6.

[48] *St. Stephen's Register, 1868,* 14.

[49] *Savannah Morning News,* April 6, 1870.

[50] *Savannah Tribune,* November 13, 1896.

[51] *Savannah Daily Republican,* March 1, 1865.

[52] *Journal of the Diocese of Georgia,* 1866, 22.

[53] Quoted in Robert C. Morris, *The Education of Freedmen in the South, 1861-1870,* University of Chicago Press, 1976, 123.

[54] Robert Porter, 124.

[55] *Daily News Herald,* March 19, 1867.

[56] Ethel M. Christler, "Participation of Negroes in the Government of Georgia, 1867-1870," (MA thesis, 1932, Atlanta University), 64.

[57] Savannah Morning News, August 11,1870.

[58] *Colored Tribune,* February 26, 1876.

[59] Otto Board of Education Document.

[60] *Savannah Morning News,* May 28, 1877.

[61] Eric Foner, 173.

[62] Alexander W. Wayman, *Cyclopaedia of African Methodism,* Methodist Episcopal Book Depository, Baltimore, 1882, 129.

[63] St. Stephen's Register 11.

[64] Susie King Taylor, *Remembrance of My Life in Camp,* Boston, 1902, 5.

[65] Quoted in Joseph Waring, 67.

[66] Johnson. 128.

[67] Whittington B. Johnson, 425.

[68] *Savannah Republican,* March 25, 1865.

[69] *Savannah Tribune*, October 22, 1904.

[70] *Savannah Morning News,* November 14, 1872.

CHAPTER 3: THE STRUGGLE BEGINS

[71] *Savannah Tribune,* October 22, 1904.

[72] *Savannah Tribune,* September 16, 1876.

[73] Savannah Morning News, May 31, 1883.

[74] *Savannah Tribune,* November 25, 1876.

[75] *Colored Tribune*, March 4, 1876.

[76] *Savannah Tribune,* October 13, 1894.

[77] *Savannah Tribune,* October 22, 1904.

[78] *Savannah Tribune,* September 24, 1953.

[79] Sylvia G.L.Dannett, *Profiles of Negro Womanhood,* Educational Heritage, vol. 1, 1964, 144.

[80] *Savannah Evening Press,* December 21, 1903.

[81] Darlene Clark Hine, editor, *Black Women in America, An Historical Encyclopedia, voL 1,* Carlson Publishing, Inc., New York, 1993, 99.

[82] *Thomas Gamble Collection,* Georgia Miscellany, Savannah Public Library. Letter Feb 9, 1938 to Thomas Gamble from Father Melchior O.S.B.

[83] *Savannah Evening Press,* December 21, 1903.

[84] *Savannah Morning News,* April 11, 1982.

[85] Susie King Taylor, 5.

[86] James L. Owens, "The Negro in Georgia During Reconstruction, 1864-1872: A Social History," (Ph. D, diss., 1975, University of Georgia), 50.

[87] Richard Haunton, "Savannah In the 1850's," Ph. D. diss, 197.

[88] *Savannah Daily Herald,* March 16, 1865.

[89] Alexander W. Wayman, 106.

[90] Ira Berlin et Al. *Free at Last*, New York, 1992, 310.

[91] Austin D. Washington, "The Savannah Education Association 1865-1867,"...............

[92] *Savannah Morning News,* January 22, 1917.

[93] Rufus Mead, Jr., "Dear Folks at Home," Savannah, Ga. January 9, 1865, "With Sherman Through Georgia and Carolina, S.C.: Letters of a Federal Soldier," Part 11, *Georgia Historical Quarterly*, 33(March 1949), 64.

[94] *Savannah Daily Herald,* March 20,1865.

[95] Robert Gadsden, *The Education of the Negro,* NAACP Lecture Jan. 20, 1967, 3.

[96] *Savannah Daily Herald,* March 29, 1865.

[97] Alexander W. Wayman, 106.

[98] The Freedman's Record, 1, June, 1865, 91.

[99] Savannah Daily Herald, March 16, 1865.

[100] Savannah Republican, March 23, 1865.

[101] *Savannah Republican,* March25, 1865.

[102] *Savannah Republican,* July 12, 1865.

[103] *Savannah Republican,* March *25,* 1865.

[104] *Savannah Republican,* March 25, 1865.

[105] *Loyal Georgian,* Augusta, March 17, 1866.

[106] *Savannah Republican,* March 25, *1865.*

[107] *Savannah Republican,* July 12, 1865: June 17,1865.

[108] *Savannah Daily Republican,* October 10, 1865.

[109] *Savannah Daily Republican,* April 19, 1865.

[110] Freedmen's Record 1, February 1 865,34.

[111] *The Loyal Georgian,* March 17, 1865.

[112] *Daily News Herald,* March 28, 1866.

[113] *Daily News Herald*, April 27, 1866.

[114] Daily News Herald, April 28, 1866.

[115] W.E.B.DuBois, *The Souls of Black Folk: Essays and Sketches,* Connecticut, 1961, ed., 31.

[116] *Savannah Daily Herald,* April 26, 1865.

[117] Blassingame, 471.

[118] Jacqueline Jones, 99-106.

[119] *Daily News Herald,* August 26, 1867.

[120] Daily News Herald, August 1,1867.

[121] *Savannah Daily Republican,* March 25, 1865.

[122] Robert W. Gadsden, 1952, 9.

[123] *Savannah Morning News,* November 13, 1878.

[124] David S. Atkinson, The *Code of the City of Savannah,* Savannah, 1918, 59.

[125] *Savannah Morning News,* September 26, 1878.

[126] *Savannah Tribune,* April 16, 1904.

[127] Colored Tribune, May 6, 1876.

[128] *Savannah Tribune,* November 20, 1889.

[129] *Savannah Morning News*, September 3, 1889.

[130] *Savannah Tribune,* November 20, 1909.

[131] *Savannah Tribune,* September 21, 1912.

[132]*Savannah Tribune,* September 21, 1912.

[133] *Savannah Tribune,* September 20, 1913.

[134] Savannah Tribune, May 22, 1915.

[135] *Negro Education,* Bulletin, 1916, No. 39, vol. 11, 197-198.

[136] *Savannah Tribune,* June 14, 1919.

[137] *Savannah Tribune,* December 11, 1920.

[138] *Savannah Morning News,* July 11,1872.

[139] R.W.Gadsden, *Negro History,* 1952, 4.

[140] *Savannah Morning News,* July 11, 1872.

[141] *Savannah Morning News,* September 3, 1872.

[142] Seventh Annual Report of the Public Schools of the City of Savannah and the County of Chatham for the Year Ending June 30, 1872, 5.

[143] *Columbus Daily Sun*, April 22, 1866.

[144] *Journal of the Diocese of Georgia,* 1872, 65.

[145] Rudolph Otto, *Negro Education in Chatham County, no date or place of publication, no pagination.*

[146] *Savannah Morning News,* January 1, 1872.

[147] Thomas Gamble, 285.

CHAPTER 3: THE STRUGGLE BEGINS

[148] Rudolph Otto, *Negro Education in Chatham County, no date or place of publication, no pagination.*

[149] Rudolph Otto, 285.

[150] Gamble, 286.

[151] *Savannah Morning News,* November 12, 1872.

[152] Albert S. Otto, *The public School System of Savannah and Chatham County,* vol. 111, no date, no pagination.

[153] Robert W. Gadsden, *Negro History,* 9.

[154] Charles L. Hoskins, 1980, 75.

[155] *Savannah Tribune,* June 4, 1892.

[156] George F. Bragg, *History of the Afro-American Group of the Episcopal Church,* Church Advocate Press, Baltimore, 1922, 271.

[157] *Savannah Tribune,* October 1, 1898.

[158] *Savannah Tribune*, November 18, 1893.

[159] *Savannah Tribune,* November 4, 1893.

[160] *Savannah Tribune,* November 14, 1893.

[161] *Savannah Tribune*, November. 11, 1893.

[162] *Savannah Tribune,* November 7, 1896.

[163] *Savannah Tribune,* November 24, 1894.

[164] *Savannah Tribune*, May 29, 1897.

[165] *Savannah Tribune,* November 2, 1901.

[166] *Savannah Tribune*, November 3, 1906.

[167] *Savannah Tribune,* November 6, 1909.

[168] *Savannah Tribune*, January 11, 1913.

[170] *Savannah Tribune,* January 11, 1913.

The Rev. Richard Bright resigned in 1913 and moved to Philadelphia. In a

[171] Savannah Tribune, June 28, 1913.

[172] Savannah tribune, July 5, 1913.

[173] *Savannah Tribune*, September 25, 1915.

[174] *Savannah Tribune*, September 25, 1915.

[175] Albert S. Otto, The Public School System of Savannah and Chatham County, vol. 111, no date, no pagination.

[176] *Savannah Tribune,* September 17, 1898.

[177] *Savannah Tribune,* September 4, 1952.

[178] *Savannah Tribune,* September 4, 1952.

[179] *Savannah Tribune,* August 1, 1896.

[180] *Savannah Tribune,* January 10, 1935.

[181] Cyprian Davis, The History of Black Catholics in the United States, Crossroad, New York, 1991, 123.

[182] Cyprian Davis, 123.

[183] *Savannah Morning News,* June 6, 1883.

[184] *Savannah Morning News,* February 9, 1885.

[185] Savannah Morning News, January 28, 1885.

[186] *Savannah Tribune,* September 19, 1908.

[187] *Savannah Tribune,* August 17, 1909.

[188] *Savannah Tribune,* January 10, 1910.

[189] *Savannah Tribune,* January 22, 1912.

[190] *Savannah Tribune,* February 4, 1911.

[191] *Savannah Tribune,* September 28, 1912.

[192] *Savannah Tribune,* September 27, 1913.

[193] *Savannah Tribune,* October 9, 1920.

[194] Savannah Tribune, December 4, 1920.

[195] *Savannah Tribune,* October 12, 1912.

[196] *Savannah Tribune*, October 11, 1913.

[197] *Savannah Tribune,* March 22, 1913.

[198] *Savannah Tribune*, October 11, 1913.

[199] *Savannah Tribune*, September 12, 1915.

[200] *Savannah Tribune*, October 9, 1915.

[201] *Savannah Tribune,* November 18, 1916.

[202] *Savannah Tribune,* October 26, 1916.

[203] *Savannah Tribune,* October 9, 1920.

[204] *Savannah Tribune,* April 11, 1896.

[205] *Savannah Tribune*, June 1, 1912.

[206] *Savannah Tribune,* January 18, 1958.

[207] *Savannah Tribune,* September 15, 1917.

[208] *Savannah Tribune,* May 15, 1920.

[209] *Savannah Tribune,* October 9, 1920.

[210] *Savannah Tribune,* January 18, 1958.

[211] Charles L. Hoskins, 1983, 22.

[212] Kermit Smalls, *Year Book of Colored Savannah,* Savannah, 1934, 77-78.

[213] Ninth Annual Report of the Public Schools, 1874, 19.

[214] Savannah Morning News, July 17, 1875.

[215] *Savannah Morning News,* May 16, 1875.

[216] *Minutes of the Board of Education,* April 8, 1895, 211: Sixteenth Annual Report of the Public Schools, April 30,1878, 30.

[217] Albert Otto.

[218] *Savannah Morning News,* April 29, 1880.

[219] *Savannah Tribune,* February 29, 1896.

[220] *Savannah Tribune,* October 3, 1914.

[221] Kermit Smalls, 23.

[222] *Savannah Morning News*, March 31, 1878.

[223] Albert Otto.

[224] *Savannah Morning News,* April 19, 1883.

[225] *Minutes of the Board of Education,* April 8, 1895, 211.

[226] *Minutes of the Board of Education,* November 12, 1894, 196: Gadsden, 7.

CHAPTER 3: THE STRUGGLE BEGINS

[227] *Savannah Tribune,* 63.

[228] *Morning News,* September 30, 1896.

[229] Robert Gadsden. 1952, 16.

[230] *WPA, Savannah Writers Project,* Coll.#1355.

[231] Albert Otto Vol 111.

[232] *Savannah tribune,* February 27, 1930.

[233] Gadsden, 1952, 7.

[234] Robert W. Gadsden, 1952, 8.

[235] WPA, Savannah Writers Project, col. #1355, item 25. Georgia Historical Society.

[236] WPA-Savannah Writers Project, col. 1355, item126.

[237] *Savannah Tribune,* July 19, 1913.

[238] A Remarkable Negro Family, Reprint from *The Southern Workman,* October 1925, 8.

[239] *Savannah Tribune*, August 15, 1914.

[240] *Savannah Tribune,* August 15, 1914.

[241] *Savannah Morning News*, August 13, 1873.

[242] Savannah Morning News, September 28, 1873.

[243] Savannah Morning News, December 10, 1873.

[244] *Savannah Morning News,* December 13, 1873.

[245] Savannah Morning News, December 16, 1873.

[246] *Harper's Monthly,* 8(August 1874), 404).

[247] Harper's, 407.

[248] Savannah Morning News, March 11, 1880.

[249] *Savannah Morning News,* October 16, 1890.

[250] *Savannah Morning News,* August 9, 1883

[251] Savannah Morning News, November 22, 1884.

[252] Savannah Morning News, February 22, 1886.

[253] Blassingame, 464.

[254] *Savannah Tribune,* October 23, 1886.

[255] *Savannah Tribune,* December 4, 1886.

[256] *Savannah Tribune,* October 8, 1892.

[257] *Savannah Tribune,* January 14, 1893.

[258] *Savannah Tribune,* January 14, 1893.

[259] *Savannah Tribune*, March 1, 1893.

[260] *Savannah Tribune*, March 1, 1893.

[261] *Savannah Tribune*, January 13, 1894.

[262] *Savannah Tribune,* January 20, 1894.

[263] *Savannah Tribune*, July 7, 1894.

[264] *Savannah Tribune,* September 12, 1896.

[265] *Savannah Tribune,* December 19, 1896.

[266] *Savannah Tribune*, December 19, 1896.

[267] *Savannah Evening Press,* November 19, 1941.

[268] Savannah Tribune, March 13, 1896.

[269] *Savannah Tribune,* March 27, 1897.

[270] Savannah Tribune, March 27, 1897.

[271] Donald Grant, 232.

[272] *Savannah Tribune*, March 2, 1901.

[273] *Savannah* Tribune, January 16, 1901.

[274] *Savannah Tribune*, February 15, 1902.

[275] *Savannah Tribune,* November 15, 1902.

[276] *Savannah Tribune,* November 15, 1902.

[277] *Savannah Tribune,* September 19, 1903.

[278] *Savannah Tribune,* September 25, 1903.

[279] Thomas M. Norwood, *Address on the Negro,* Savannah, Ga., n.d., .26-27.

[280] *Savannah Tribune,* March 17, 1906.

[281] Minutes, 224.

[282]*Savannah Tribune,* June 23, 1906.

[283] Savannah Tribune, June 23, 1906.

[284] *Minutes of the Board of Education,* June11, 1906, 224.

[285] Board of Education Minutes, 224.

[286] *Savannah Tribune,* January 28, 1911.

[287] *Savannah Tribune*, June 14, 1913.

[288] *Savannah Tribune*, October 2, 1915.

[288] *Savannah Tribune*, October 9, 1915.

[289] *Savannah Tribune,* October 7, 1916.

[290] *Savannah Tribune,* August 19, 1916.

[291] *Statistical Report of the Public Schools,* 1915-1916, 21: *Minutes of the Board of Education,* October 8, 1916, 3.

[292] *Savannah Tribune,* October 14, 1916.

[293] *Savannah Tribune,* November 18, 1916.

[294] *Savannah Morning News,* May 12, 1917.

[295] *Savannah Tribune,* June 21, 1919.

[296] *Savannah Tribune,* June 28, 1919.

[297] *Savannah Tribune,* October 4, 1919.

[298] *Savannah Tribune,* February 14, 1920.

[299] *Savannah Tribune,* February 21, 1920.

[300] *Savannah Tribune,* March 6, 1920.

[301] *Savannah Tribune,* March 13, 1920.

[302] *Savannah Tribune,* July 31, 1920.

[303] *Savannah Tribune,* October 2, 1920.

[304] Asa H. Gordon, *The Georgia Negro,* Ann Arbor, Michigan, Edwards Brothers, Inc., 1937, 164-165.

[305] *Savannah Tribune,* September 11, 1897.

[306] *Savannah Tribune,* October 22, 1904.

CHAPTER 3: THE STRUGGLE BEGINS

[307] Savannah Tribune, July 14, 1888.

[308] *Savannah Tribune,* October 28, 1893.

[309] *Savannah Tribune,* December 14, 1918.

[310] *Savannah Tribune,* December 14, 1918.

[311] *Savannah Tribune,* December 28, 1918.

[312] *Savannah Tribune,* May 8, 1915.

[313] *Savannah Tribune,* April 16, 1921.

[314] Frank Bynes, *History of the Mutuals,* unpublished document.

[315] *Savannah Tribune,* February 18, 1888.

[316] Savannah Tribune, July 7, 1894.

[317] Savannah Morning News, April 13, 1921.

[318] *Savannah Morning News,* April 13, 1921.

[319] *Savannah Tribune,* July 16, 1926.

[320] *Savannah Tribune,* January 17, 1935.

[321] *Savannah Tribune,* January 17, 1935.

[322] *Savannah Tribune,* January 24, 1935.

[323] *Savannah Tribune,* January 17, 1935.

[324] *Savannah Tribune,* May 28, 1921.

[325] Robert W. Gadsden Papers.

[326] Robert Gadsden Papers.

[327] Robert Gadsden Papers.

[328] *Savannah Evening Press,* April 26, 1969.

[329] Robert Gadsden Papers.

[330] The Atlanta University Bulletin, December 1947, 16.

[331] *Savannah Tribune,* December 13, 1902.

[332] *Savannah Tribune,* January 16, 1904.

[333] *Savannah Tribune,* April 27, 1907.

[334] *Savannah Tribune,* July 7, 1938.

[335] *Savannah Tribune,* January 24, 1929.

[336] Savannah Morning News, October 27, 1938.

[337] *Savannah Tribune, May* 16, 1940.

[338] *Savannah Tribune,* November 3, 1955.

[339] *Savannah Tribune,* September 15, 1906.

[340] *Savannah Tribune,* September 19, 1903.

[341] *Savannah Tribune,* April 18, 1903.

[342] Bynes-Royall, *Funeral Home Records*, 1957, 78.

[343] Note from Mrs. Margie Caution, December 21, 2000.

[344] *Savannah Morning News,* May 1, 1976.

[345] *Savannah Tribune,* February 27, 1930.

[346] Savannah Evening Press, April 27, 1974.

[347] *Savannah Evening Press,* April 21, 1968.

[348] *Savannah Evening Press,* June 23, 1979.

[349] *Savannah Morning News,* May 1, 1976.

[350] Charles l. Hoskins, 1995, 59.

[351] Charles l. Hoskins, 1995, 60.

[352] *Savannah Tribune,* January 30, 1930.

[353] *NAACP Brochure.*

[354] *Savannah Tribune,* September 25, 1955.

[355] *Savannah Tribune,* February 2, 1956.

[356] *Savannah Tribune,* February 2, 1956.

[357] *Savannah Tribune,* July 14, 1949.

[358] *Savannah Tribune,* December 27, 1951.

[359] *Savannah Tribune,* November 12, 1918.

[360] *Savannah Tribune,* January 12, 1918.

[361] *The Chatham County Teachers' Association, 1913-1965,* Savannah, 1965.

When Jim Crow was King

After the fall of Confederate Savannah in 1864, whites still maintained their previous obsession to keep blacks "under due order and subjection." Eventually they latched on to a new dispensation-the Jim Crow era. The two Savannahs were carefully crafted to parallel each other but never touch. Jim Crow laws and customs guaranteed this outcome despite Federal Civil Rights laws, Reconstruction Acts and the 14th Amendment. Blacks were forced to "fend for themselves." No area of life perhaps, better demonstrated this resolve better than health.

The urban milieu of Savannah exposed blacks and whites to many health hazards. Several rice fields, swamps, unkept privies, dirt roads and an abundance of mosquitoes, enclosed the town. In 1802 smallpox, which was as dreaded as yellow fever, broke out on several plantations around Savannah. Infected blacks were removed to Tybee Island and placed under guard.[1] The port, over the years, also proved to be a source of communicable diseases. Charles Hardee wrote that Savannah's reputation, as an unhealthy place was "not undeserved."

Blacks were said to be somewhat immune to malaria but relatively more blacks than whites succumbed to respiratory diseases. Cholera was very common among blacks. Part of the black health problem stemmed from unhygienic living conditions. On September 8, 1804, a hurricane wreaked havoc in and around Savannah from nine in the morning until about 10 at night. The river rose above the wharves and covered Hutchinson Island and the rice plantations around the city." Every vessel in the harbor was thrown down. It was reported, " Over one hundred Negroes were drowned on Hutchinson Island and on the rice plantations near the city."[2]

According to Mary Sowell, two doctors operated a hospital for sick Negroes.[3] However, deaths among slaves were "poorly reported."[4] In 1816, Dr. James Ewell suggested that a separate hospital for blacks should be built. Thomas F. Williams, a white man, who died that same year, bequeathed a sum of money for the "relief and protection of afflicted and aged Africans." This fund, together with a donation of 50 acres, was used to establish what became the "Georgia Infirmary for the Relief and Protection of Aged and Afflicted Negroes." The Georgia Infirmary was chartered on December 24, 1832.[5]

By August 1823, William C. Daniell and J. P. Screven reported that his group had bought the Poor House, and would open it on the first of May, "for sick seamen and Negroes." They assured all slave owners that "the patients will be kept in strict discipline and will be prevented from visiting the city."[6] Historian Donald Grant claimed that official medical attention was insufficient and slaves had to depend on "folk remedies" and "medicinal plants."[7]

Carter Woodson wrote that a dentist Dr. Zeke, who had studied in Scotland, and practiced in Savannah before the Civil War, was driven from his home and settled in Augusta.[8] Historian Richard Haunton states that slaves were sent to private hospitals such as the *Savannah Infirmary,* opened in 1852, or another hospital, which had separate slave sections.[9] Nonetheless slave mortality was high.

The yellow fever epidemic in the August heat of 1876, the third disastrous epidemic to hit Savannah, created havoc among the inhabitants and changed Savannah's way of handling health matters.[16] At that time medical science did not know that the female mosquito spread the disease. The wealthy left town as soon as the news became public and the city became a ghost town. Blacks and poor Irish had no choice but to remain in place and hope for the best. The *Savannah Tribune* advised, "Every person should use Carbolic acid, Chloride of lime or other disinfectants freely about his premises, in order to stay the increase of the disease as much as possible."[17] It was estimated that about 20 persons died each day of the disease. By the fall over 1,000 had died of the plague. This event triggered efforts to solve these outbreaks.

The black paper reported "Those of our people remaining are calm and hopeful, doing what they can to help the sick and destitute." The Benevolent Association cared for about 36 blacks. African Americans established this organization specifically for that purpose.[18] The Rev. Ulysses H. Houston opened his church "from 4 to 6 o'clock for prayer and supplication to Almighty God." All Christian brethren were invited to attend.[19] The Rev. A. Harris headed a committee in early 1887, to ameliorate health conditions at the Georgia Infirmary. The Rev. M.R. Wilson was secretary and the Rev. S.H. Robertson was treasurer. They hoped to "raise enough money through contributions from churches to employ a night nurse at $10 per month." Black health dropped as economic resources prevented many from seeing their doctor. The black death rate dropped to about, .05 to 38.0 per thousand greater than that of whites.[20]

Dr. A. T. Augusta, who headed the Federal Government's Freedman's Hospital in 1865, was probably the first African American medical doctor to practice in Savannah.[21] He died in Washington December 22, 1890.[22] The city directory of 1870 listed the presence of **Dr. Charles H. Taylor,** who lived at 98 State Street and had his office at 112 York Street. The directory also listed a black nurse, Rebecca Sneed, who lived at 22 Taylor Street. These Directories, over the years, omitted many blacks.

Dr. Patrick Henry Coker was listed as a colored physician at 21 York Street.[23] In 1870 he ran for coroner but lost.[24] He died September 8, 1886. The community held him in "high regard." St. Philips A. M. E. Church was "crowded with an audience of refined and cultured people who fully appreciated the worth of the lamented dead." The Revs. William H. Harris and James M. Simms conducted the service while Col. John H. Deveaux gave remarks. The services were very impressive and the "people were visibly affected by the solemnity of the occasion."[25] In October, an earthquake shook the city but no damage was done to the buildings.[26] Health Officer McFarland opined that the deaths among blacks had increased since freedom.[27]

Prof. Samuel B. Morse, and a club of young ladies, gave a concert for the benefit of the Georgia Infirmary.[28] In July 1888, The *Savannah Tribune* reported on a proposal "to turn over to the colored people the management of the Infirmary." The paper considered this a "move in the right direction and there is no doubt that a colored board of managers can manage an institution as well as a white board can."[29] Some women organized the Christian Workers Association for the express purpose of assisting the unfortunate patients at the hospital. On the fourth Sunday of each month, they held religious services at the hospital attended by nearly all the patients. Several members of the black churches aided them in this endeavor. In September, eight colored nurses "left for Jacksonville to care for yellow fever victims."[30]

Captain William Woodhouse's group attempted to organize a hospital for blacks to be operated by the Catholic Sisters of Mercy.[31] The hospital was to be located at the corner of West Broad and Pine Streets in a building occupied by a school. William H. Royall a wealthy mortician also organized the Georgia Relief Association, which raised money for the improvement of Georgia Infirmary and in addition, a home for the aged. In the early 1890's, many blacks still claimed that they were not receiving "adequate care at the Georgia Infirmary." In 1891 Dr. S. C. Snelson and his bride arrived in the city and was given a public reception.[32]

Letters to the *Savannah Tribune* charged that the white staff at the facility "had no interest in black patients, and called for the removal of the white directors and their replacement by blacks." In February 1892, trained white nurses were "placed in charge of the Georgia Infirmary in lieu of Mr. W. W. King, the efficient superintendent. King had charge of the Infirmary for about five years. When he was appointed "the place was not fit for the purpose for which it was used. He went to work energetically and renovated the entire building and has made it with outside aid what it is today." No reason was given for the dismissal and the paper reported that "it was not called for and they (the white nurses), are not able to cope with the patients therein, or may hereafter be confined."[33]

In early January 1893, the paper carried an article entitled "Better Management Needed," in which a reporter dispatched to the Georgia Infirmary, as a follow-up to many complaints from readers, wrote a scathing account about conditions at the facility. He found that the patients were "cooped up in two temporary constructed buildings" and added "several men in critical condition said that the physician pays no attention to them." The building was not well insulated from the cold and some people felt that "a trained nurse was needed." The reporter ended his tirade with the hope that "every colored person would lend his assistance to the poor unfortunates who are confined out there." The following week, an editorial stated: "I could never see the philosophy of having white attendants in a Negro hospital and, no white nurse will take the interest in caring for a sick Negro as he deserves." The writer called for a meeting of the people for the purpose of looking into the matter and making some recommendations to the proper authorities.[34]

William W. King finally stepped into the breach with a letter to the *Savannah Tribune*, which stated that he was gratified to see that the paper had "undertaken to show up to the public the gross mismanagement and inhuman and criminal neglect on the part of those who have the care of the poor unfortunates in the Georgia Infirmary." King claimed that five years of toil enabled him to "know better than those who are at present in control of the affairs the needs of the place and the inmates whose welfare are in their charge."

He thought that the two white women who replaced him were brought in from the North with the assumption that they were better than he. King claimed that they were "not physically fitted for such work and that they were entirely out of place among Negroes." Finally King suggested that the deplorable conditions could be improved if the institution was placed under the rule of an intelligent colored man: "One who knows the characteristic feelings of his own people and will treat kindly and humbly protecting them from the harsh treatment of the physician in charge." King reminded the authorities that the patients were "human and not brutes." By the 1890's, it had become evident to blacks that in health matters, at least, they had to "work out their own salvation."[35]

Dr. Cornelius Mc Kane (1862-1912) was born February 2, 1862, in British Guyana, South America. His grandmother was stolen from Liberia and sold into slavery in Dutch Guyana. She impressed the young McKane that his great-grandfather was an African King, Mannah Funacai, and that it was his obligation to return to Mother Africa and work for the regeneration of his race. Pursuant to this charge, young Cornelius was sent to New York City at 10 years of age to further his education. Deacon Moses F. Wester took him into his house and sent him to high school in New York. In 1882, on completing his studies, Cornelius McKane went to Monrovia, Liberia, and became principal of a school and served as chief of the treasury.

He resigned in 1888 and returned to New York. Mc Kane studied at Dartmouth, with the intention of returning to Africa as a doctor. He received his M.D., degree from the Medical College of the University of Vermont in 1891 and was later appointed Medical Examiner among colored people for the New York Mutual Life Insurance Company. This 30-year-old physician came from a remarkable lineage. In fact, he was the "great-grandson of a king."[36] Available sources do not indicate why Dr. Mc Kane chose to come to Savannah. It is known, however, that Dr. McKane was at that time mulling over an offer from the American Colonization Society.[37] It is possible that he knew or had heard of West Indian born Dr. T. James Davis, one of the first back doctors to practice in Savannah. A notice in the

Savannah Tribune stated, "During my absence from the city Dr. C. McKane of 107 Montgomery Street will attend my professional practice." It was signed, T. James Davis, M.D.

The four physicians in the city met in Dr. Cornelius Mc Kane's office at 107 Montgomery Street and formed the Southern Medical Association. Dr. T. James Davis was elected President, Dr. Cornelius McKane, Vice-President, Dr. S. C. Snelson, treasurer, and Dr. C. Bryan Whaley, Secretary. The purpose of the organization was to enhance the "mutual benefit and the best interest of their patrons and the advancement of science, also the physical and hygienic improvement of the condition of our people in this city and adjacent parts." The paper commended the doctors for this move and declared that the doctors were, "race lovers and are ever ready to do anything to upbuild the race." The editorial concluded, the doctors were, "the ablest the country affords."[38]

Dr. McKane, a physician and surgeon, reportedly was "pleased to see those who are in need of medical attention." His hours were 8 to 11 A.M. and 1 to 4 p.m., and 6 to 8 p.m. Sometime later the *Savannah Tribune* reported that the doctor's office was "well fitted up, backed by a growing practice, which he justly merits." The paper regarded Dr. Mc Kane as having "great ability and sagaciousness" and claimed that he was "bound to be a success."

The newly organized doctors' group soon had to demonstrate its usefulness to the community. The group denounced the newly formed Provident Benevolent Association as "injurious to the well-being of blacks." A letter signed by "A Negro Physician," claimed that "Negroes will not be led by Negroes and that they have no confidence in each other." The writer further accused the Benevolent Association of slander by claiming that Negro physicians were incompetent. Dr. Cornelius Mc Kane gave a lecture on physiology at the Peabody Institute held in the city. G. B. Lamar left a bequest of $10,000 to the Georgia Infirmary.

The controversy between the black doctors and the Provident and Benevolent Society raged on for months in the *Savannah Tribune.* In November Drs. T. James Davis, J, Henry Bugg, S.C. Snelson, Cornelius Mc Kane, W. C. Smalls and C. Bryant Whaley signed a letter to the editor of the *Savannah Tribune.* They stated: "The South East Georgia Medical Society desires to put herself on record as being uncompromisingly opposed to any and all such organizations for it is the hand of Esau but the voice of Jacob." The group further professed itself "to have no sympathy, nor does it ever intend co-operating with any such organization, because we believe them to be detrimental to, and an imposition upon our people and advise that our people take a similar position." Two weeks later the *Savannah Tribune* reported that Dr. Cornelius McKane and Major Royal had just returned from Augusta, feeling "highly elated over the hospitality extended by the citizens of Augusta." At the instigation of the *Tribune* a group of black Savannah's worthies met in Dr. McKane's office to plan the "proper celebration of emancipation day."

Dr. Alice R. Woodby passed through the city on her way to Augusta, where she was expected to take up a position as an instructor in physiology and chemistry at Haines Institute and also to practice as a physician in Augusta.[39] She was born during the Civil War in Bridgewater, Bucks County, Pennsylvania. Young Alice lost both parents at an early age, but by perseverance, she completed her education at the Youths Institute of Philadelphia, and graduated with honors in 1889. Miss Woodby then entered the Women's Medical College of Pennsylvania, from which she graduated with honors. She was also a published poet.

Later the *Savannah Tribune* reported: "The engagement of Dr. C. McKane of this city and Dr. Alice R. Woodby of Augusta is announced."[40] Dr. Woodby was regarded in Augusta as "a modest unassuming business woman," and the *Savannah Tribune* predicted that she "will be a great addition to Dr. McKane and the people of Savannah." Later the paper reported: "Two Made One," which stated: "On Thursday last about 4 o'clock, Dr. Alice R. Woodby of Augusta and Dr. Cornelius McKane of this city, were united in sacred wedlock by Rev. Alexander Ellis of Beth-Eden Baptist church." It further reported: "Mrs. Dr. McKane will leave tomorrow for Augusta, but will return in a few days when she will remain permanently."[41]

Dr. Simeon Palmer Lloyd (1866-1909) was the first Savannah born African American to become a medical doctor and return to his hometown to practice. He was born in Savannah June 16, 1866, the son of Josiah Lloyd, a well-known grocer who operated his business on the corner of Jones Street Lane and East Broad Street. Young Lloyd attended East Broad Street School then called Fairlawn, and graduated in 1881 with honors. He won a scholarship offered by First Congregational Church for one year's tuition at Atlanta University. Prof. J.H.C.Butler, Miss Alice Miller and Mrs. Sarah F. Butler, all of West Broad Street School, examined the twelve students and awarded the scholarship to young Lloyd.

Lloyd enrolled in Atlanta University in 1881 and graduated in 1889 with distinction. He returned to Savannah and was appointed Assistant Principal of East Broad Street School. He also studied medicine under Dr. T. James Davis, who thus became Lloyd's "medicus pater." Later Lloyd went to the University of Pennsylvania Medical School and graduated with his M. D. in May of 1893.[42] Returning to the city, he set up office at the corner of South Broad and East Boundary Streets. Lloyd was "portly, unassuming, but capable and efficient." He went to work "with vigor and built up a remunerative practice."

In June of 1893, the city's black elite presented Dr. Lloyd to the public, at the home of Prof. Sam B. Morse, 26 Gwinnett Street. The Rev. L.B.Maxwell, Pastor of First Congregational Church and a trustee of Atlanta University spoke eloquently of Dr. Lloyd. Dr. T. James Davis then rendered the beautiful solo, "No tongue can tell." At the end, Dr. Lloyd thanked all his friends for their kind remarks and their words of wisdom. He assured them that he would "always be found where duty calls."[43] Blacks petitioned city council to appoint a black city physician and the notion was favorably received.[44] Mayor Herman Meyers and council appointed Dr. Lloyd as the first black city physician, in part as a reward for previous black political support.[45] It was the responsibility of a city physician to attend "all sick persons residing in the city who were unable to pay for medical services."[46] In 1896, Dr. Lloyd made his report to City Council as one of the city physicians. Dr. Lloyd treated 6,712 colored patients and 224 whites. He made 6,189 house visits, received 4,515 office calls, and issued 108 hospital permits.

Dr. Lloyd's activity as city physician was highly praised in the mayor's report. Out of his large number of patients, he only wrote 94 death certificates. His office as city physician was located at 38 New Street near St. Philips A.M.E. Church. The doctor had also made several suggestions in connection with the unhygienic living conditions in some sections of the city. He recommended the enlargement of the Georgia Infirmary and said that several times patients had been refused admission because of this and sent to some shanty or out-houses and suffered, and occasionally died for lack of proper attention.

The paper obviously felt very pleased with the doctors performance and claimed that "the entire colored population feels elated over the record that Dr. Lloyd has made, knowing that he has given satisfaction to the authorities, gained credit for himself and is an honor to his race." Dr. Lloyd gave the Emancipation address on January 1896.[47] In 1897, city physicians treated 6,189 whites were treated and 25, 811 coloreds. By 1900 however 6,2264 whites and 26, 144 coloreds were treated. Blacks made up about 40 per cent of the population but accounted for 80 per cent of those treated by city physicians.[48] Colored prescriptions rose from 19,667 in 1897 to 35,662 in 1900.[49]

McKane Training School for Nurses / Hospital for Women and Children

Dr. Alice Woodby McKane, principal and founder opened the McKane Training School for Nurses, September 1, 1893, in her home and office combined, a two-story frame building located at the Northwest corner of Liberty and Montgomery Streets.[50] The school aimed to be as convenient as possible for the students, due to the "alarming death rate among our people, the people of the Negro race, due in large measure to ignorance and incompetent nursing," The goal of the school was to "assist in remedying this evil."[51]

Several students registered and paid the small tuition fee. An entrance examination was held in reading, spelling, writing, arithmetic, grammar, and geography. The nursing course was a two-year program with practical as well as theoretical subjects. The course included anatomy, physiology, hygiene, midwifery, therapeutics, chemistry, medical nursing, surgical nursing, care of women in confinement, and cooking for the sick. Boarding was available near the school for $1.50 per month, while tuition was set at $4.00 per month and was to be paid in advance. Those who intended to go to Africa as missionaries and those preparing for the ministry received free tuition. In addition, special arrangements were made for a few industrious students.

Over one hundred students were admitted to the school. The work however was misunderstood and "students became discouraged." The more industrious and serious minded persevered and two classes of nurses graduated before the Drs. McKane left for Liberia.

Since the students needed practical experience, children were at first "hired for small pay to act as patients." This approach led to talk by the parents that the practice would "cause sickness to come to them." It was after this experience that a small public dispensary was opened in connection with the work. Students were then sent to the homes of the needy sick to render services if they were ordered to bed and Dr. Alice McKane would follow and instruct. When Dr. Alice McKane became ill her husband, Dr. Cornelius McKane substituted for her in the school. As it happened, Scipio wrote the *Savannah Tribune* complaining that Dr. Mc Kane was allowing "a policy shop to be next to his office and his training school for nurses."[52]

The McKane Training School for Nurses decided to assist the deserving poor of the city by opening the dispensary from 4 to 5:00 p.m. daily. During those hours patients were treated free of charge, though a small fee was charged to cover the cost of drugs. The paper boasted "This is the only enterprise of the kind that is managed and supported entirely by Negroes. Our people should appreciate it." The McKanes had done all the preparation for the school without help from others. As the *Savannah Tribune* put it, "unaided and alone they are doing a good work for our people."

The *Savannah Tribune* ran a special section during September 1893 under the heading, "Our Doctors." The paper listed the resident doctors as follows: Drs. Jas.H.Bugg, T.James Davis, S.C.Snelson, W.C.Small, C.Bryant Whatley, C.McKane, A.W.McKane, S.Palmer Lloyd, and F.C.Lambert. These nine doctors were regarded as "competent physicians and surgeons. Eight are regular physicians and surgeons, one lady physician and a surgeon dentist." Then it concluded, "what do you want the earth?" There is no excuse. You "can have your choice and if there is race pride in you, you will patronize them." All were said to be "able, worthy and efficient."[53] In November, the *Tribune* boasted that Dr. C. McKane, assisted by Dr. C. Bryant Whatley, successfully removed a very large tumor in the pelvic region from a patient of 24 Pine Street. The patient was reported to be "doing well." This was only one among the many successful operations performed by Dr. McKane.

The McKane Training School for Nurses held its first commencement exercises May 1895. The schoolroom was elaborately decorated with flowers. The Rev. R.R. Downs opened with a prayer and Dr. Cornelius McKane gave a brief history of the school. He stated, "it was organized at the suggestion of his wife Dr. Alice McKane, the principal, in 1893 with a class of fifty." Dr. Alice McKane then addressed the audience, "in an effective and feeling address to the graduating class," urging them to be "vigilant and not content with yesterday's or today' knowledge but always seeking and learning." She then presented diplomas to the first nurses trained at the institution. They were Gussie E. Freeman, Anna E. Randolph and Emma G. Collier. Miss Freeman, "in an artistic and business manner," then gave an object lesson in bandaging a boy "from head to foot." The Rev. M. W. Gilbert, John H. Deveaux, the Rev. Downs and J.T. Lee of New York then gave remarks on the importance of trained nurses and the good work the school had accomplished.[54] A report published in 1935 listed "twenty pupils comprising this class, eight of them completing the course." [55] These graduates would go on to render "yeoman service in Savannah during the early years when Negro nurses were very rare."[56]

No sooner had the first graduation of the Training School taken place, than the Doctors McKane, seized by the "Liberia Virus," decided to leave for Africa, and on May 17, 1895, they left Savannah for New York. Dr. Cornelius McKane said he was going to Africa "in accordance with a sense of duty and high obligation." The *Savannah Tribune* stated: "no man has ever come to our city and won a better station in life and warmer place in the hearts of her people than Dr. McKane, and our people part from him in great regret." It added, "The doctor has been in Savannah for five years and has won for himself an enumerable record as a physician and a man."[57] The Hospital was incorporated June 1, 1896.[58]

Dr. William C. Blackman took over the running of the Training School. Like Dr. McKane, he was born in Georgetown Guyana, South America. In fact, Dr. McKane had helped him to come to America and on learning that he was about to graduate, Dr. McKane asked him to come to Savannah and take over the Training School and Hospital. Dr. W.C.Blackman graduated from Leonard Medical College. The doctor "took an examination last week before the state board, along with several whites. He received notice that the examination was a successful one and he was licensed to practice in the state."[59]

Blackman occupied the office of Dr. Cornelius McKane at Montgomery and Liberty Streets and ran the training school. He "appeared austere to many, but within there glowed a fervent heart." However he enjoyed "a practice among a loyal class of patients." He was a "pleasing conversationalist with a fund of information. The paper regarded the new doctor as "a quiet and unassuming gentleman and will no doubt do well in his new field," and years later the paper would say: "His efforts for Charity Hospital will remain as a memorial to him." When Dr. Blackman died in 1930, the *Tribune* reported: "No other person has given more freely to the needs of the hospital."[60] The McKanes had a daughter in Monrovia, Liberia, on August 22, 1895.[61] Within months, however, Dr. Alice W. McKane suffered a life threatening attack of the African fever and the McKanes were forced to leave Liberia. Their Savannah friends and the graduates of the Training School urged the McKanes to return to Savannah to "save the institution because in their judgment, the people appeared to be losing interest in the work."[62]

Dr. Cornelius McKane and Dr. Alice B. McKane, accompanied by Alice their little daughter, arrived from Boston, Mass, on the Steamer *Tallahassee*. Many friends here were glad to greet and welcome them. The doctors opened offices at West Broad and Alice Streets.[63] No sooner had the McKanes arrived back than a controversy arose as to the relationship between them and the officers of the Migration Society. The Society apparently made the case that Dr. Cornelius McKane had ulterior political motives while in Liberia. The *Savannah Tribune* claimed that Dr. McKane was on the right line "in letting his people know of the true conditions of affairs, and in this, he will be supported by the true element of the race."[64]

Meanwhile, the McKanes were hard at work reorganizing their Savannah project. They discussed the possibility of adding a hospital to the Training School. Dr. Blackman did not agree with the idea at first. Dr. McKane called all the colored doctors in the city to a meeting to discuss the proposition. After many discussions the McKanes were the only ones who were in favor of the project for it was viewed as an expensive affair. The colored people were also consulted as to the wisdom of starting a hospital. Some white people were in favor of the project. Finally most agreed and rallied enthusiastically to the cause. McKane Hospital for Women and Children and Training School for Nurses was incorporated June 1, 1896. C. McKane, M.D., A. W. McKane, M.D., Mrs. Emma Collier, Mrs. Ann E. Randolph, Mrs. A.B.G. Carr, Mrs. Lula Johnson, Mrs. Ellen Bennett and Mrs. Anna Nutall were the incorporators.[65] The McKanes secured the property of Mrs. Lucretia Baker on New Street for a Hospital.[66]

The McKanes re-organized the Board of Directors. The new officers were Dr. S. P. Lloyd, major Royall, and Lieut. Sol Johnson and R. M. Bennett. The bylaws of the corporation made every colored physician in the city "who cast his lot with the enterprise a member of the advisory board." It was hoped that the "churches, societies and other organizations will help this worthy cause which means much primarily for Savannah and add not a little toward the onward progress of the race." The paper concluded, "The time has arrived when we ought to attempt to do something for ourselves."[67]

Dr. C. McKane addressed the congregation of St. James A.M.E. Church and appealed for contributions for the proposed hospital. On subsequent Sundays, many black doctors fanned out through the black churches and appealed for contributions. Drs. McKane and Lloyd spoke at St. Philips A.M.E. and collected $6.[68]

The entertainment given for the benefit of the McKane Hospital at Ezra Presbyterian Church was said to be quite a success, but no dollar figure was listed.[69] The *Savannah Tribune* carried this sad notice: "Alice Frances, the little daughter of Dr. And Mrs. C. McKane, died early yesterday morning. The body will be interred this morning at 10 o'clock. The afflicted parents have our sincere sympathy."[70]

Efforts continued to raise money for the new hospital. The *Savannah Tribune* thought it "gratifying to the trustees and the public at large to notice with what marked success the proposed hospital is meeting on every hand." William B. Woodby, the brother of Dr. Alice McKane donated $30 to the proposed hospital.[71] The churches fully supported the project though the amounts raised were rather small. Seven churches contributed $32.50 in September of 1896. Mrs. Nutall gave a lawn party at Florence and Seventh Streets in Brownsville for the benefit of the hospital. Admission was 10 cents and guests were to receive free ice cream. Florence A. Lewis gave a dime party for the benefit of the new hospital.[72]

The new McKane Hospital for Women and Children and Training School for Nurses opened November 1, 1896. The *Savannah Tribune* expressed the fulsome pride of the black community thus "the colored people of Savannah might well feel a sense of pride in the opening of the McKane hospital for Women and Children and Training School for Nurses." The paper thought the successful opening reflected "great credit on the noble and heroic women who gave of their means and influence to this worthy cause and charitable institution."[73] The Hospital was the first in the state, and was said to "speak volumes for the upward tendency of the race in Georgia." The group bought a house on Florence Street in Brownsville.

Mrs. Annie Nutall donated the building at the corner of Florence and 36th Streets. It was remodeled at a very moderate cost, and the school equipment was removed from Montgomery Street to the new site. The hospital was incorporated by Superior Court on June 1, 1896. The Board of Trustees included the McKanes, Annie Nutall, A.B. Carr, Mintie Canal, A.E. Randolph, Lula Johnson, Fanny Hamilton, Ellen Bennett Major W.H. Royall and Sol. C. Johnson. Later the Rev. L.B. Maxwell was added and he became the President of the group.

Dr. Cornelius McKane was selected as the Superintendent of the hospital and Dr. Alice McKane was placed in charge of the Nursing Training School. A head nurse was also appointed. Emma Lewis, President of the Hospital Relief Association, gave a report on the group's effort to aid the hospital. The Solomon C. Johnson Club and the Palmer Lloyd Club, assisted by several prominent ladies of the city, made up a surprise party and donated several useful articles to the hospital. A Thanksgiving offering was taken up at many schools. Anderson Street School collected $11.23. East Broad Street School contributed six blankets, three white spreads, one dozen towels and other items. West Broad Street School contributed $22.20 and a pair of pillowcases, Beach Institute seven cents and two baskets of groceries. The hospital represented clear evidence that local blacks were "on their way up."

The *Savannah Tribune* carried yet another appeal to blacks to support the hospital. It gave three reasons that it had been organized and was managed by "our own people," that "it would afford relief to many suffering women and children who without its shelter and treatment might meet a miserable and untimely death." The final justification for support was the fact that the hospital "offered an opportunity of reputable livelihood and usefulness to our young women who have heretofore been limited to the work pot, the schoolroom, the work tub, or the sewing machine." The *Savannah Tribune* retaliated against certain "so called intelligent persons whose purpose in life seems to be to misrepresent, destroy and pervert every good effort put forth by the colored people, to better their condition."[74]

Furthermore, Sol Johnson claimed the hospital was "a free hospital, not one cent has been received from any patient as fee." The managers and attending physicians gave their services without compensation. The nurses received no pay but the laundress, received a small compensation. Two nurses together gave $5.00 per month, this money was used for fuel, and such things as were needed. So you see, friends, it was done on a strictly common sense business basis. A "Trustee" signed the letter.[75] A prayer meeting was announced for every Sabbath afternoon from 3 to 4:00 p.m. at the McKane Hospital. The public was invited to attend. A benefit for the hospital held at Asbury Methodist Episcopal Church was said to have been "a rare literary and musical treat." The young children from Haven Home under the direction of Ada Johnson won the admiration of the whole house. Little Jennie Boozer was the accompanist on the organ. Proceeds amounted to $7.35.

A conference on black mortality was held at Second Baptist Church. Drs. Lloyd, McKane and Buggs read papers on health requirements. Mrs. Emma Collier of the class of 1895 of the Training School then read a very interesting report of a case under her observation. Two other nurses gave talks and a discussion period followed. Mrs. Laura Williams then moved that all present give a donation to the McKane Hospital. Dr. Alice McKane objected to this proposal on the grounds that it clashed with the announced purpose of the meeting.

The Training School re-opened in September, 1897, with quite a number of students. The *Savannah Tribune* felt that "the great good that this school has done is apparent not only to the efficient nurses who have graduated, but to the patients whom they have attended and their friends." The paper chided its readers that the hospital was "a worthy cause and there is no reason why it is not helped more by the citizens." A board of lady managers was appointed from the various churches with the sole purpose of assisting in raising means for the hospital.

It was felt that the enthusiasm displayed in behalf of the hospital, assured that much good would be accomplished. The white papers throughout the state reported that the first colored woman had applied to the state for authority to practice medicine. The *Savannah Tribune* stated: "In our midst we have a lady, Dr. Alice W. McKane, who has been practicing medicine in the state for six years. Mrs. McKane is a physician of no mean ability, and has given much satisfaction."[76]

One month later, the paper reported that the citizens were becoming "very liberally disposed towards the McKane Hospital and Training School for Nurses, even school children are imbued with the spirit." Three black schools, Anderson Street, West Broad Street and East Broad Street, donated $49.91 to Charity Hospital. Dr. J. Henry Bugg, one of the two colored city physicians, gave his report for the previous year. He had a reputation of being an able physician. Dr. Bugg attended to 1,417 persons, made 983 and 941 office calls. He vaccinated 235 persons.[77]

Dr. Bugg recommended the "teaching of hygiene in the public schools, and added that many of our people are not aware of its benefits and the children who are now being raised should be though about it." The City Council, however, proposed an ordinance prohibiting black city physicians from treating whites or white physicians from treating blacks. The *Savannah Tribune,* after ridiculing the ordinance, hoped that the Council would "not pass such an unjust unreasonable and uncalled for ordinance."[78]

A conference on mortality held at Second African Baptist listed vice, quack midwifery and ignorance of hygiene as causes of early death among blacks. In December that year Mrs. Overton donated a glass of pineapple jelly, half a dozen eggs to the Hospital while Mrs. E.L.Hazel donated two cans of tomatoes and a quart of beans. Mrs. Lavinia Willis donated two pounds of lard. St. Stephen's Episcopal Church donated two quarts of beans, half dozen bananas, half a bushel of apples, half a pack of sweet potatoes and three cans of tomatoes.

By January 1898, the upsurge in black pride and self-help seemed to be ebbing. McKane and others made several speeches on Sundays at the local churches in an effort to increase donations. The *Savannah Tribune* decided to upbraid its readers. It reported that the attendance at the Board of Trustees meeting was described as fair. Monthly donations from the churches had not produced the required funds. The paper warned that the interest in the hospital should be unabating. In February 1898, the Board of Trustees of the McKane Hospital appointed a committee to submit plans and cost estimates for enlarging the hospital.

Dr. Cornelius McKane bought some property, apparently with the intent of setting up an office just beyond Woodville, on Augusta Road. The people hailed his coming with much gratification. The doctor also secured the former offices of Dr. Sheftall on the northwest corner of Jefferson and Liberty Streets.[79] The Hospital "is doing a noble and great work both in alleviating suffering among our people and in training nurses to care for the sick," it reported and "the McKane Hospital has received less from the general public and done more for our people than any other institution attempted or put in operation by our people in this city."[80] Mrs. S. Louise Ward and Mrs. Leonora Kaintuck Wayring graduated from the McKane Nursing School at a function held at St. Philip's A.M.E. Church. Mayor Meldrim and Dr. T. James Davis addressed the graduates. The mayor complimented the institution very highly "and made many encouraging remarks upon the value of such an institution among our people."[81]

The Hospital Trustees appealed to the city council for financial assistance. On becoming aware of this move on the part of the board, the Drs. McKane sent a note to the council vigorously opposing this move. Attorney Abraham L.Tucker, the Rev. J.J.Durham, Dr. Henry Bugg and Dr. T.James Davis represented the hospital before the council. Their appeal to Council was that the Hospital had been doing great good for the poor of the race. Dr. McKane and about a half dozen others were present to protest against aid given this worthy institution. After listening to the Hospital representatives, Council refused to hear from Dr. McKane or his group. The *Savannah Tribune* reported that the trustees by their action "won the commendation of the colored citizens and gave a just rebuke to those Negroes who are against enterprises that is of benefit to the race." The Council subsequently decided to give the hospital $25 per month.[82]

The black public expressed increased interest in the future of the Hospital and the paper reported that each physician in the city was actively engaged in making the hospital a success. A "large number of prominent citizens has been elected on the board of trustees. New rules will be adopted at the meeting next week and the name will be changed."[83] The institution had struggled onward for nearly three years with little space only able to accommodate seven patients. Not surprisingly, the trustees ordered the building enlarged to accommodate at least 35 to 40 patients. The paper wondered whether the colored people of Savannah would help in the work. It stated, "The time has come when we must look to ourselves to maintain our own institutions and God grant that we will do what we can to hold up this Institution as something we have done for ourselves." Presumably with this sentiment in mind a musical and soiree was given at the Ford Opera House, St. Julian and Whitaker Streets for the benefit of the Hospital.

The *Savannah Tribune* announced the hospital's new name, Charity Hospital. The report stated: "Let the colored people of this city prove to everybody that they can foster an institution of their own, by helping the Charity Hospital and Nurse Training School, located on the corner of Thirty-sixth and Florence Streets. This is an institution that has already done much good. To put it on a solid basis, it needs several hundred dollars, which can be easily raised without the least hardship on any one if the bulk of the citizens would only do a little.... This institution belongs to the colored citizen and they have a chance to make it the best of its kind in the country thereby raising themselves in the estimation of the opposite race."[84] With the February 1901 name change, men were admitted as patients and some adjoining lots were subsequently bought.[85]

Past Grand Master John H. Deveaux and other masons laid the cornerstone of the new Charity Hospital and Nurse Training School. Several groups processed from Liberty and East Broad Streets, headed by the College Band, to the hospital at

36th and Florence Streets for the ceremony.[86] Appeals continued to be made to assist the Hospital. A group of volunteers, whom the paper described as "race loving members of the Silver Star Association," collected pennies from their several friends for the Hospital in the sum of $15.66.[87] The group was organized to aid members in sickness and death, but whenever a call of charity or anything that would benefit the race "these members are always found ready and willing to do their duty. Mrs. Henrietta Owens was president and Mrs. F.P. Edwards was secretary. The commencement exercises of the Nurse Training School were held at the First African Baptist Church, Franklin Square in June 1901. Mrs. A.N.Wilson of Limerick, Georgia, was the only graduate that year.

Continuing its stern rebuke of the Drs. McKane and their followers, the black paper claimed that all the colored citizens of Savannah, those who were truly identified with the best interest of the city, were in favor of the Charity Hospital and its current management. "They look upon it as great need and should be helped by the city. This class of the better element of the colored citizens strongly protests against the nefarious action of a few malcontents and their misguided followers."[88]

In 1902 City Council voted to give Hospital $25.00 per month. Later this amount was increased to $75.00 per month. African American physicians continued to visit churches and appeal for funds. One such visit was to First Bryan Church on February 2, 1902, when $9.15 was donated to the Hospital. The *Savannah Tribune* stated: "We are glad to say Charity Hospital has many substantial friends in Yamacraw as in evidence by the useful articles and money donated from that pert of the city." By 1902, Dr. T. James Davis stated that "a number of the leading white physicians of the city are interested in the institution and a large number of them practice there." He boasted that the hospital "was free and open to all reputable physicians in the city whether white or colored." However, he bemoaned the fact that the Hospital "had no endowment, absolutely none."

The institution struggled onward "for nearly three years with limited space, being able to accommodate only seven patients." The Trustees had ordered the building enlarged to serve 35 to 40 patients and an operating room was added. The paper ended its tirade by claiming: "The time has come when we must look to ourselves to maintain our own institutions as something we have done for ourselves." The Rev. L. B. Maxwell headed the board. The new Superintendent was Dr. T. James Davis, with Drs. C. B. Whaley, P. E. Love, S. P. Lloyd, James H. Bugg, J. Walter Williams and William C. Blackman, as staff. The Council later increased the appropriation to $75 per month.

From 1893 to 1913, there had been 37 graduates 16 of whom, were practicing in the city. The Hospital had 40 beds 8 of which were in private rooms with two wards male and female. In addition, there was a splendid operating room with a modern kitchen.

After the McKanes disconnected themselves from the hospital and Nurses

Training School, they remained for a few years in the city then left for Boston around 1909, "in order that his boys may enjoy better educational facilities."[89] Dr. Cornelius McKane died in Boston in early March 1912. The *Savannah Tribune* reported that the news was received "with regret from his large circle of acquaintances in the city and especially by his former patients." The paper noted that "the memory of Dr. McKane should be revered, and appreciation should be shown Mrs. Dr. McKane for giving to Savannah such an Institution."[90] Deep sympathy was expressed for the bereaved widow and children. In 1939, Governor Leverett Sattonstad "made history" when he appointed First Lieutenant Cornelius McKane his personal aid. McKane the son of Drs. Cornelius and Alice McKane was born in Savannah and educated in Boston schools and an honors graduate of the Massachusetts Military Academy of the class of 1933. The *Savannah Tribune* claimed that the "Savannah friends are proud to note the prominence of young McKane who was born in Savannah." [91]

During 1913, four private rooms were added to Charity Hospital. Some 819 patients were treated and 327 operations were performed with nearly half of them done by physicians on staff. By the next year E.E.Desverney was President of the board Miss Emma Lewis Secretary and Dr. I.D.Williams Treasurer. Mrs. Mary Woodhouse Long was Matron of Nurses and Dr. William C. Blackman was Superintendent. The paper appreciated the audacity of the founders and successors of this endeavor. It stated: "In the beginning it would have been a brave prophet indeed who would have attempted to prophesy as to the outcome of the efforts started by the McKanes."

On April 25, 1919, at a meeting called for that purpose, the Trustees told the Federation that unless they had a full report of all monies collected the canvass would be terminated after May 1, 1919. A drive by the Federation of Negro Women's Clubs to raise $50,000 for building the new Charity Hospital had ended.[92] It was. During 1912 to 1915, about 3,322 patients were treated with 1,351 charity patients. January 1, 1919, was Brick Day for Charity Hospital beginning a 30-day drive. Bricks sold for 10 cents. Dr. Davis put the operating rooms in order.

The Hospital had served 902 patients with a small death rate and had received a $900 appropriation from the city. Efforts were a foot to build a new modern hospital of 45 beds. Dr. William Harris headed the hospital.[93] Drs. W. H. Harris, C.E.Rent. E.K.Love, C.C. Middleton and I.D.Williams were on the staff. Miss Mary Ellen Davis, Miss Alice Pelacher Linder and Miss Elizabeth Ann Williams graduated that year.

Dr. Philip E. Love was born in Auburn, Alabama and came to Savannah in 1887, "when quite a lad." His brother the Rev. Emanuel K. Love pastored the First African Baptist Church in Savannah, "one of the most outstanding and most colorful ministers the local pulpit has ever had." Dr. Philip E. Love graduated from Leonard Medical College, Raleigh, North Carolina. He passed his final examination in March

1896.[94] Love returned to Savannah where "he enjoyed a most lucrative practice until his health began to fail him." He was the second colored city physician appointed by the city council.[95] Black city physicians were overworked and underpaid, the paper complained: "the two colored physicians do more than twice as much work as all of the white physicians combined and receive less compensation." City Council should at least increase the pay of the two physicians and give an additional one in the growing Southside."[96]

Love was an ardent supporter of Charity Hospital and was dean of its medical staff. He was a member of Eureka Lodge, No. 1, Ezra Consistory, No. 27, Scottish Rite Masonry and Omar Temple No. 21, Mystic Shrine. From early youth he was a faithful member of African Baptist Church and "one of its staunchest supporters throughout his long life." Dr. Love died in 1942. [97]

Dr. T. James Davis Sr., was born in Jamaica, West Indies, in 1860.[98] He was the first Negro graduate of the University of Vermont and "took very high rank as a student." Davis came to Savannah "directly after the death of Dr. P. H. Coker and was therefore the oldest of our physicians in the city. He was well known and considered an able physician."[99] Davis was regarded as a "thorough scholar, a profound thinker and a courteous unassuming gentleman," and there were "few men in the state that stand higher than himself."[100] He was a prominent member and Grand Chancellor of the Knights of Pythias,[101] and was Past Grand Chancellor and Chancellor Commander of Crescent Lodge No. 2. Toward the end of September 1893, one of the ten black physicians in the city, Dr. T. James Davis, "Savannah's oldest resident Negro physician," left on a business trip to New Orleans.

The *Savannah Tribune* stated: "He was a man that is well liked by his patients and the community generally." He was regarded as "a doctor of the old school" who believed "in doing much and saying little." He died in 1903 and was buried from Beth Eden Baptist Church. The church was "crowded with friends of the deceased," and "a large number of friends of the deceased from other cities were present."[102]

Dr. T. James Davis Jr., the son of Dr. T. James Davis Sr., and Mrs. Luella H. Davis, a teacher at Paulsen Street School until her death in 1948, was born in Savannah. He attended local schools then went away for his medical education. Dr. Davis returned to the city and opened an office at 545 East Gwinnett Street near East Broad Street. He specialized in x-ray diagnosis and cancer detection and treatment. Dr. Davis practiced in Cleveland, Ohio, where he was a member of the Medical faculty of Western Reserve University and was on the staffs of Crile Hospital and Cuyahoga County Hospital.[103]

Former student Dr. Thomas J. Davis installed new officers of the Paulsen Street School Student Council and other school organizations. Freddie Mae Johnson was elected president of the school by a wide margin. She was an outstanding student and a very active in church and civic affairs. Veronica Carpenter was installed as vice president, Bessie l. Brown, secretary, Margaret Gould, assistant secretary, Joyce Young Bennett, treasurer; Leroy Ladson and Doris Jones, reporters. Betty L. Johnson, parliamentarian; Beverly Williams, chaplain; Jerome Roberts, captain of patrols and Roy Rosier, fire chief.[104]

The Doctors Collier. Dr. Henry Morgan Collier, Sr., was born June 12, 1889, in Augusta, Georgia, to the Rev. John B. Collier and Mrs. Mary Jane Morgan Collier, the daughter of the Rev. Henry Morgan.[105] The Rev. John B. Collier was born in 1861 and died in 1919. His wife Mary Jane was born in 1864 and died in 1918.[106] The Rev. Collier's father-in-law Henry Morgan was born in 1844 and died in 1917. The Rev. Collier's mother-in-law Dora Morgan was born in 1866 and died in 1923. Dora Morgan's father Jessie Stewart was born in 1835 and died in 1925.[107]

The Rev. John B. and Mrs. Mary J. Collier moved to Savannah where young Henry Collier completed his elementary and secondary schooling in the public school system. Young Collier did his normal course at Georgia State College and his college work at Shaw University in North Carolina. He later matriculated at Meharry College, Nashville, Tennessee, in 1908, and graduated with the M.D. degree in 1913 from Meharry Medical College. During the summer Collier worked on board ships and in the dining car service, which enabled him to pay his way through school. Dr. Collier passed the Tennessee Board during his junior year at Meharry and after graduation, practiced in Dixon, Tennessee, and then he returned to Savannah.[108]

Dr. Henry M. Collier, Sr., married Miss Annie Beatrice Gilliard, the daughter of America Gilliard,[109] October 28, 1915. Eight children were born from this union: Dr. Henry M. Collier, Jr., Mrs. Ruby Collier Bryan,[110] a teacher, John B. Collier a general contractor; Lucius E. Collier, registered X-ray technician; Dr. Charles N. Collier a dentist; the Rev. Merrick W. Collier, Dr. Harold R. Collier, and Toland J. Collier. Writing to a friend in 1952, Mrs. Annie Collier stated, "I am proud of my children. They have made me happy each in his own way. I think that a sacred trust was given me when God Almighty saw fit to make me a mother."[111]

In 1920, Dr. Henry M. Collier, Sr., specialized in the X-ray diagnosis and pioneered the field and Physical Therapy at Charity Hospital as head of the Department. He also served for many years as chairman of the X-Ray division of the National Medical Association and was a member of the Georgia State Medical Association and the South Atlantic Medical Society. He was a member of the Mid-Town Chamber of Commerce and a 32-degree Mason and a Shriner. Dr. Collier practiced medicine in Savannah for over 47 years.[112] He served as city physician and was an examiner for the North Carolina Mutual Insurance Company. Collier built a large house at 1002 East 37th Street. He was an ardent member of the First African Baptist Church.

In 1950 he was accosted by a knife-wielding burglar in his office at 707 West Broad Street but was saved by the arrival of his son Dr. Henry Collier Jr.[113]

His son Toland J. Collier, a soldier in the US armed forces in Korea, died in Korea in 1951. He graduated from Beach High School and received his A.B. from Savannah State College in June, 1950. Prior to going into the army he and William B. Haynes formed the Collier and Haynes Construction Company.[114] The South Atlantic Medical Society named Dr. Henry M. Collier, Sr., "Doctor of the Year" in 1958. He died at his residence 1002 East 37th Street in 1961, [115] having practiced medicine for forty-seven years. His wife, sister, 7 children and 16 grand children survived him.[116]

Dr. Nathaniel H. Collier, brother of Dr. Henry Collier, Sr., was born November 6, 1900, in Savannah, where he received his early education in the local public schools. He later attended Savannah State College and went on to obtain his dental degree from Meharry Medical College Dental School, in Nashville Tennessee. Dr. Collier built up "a most lucrative practice and at the time of his death was reputed to be worth in the neighborhood of $200,000. His home on Victory Drive is one of the show places of Savannah."[117]

He was president of the Brotherhood of First African Baptist Church and was actively involved in the Masons, the Mutuals and other social organizations. For over ten years he conducted a free dental clinic for the public school children "until a publicly supported one was established." He was named Kappa Man of the Year in 1952.[118] Collier served on the staff of Charity Hospital and was director of the Negro Division of the Red Cross Feather campaign and was a member of the United Community Services. Dr. Collier practiced dentistry in the city for 32 years.[119]

Collier served on the Board of the West Broad Street branch of the YMCA, a member of the Hub. He was President of the South Atlantic Medical Society, past polemarch of Savannah Alumni chapter, Kappa Alpha Psi Fraternity. He was past illustrious potentate of Omar Temple, Nobles of the Mystic Shrine; past president of the Frogs, Inc. Dr. Collier died February 19, 1954. His wife Nancy Thomas Collier and a brother Dr. H.M. Collier Sr., and a sister Anna Collier survived him.[120]

Dr. Henry Morgan Collier, Jr., was born in Savannah, August 7, 1916, to Dr. Henry Morgan Collier, Sr. and Mrs. Annie B. Collier. Young Henry Collier Jr. attended the local public schools and then went to the Georgia State Industrial College, graduating with a B.A., in 1935. He wrote Richard Wright Sr., informing him of his graduation. Bank President Richard Wright replied June 3, 1935,

> "Nothing gives me greater pleasure than to know that you, my great-grandson, graduates from the school which I founded and of which I was President for so many years. Your father graduated under me. Your grandmother graduated under me, and so now I am writing to you. I trust that you will be as good as your great grand father, as intelligent and kindly as your mother and as enterprising and successful as your father. You have a great task before

you and I have no doubt that you will measure up to it."[121]

One year before graduation he contributed an article on health in Kermit O. Smalls' book.[122] Collier was a science teacher at Dickerson County Training School, Vidalia, from 1935-36.[123] He later studied at Meharry Medical College and received his M.D. degree in 1942 and did post graduate work at the School of aviation medicine, U.S.A.F. He did his residency at Kate Betting Reynolds Memorial Hospital in Winston-Salem, North Carolina, where he met his future wife, Mozella Gaither.

Mozella Gaither Collier was born in North Carolina in 1924, but lived most of her life in Savannah. She was an honors graduate of Savannah State College. Their wedding reception was held at the residence of Dr. Henry Collier. Sr., for Dr. and Mrs. Henry M. Collier Jr.[124] The couple had three children; Vincent, Henry, 1V, and Roberle. Mozella Collier was a member of the Gamma Sigma Omega Chapter of the Alpha Kappa Sorority, Inc. The Savannah Chapter of Links, Inc and the Jack and Jills of America chose her Woman of the Year. She died December 15, 1984.

Dr. Collier opened his office at 705 West Broad Street, "taking the suite of rooms formerly occupied by his father." The father moved his offices downstairs at the same address.[125] In 1950 Collier served as chairman of the education committee of the local NAACP chapter.[126]

From 1952-55, Dr. Collier was a Flight Surgeon and Captain in the United States Air Force. He was stationed at Yokota, A.F.B., Japan, and served as Commander of the 35th Tactical Hospital and Base Flight Surgeon.[127] His wife was with him during his tour of duty in Japan. Dr. Collier and his wife returned to Savannah and he became chief of staff of Charity Hospital in 1959. Dr. Collier was president of the Beta Phi Lambda Fraternity, Inc., chapter of the Alpha Phi Alpha.[128] He was Savannah State's College physician for many years and practiced medicine in Savannah for over forty years. Dr. and Mrs. Collier were active Episcopalians and both served several terms on the Vestry of St. Mathew's. A stained glass window in the church, which they donated, honors their memory.

Dr Charles N. Collier was born in Savannah July 31, 1927, and was educated in the local schools. He graduated from Beach High School in 1944 and received his B. S. degree from Savannah State College then went on to Meharry Medical College School of Dentistry. After graduation he entered the U.S. army and served for two years as a dental officer serving in Korea. He was honorably discharged with the rank of Captain.

The *Savannah Tribune* described Dr. Collier as "one of Savannah's promising young dentists," noting that he came from "a family whose name for many years has prevailed in the medical field of the Savannah area among the leading dentists and physicians of the city."[129] Dr Charles N. Collier practiced dentistry in Savannah for more than forty years and died in 1989. A son and four daughters survived him.[130]

Dr. Harold Roland Collier was born May 10, 1936 and attended the public schools of Savannah. He graduated from Beach High School and then from Lincoln University in 1956. He did further graduate work at Howard University. He later graduated with an M.D., from Meharry Medical College, Nashville, Tennessee in 1964. Dr. Collier completed his internship at Unity Hospital, Brooklyn, New York, from 1965 to 1966.

He served in the United States Army from 1966-1970 and then practiced for a short time in Los Angeles, California. Dr. Collier returned to Savannah and joined his brother in the practice of medicine and surgery. He was active in the Boy Scouts of America and attained the rank of Eagle Scout. He served on the Executive Board of the West Broad Street Y.M.C.A, the Falcons, Inc., and was an active member of Butler Presbyterian Church.[131] Dr. Harold R. Collier died in February 1975. The Collier family has served blacks in Savannah as physicians and dentists for over 160 years.[132]

Dr. Linton Stephen Parks, "pioneer colored dentist of Savannah," was born in Lincoln County on August 16, 1860, to Harrison and Anna Parks.[133] He went to school in Augusta and while working as a drayman, studied dentistry under Dr. Spears. Parks came to Savannah some years later and again while working as a drayman, he continued to study dentistry, this time under Dr. A. H. Best, with whom he shared an office for ten years. He then opened his own office, and eventually had a very prosperous dental practice in the city.

During 1904, Dr. Parks took a very extensive vacation trip through the West and Northwest. At that time he was described as a "skilled and expert dentist, one who enjoys years of experience and wide reputation and possibly the oldest colored dentist in the state." His work and worth as a dentist "has stood the test for many years; he has been of great service and value to his people." Dr. Parks had his office at 240 Barnard Street near Perry Lane.[134] He was a Mason and a member of the Pythians. A fervent Episcopalian, Parks served St. Stephen's Episcopal Church as Junior Warden for several years.

An advertisement in the *Savannah Tribune*, listed him as offering "gold fillings, cement fillings, and silver or amalgam fillings, from nine to a full set of teeth $7.00 and $3.00." When the Seventh Annual Session of the Georgia State Medical Association of Colored Physicians, Dentists and Pharmacists met in Savannah in 1910 he was a member of the reception committee and gave a demonstration on dental procedure. Dr. Parks was described as "the pioneer dentist of Savannah, if not of the state. He is widely known and has stood the test and proven one of the best dentists in this state. He is well liked and respected by all who know him. He will give a demonstration in the clinical department next week."[135]

Dr. Fannin Saffore Belcher was born in Augusta, October 24, 1871. His father, the Hon. Algernon S. Belcher, was prominent in Georgia politics. Young

Belcher attended Augusta Grammar School, Haines Normal and Industrial Institute in Augusta and later did some of his college work at Wake Forest, North Carolina, and graduated from Lincoln University in 1895. He was Principal of Eddy High School, in Milledgeville, from 1895 to 1898. Belcher entered Howard University Medical School, in Washington, D. C., and graduated with his medical degree in 1902. Belcher then went on a two months tour of the Far West.[136] Dr. Belcher began practicing medicine in Savannah in 1902. Dr. Belcher received his license to practice in Savannah, June 11, 1902. He married Mamie Elizabeth Sheftall, daughter of Jackson Benjamin Sheftall, May 19, 1905. They had four children, Fannin S., Jr., Ursuline B., Doris B., and Algernon S. Belcher.

Throughout his 53 years of practice in Savannah, he served his people in several capacities. He sponsored many church and civic medical projects. During World War 1, Dr. Belcher helped organize and was the first instructor of the Toussaint L'Overture chapter of the Red Cross and chairman of the Red Cross drive. Dr. Belcher was political chairman of the colored division of the Citizen's Club, and President of the first local branch of the N.A.A.C.P., and a charter member of the colored library in 1905. He served as chairman of the colored library board for 30 years and as a member for 46 years. Dr. Belcher was an active member of the Knights of Pythians for 30 years serving at one time as Commander.[137]

He was appointed city physician in 1917 and served in that capacity for 14 years. For many years, he served as an officer of the South Atlantic Medical Society and the Georgia State Association of Physicians and Pharmacists. In April 1951, Dr. Belcher was awarded a Certificate of Distinction by the Medical Association of Georgia for his 50 years of practicing medicine. In November his children planned a surprise 80th birthday party for their father. All except, Dr. Fannin S. Belcher, Jr. The Belchers and Mrs. Sarah Ann Jackson, sister of Mrs. Belcher, enjoyed " a sumptuous turkey dinner on the afternoon of Dr. Belcher's birthday."[138] He was a devoted member of First African Baptist Church and served for 10 years as Chairman of the Deacon Board. Dr. Belcher died in 1956. The black paper described him as "the dean of local physicians."[139] His wife died February 9, 1955, shortly before their fiftieth wedding anniversary. At the time of his death, his daughter Ursuline Ingersoll was his only child still residing in Savannah.

Dr. Simon Fenimore Frazier was born in Limerick, Liberty County, October 22, 1888. His father, Plymouth Frazier, was a farmer and his mother, Rosa Dyer Frazier, was the daughter of Joseph and Margaret Dyer. He worked with his father on the farm and attended the Dorchester Academy. His mother encouraged him to become either a physician or a minister. Young Frazier taught school in Liberty County and so earned enough money to go to college. He attended Biddle University later called Johnson Smith University in Charlotte, North Carolina. During his days at the university, he did hotel work in the city. Later he went to Meharry Medical College and earned his medical degree in 1915.

Dr. Frazier came to Savannah in 1916, "with no money and only such equipment as he had brought with him from College." However, he entered the practice of medicine with gusto, setting up offices on East Gwinnett Street. He practiced medicine in Savannah for 46 years. Dr. Frazier served on the staff of Charity Hospital for many years and on the Board of Directors of Carver Savings Bank. He was an ardent elder of Butler Presbyterian Church and a Mason and an Odd Fellow. He was married for forty-one years to Lucile Dawson Frazier. They had three children Muriel Eneas, Ouida Thompson and Wahwee Scott.

Dr. William Augustus Harris was born in Morgan County, on December 17, 1877. He attended Georgia State Industrial College in Savannah and later went to Lincoln University where he obtained his bachelor's degree in 1900. Harris then attended the College of Physicians and Surgeons, gaining his medical degree in 1905. He went to England for further study and completed his postgraduate studies there in 1911. That same year he came to Savannah and began his practice of medicine. Harris served as President of the South Atlantic and the State Medical Societies and was on the staff of Charity Hospital. Dr Harris was appointed medical examiner for the Westside Draft Board.[140] The Anti-Tuberculosis League was organized "a few years ago as an adjunct of the Men's Sunday Club," and he did "regular and effective work among the sick of our city."[141] By 1935 he had become "one of the senior practicing physicians in the city," and by his unobtrusive manner had "gained a place the esteem and confidence of the citizens which is enjoyed by but a few." He served Charity Hospital as a trustee and superintendent. He got the officers of the Georgia Medical Society in Augusta to "open a clinic to the colored physicians of the state."[142]

The Doctors Jamerson. Dr. John William Jamerson, Sr., was born October 15, 1874 in Ridgeway, Henry County, Virginia, to farmer John Jamerson and his wife, Elizabeth Burgess Jamerson. At four years of age, young Jamerson lost his father and shortly thereafter his mother also died. A white family in Patrick County adopted him and he lived with them for eleven years. Since he had not received any formal education, eighteen-year-old Jamerson began his education[143] in the first grade of Grace Presbyterian Church mission school.[144] Within a few years he matriculated at Biddle University, now named Johnson C. Smith University in North Carolina and obtained his A. B., degree in 1900.

Emboldened by this success, young Jamerson determined to study dentistry at Walden University now known as Meharry Medical College in Nashville, Tennessee. While in dental school, Jamerson worked at a boarding house and during the summer he worked in several hotels. Jamerson graduated from dental school in 1905 and relocated to Savannah where he remained for the rest of his life and had a very successful practice. It is possible that his Presbyterian Church contacts suggested Savannah as a good location for a young dentist. He was one of the first black dentists to practice in Savannah.[145] Buttressed by a loan from George Peabody of New York, the young dentist devoted his energies to establishing a sound practice at his Eastside office. This investment became so successful that within a short time he paid off the Peabody debt.[146]

The financially secure Dr. Jamerson married Julia Aline Belcher of Augusta on September 8, 1909, at her parents' home. She was the daughter of Algernon Belcher and Sarah Stevens Belcher, a well-established family of Augusta and sister of Dr. F. Belcher of Savannah. Savannah born the Rev. George H. Dwelle performed the ceremony. The wedding party left immediately after the ceremony, took the train for Savannah and went to the Jamerson home on Ogeechee Road. The bride was regarded as "a very estimable young lady." She was one of the popular teachers of the public schools of Augusta, and "beloved by all of her friends." The groom was described as "one of the leading dentists and holds a popular place in the esteem of our citizens, all of whom join in welcoming the bride to our city and wishing for both a happy sail on the matrimonial sea."[147]

The couple had four children: John W. Jr., and his twin Mayaline Wallace of Silver Spring, Maryland; Juanita Syphax of Washington D.C., and Dorothy Days of Silver Spring, Maryland. The first two were born in 1910. In that year the *Savannah Tribune* reported: "No young man has made greater strides than our young dentist. Coming to this city nearly a total stranger, has added to his list a large number of substantial friends, and by his indefatigable efforts, has built up a practice that equals, if not surpassing the younger dentists of the state."[148] The paper later announced the birth of his twins, reporting: "the mother, son and daughter are doing well, while the doctor is all smiles and receiving the congratulations of friends."[149]

The first Dr. Jamerson was an astute businessman. When the Wage Earners Bank was built at 458 ° West Broad Street, Jamerson moved his office to the bank building and was one of the directors of the institution. In addition, he functioned as an "unofficial bank" loaning money to customers and others who could not obtain regular loans from the bank. He lost "a big part of his fortune when the Wage Earners Bank crashed."[150] Jamerson was ardent member and official of Butler Presbyterian Church for many years. He was treasurer of the Carnegie Colored Library and served as treasurer of his Masonic lodge. He was active in the local Red Cross movement among blacks in the city and served on the executive committee of the local branch of the NAACP. In 1938, Dr. Jamerson was elected the first president of Georgia Dental Society. This group withdrew from the Georgia Medical & Pharmaceutical Organization after forty years to form their own organization.

Julia Aline Belcher Jamerson died at her home, April 27, 1927. The following year Dr. Jamerson married Minnie Carwell Jamerson of Washington, D.C. She died February 13, 1952 in Savannah. Dr. Jamerson next married Harriett Lewis Jamerson February 19, 1955 in Pittsburgh, Pennsylvania. She died December 18, 1962 in Savannah. Dr. John William Jamerson died in 1963, having practiced dentistry for an incredible 58 years.[151]

Dr. John William (Bill) Jamerson, Jr., was born in Savannah, September 22, 1910, to Dr. John. W. and Mrs. Julia Aline Belcher Jamerson.[152] He attended East Broad Street School in Savannah and was sent to his maternal grandparents in Washington, D.C., where he attended Paul Lawrence Dunbar High School.[153] Jamerson then went to Lincoln University in Pennsylvania from which he graduated in 1933. As the oldest child he had to suspend his educational pursuits and earn some money so the family could educate the younger ones. He worked at various jobs in Washington, D.C. Jamerson later followed his father and studied dentistry at Meharry Medical College in Tennessee graduating in 1941.[154]

A year before graduation, September 28, 1940, Jamerson married Dorothy Louise Breaux of Endsley, Alabama, the daughter of Louis Felix Breaux, Jr. and Minnie Nesbitt Breaux of Montgomery Alabama. She was educated in the public schools of Chicago, Illinois, and graduated from Dowagiac High School in Dowagiac, Michigan, in 1934. Dorothy Breaux obtained her B.A. degree in biology from Fisk University, Nashville, Tennessee, in 1939. She graduated from Atlanta University with a B. S. degree in Library science and in 1963 she received her Ed. S degree in library science from George Peabody College of Vanderbilt University in Nashville, Tennessee.[155] Dorothy Jamerson worked as a librarian at Carnegie Public Library, Beach Adult Education Center, Sol Johnson High School, and Savannah State College. Prior to her illness Dorothy Jamerson was an active member of St. Matthew's Episcopal Church, a Sunday school teacher and a member of St. Stephen's Guild. She died May 24, 1999.

Dr. Jamerson, Jr., returned to Savannah, joined his father's office, practicing dentistry at 458° West Broad Street from 1941. In 1951 he and his wife drove to Shepherd Field, Texas to enter the dental service of the Air Force.[156] to 1983; then he joined his son, Dr. Jamerson III, in his new office in the Victorian District at 315 East Henry Street until he retired in 1986. Jamerson served as past president of the Georgia Dental Society and Chatham Dental Society, a life member of the American Dental Association, Georgia Dental Association, and the Southeast District Dental Society. He was a fellow of the Academy of General Dentistry and the Academy of Dentistry International. He served as a dentist at the Chatham County Health Department and was secretary to the dental staff at Memorial Medical Center.

In 1986 the local branch of the NAACP honored him with the Freedom Award for his civil rights activity, his commitment to the organization as a life member, and Vice President for more than twenty-five years. As an advisor to the Youth Council he helped to integrate Tybee Beach. He was a plaintiff in several suits, which eventually legally desegregated Savannah. The Economic Opportunity Authority honored Dr. Jamerson for his civil rights work at their 23rd annual meeting.[157] He was also active in the Hub, a group of black professionals and business people who worked for the improvement of social conditions.[158] *Savannah Morn-*

ing News, February 15, 1997. Dr. J. W. Jamerson served in the United States Air Force as a Captain during the Korean War.

A devout churchman, Dr. Jamerson served St. Matthew's Episcopal Church as Church School teacher, Choir member, Bible Study Co-coordinator, Men's Club member and Vestry member for several decades. Episcopal Bishop Albert R. Stuart appointed him to Savannah's Bi-racial Committee. He was a volunteer at the Emmaus House project of Christ Episcopal Church. Dr. Jamerson was a long time member of Omega Psi Phi, Inc. since 1930. In 1963 he became an Omega Life Member # 1701. That same year St. Matthew's Men's Club saluted Dr. Jamerson. He was described as "a great asset to his church, family and community and has shown a willingness to serve whenever and wherever he might be needed."[159]

He was a member of the Hub Civic Club, the Human Relations Council of Savannah, and the Board of Directors of the Carnegie Library, the Dixon Park Neighborhood Association. He loved to read and was a co-leader with E. J. Josey, College librarian, of the SSC Great Books discussion group opened to faculty, students and the public.[160] He and his wife had three, daughters: Dr. Dorothy Aline Jamerson, who married Dr. R. L. Anders of San Jose, California; Kathleen Amelia O'Quinn of West Bloomfield, Michigan who married Milton O'Quinn; Patricia Ann Manson of Miami, Florida, who married Ernest Manson; and a son: Dr. John William Jamerson, III, of Savannah, who married to Shearon Brown Jamerson.

Dr. John William Jamerson, Jr., died Christmas Day, 1998, in his 88th year, as his father before him. Almost a century earlier in Savannah, he would have been called a "race man," because, as was said of James Porter, "he was a lover of his race. Almost his whole life was spent in his effort to improve and ameliorate their condition."[161]. "Doc," as he was affectionately called by all, was one of those rare individuals who when they enter your life, they demand a whole lot of you, "mess with your mind," and when they depart from you, they leave you roughed-up a bit, but changed for the better. That was the effect "Doc" had on me after over twenty years as his pastor.

Dr. John William (Billy) Jamerson, III, was born in Savannah, April 26, 1951 and was educated in the public schools of the city. He graduated from Savannah High School in 1969. He then studied at Morris Brown College in Atlanta and graduated from Savannah State College in 1974. Jamerson went to Howard University Dental School, from which he received his doctorate in dental surgery in 1980. Maintaining the tradition, he joined his father's practice at 458 ° West Broad Street and so for the second time Savannah had two doctors Jamerson. In the 1940's Dr. Jamerson Sr., was called "old doc" and his son, "young doc." Forty years later the custom was not repeated. The Drs. Jamerson had rented their offices from 1905 to 1982. Dorothy Jamerson had a better idea. She urged her son to build his own office. Once the building was completed father and son moved in and practiced together until the senior Jamerson retired in 1986, having practiced dentistry in

Savannah for 45 years.

The third generation Dr. John W. Jamerson, and his wife Shearon Brown Jamerson, were married December 28, 1977, and have six children: Desiree Maria, Elizabeth Rene, Amanda Louise, John William 1V, Charles Martin Breaux and Amelia Morgan. Dr. Jamerson is affiliated with many local state and national dental associations. Jamerson has also preserved the family tradition of involvement in the community. He is board chairman of the Chatham County Department of Family and Children Services.[162] As his father before him Dr. Jamerson also serves as a Vestry member of St. Mathew's Episcopal Church and is a life member of the NAACP. He too has received several honors and fellowships in the dental profession. He was Alpha Phi Alpha Fraternity man of the year on several occasions. These three Jamerson dentists, with 123 years among them, are unmatched in black or white Savannah. At the Martin L. King Celebration January 2000, the Jamerson dentists received a special recognition for their contribution to Savannah. They have surely set an admirable record of service in black Savannah if not in the two Savannahs.

The Doctors Cooper. Dr Herbert Lee Cooper was born "on a little cotton farm in South Carolina," December 6, 1875, to farmer Henry Cooper and Elsie Barr Cooper, but lost his mother when quite young. Cooper attended the public school and night school taught by his brother. He next went to Allen University and finally to Meharry Medical College graduating with his M. D. degree in 1907. Dr. Cooper practiced for a short time in Hemingway, South Carolina. In 1911 he moved to Savannah and eventually built a lucrative practice.

He married Ollie Rutherford, the daughter of Peter and Ellen Rutherford. They had three children: Elsie Lee, Herbert Lee, Jr., and Wendell Phillip Cooper. The mother died when the children were young.

Dr. Phillip W. Cooper was born in Savannah and was educated at St. Benedict School and Benedict College, Columbia, South Carolina, the University of Indiana and Atlanta University. He was an instructor at Beach-Cuyler High School. In 1944 he was homeroom teacher of the 10th, 11th, and 12th grades. In that capacity he made an indelible impression on several young minds, inspiring them to "make something of themselves." Cooper would take his class to Derricks Inn on Ogeechee Road for picnics. He postponed leaving for dental school in order to be present for the graduation of the class of 1946. This sense of "togetherness" enabled the class to remain together even to the present time. Walter Simmons, better known as 49, was inspired to go to college because he wanted to be "as good a teacher as Mr. Phillip Cooper and as good a coach as Mr. Joe Greene."[163]

Cooper received his D.D.S. degree from Meharry Medical College School of Dentistry in June of 1950, "maintaining the highest scholastic average over a four year period."[164] He subsequently passed the National Board of Dental Examiners of the American Dental Association. Dr. Cooper was a member of Butler Presbyterian Church, Omega Psi Phil. Fraternity, and Kappa Sigma Pi Honorary Fraternity, Omicron Kappa Upsilon National Dental Society for Children and the Frogs Club. Dr. Cooper opened his office in Savannah at 530 West Broad Street in 1950.[165] He served as treasurer of the local branch of the NAACP.[166]

The class of 1946 dedicated their twenty-fifth class reunion December 28, 1970, to "their beloved former teacher, Dr. Phillip Cooper, for outstanding leadership in education, athletics, community services, his skillfulness as a master teacher and counselor."[167] In 1975 Dr. Cooper was awarded a fellowship in the American College of Dentists. Since 1920 this organization had recognized, through its fellowship, dentists who had "contributed to the advancement of the profession."[168] That same year the Georgia Dental Society presented several awards to Savannah dentists. Dr. Cooper, Sr., received an award for his 30 years of practice in Savannah.[169] Dr. Cooper died in 1980.[170]

Dr. Phillip Wendell Cooper, Jr., the son of Dr. Phillip W. Cooper Sr., and Mrs. Agatha Cooper was born ion Savannah and graduated from St. Pius X High School. He did his post secondary studies at Benedict College in Columbia, South Carolina, and then entered Meharry Medical College School of Dentistry in Nashville, Tennessee. Cooper received his D.D.S., degree from Meharry in 1975 and returned to Savannah and opened his practice with his father at 413 West Duffy Street.[171] Cooper served as president of the Georgia Dental Society in 1980 when he distributed awards to his father. Dr. Albert S. LaFayette, a 1917 graduate of Howard University received an award for his 63 years of practice in Savannah. Dr. J. Wilmette Wilson, a 1930 graduate of the University of Iowa received an award for his 51 years of dental practice in the city.[172]

Dr. Clarence Bailey Tyson was born in Monticello, Florida, on October 15, 1872, to George and Janie Tyson. He worked on a farm until age eighteen when he worked in hotels in order to put himself through Talladega College in Alabama. After a short teaching spell in Alabama, young Tyson went to Meharry College, where he graduated with his M. D., in 1897. Dr. Tyson worked for a while in Waycross, and then relocated to Savannah where he established "a large general practice."[173] He was an active Mason, city physician for five years, and a member of several societies. Dr. Tyson married Rosa B. Moody, a teacher who was educated at Morris Brown University. They had three children Alma V., William G., and Clarence B., Tyson, Jr.[174]

On a Tuesday evening in the fall of 1912, Dr. Tyson's wife gave her husband "a very pleasant surprise at his residence, 811 Gwinnett Street. It was the doctor's birthday. And many of his friends gathered at the home to celebrate the event." The affair was "most delightful" and the doctor "not only expressed himself as feeling many years younger on account of the evening's surprise but looked the part as well." The Metronome Orchestra supplied the music and Mrs. R. B. Tyson, Mrs. William Durden, Mrs Pearl Thomas and Mrs. Ida Hopkins served refreshments. Drs. W. A. Harris, G. W. Smith, P. E. Love, N. W. Este, I. D. Williams, J. W. Jamerson,

H. L. Cooper, F. S. Belcher, L. W. Leftwich, C. C. Middleton, L. S. Parks, Messrs L. E. Williams, R. L. Jones, M. W. Bryant, Henry B. Wright, A. Holbrooks, J. E. Weston, Thomas Green, Samuel King, Willie Blair, Herbert Desverney, D. J. Scott, Milledge Anderson, and D. M. Patterson attended the gala affair.[175]

Dr. William G. Tyson, son of Dr. and Mrs. C. B. Tyson of 211 East Gwinnett was born in Savannah and educated in the elementary public schools. He graduated from Cuyler Junior High. In May of 1926, Tyson completed his professional course at Meharry Medical College, graduating with honors. Tyson successfully passed the Georgia Medical Board in 1926. Dr. Tyson returned to Savannah and opened a practice with his father, "Savannah's old reliable practitioner of many years experience with offices in the Wage Earners Bank building." His friends wished him "much success."[176]

Young Dr. Tyson was "highly commended" for his study of syphilis among Negroes, which he conducted at the Cuyler School clinic. The study was published in a national journal. Nurse Laura King assisted Dr. Tyson in this study. This project was partly sponsored by the Savannah Federation of Colored Women's Clubs and a small monthly donation from the city of Savannah. [177]

Nurse Alethia W. Saulter was born in Charleston and attended Avery Institute in that city. She graduated from Allen University and taught for four years. She came to Savannah and took the nursing course at Charity Hospital graduating in 1915. Nurse Saulter was promoted to Superintendent of nurses and matron in 1916 and remained at Charity until her death in 1933.

In 1923, Nurse Saulter took a postgraduate nursing course at Freedman's Hospital in Washington, D. C., and a six-week course, in 1930, at Harlem Hospital in New York City. Nurse Saulter was a "most popular nurse among both white and colored doctors and had a very unusual character in that she had "the ability of being able to readily make friends and to hold them. She was efficiency plus and possessed rare executive ability." A report in the *Savannah Tribune* announcing her death in 1933 claimed that during her stay at Charity Hospital, "the hospital grew to its zenith under her reign and much success attained by the Institution was due to her skillful management and her wonderful personality."

During 1933 while at work at the hospital, she succumbed to blood poisoning. After a frantic search to find matching blood, the *Savannah Tribune* of April 20, 1933, reported that "a white man whose blood did match readily gave his blood for the transfusion in an effort to save the life of Mrs. Alethia Saulter." Nurse Saulter died and was buried from St. Phillip's A.M.E. Church. Her funeral was "largely attended."[178]

Nurse Lula B. Johnson celebrated her 77th birthday with her family and friends at her residence at 214 East Park Avenue. Nurse Johnson was "a member of the first class to graduate from Charity Hospital Training School for nurses at that time the McKane Nurse Training School." In 1935, "she and two other ladies being the only surviving members of that class." Nurse Johnson followed her profession for many years and was at that time, "one of the best known nurses in this city."[179]

Nurse Ella Reid Sams retired from her profession in 1957 after more than fifty years of "outstanding service." She had "the distinct honor of being one of the first graduate nurses of Georgia Infirmary, having graduated April 2, 1908." Nurse Sams did her early schoolwork at Dorchester Academy in Liberty County. When she received her certificate at graduation from the Georgia Infirmary, she was given a pair of scissors, which she kept and used till her retirement. She was "the first colored nurse to be called for private duty at the old Savannah Hospital."

She was a devoted member of Bethany Presbyterian Church and an elder of the church. The *Savannah Tribune* claimed "many citizens both white and colored will long remember Nurse Sams for her loyal, kind and devoted care administered to them during their illnesses. She is a fine example for young womanhood to emulate. In the thinking of many persons, she is truly a twentieth century Florence Nightingale."[180] Nurse Ella Reid Sams served as a private nurse, a public health nurse and a nurse for the Henry Ford plantation in Bryan County. She served as an elder at Bethany Presbyterian Church. The *Herald* claimed that many citizens of both races would long remember nurse Sams "for her loyal, kind and devoted care administered to them during their illnesses. She has been referred to as a fine example for young nurses to emulate."[181]

Savannah Pharmacy

The **Savannah Pharmacy** is the second oldest African American owned business, after the Bynes Royall Funeral Home, in contemporary Savannah. It is located at 918 Dr. Martin L. King Jr. Blvd., the former West Broad Street, which was the location of a black business strip, stretching from Gaston to Henry streets. Earl Fonvielle, the present owner, is the third generation to operate the pharmacy.

In 1893 Professors D.C.Suggs and L.B. Palmer of the Georgia State College for Colored Youth and Dr. R. C. Williams opened the first African American pharmacy on Broughton Street near Montgomery Street.[182] African American doctors vied with one another to be the first doctor to have his prescription filled at the new pharmacy.[183] As it turned out, Dr. McKane won the competition, but Dr. Snelson's prescription had the larger dollar amount. Sol Johnson gloated: "The patronage already given is a reasonable guarantee that the enterprise will be a grand success." Prof Suggs sold his store in 1894.[184] In August, Dr. Dingle, formerly of South Carolina, took charge of the Forest City Drug Store on Liberty Street. The *Savannah Tribune* reported, "The doctors and ministers have been enthusiastic in their support." Meanwhile J.M. Benson joined Forest City Pharmacy. He was regarded as "a young man of considerable experience in compounding medicines and coming from one of the best pharmaceutical schools in the country, Leonard Pharmaceutical Department of Shaw University."

The *Savannah Tribune* asked the question, "should we as intelligent citizens patronize such places?"[185] The writer expressed his distaste for boycotts but wondered whether the time had not come for blacks to "spend their money on drugs only in those drug stores which did not practice any form of discrimination."

Later, proprietors Drs. J. H. Bugg and S. C. Snelson opened a second pharmacy at Liberty and East Broad Streets. The paper reported, "To say it is very handsome does not express the beauty of it." All ladies who made a purchase on the first Saturday received a nice glass of soda water.[186] In 1905 the West Side Pharmacy at 511° West Broad Street at the corner of Minis Street, advertised itself as the "Colored Drug Store." Drs. C. P. Watts and J. F. Ford were the Druggists.[187]

Dr. C.W. Smith and **Dr. J. E. Smith** of Brunswick, Georgia, came to Savannah around 1910, and opened a drug store called the Savannah Pharmacy, at the southwest corner of West Broad Street and Gwinnett Lane. They conducted the business for about two years and then the Lee Chemical Company of Atlanta and Albany bought them out and placed pharmacist Dr. J. B. Gannt "an old druggist of Yonkers New York, will have charge of the store and Dr. G.W.Smith pharmacist, will remain with the firm for awhile," in charge. Plans were to stock the establishment with a full and complete line of drugs, cigars, cigarettes and toilet articles.[188]

Dr. W. T. Pritchett was born at Oak Hill, Virginia, and was educated in the schools there. He afterward attended Hampton Institute, and then Shaw University, taught school for sometime, and then finally took a course at Leonard Medical College. He went to Augusta and practiced there for many years. Pritchett came to Savannah in early 1913 and opened the Eastside Pharmacy at 225 Randolph Street. This was the second Negro drug store in the city. The *Savannah Tribune* boasted: "This makes the second Negro drug store in the city, and its opening is welcomed by the Negroes throughout the city."[189] He was a specialist in women and children diseases.[190] Dr. W. T. Pritchett "stood among the foremost in the profession." After "practicing several years he went before the Georgia Board of Pharmacy and was one of the sixteen successful applicants out of the fifty nine who entered the examination."[191]

Dr. J. E. Peters of Columbus worked for a few months in Waycross then came to Savannah in July 1913. He joined Dr. Moody, who had been working alone since the departure of Dr. Grant for New York. Peters graduated from Flint Medical College in New Orleans and was "well versed in the drug business."[192] The Lee Chemical Company bought property at the southwest corner of West Broad Street and Maple Lane and erected a new two story brick building. Pharmacist Dr. W. F. Moody succeeded Dr. Grant as local manager of the Lee Chemical business. Dr J.

E. Grigg worked with Dr. Moody. In 1914 Savannah Pharmacy began the erection of a new building with black contractor W. B. Brown in charge of the work.[193] The pharmacy carried a "fresh stock of drugs, a select line of toilet articles and accessories. Its soda fountain trade is extremely large." The store maintained a quick delivery, using two boys in this department.[194]

Dr. Walter F. Moody, a New Yorker and graduate of a college in upstate New York, migrated south and was employed as a chemist at the Lee Chemical Company in the 800-block of West Broad Street. This site later became the famous Neptune Café on West Broad Street.

Dr. Joseph Earl Fonvielle was born in Goldsboro, North Carolina, and graduated from Livingstone College in Salisbury, North Carolina. He subsequently studied at Howard University School of Pharmacy and graduated in 1914. Fonvielle headed south to Camilla, Georgia, to work as a pharmacist. Racial animosity subsequently forced him to escape from the town at "dead of night." Fonvielle made it to Albany and contacted a prominent black physician who promised to keep him there until he was able to get enough money to return home. In the meantime, the physician learned about a Savannah pharmacist, Dr. Walter Moody, who was employed at Lee Chemical. Arrangements were made for Fonvielle to go to Savannah to meet Moody.

When Drs. Moody and Fonvielle finally met, they immediately "got along well." In early September 1915, they bought the Savannah Pharmacy, the "only Negro Pharmacy in the city." The pharmacy was described as "the most attractive Negro Drug Store in the State." The *Savannah Tribune* declared that the proposed deal "will prove of much interest." The two men had expansive visions for the business and succeeded in getting the Lee Chemical Company to sell them the entire business and building for about $20,000.[195] That same year the paper announced the arrival of Joseph E. Fonvielle, the son of Dr. and Mrs. Joseph E. Fonvielle of 2310 Florence Street. Baby and mother were said to be getting along nicely.[196]

The new owners, described as "the most astute young Negro business men in Savannah," launched a massive development strategy. First, they built up the patronage of the West Broad Street store; then they bought out Champion Drug Company, a small drug store on at 140 Fahm Street on the corner of Fahm and York Streets. Dr. I. C. Harris of St. Paul Minnesota, a graduate of Meharry Medical College, was added to the staff of the pharmacies.[197] Throughout their years of partnership, Fonvielle and Moody never had a written legal contract but "operated on a gentleman's agreement," and obviously did well at it.

The Savannah Pharmacy purchased the two story brick building at the southwest corner of West Broad and Maple Lane.[198] This property included a two-story building on West Broad Street and several frame houses in Maple lane. African American real estate dealer G.H.Bowen arranged the deal and the Wage Earners Bank financed the purchase. The brick building fronted West Broad Street for about

40 feet and extended back about sixty feet. In April 1918, the Savannah Pharmacy installed a new fountain in order to "better its soda and ice cream trade." It was reported to be "the latest design and will greatly facilitate the handling of the big Sunday and after theatre soda trade. The service given at this pharmacy is first class in every respect."[199] The Savannah Pharmacy opened a third store on the southeast corner of Randolph Street and Oglethorpe Avenue in a building previously purchased by Dr. Henry M. Collier. The company conducted a "Negro drug store in the city, the other two stores being located one at West Broad and Maple Lane and the other at Farm and York Streets." The new store was "advantageously situated and will doubtless have a very large patronage from those who live in the Old Fort."[200]

By 1924 the Savannah Pharmacy had four stores and the *Savannah Tribune* regarded the chain as "a most thriving business, with a staff of five pharmacists, five clerks, two motor deliverymen and two porters," and "one of the largest and most successful Negro business enterprise." Aside from the usual outlay of drugs, candles, toilet preparations and other commodities, the store had a large soda fountain. The Savannah Pharmacy was regarded as "one of the high spots in local Negro business enterprises." The company also employed Dr. J.H.Eberhart of Athens, a graduate of Howard University, Dr. R. I. Peters of Anniston, Alabama, and a graduate of Meharry Medical College and Dr. Inez Ralford of Aiken, South Carolina, a graduate of the Rhode Island School of Pharmacy.[201]

The branch store at Fahm and Margaret Streets was moved to 615 West Bay Street, "In accordance with its custom to follow the drift of the city's population in locating its branch stores, the removal of this store was decided upon." In 1926 Savannah Pharmacy operated its main store at 719 West Broad Street with a branch at 202 Randolph Street, Augusta Road and Eagle Street.[202]

The four chain stores were displayed in the *Savannah Tribune.* The ground floor of the Savannah Pharmacy building West Broad and Maple Lane housed the drug store and the Mechanics Savings and Investment Company. Upstairs contained the offices of three physicians, one dentist, a contractor and the Liberty Mutual Insurance Company. Mrs. Ella Payne and Miss Martin Hurd were clerks in that building. Mrs. Janie Clanton was a clerk in the Fahm Street building. Miss Emmaline Epstein clerked at the Randolph Street outlet.

Fonvielle and Moody continued to work hard and in the late 1920's, they learned that there was a desperate need for a black drug store in Augusta. After making some contacts and the necessary arrangements, both men made plans to go to Augusta. Unfortunately, on the morning of their departure the largest black bank, the Wage Earners bank failed. Since most of their savings were in the bank, they had to scrap their plans. All of the above locations, except one, were gobbled up by urban renewal or black removal as some have called it.

The Savannah Pharmacy later began the manufacture and sale of ice cream. This became a bonanza. For a while, the drug business was pushed into the background. They furnished ice cream for weddings, parties, picnics, groups and individuals. They experimented with new flavors, new ideas and had all of the modern facilities for experimentation and production. In addition, it all paid off for a while. Not for the first time in Savannah's history, Jim Crow's twin sister, white supremacy, took control of the situation.

As whites in the ice cream business discovered how successful the Savannah Pharmacy's ice cream business had become they made it impossible for Savannah Pharmacy to obtain the ingredients locally. For a time, supplies were purchased from a dairy supply house in Smyrna, Georgia. Eventually, this became so inconvenient and costly for the good product that they wanted to produce that the Pharmacy had to abandon the ice cream business and concentrate on the drugs. In 1939 Frances Fonvielle was the ranking student of the graduating class and the principal speaker at the commencement exercises of Beach High School.[203] Frances Fonvielle graduated from Bennett College, Greensboro, North Carolina, in 1943 with the B. S. degree. She majored in nutrition. She was an outstanding student during her four years at the school and was active in the Little Theatre Guild and the Marshall club. She was the class salutatorian.[204]

Dr. Walter Moody died in August 1942, and Dr. Joseph Fonvielle purchased the Moody interest from his wife, Mrs. Mary Moody in 1952. By then there were pharmacies at Oglethorpe Avenue and Randolph Street, Eagle Street and Augusta Avenue and at West Broad and Henry Streets. Because of a drastic decline in the black population of the Fort district, the company discontinued the store at Oglethorpe Avenue. The firm employed three registered pharmacists, two managers, a bookkeeper, five clerks, two soda fountain attendants and five delivery boys. [205]

Dr. Fonvielle died in 1954 around the same time as that "drum major extraordinaire," Sol C. Johnson. An editorial in the *Savannah Tribune* commented on his death in this wise:

> "The passing of Dr. Fonvielle leaves the Negro Community so much poorer. A successful citizen of Savannah for more than 30 years, he endeared himself to a host of friends and made for himself and his business an enviable standing among businessmen in this city. His dependability so impressed itself on the community that he was often requested to be a worker in the community chest drives. He was a charter member of the Citizens Committee for Negro Social Service and of the West Broad Street YMCA. We pay this tribute to a dutiful father and husband and valuable citizen and acknowledge his passing as a positive loss to which we bow with humble resignation."[206]

Fonvielle's civic activities centered on the boards of the West Broad Street

YMCA, Charity Hospital, and the United Community Services. In 1948 Fonvielle directed the campaign for donations from Negroes, "the most successful drive ever put on by this group for the United Community Service." Dr. Fonvielle was a member of the South Atlantic Medical Society, the Mutual Benevolent Society, the AME Church and the Hub. His widow, Lillian P. Fonvielle, two sons, W. Earl and R. Ulysses Fonvielle and one daughter, Frances Fonvielle, and several other relatives, survived him.[207]

Dr. Julian H. Eberhardt was born in Athens, Georgia, March 26, 1886. He moved to Chattanooga, Tennessee, with this family at an early age and later graduated from Howard University School of Pharmacy receiving his doctorate in that field. Shortly after graduation Eberhardt came to Savannah and remained with the Savannah Pharmacy for 35 years until his death at his residence 607 37th Street in July 1956. Dr. Eberhardt was prominent in Savannah civic affairs and was a member of Omega Psi Phi Fraternity, the South Atlantic Medical Society and the First African Baptist Church.[208] In 1956 a robber shot to death W. Earl Fonvielle in the pharmacy. (*Savannah Tribune,* February 16, 1956.), and his daughter carried on the business. In the latter part of the 1950s, Savannah Pharmacy found itself in the way of "city progress," urban renewal-or black removal, as some say. Rather than close out the era on that note, the business relocated. Because of this decision, the business was moved to the present Fonvielle Office Building at 914-918, Martin L. King Jr. Blvd. William E. Fonvielle, the grandson of the original Fonvielle, took over the operation of the Pharmacy in December, 1980. Francis Fonvielle became secretary-treasurer of the business.

Self-Help

During the years following Reconstruction, African Americans lacked the collateral to obtain loans to start new businesses or improve existing ones. Jim Crow laws and mores further seriously handicapped their economic advancement. In 1870 blacks owned more than $4000,000 in property. From 1866 to 1874 blacks had deposited $153, 000 in the Savannah branch of the Freedmen's Savings Bank.[209] A group of "a number of respectable colored citizens" organized the Self Insurance Association of Georgia for mutual protection and benefit. Each member was expected to pay one dollar on entrance into the Association and an assessment of one dollar and ten cents upon every death, one dollar to go to the family of the deceased member and ten cents into the treasury as a general fund to meet current expenses. Seventy-five members joined up at the first meeting.[210]

Never at their wits' end, African Americans decided to establish their own banks. The black press strongly supported this attempt. It stated: "What the colored man can do in the commercial world is clearly shown by the handsome working of the Workingmen Loan and Building Association during the past year. The Association is in splendid trim and will declare a dividend to each one of its share holders." The Officers obtained their charter from Judge Faligant.[211] Later the paper added: "Savannah needs a colored savings bank, drug store, dry goods store, shoe store, several first class grocery etc.," and added "this is an excellent chance for some men with money, pluck and tenaciousness." A letter to the editor signed by "The Workingmen Loan and Building Association" claimed that the Association "will help its members to get homes and save money."[212] The Association paid 5 percent on the dollar on sums of $25 or $50 and upward.

By 1892 the *Savannah Tribune* touted the need for a black bank, drug store, dry goods store, shoe store, and several first class grocery stores.[213] On the other hand black Savannah had a newspaper, job printing offices, a building and loan association, physicians, a lawyer etc.[214] Plans were to organize a bank. A letter in the *Savannah Tribune* concluded: "We are one year old and have loaned out $3000 to members." The Association soon increased its capital to $10,000. A well-attended meeting was held at the home of Mr. J. W. Searles "for the purpose of organizing a savings bank among the colored people." A committee was appointed to report on the advisability of establishing a bank.[215] One week later, the paper reported that the proposed bank had met with "hearty approval by the people in general." Shares were to be at $100 each, ten percent of which had to be paid down and the remainder either in monthly or quarterly installments.[216] The paper expressed the view that these actions proved that "the colored people of Savannah have the ability and good intentions of launching out in the commercial world."[217]

The Peoples Savings Bank was organized and J. W. Searles was elected president.[218] The Board of Managers of the People's Savings Institution called a meeting of the subscribers at the residence of Mr. J.W.Searles at No. 26 Harris Street "for the purpose of collecting 5 percent of the amount subscribed."[219] Later the paper stated: "Our savings bank is now an assured organization. Every colored person should encourage it, by their patronage as soon as the books are open for business."

Savannah had two incorporated Loan and Building Associations, a savings bank, "all managed by colored men. Hurrah for the colored citizens of Savannah." In addition, the paper boasted that the city had "three colored job printing offices, two newspapers, four physicians, two lawyers and several other men doing excellent business, all of which the people should be proud and show their appreciation by patronizing unstintingly and encouraging others to launch out in some other branches."[220] One month afterward a mass meeting was held at First African Baptist Church at which the audience was urged to buy stock. The following week another meeting for the same purpose was held at St. Philip's Church.

The paper praised J. W. Searles, "Though his residence among us has been but a few years," for making his contribution to the quality of life in the city by "up building of race enterprises."[221] He had organized the Workingmen's Loan and Building Association, the People's Saving Bank and lately a "well established shoe store." The paper expressed the hope that the "young men imitate him in his progressiveness and we assure them that they will be successful." In 1896 the Mechanics Investment Company, with offices at 20 State Street opened for business. Lindsey Reed was one of the pioneers among blacks in the banking business in Savannah. These banks eventually failed.

In early 1900, about a dozen black businessmen met and decided to pool their resources and start a bank. They came up with $102. A mass meeting was to be held at Ford Opera House on Monday July 8, 1901. This meeting was to be under the auspices of the Wage Earners Loan and Investment Company, "which desires to interest the people of Savannah in the organization and to this end will hold the meeting and the attendance of all adults, both ladies and gentlemen are requested."[222]

There was to be no admission fee and cold refreshments were to be served. The *Savannah Tribune* had previously reported that the meeting should "receive the support of the public at large, and should command the attention of all thinking people." It did. A large number of African Americans attended and were apprised of the plans that the directors had for the community. Attorney Abraham L. Tucker and Prof. N.B.Young of the Georgia State College were the principal speakers. The facts presented were said to have "opened the eyes of all who heard them. Especially what was called the painful truth that the Negroes of Savannah spend yearly upwards of two million dollars, and not ten percent of that amount is spent among our people." The bank was located at 22 West State Street. Aware of previous failures of black banks, and though organized less than a year earlier, the directors stressed the probity of its members and especially that of its president, Albert Jackson.

President Albert Jackson (1852-1901), "one of Savannah's best known and highly respected citizens," was born in Savannah around 1852 and "after attaining such education as was obtainable here in his boyhood,"[223] most likely in one of the black underground schools in the city, he was sent to the Harvard Institute in Boston, Massachusetts. After graduation the "Liberian bug" bit him, as it had several other black Savannahians before him, and he lived in Liberia for a few years. Jackson returned to Savannah and opened a locksmith and machine shop. During Reconstruction, the City Board appointed Jackson "assistant city register for the colored population of this city."[224] He distinguished himself in that capacity, and "by his courtesy and conservatism won the respect of the people of Savannah, especially of the white people who were required to take the oath of allegiance to the United States Government."[225]

In January, 1869, while employed as a bookkeeper, he married Jeanette

Bullock, the daughter of Josephine Mirault.[226] She died in 1872 aged 26 years.[227] Albert Jackson later married Mary Louisa Scott June 10, 1874. She was the daughter of Thomas Scott, a free mulatto barber. The Rev. Joseph S. Atwell, rector of St. Stephen's Episcopal Church, performed the ceremony.[228] The couple lived in a two-story house with a stable, at 307 Charlton Street, which Jackson bought for $1,500 in 1876.[229] They had three children, Joseph, Sidney and Mary.[230] The Jackson family was one of the founders of St. Stephen's congregation.[231] Albert Jackson was elected a Vestry member of St. Stephen's in 1874,[232] and was in charge of caring for the "sick and destitute" as a member of the Forest City Benevolent Society.[233] His seven-year-old eldest son fell victim to the third fiercest yellow fever scourge to hit Savannah.[234]

Albert Jackson worked in the cotton exporting business for the firm of Deas & Johnson. When Deas died in 1872 the firm changed to Johnson and Jackson.[235] Later when Johnson died in 1884, Jackson became the sole owner of the new establishment, Jackson and Sons located at 84 Bay Street.[236] Jackson's daughter, Mrs. Moore, the wife of J.F.W. Moore died in 1892.[237] Albert Jackson conducted a very profitable business up to the end of his life and acquired a great amount of real estate, which provided him with a sizable rental income.[238] He was a man of "the strictest integrity and his judgment on all business matters was frequently sought and appreciated by many." He had "always been intensely interested in the welfare of the race, and no one felt the pangs of insults and discriminations more than he did."[239] Jackson was a prominent Republican and served on the permanent committee of the party. In 1878 Jackson and William H. Royall established the first black funeral home in Savannah.

Editor Sol Johnson hoped that: "The life and business transactions of this noble man, should be and example for all of our young men, and should be the cause of giving them an incentive for greater achievement." He concluded the editorial with: "The death of Mr. Jackson is a distinct loss to the Negro, but he has left an excellent legacy for uprightness and business integrity that we can profitably emulate."[240] The Vestry of St. Stephen's Episcopal Church passed a resolution recording the "loss of a true friend and co-worker, whose council and advice was alike valuable and unselfish."[241] Albert Jackson left his wife Mary, his children Albert Jr. Joseph, Sidney and Mary, and a sister Maria Jackson to cherish his memory.[242] The following year his son, Joseph L. Jackson, an "enterprising young business man" with a "successful plumbing business," married Miss Sarah Ann Sheftall, eldest daughter of Jackson B. Sheftall and a "lady of excellent qualities."

The Board of Directors elected Lucius E. Williams, the vice-president, to the presidency of the bank. W. R. Fields was elected vice-president, and Walter S. Scott, secretary/treasurer. The other members of the board composed the elite of black Savannah Attorney Abraham Tucker, Edward E. Desverney, Dr. J. J. Durham, Paul E. Perry, J. L. Jackson, L. M. Pollard, Dr. J. W. Williams, J. H. Rogers, and Sol

C. Johnson.[243] The *Savannah Tribune* featured a reflective editorial on banking and African Americans in the city. It stated:

> "Our people had been greatly discouraged after emancipation by the failure of the Freedman's bank and several other enterprises inaugurated by men who hadn't even the rudiments of business training. Because this is so, there is no reason why they should continue to feel discourage. Things now are not what they were then. Our men are more enlightened and many enterprises among them are conducted on the plans of business."[244]

President Williams visited Birmingham, Alabama, and reported on his trip in the *Savannah Tribune.* Williams found the success of African Americans in that city "a revelation, particularly so when compared with Savannah which affords so many more and greater opportunities than Birmingham." He visited the Alabama Penny Saving and Loan Company located in its own "three story brick building on the main business street of the city." The bank had nearly $100,000 in deposits and had been in business for twelve years. Williams concluded his signed article with these words: "It is this same spirit of confidence and combination that we need in this community, that it will be felt and enjoyed by the most humble citizen. The question is, shall we sit still, divided, and be forever crushed down or shall we bestir ourselves with a united rank, and prosper as the proverbial Rose of Sharon."[245]

Sol Johnson joined the fray with an editorial that stated: "The *Tribune* deplores the fact of the absence of that public spirit and ambition for race enterprises among our people in this city. There are opportunities at hand that would result in great benefits to the promoters if they would only come together and inaugurate methods and take hold of them."[246] He gave as an example the fact that local African American physicians could come together and establish a first class pharmacy. The *Savannah Tribune* re-introduced Lucius E. Williams, the new President of the Wage Earners Loan and Investment Company, to the African American community, in an article entitled "A Worthy Enterprise: Presided Over by a Worthy Young Business Man."

Lucius E. Williams was born April 20, 1871, in Americus, Georgia, to Edward and Mary Williams, and was educated in the local grammar schools of Americus. Later he was employed in a large cotton exporting business. Around 1891 he, his wife and four daughters moved to Savannah and he was employed as a mail clerk in the Railway Mail Service. During his employment the "chief clerk or superintendent has never had occasion to reprimand or fine him for a dereliction of duty or for non efficiency."[247] Within a few years, Williams had amassed the sum of $4,000 and was establishing himself in the city. Mutual Benevolent historian Frank Bynes informed the author that Lucius Williams was injured on his railroad job and was awarded a huge sum in a settlement. Within a short time Williams had "grown from a stranger in Savannah to be recognized as one of the leading men of this people." He attained that position of confidence because of his "great heart, his intense race interest, and his great hopes in the future of the race."[248]

In addition, Lucius Williams was also President of the Adelphia Club, "the leading social club of the city for colored youth," and served as a member of the Trustee Board of the First Congregational Church of Christ of Savannah. He was regarded as "modest and unassuming, a patron of the advancement of our people, a firm believer in the future of the Negro." The paper felt that the success of the bank was "in large part due to him." By 1902 the company was capitalized at $10,000 with an authorized capital of $50,000. Shares were $10 each and there was "a very large number of shareholders and among every class of the colored citizens of Savannah." The company planned to start a savings department on January 1,1903.[249]

In November 1902, the Wage Earners Bank held its annual meeting in the parlors of the Adelphia Club. President Williams gave a concise report of the company's work and a survey of its prospects. Secretary/Treasurer Walter S. Scott reported that the company was in a "progressive condition." Each stockholder was urged to "increase his shares and encourage others to take shares." The *Savannah Tribune* took "pleasure in commending it to the public," and the directors visited the churches to spread the usefulness of the bank for black Savannah.[250]

The Southern Bank of Savannah established "separate windows for the use of white and colored depositors." The *Savannah Tribune* reported: "as a consequence nearly all of its colored patrons have withdrawn their accounts."[251] This report was a by-line from the *American Baptist.* The paper did not explain why it had to quote an outside source for a matter of this importance in its hometown. An editorial in the same issue expressed pride that, "all of the self-respecting colored men and women, who are depositors in the Southern Bank have either withdrawn their deposits or will do so at the end of the quarter."[252]

A mass meeting, to publicize the Wage Earners Bank and the Pembroke Loan Company, was held at the Harris Street Hall. Since this was the first meeting of its kind held in the city, several hundred people "who are interested in the welfare of the race. The most gratifying result was the attendance of a large number of ladies, each of whom lends endorsement to race enterprises and rebukes those who say not a word of encouragement or act in that direction."[253] Walter S. Scott announced that after placing twenty percent of the net earnings in the reserved fund, it was decided to declare a dividend of twelve per cent. So gratified were the directors over the result until they had to give vent to their feeling by hearty applause."[254]

The Wage Earners Loan and Investment Company relocated its offices from State Street to 468 West Broad Street near Gaston Street, in order to facilitate access and increase office space. The Guaranty Aid and Relief Society was located in the same building. Both businesses were "managed by some of the most prominent men in the city of business experience and ability." These companies had "done more to stimulate confidence in, and a desire to establish enterprises among our people than any other agency."[255]

The Union Saving and Loan Company, "one of the latest banking concerns to come out for business is among the many Negro concerns doing a creditable business among our people." A reporter felt that L. S. Reed the founder of the Union Benefit Insurance Company and the Union Saving and Loan Company "deserves credit for his untiring push and business ability and his effort to give work to Negro boys and girls." L. D. Thompson was the general agent and he was said to be "doing much for the success of the company."[256]

The Wage Earners Loan and Investment Company in its sixth year, was attracting "the admiration and support of the people of Savannah and the state of Georgia…for the practical and constructive work that it has done since accepting its charter under Georgia laws. Organizing in October 1900, with a paid in capital of $112, it has slowly but surely laid a foundation for future success that is almost unparalleled in corporate existence and at the present time has combined resources amounting to more than $33,000." Its business activity has increased by about 75 per cent. Stocks were $12 per share, either in cash or the payment of $1 down and fifty cents per month until the full amount was paid. The Savings Department was paying 5 per cent per annum compounded quarterly.[257]

As the business of the Wage Earners bank Increased the directors asked Williams to "give his entire service to the company. Seeing the necessity of this and having confidence in the success of the company, he readily tendered his resignation to the government." The paper regarded Williams as "among the ablest financers of the race. Through his keen discernment, business sagacity, conservative actions and untiring efforts the business of the Wage Earners has grown to a great proportion. He is sunny in disposition and friendly with everybody." The editorial predicted that 'assisted by the able secretary and treasurer, Mr. Walter S. Scott, that the company's business will increase in a substantial and wonderful manner."[258]

The Union Savings and Loan Company, "the first Negro Savings bank in the state to buy its own banking house," purchased property at 12 State Street West. The building was said to be "in the heart of the business district of Savannah, and commands a beautiful view of the post office and Bull Street." The board of directors planned to erect "a first class Negro bank house and office building."[259]. The Afro-American Union Saving, Loan and Trust Company located at 216 Whitaker Street was capitalized at $5,000 was paying 5 percent on all annual deposits.

The Directors felt "encouraged over the flattering prospects of business and hope that during the coming year to be able to do twice as much business as was accomplished during the past year." All these banks eventually failed. Prof. Robert Gadsden, in a letter to Savannah's first African American City Alderman Bowles Ford, was of the opinion that this surge by blacks was piloted by Lindsey Reed, a pioneer in business as well as in selling insurance to Negroes. Reed, who shared a building with Attorney Abraham L.Tucker on the north side of State Street near Whitaker Street, was part of the group credited with the establishment of the Wage Earners and the Mechanics Banks.[260]

In 1912 the Wage Earners Loan and Investment Company was declared the "pride of our people." It was said that the company "was organized something more than six years ago by a few of our citizens and paid in at its organization the small sum of $102. But by a careful and conservative management the bank's combined assets amounts at this time to near $50,000. We are informed they have 1280 depositors and several hundred stockholders."

The article went on to claim that: "since they have been in business they have built, bought or otherwise assisted over 100 colored citizens of this community in securing or owning homes besides helping scores of our young men in carrying on business enterprises." The bank was in the process of constructing seven houses on Burroughs Street near Thirty-Third. It also bought a large tract of land in the southeastern section of the city.[261]

Abraham L. Tucker bought a piece of property on the southwest corner of York and Barnard Streets for $18,000. This piece of property was "but one of the many valuable real estate holdings in this city owned by Mr. Tucker." The plan was to raise the building located on the lot and construct a new up-to-date bank, which was to provide luxuriant quarters such as a "waiting room for ladies fitted out in the new building with all the modern conveniences and will supply a long felt need for colored women when down town."[262] In 1913, the bank moved from the ground floor of the building at 20 State Street west to new quarters at 139 Barnard Street.

The new quarters of the bank consisted of the President's room, the banking department, the ladies waiting room, and a general utility room in the rear. It was felt that the ladies waiting room finished in white and very beautifully furnished with every convenience, filled "a long felt want by ladies of the city when uptown." The Mechanics bank paid out a dividend of seven per cent. Henry Pearson was elected president D. Simmons, vice-president; Abraham L. Tucker was chairman of the Board of directors and F. D. Tucker was secretary treasurer.[263]

The Wage Earners acquired property at the northeast corner of West Broad and Alice Streets for its new bank. The site was regarded as "a splendid one, being but a block's distance from the Union Station and but one half a block away from the present location of the bank." The bank's combined assets were put at about $200,000. In July 1912, the paper was very sanguine about the Wage Earners and the Mechanics Banks. Sol Johnson reminded his readers that it had always been the policy of the paper to "commend to our people the institutions of worth among us." These two institutions entered the field of fiercest competition and performed so well that they merited the praise, confidence and continued support of the people. They passed the experimental stage in their growth and were declared "now firmly established among us."[264]

The Wage Earners Bank chose Robert Edward Pharrow to build its new bank. Pharrow was born in Wilkes County, March 8, 1868, the son of Isom and Isabella Pharrow. At fifteen years of age, he went to Augusta and began work as an apprentice with a builder. He later moved to Atlanta. Among many other projects, he designed and built the dormitory of Morris Brown College in Atlanta and constructed St. Philip's A. M. E. on Charles and West Broad Streets for $35,000. The *Savannah Tribune* claimed that Pharrow was the "largest Negro contractor of the South."[265] In 1919 Lucius Williams was elected vice-president of the National Negro Business League.[266]

The new building was to be three stories high and constructed of buff bricks. The bank was to occupy the first floor while the second and third floors were to be used for offices. The *Savannah Tribune* regarded the Wage Earners as the "pioneer Negro banking institution of the state and the second largest institution of the kind among Negroes in the country."[267]

In October 1913, the bank's combined assets were $221, 414.22 with "over 5,000 depositors, a few of whom are, and has erected hundreds of houses in and around the city." The bank was capitalized at $50,000 with $48,417.10 paid in. The combined assets were shown to be $267, 646.58. Reserve and undivided profits amounted to $51,796.90, while unpaid dividends were $179.20, with bills payable amounted to $34,000 and deposits were $133,253.38.

The newly built Wage Earners Bank opened in October 1914 with much fanfare. The first person to reach the cashiers window was "one of the leading Negro businessmen Mr.T.T.Freeman, whose business is on Randolph Street." By October 1915, the Wage Earners had increased its operation by more than $35,000, a truly remarkable showing as the "the past year was one of the worst financial years ever." The directors announced a dividend of 12 per cent. Towards the end of October J. Pierpoint Morgan invited Wage Earners "to participate in the half million dollar bond issue for the allies of Europe." By December, the state bank examiners gave the bank a favorable report. With three black-owned banks and four black-owned real estate firms, Savannah was becoming a leading center of black commerce.[268] During May of 1916, the Mechanics Bank moved to new quarters at 721 West Broad Street next to the Savannah Pharmacy.

The *Savannah Tribune* reported that $30,000 of Christmas club money was distributed by the colored banks in the city.[269] The bank paid out a dividend of 7 percent on the year's earnings.[270] The following year, Paul Edward Perry, former Vice-President and one of the organizers of the Guaranty Insurance Co: and the Mutual Health and Life Insurance, the Wage Earners Bank and of the Savannah Savings and Real Estate Corporation: and who had recently acquired an interest in the People's Health and Life Insurance Company, was elected Vice-President of the Mechanics Banks. By 1919, the Wage Earners Bank had bought more property in

Savannah and a year later, some property on the southwest corner of 7th Avenue and 135th Streets in Harlem, New York, for $200,000.

The Wage Earners bank had nearly 20,000 depositors amounting to over $900,000. There were also three other Negro banks in the city. It was estimated that approximately one third of the Negroes owned their homes and that three of every five had a bank account. The 1919 Chatham County tax digest showed that Negroes had property worth around $3,500,000. Blacks had approximately $6,000,000 in banks.

The Wage Earners Bank spawned many other businesses such as insurance companies, funeral homes, and true to its motto, "own your home" enabled hundreds of black families to buy their own homes. The Wage Earners was said to have "helped more Negro business ventures to success than any other Negro bank." Sol Johnson reported the consultation between Lucius E. Williams of the Wage Earners Saving Bank and Brown and Stevens bankers of Philadelphia concerning the Payton Apartments Corporation representing New York apartments properties valued at $2,500.000.[271] The properties were reported to be "among the finest in New York and certainly the most valuable and handsome controlled by Negroes in the world, are put upon a sound business and financial basis and preserved to the Negro race."

The buildings were constructed at the cost of more than one and a half million dollars. The properties covered "two acres of ground in the heart of the Harlem district." Two weeks later, the Wage Earners Bank had "attracted national attention and attained national prominence in its most recent business venture of large proportions that in which its resources and splendid business acumen of its president were drawn upon by the Payton Apartments Corporation of New York City, involving New York properties amounting to nearly three million dollars."[272]

Towards the end of November 1918, the state bank examiners found the Wage Earners to have all accounts "correct and the business conducted on the highest basis. The examiners were unstinted in their commendation of the excellency of the bank's condition." At the end of December two black banks in the city distributed $35,000 in Christmas saving clubs of which the Wage Earners paid out $25,000.

The annual meeting of shareholders was held in the director's room at the bank. Reports presented showed that the bank "had a most remarkable business during the last fiscal year, the increase over the business of the previous twelve months being $167,251.78. The number of depositors which the bank has was shown to be 11, 315 a gain of 2,5518."[273]

In 1919, the Wage Earners Savings Bank, the Savannah Savings and Real Estate Corporation and the Mechanics Savings Bank had about 15,000 depositors "indicating that one Negro in every three has some sort of bank account." The *Savannah Tribune* announced the: "Biggest Financial Transaction That Has Yet Occurred In This City Among Negroes."[274] The Wage Earners Savings Bank and allied interests planned a huge complex that included a modern theatre-auditorium and a first class department store, at the cost of about $75,000. The bank acquired the remaining 80 feet of the block of West Broad between Wayne and Alice Streets.

The Enterprise Mercantile Company, which was already operating "the most up-to-date fancy grocery store in the city run by Negroes," was to be one of the partners in this massive enterprise. Sol Johnson in an editorial July, 1919, thought that "it was gratifying and inspiring that a Savannah Institute, founded in Savannah, and on Savannah money, should so stand out as a pioneer and a leader in these (big things) of the new day in Negro business."

To cap it all, the *Savannah Tribune* announced that twenty-five of "Savannah's leading Negro business and professional men" would leave for the annual session of the National Negro Business League in St. Louis.[275] The paper estimated that "the aggregate value of the business and other interests represented by the party will run beyond a million dollars." Lucius E. Williams, President of the Wage Earners bank, was the Chairman of the delegation, which arrived at St. Louis aboard a special "Gold Coast Pullman." Not surprisingly, Lucius E. Williams was elected Vice-president of the National Negro Business League.

In December, it was estimated that over $125,000 in Christmas club funds were to be distributed to blacks in the city. About 6,205 persons contributed to these clubs. Wage Earners Savings bank was due to pay out about $40,000 to 4,000 depositors. The Savannah Savings and Real Estate Corporation was to pay out $20,000 to 1,005 depositors. The Mechanics Savings Bank was due to pay 1,200 depositors about $14,000. It was estimated that the white banks would pay out $50,000, making a total of $125,000.

A New York paper reported that some property was purchased by "the Wage Earners Savings bank of Savannah, Ga., whose deposits represented in the month of February $875,184.36 and having 14,000 depositors." A. Pope, a New York lawyer and former College instructor at the Georgia State College in Savannah, did the legal work for the deal. The Wage Earners bank purchased some property in Harlem, New York worth about $200,000. The sale was said to be "one of the biggest transactions handled by colored investors in this section for a long time." The paper quoted the *New York Times* as identifying the property "at the corner of 135th Street and Seventh Avenue."[276]

The *Savannah Tribune* carried a report that the Wage Earners bank had passed one million in assets. It shouted in a proud headline: "WAGE EARNERS PASSES MILLION. A Negro banking institution had never before attained the $1,036,195.61 figure.[277] The bank, the paper reported, "continues to be strongest Negro bank in the world...a figure never before attained by a Negro banking institution." The bank had had a "phenomenal growth in the past five years." Depositors increased to 17,000 and the bank was "under state supervision and is heavily interested in real estate in this city and the north."

The white press stated: "Every white man and every colored man in Savannah must be proud of the growth and increase. It speaks volumes for the colored race and is better than all of the political stuff, which is paraded in accentuating the race issue in the south."[278] The following year the *Savannah Tribune* boasted that the bank's building was appraised at over $95,000 and the depositors had increased to 20,000 from all over the country and even in the West Indies, Cuba, Europe and Africa. Wage Earners offered a specialty called "banking by mail." Plans were to enlarge the space of bank activities given over to banking.[279]

Lucius E. Williams was president of the bank, Sol C. Johnson, Vice-president, R. A. Harper, cashier and Edgar C. Blackshear was assistant Cashier. Samuel J. Brown, Dr. Henry M. Collier Sr., J. M. Ferreebee, Thos. M. Holly, Jos. L. Jackson, Dr. J. W. Jamerson, John F. Jones, Nathan Roberts, J. C. Lindsay of Atlanta: Daniel Simmons, A. B. Singfield, I. R. Spaulding, R. A. Harper, Sol Johnson and Lucius Williams were Directors.

Sol Johnson in an editorial expressed the view that the bank's success was due to "an unwavering policy of uniform courtesy, an ever-ready willingness to serve and an unselfish interest in the advancement of the people and the community." Johnson thought the success of the bank would "mean volumes in encouragement and hope to younger generations, and will pave the way for many efforts which, but for this singular and distinctive success may have been made at all. It is going to establish confidence and faith among the people of other races in the Negro's capacity to do big things."

The *South-Western Christian Advocate* ran an article concerning the Wage Earners Bank stating:

> "It is a startling revelation that in the year 1900 this institution began with about $100 and that today, just twenty years thereafter, it boasts of a gross business of $1,036,195.61. Of course compared with the great moneyed institutions of the country this showing is not so flattering, but when the handicaps of race and section are considered in the equation this is a truly remarkable showing. It is strong testimonial of the business sagacity, ability and integrity of the small group of men who have built such an institution and given this asset to the race."[280]

Meanwhile the *Savannah Tribune* again quoted an outside paper extolling the Wage Earners Bank. This time it was the turn of a Harlem *Trade Magazine*, which commended the black Southerners, who had invested heavily in Harlem. It regarded Lucius E. Williams as "a pioneer Negro banker and splendid type of that excellent group of Negro business men developed in the south during the past decade." The article stated: "The Wage Earners bank now has interest in New York aggregating around a quarter of a million dollars. These include the Quality Amusement Corporation and other theatrical interests, besides such real estate and mortgage loans." Williams was Vice-President of Quality Corporation and was "personally interested in several business movements in Harlem."[281]

The afterglow of the Wage Earners Bank's crossing the million-dollar mark did not save Savannah's African Americans from the whites' obsession to keep them "in due order and subjection." At the downtown Citizens and Southern Bank, a Negro woman "was severely handled Monday morning," simply because "she insisted in being properly addressed by the clerk who was waiting on her." The woman objected to being addressed by her first name. At the end of the altercation the clerk "came from behind the cage, handled the woman roughly; finally pushing her out of the bank, and is then said to have kicked her."[282]

About 6,000 depositors could collect their 1920 Christmas club money from the four Negro banks in the city. The sum in 1920 was estimated to be $100,000, which was $38,000 more than the previous year. The Wage Earners distributed $60,000 to 2,000 depositors: Mechanics Savings Bank distributed $15,000 to 2,000 depositors and the Fidelity Savings Bank distributed $4,000 to 500 persons. Financier John Jacob Arnold called the meeting for African Americans from around the country to discuss the formation of an entity to help black business.

By July the Mechanics bank announced that in seven months assets had increased $92,404.73. The paper claimed that the bank was "making rapid progress in increased business." The bank was "reorganized under new management during September of last year." Total assets were put at $123,928.67. The Mechanics Bank bought property on Maple and West Broad Streets.[283] The paper suggested that "The officers and directors are all wide awake businessmen and there is no doubt that the future is bright for the Mechanics Saving Bank." The stockholders of the Mechanics Savings Bank held their annual meeting and heard reports that indicated that the bank's assets had increased over the previous year.[284] Paul Edward Perry headed the Mechanics Bank in 1920. The bank's assets had increased during the previous year from $32,000 to $121,500. Plans were to erect a new building on West Broad and Maple Streets. Dividends of 8 per cent were paid.[285]

The **Savannah Savings and Real Estate Corporation** located at 408 West Broad Street, began operation in October 1915.[286] At that time there were five black banks in the city. The *Savannah Tribune* thought that the city was "large enough for all of these institutions, especially if our people will give them all unstinted patronage." The bank had an authorized capitalization of $100,000. Stocks were sold at $10 a share, payable one dollar down and one dollar per month. The *Savannah Tribune* thought the bank began its career "under favorable auspices and will no doubt serve as a stimulus to the saving habit of the local public."

Walter S. Scott former secretary/treasurer of the Wage Earners Bank was President of the organization, Paul E. Perry was vice-President, and Robert E. Scott was secretary and Treasurer. The paper expressed the hope that this new bank would "serve as a stimulus to the saving habit of the local public." St. Louis Ponder was Vice-President, Robert E. Scott was Secretary-Treasurer; Joseph H. Green Assistant Secretary-Treasurer and F. B. Pettie Attorney. Lachlan M. Pollard, R. R. Wright Edward Sherman, Howard Stiles, Henry F. Skipper, Robert E. Scott, Cato Young, John W. Hubert, Jos. H. Green, St.Louis Ponder, Walter S. Scott, E. A. Williams, Paris Hamilton, Frank Cain and H. T. Singleton were Directors of the company. The first annual meeting of the Savannah Savings Real Estate Corporation took place August 10, 1916. The reports of the company's officials showed that the "affairs of the company were in excellent condition and the success attained during the nine months of its existence proved that the people of Savannah are anxious and willing to support a reliable institution."

Towards the end of 1920, the Savannah Savings and Real Estate Corporation decided to build what the *Savannah Tribune* described as another monumental Negro office building. The Savannah Savings Bank proposed to build a $200,000 structure on the northwest corner of West Broad Street and Gaston Streets. Contractor William McKelvey, "one of Savannah's leading young business men," was in charge of the building project. There were to be three floors to include a 1,540 square feet bank space, a 45 feet by 73 feet theatre seating 800 to 1,000 persons.[287] Located at the northwest corner of West Broad and Gaston streets, the complex contained several offices. Three stories high and costing approximately $200,000, the building was 73 feet on West Broad and about 100 feet on Gaston Streets. Assets totaled $21,413.24 and the Christmas Savings Club had 853 members with a payout of about $10,000. More than $4,000 worth of stock was subscribed for by those present and "all promised to double the business of the company in the coming twelve months." The report of Certified Public Accountants Charles Neville and Company showed that the above report was correct.

The bank of 1,540 square feet floor space occupied the corner; the Real Estate section 28 by 55 feet, the Theatre in the center occupied 45 by 55 feet and had a seating capacity of about 800 patrons. Two stores on the northern end had 18 by 55 feet each. The second and third stories contained offices while the Guaranty Life and Health Insurance Company used the third floor. William McKelvey was the contractor.

Daniel Simmons was born in Allendale, Barnwell County, South Carolina, on October 22, 1875. He lost his father, Handy Simmons, when he was nine years old. He also lost his mother, Clementine Bowers Simmons, within a few years, but although merely a youth, he remembered her "with peculiar gratitude for her beneficent influence on his life." His paternal grandparents were Sam and Hester Simmons and his maternal grandparents were Thomas and Candice Bowers. Though poor and living on a farm, young Simmons received his elementary education at Brinson. Without a dime, he walked to Savannah in 1892 and did odd jobs, such as sawing wood, for a while. Later he became a telegraph messenger.[288]

Simmons married Hattie Eugenia Davis on August 2, 1897, and they had five children. He went into business for himself in the early 1900's. He purchased a two story building on East Bay Street for several thousand dollars, remodeled it and added a second story. Simmons used the first two floors for his business and leased the third story to the Southern Cotton Oil Company. His business acumen was such that his patrons were among the large furniture and department stores of the city. He was the only colored man owning property on the bay, with an opening on the river. The business opened a branch at Beaufort, South Carolina. The firm specialized in the renovation of bedding with modern sanitation and equipment.[289] Simmons was a director of the Wage Earners Bank and the Mechanics Bank and Grand Treasurer of the Odd Fellows. He was a member of Eureka Lodge No. 1 and a past master and member of the Grand Lodge. He was also a Royal Arch Mason and Knight Templar, as well as Pythian Knight and Eastern Star.

For more than thirty years, Simmons was an ardent member of St. John Baptist Church and celebrated his 20th anniversary as Superintendent of the Sunday school.[290] The paper regarded him as "one of the best known Sunday school workers in the city," and "one of the most successful Negro business men in the city." Despite his pressing schedule he "always found time to give the best services he is capable of to his Sunday school." His mattress business was "one of the largest concerns of its kind in the city." Simmons attributed his success to the advice and liberal support that the white furniture dealers of the city gave him. The Savannah Mattress Company, a growing Negro business, owned its place of business on the city's waterfront.

The Company, owned and operated entirely by Negroes, manufactured and renovated felt, cotton, moss, and wool and curled hair mattresses. It was located at 318 to 320 East Bay Street. The workspace was 100 feet by 100 feet and there were six employees who worked by hand and machinery. Daniel Simmons died in 1926. Editor Sol Johnson regarded him as, "Amiable in disposition, humble in action, unselfish towards others, charitable to a considerable extent."[291] After his death in 1926, his two sons, Edward J. and Herman D. Simmons, continued the business. In the late 1930's, the company sponsored a choral group called the Simmons Singers.

Beauty Culture

Many white observers of nineteenth century Savannah noticed the importance African American slaves or free persons of color attached to grooming hair and the style and pattern of clothes they wore. The *Savannah Republican* reported

"This ambition of dress is absolutely a disease."[292] This love of finery was destined to remain with their descendants throughout the new world. In time, the love of "dressing up" provided an outlet, as perhaps nothing else could, for hundreds of black women in Jim Crow Savannah to earn a living and some measure of economic security.

Madam Birdie Freeman was born in Hampton, South Carolina and was reared in Beaufort, South Carolina. She married her husband in Beaufort, South Carolina, September 15, 1903. Shortly afterwards they came to Savannah. Her husband operated a grocery and she went into the beauty culture business. A *Savannah Tribune* editorial in 1912 did not seem to look favorably on her future business prospects. The writer stated:

> "One of the modern abominations against nature is the hair straightening and face bleaching craze. If God intended certain ones of our race to have straight hair or that their faces be other than dark He would so make them. All of us should be commended for beautifying ourselves, but not at the expense of nature. This craze has gone to quite an extent. The pages of many of our leading journals are filled with ads of these hair straightening and face bleaching concoctions.
>
> These journals should maintain a more exalted standard. Under no circumstances would the *Tribune* accept a hair straightening or face bleaching ad nor those of whiskey dealers or any other class of business unless we can safely recommend same to our readers. The class of ads in our columns is proof of our assertion."[293]

Nonetheless, the black paper reported that the couple "have met with much success in their respective lines and through strict application to business and unusual foresight, they have become two of Savannah's most substantial citizens." Master beautician, Madam Freeman was thought to hold a "front rank among the beauticians of this section of the state."[294]

She opened her first beauty parlor in 1914[295] and in 1917 she began her beauty culture parlor in earnest. Two years later, she took a twenty-one day diploma course at the Poro College at St. Loius, Missouri. The course included fancy hairdressing, American bobbing and waving. Madam Freeman's parlors were located at 456° Montgomery Street. She specialized in the Poro system and performed manicuring and messaging. Her College of Hair and Beauty Culture offered a diploma in beauty culture.

In 1930, Madam Freeman did extensive renovations to her place of business and opened a flower shop. The facility was regarded as "the most complete and up-to-date shop of the kind in the city." There was a large show room to the right of the reception room. In an effort to boost her business, Madam Freeman published "a very clever little booklet, which she is distributing among her friends." By the 1930's, Madam Freeman had branched out to the Apex System of Beauty Culture. A complete supply was on sale and the Apex system taught.

Madam Freeman won first prize in a 1930 competition sponsored by First Bryan Church. The prize was a round trip to Chicago and ten dollars in gold. Madam Freeman was regarded as "an indefatigable worker in any cause she enters and her wide acquisition and attractive personality always stand her in good stead." In addition, she was said to be "one of the most astute businesswomen of Savannah and her beauty parlors enjoy a most lucrative patronage."

She and her husband celebrated their 35th wedding anniversary in 1938. By that time, the husband had retired from active business while his wife was still active in the beauty business. The following year she enlarged the school. The new addition was used for classes in theory and other activities. Her shop was said to carry "one of the most complete stocks of cosmetics, hair combs and general beauty culture equipment in the city."

The establishment enjoyed "a very high rating from the State Board of Barbers and Hairdressers and its unusual success is attributed directly to the close and careful supervision of Madam Freeman, who is recognized throughout the State as an outstanding authority in her work."[296] Her Beauty School was credited with being, "one of the foremost such establishments in the Southeast."[297] She was a "foremost figure in the civic, business, religious and fraternal life of the city." She was a trustee of St. Philip A.M.E. Church, president of the Evening Call Aid and Social Club, a member of the Elite Temple Daughters of Elks; the Pilgrim Christian Band and the Twelve Sisters.[298]

Madam Carrie Dixon Cargo was born in Augusta and received her elementary schooling and two years of study at Paine College, Augusta. Cargo then went to Howard University to study medicine. Within a few months she came to Savannah and after "a careful study of Poro System of beauty culture, she opened her place of business in 1915," and for the next several years devoted herself to the hair dressing industry. After graduating from beauty school Madam Cargo studied at various institutes in California, and clinics in North Carolina, Augusta, Alabama and Washington. She also studied the Poro System at Poro College in St. Louis. In 1916 she opened Cargo Beauty Salon and in 1928 the Cargo School of Beauty Culture.[299]

In time, it would be said, "hundreds of successful operators, scattered all over the country attribute their success to the thorough foundation acquired while being trained under Mme. Cargo." Malone's Poro products and the system of beauty culture popularized by Madam C. J. Walker were very popular in the Savannah market. Madam C. J. Walker, "well known hair culturist" of Indianapolis, was in the city attending the National Baptist Convention. During her stay, she was the houseguest of Miss R. G. Houston at 506 Hartridge Street. Madam Walker gave a lecture on the Negro woman in business.[300] She was reported to be the "most widely known Negro hair culturist in the country and a woman of considerable means and her preparations are on sale throughout the United States."

Madam Walker was said to be "very much interested in the uplift of the Negro." She "held shop" at the hair parlor of Mrs. Ethel Durden Young at 461 West Broad Street, from 9 a.m. to 5:30 p.m. The *Savannah Tribune* expressed the hope that "Every woman of pride and who is anxious to make money should avail herself of this wonderful opportunity to learn the art of hair growing from her personally."[301]

Hair grooming shops sprang up all over the city. The trade demanded a small amount of capital for material; it was easy to learn in a short space of time locally, and there was a "hungry" clientele. Apart from a few teachers, nurses, dress makers, and a large number of domestics, there were few other jobs available for African American women in the city. Hair care could even be done in one's home. Drug stores did a brisk business in hair straightening products.

By 1919, the Nu-Life system of "culturing and beautifying hair was becoming very popular among the city's blacks." Women were encouraged to "make yourself an independent living by becoming Nu-Life agents." Thirty-day courses in hair culture were offered at $10.00 each. Facial massage was done for $ 10.00. Manicuring was done for $5.00 and hair weaving for $10.00 or all for $25.00. Mrs. Simpkins and Mrs. Roberts conducted their school at 530 West Broad Street.

The Alpha Chi Pi Omega Sorority presented a plaque to Madam Carrie Cargo in 1958 naming her "The Most Outstanding Beautician of 1958." She held membership in the United Beauty School Owners & Teachers Association, and served on the Board of the Southern Beauty Congress. Madam Cargo was second vice-president of the West Broad Street YMCA.[302] The following year a local branch of the National Beauty Culture League was organized composed of nearly all the heads of the different hairdressing and beauty culture systems in the country. They claimed that they were "desirous of being on the map." In 1926, Madam Cargo took a course at one of the best-known schools of beauty culture in New York City.

While perhaps not totally against beauty culture, a *Savannah Tribune* editorial entitled "The Stocking Cap," took a decidedly negative view of men wearing a stocking on their heads.[303] It claimed that women used the stocking to cover their legs or as "knee banks, that is, a place to hide their money." Now, it mourned, "a large proportion of the young male population has adopted it in a rather odd manner, they wear the stockings on their heads, to keep their hair from becoming ruffled." At that time, the special hair pomade in vogue required wearing the stocking in order to prevent the hair from getting out of place. The paper added, "The average boy has appropriated unto himself one of his sisters pedal covering." Though perhaps permissible at home, the *Savannah Tribune* thought boys who wanted to keep their hair "properly groomed should not wear the stocking on their head in public." Bluntly, the paper claimed "It is vulgar, unbecoming and highly improper to use the stocking cap in public and, if our young men must use it, let them confine it to house wear and not on the streets."[304]

In April 1929, Second Baptist Church ran a fund-raising contest to determine the most popular hairdresser in the city. Madam Cargo won first prize as the most popular hairdresser in the city. Madam Cargo's first prize was $230. Mrs. Birdie Freeman, Mrs. Willie Lampkin, Mrs. Oliver Smith, Mrs. Jenne Williams, Mrs. McTier won other prizes. The church realized a profit of $507.75. Mrs. Mittie Foulke-Johnson, special representative of the Poro College in St. Louis, Mo., visited Savannah in 1929. The *Savannah Tribune* reported that she was "well pleased with the showing the many Poro agents in this section ere making."

In 1932, Madam Cargo celebrated the anniversary of the opening of her shop. She was reported to have climbed "from the ranks to a commanding position in her special line." In early March, Madam Cargo returned from a trip to New York City, "where she took some advance work, specializing in the latest beauty fad, finger waving." This additional feature in beauty culture represented the latest discovery of a master beautician. She explained the difference between the old and the new method of hair care by adding: "Hot irons of any sort are done away with in the new finger wave." As part of the anniversary celebration, she had several exhibits and artificial flower designs. Madam Cargo also taught the art of artificial flower making. She advertised a pre-Easter special in 1932. A Shampoo was 40 cents; marcelling, 35 cents; massaging, 25 cents; haircut, 25 cents, eyebrow arching, 10 cents, manicuring, 35 cents; hot oil treatment, 25 cents and oil shampoo, 40 cents.

An editorial in the *Savannah Tribune* touched gingerly on the delicate issue of skin whitening and bleaching concoctions and whiteners, then very popular among the city's dark skinned African Americans. It quoted the National Drug Administrator as stating that several colored women of Washington were suffering from mercuric poisoning sustained from the use of a cream purporting to lighten the skin. The paper concluded "It must not be understood that we are against the use of face lotions, but our women should be careful to secure only the best articles to be used on their face."[305]

In the matter of color, or shades of blackness, Savannah's African Americans shared a past with those of New Orleans, Louisiana, and above all Charleston, South Carolina. The concern about color in part at least, grew out of the reality of slavery. Light skinned blacks, or "high yellows," often enjoyed, if recognized by their white father, advantages of education or a higher economic status. This gave them a head start over the impoverished blacks.

The *Savannah Tribune* reported that Madam Cargo had "built up a very satisfactory business and a remarkable reputation not only as a beauty expert, but also as a leader in training others."[306] The paper opined that she was looked upon as "the one and only real beauty artist in the city, and her work is unquestionably outstanding." Madam Cargo introduced marcelling, which became the most popular mode of hair care in the city. Madam Cargo's Parlor was the supply station for the hundreds of Poro representatives in the city. Her husband Harry, a cabinet-maker and wood worker, was seriously wounded in a tussle with an intruder in his workshop. He required twenty stitches.

Madam Cargo opened a new Beauty Parlor, 1219 West Broad Street, at the corner of Henry Street. The new establishment was said to be the "most up-to-date beauty salon in the city and affords its patrons every convenience known to these popular emporiums, which cater to the beauty culture of women."[307]

Mrs. Malvin C. Wheeler, Madam Cargo's daughter, operated the new shop. A *Savannah Tribune* columnist writing in "Lights and Shadows," stated, "The young men's hats are off to you, Madam Cargo in congratulations for your swell new beauty parlor. We trust that you and the others will soon eliminate the entire pepper head family so that men will no longer have to go to New York, Chicago, and other places to find a variety of feminine beauty."[308]

Madam Carrie Cargo, of 919 West 36th Street, who operated two beauty parlors on West Broad Street, received the highest marks in the examination held by the State Board of Barber Examination. The *Savannah Tribune* regarded her as enjoying "an enviable reputation among the beauticians of the state."

Her parlors were described as the "most completely equipped and the most ornate and comfortable in design and arrangement of any to be found in Savannah." Located at 1219 West Broad Street, they were completely remodeled and renovated. The interior woodwork and furnishings were done in maroon and white. The parlors employed seven graduate master beauticians. The entire teaching and operating personnel were under state regulation. In the 1930's the firm specialized in the newly styled "up-sweep" coiffure, "with special Cargo "up-sweep" wave. [309]

The state examination for beauticians for 1950 was held at Madam Cargo's facilities at 1210 West Broad Street. The forty students came from several cities including Brunswick, Waycross, Pembroke, Millen and Augusta. The test consisted of a hairstyle and facial during the morning session and a written test during the afternoon. Cargo Beauty School, Freeman's Beauty School and Kings Beauty School presented students for the examination.[310] Madam Cargo died in 1982 at 606 West 45th Street.

Mrs. Elmus Johnson, proprietress of Elmus Beauty Salon, 524 West Anderson Street, returned from New York City, where she completed a new course in the technique of beauty culture at the Apex College. Mrs. Johnson was one of the more progressive of the younger beauticians of the city and her shop was the Mecca for a large number of ladies who appreciated the best in hair work and beauty culture.

Madam Ruth Curry Williams was founder and operator of Rudie Salon and Rudie College of Beauty Culture at 815 West Broad Street. Her businesses had "won their place in the hearts of Savannah women because of the marked results which have been accomplished by Rudie beautician-operators in improved and stylish hair dressing, scalp treatment and in skin and facial improvement." It was reported, "You hardly know them when they leave the Rudie Beauty Salon." Madam Williams had built up a "high reputation for complete hair and beauty treatment and guarantees permanent improvement in every feature of the work." She employed 10 master beauticians.[311]

Each year a large class of graduates left the College and they either established their own school or worked in other beauty shops around the city. The facility was extensively renovated in the late 1930's and was able to accommodate about fifty students. The tuition for a full instruction and certificate was fifty dollars, payable at two dollars down at enrollment and one dollar and a half each week until fully paid. As one advertisement put it, "Madam Rudie urges all ambitious women who desire a career in business which will bring large success to enter the Rudie College of Beauty Culture."

The Rudie School of Beauty Culture was located at 1827 Ogeechee Avenue. The paper claimed that the school was "one of the best-known and most popular institutions of the kind in the city." Mortician Sidney Jones and N.H.G.Williamson, representative of the State Board of Barber examiners, addressed the graduates. Ella Merkerson, Minnie Green, Hattie Miller, Louise Kennedy, Julia Brown, Ethel Reddick, Gertrude Collier, Gertrude Pringle, Onnie Mae Golden, Genevieve White, Rachael Baldwin, Rosa Gregory, Alberta Jackson and Rebecca Douglas graduated as the class of 1937.[312] Attorney J. G. Lemon, in an article in the *Savannah Morning News* reported that there were about 12 beauty concerns in the city. He claimed that the business had grown "so large and so rapidly that it has been brought under state regulation." Each place of business "having such sharp competition for patronage that each maintains a well-appointed, absolutely sanitary, fully-equipped parlor and class room for its work." Lemon concluded "This business has grown to large proportions because every woman and child wishes to be made more beautiful."[313]

Beacon For Race Progress

With the imminent collapse of Georgia's limited Reconstruction, African Americans in Savannah looked for other means of "working out their salvation." The newspaper appeared to be one such avenue. The overtly partisan black press was, in part at least, a reaction to the white press, which was anything but objective, especially as far as reporting on black news items. In the battle for minds, however, black pressmen were "soldiers without swords." They lacked the economic or political clout to impose their wills on the white power structure.

In one sense, African Americans had some "limited experience" with publishing newspapers. The *Daily Morning News* reported that it had changed to steam operated machinery. Prior to that move the equipment was operated by "several relays of the peculiar institution by which our press has hitherto been propelled."[314] The 1930's W.P.A. summary of that report omits any reference to the slave labor contribution.

The Reverend James M. Simms was the first African American to publish a newspaper in the city. The white paper reported, "The *Southern Radical and Freedman's Journal* which has been contemplated for sometime past, will be published on the fourth of July. [315] It was to be an Evening paper. In the following year, the name was changed to the *Freedmen's Standard.* This paper had a short life span.

Editor and manager John H. Deveaux, a colored customs clerk, Louis B. Toomer also a colored customs clerk and sometime teacher, Richard W. White a colored rail agent and former teacher and union soldier and Louis Pleasant a colored U.S. inspector, published the first issue of the *Colored Tribune,* on Saturday, December 4, 1875.[316] Miss Emma DeLamotta, sister-in-law of editor Deveaux, was the paper's first secretary. White printers produced the first issue in a building at the corner of Price and Harris Streets opposite the Beach Institute. The *Colored Tribune* was a three-column folio printed on a sheet 11 by 16 inches. The editorial of the first issue stated its mission as "devoted to the advancement and elevation of the colored race and will endeavor to teach them their duties as citizens."[317]

An editorial in March commenting on the celebration of St. Patrick's Day, appealed to the colored people to learn from the Irish. It lamented: "with six times the population of our Irish friends, and a cause that should be as dear to them, the colored people have been hitherto incapable of making the display of strength and maintaining organizations that would make them respected in accordance with their numbers...If you desire to right your wrongs, organize yourselves and show your power by being true to your race and the rights you hold dear."[318] The following month the paper bemoaned the habit of "these dirty colored women, of arresting their husbands every time they have a family quarrel is becoming intolerable, and should be either stopped or colored men should stop marrying." An incident was reported in the white press of Elisabeth Johnson who had a warrant issued against her husband, James Johnson. James was drowned in the Savannah River attempting to escape from the arresting officer.[319]

The city's African Americans liberally supported the *Colored Tribune.* In June the paper reminded its readers that "the wrongs upon our people must be constantly exposed and this cannot be done unless you have your own medium...we must fight against this hateful prejudice and for equal rights in every respect, and this cannot be effectively done without the aid of a newspaper, the general educator and moulder of public sentiment."[320] A letter to the editor signed Tax Payer, related two incidents in which colored jurors were summoned to court only to be told that there was a mix-up on names. [321] Louis B. Toomer signed a letter informing his readers: "During the absence of the editor from the city we shall endeavor to present such facts to our patrons that will advance their interest and tend to the advancement of the great Republican party of which we are a component part."[322]

In November the paper rebuked the *Savannah Morning News* for accusing the colored people of being "ungrateful to the whites in connection with the recent issuing of rations." The paper asserted "the News forgets that but for the colored people, hundreds of white men and women would have perished for want of nurses. These attacks upon the colored people are untimely, unjust and uncalled for."[323] The editor advised his readers "Men who wish to serve their people must not expect to sail on a smooth sea, or run on an easy track."[324] John H. Deveaux resumed publication of his paper, after an absence of a few years, in October 1886, this time calling it *The Savannah Tribune.*[325]

John H. Deveaux was the sole owner publisher and editor of the five-column folio. A job-printing department was also added. The paper changed its name

> "For reasons that are perfectly satisfactory to ourselves but unnecessary to be now stated, we change its name to the *Savannah Tribune.* With the change of name however, the paper will suffer no change in principle. It will still be devoted to the advancement and elevation of the colored race and be unflinching in its defence of the rights of our people and we say to them again the Tribune's yours if you will have it."[326]

Meanwhile, another publication appeared on the scene. The Harden Brothers and Griffin published the *Savannah Echo* in 1879.[327] The success of these two papers apparently stimulated the growth of others. Alex McHardy published the *Phoenix,* edited and managed by James A. Sykes. This publication lasted from 1885 to 1886 and then bowed out.[328]

The *Savannah Echo* was later called the *Savannah Weekly Echo*. It took a more independent political position and had a wide circulation. It lasted from 1878 to 1884.[329] Some black workers also published the *Labor Union Recorder,* which was edited by I. W. Lewis and existed from 1891 to 1896. Eugene Browning and John H. Toomer published the *Savannah Journal*, a monthly.[330] The *Savannah Phoenix* began publication in 1885 but closed the following year.[331] The *Advocate* began in 1896 and lasted for two years. The *Baptist Truth* began in 1898 and closed in 1914. The *Gazette* began in 1897 and closed in 1903. The *Savannah Sentinel* started in 1884 and closed in 1887. The *Southern Gazette* began in 1897 and ended publication in 1916.[332]

Solomon Charles Johnson, at 23 years of age in 1889, began an editorship that lasted for 65 years and had a profound influence on the life of African Americans in Savannah. Sol, as he was called most of his life, was born in Laurel Hill, South Carolina, March 1, 1866, but came to Savannah as a child. His father, John H. Johnson, was a carpenter and millwright. During the summer, young Johnson secured a route selling the *Savannah Morning News* and worked in the ruling department of the largest print shop in Savannah. On completing his schooling at West Broad Street Elementary School under Principal James H. C. Butler in 1883 Johnson took a job at the *Savannah Echo* as a "printer's devil,"[333] and eventually became a first class printer. Johnson later went to work for John H. Deveaux at the *Savannah Tribune.*

Within months of taking over the operation of the paper, Johnson increased it to a six-column folio, added a mechanical department and secured a larger office at 562 West Broad Street. After the move, he increased the paper to a seven-column folio. He later recalled that he had to be "janitor, clerk, pressman and editor," of the *Savannah Tribune* in those early days. A year after Deveaux's death, Johnson purchased the business and became the sole owner of the *Savannah Tribune*. In 1911 he bought a lot at 1009 West Broad Street and erected a new building to house the press. By the end of this building activity in 1912 Johnson again increased the size of the paper. He bought a linotype machine was bought. Eventually the paper became "one of the prosperous business concerns of the city."

Johnson obviously admired Deveaux; he surely shared Deveaux's middle of the road philosophy. Under Johnson, the paper continued to endorse Republican candidates. Johnson was a devout Mason. He was at one time Illustrious Potentate of Omar Temple 21, Past Master of Eureka Lodge #1, Mason-in-Chief of Ezra Consistory #27, and Chairman of the Masonic Building Association. Johnson was also an ardent Republican and was a delegate to the National Convention in Chicago in 1916. He served as Secretary of the Georgia State Executive Committee. He was Vice-president of the Wage Earners bank, vice-president of the Enterprise Mercantile Co., and a Director of Standard Life Insurance Company.

Sol Johnson served as clerk and a trustee of the Congregational church, Grand Secretary of the Masons from 1895 on,[334] and was Grand Patron of the Order the Eastern Star and the Odd Fellows. He was Grand Secretary of Prince Hall Grand Lodge in Savannah, and had organized the Order of the Eastern Star in Georgia. He was also very active in the local African American militia and attained the rank of lieutenant. He still seemed to have had time to do his main task, which was to run a newspaper. In the press, he strongly advocated the need for businesses among African Americans in Savannah and rare was the occasion when anything for the "upliftment of blacks in the city," did not have his name almost first on the list. When the Wage Earners Loan-and Investment Company was organized in 1900,

Johnson was among its directors. In the terminology of the day, Johnson was the quintessential "race man." He was completely and selflessly devoted to the uplift and improvement of his people.

In his newspaper, Johnson followed the Tuskegee model of economic cooperation, racial solidarity and self-help. He held education in very high esteem as a tool for the advancement of African Americans, and opposed the migration to Africa or to the North. The spread of Jim Crowism increased his militancy somewhat and he complained about the city's vagrancy ordinances. Sol C. Johnson was never the objective, impartial observer of black life in Savannah. He was an active chronicler of the vagaries of race relations and even urged blacks to boycott streetcars in 1906. He spoke out often against black on black crime, gambling, and black "low life" in some sectors of Jim Crow Savannah.

When the Cotton States International Exposition was held in Atlanta in 1895, Johnson carried the speech of Booker T. Washington, advocating racial accommodation as the best strategy for blacks. However, he differed from Washington's stand against blacks running for Congress. The paper kept blacks informed about lynching in other parts of the state and the country.

The *Savannah Tribune* was not above extending a hand of friendship to whites. A letter published in 1893 was headed: "A love letter to our white friends who are our best friends." The letter blamed a "foreign element" for the destruction of the "good old days of friendship" between the races locally. Sometimes the *Savannah Tribune* seemed comfortable with white paternalism, especially when blacks got what they wanted from the interaction. The *Savannah Tribune* both reflected and influenced African American life in the city. When necessary it could castigate white "disfranchises" who hindered black participation in elections, but reserved some of its harshest volleys for those African Americans who acted in ways the paper believed, were inimical to black progress. Johnson stated: "When colored men learn to be above petty spite and jealousy, they will unite for the common good until then, there will be little or no progress among them; they are at present, hopelessly divided as to the proper course to be pursued to advance the interest of the colored citizen."[335]

The column "Georgia School Notes" carried reports about the McKane Training School for Nurses and the Georgia State Industrial College for Colored Youth, as well as the black State Teachers Industrial College for Colored Youths, and the black State Teachers Association. Church news featured prominently on its pages, occasionally with complete sermons, though the more prestigious churches tended to dominate the columns. In 1893 the paper called for black policemen to be appointed in the city.[336] In summary, the paper was a decidedly race paper. It lasted for 85 years and was one of the strongest African American enterprises in Savannah's history.

The *Savannah Tribune* was said to enjoy the "patronage of every class of citizens." It was sold in every state of the Union and in some foreign countries. The *Savannah Tribune* boasted that it enjoyed "the confidence of the community, and that it had led every public endeavor and no worthy cause has ever been slighted."

Sol Johnson found it necessary to remind his readers that the paper belonged "to no faction, pulls no wires, but is bold and outspoken for the interest of the race and the principles of the Republican Party." He also emphasized that the colored vote in the city outnumbered "the Jews, Germans and Irish, who have representatives on the Aldermanic board and why not the colored."[337]

Perhaps tongue-in-cheek Johnson reported, "A Niggardly white man in front of the Pulaski house on Sunday night last, wanted to know "why is that a nigger is black." He is undoubtedly unaware that they come white as well as black."[338] But his own people did not escape his tongue-lashing. Johnson stated, "Negro "pimps" for white officers predominate in our city, it is this class of our people who has a tendency of retarding the progress of the race."[339]

The year 1912 apparently began with a lot of hope, on the part of African Americans in the city. The *Savannah Tribune* greatly increased the decibel level of its "bully pulpit" role in the African American community. An editorial stated: "This year should be surpassed. This year should find many more of our young men investing in real estate or in some safe stock concern."[340] Sol C. Johnson admonished each family to try to secure at least a good home. Those holding lucrative positions, he advised, "should systematically save a part of their earnings." Incidentally, almost as if the bolster this movement, the city began putting uniform sidewalks on West Broad Street.

Another editorial stated bluntly: "In recent years the breach among certain of our leading men has resulted mainly in retarding the spirit of progress and dwarfing the aspiration of many." It bemoaned the fact that much advancement of blacks was stymied because of this breach.[341] Johnson presented "a white dove of peace" and called on all concerned to accept it; "let the actions and words of the past be buried with the past and all join hands now in laboring for the uplift of all the people." The editorial also complained that "one of the most notable faults of Negro business enterprises in the past was that lack of attractiveness."

This editorial led to a response. Mannie Houston wrote a letter to the editor, entitled "Get Together." Houston claimed that the previous editorial was "a hummer, though it was saturated with truth." Houston admitted that the editorial laid "some very heavy charges at the door of the colored people of Savannah. Charges, which should cause all of us to do some tall thinking."[342] Houston stated: "At random I pick the following men: Johnson, conservatism; the Scotts, shrewdness in business; DesVerney, accuracy; Tucker, frankness; Grant, modern; Gadsden, amiable; Gary and Styles, economy; McIntosh and Sherman, boosters; McDowell, advertising; Williams, G.S, orator; Williams, J. W., public spirited; Butler, reclusive; Williams, L.E., wise."

In a second letter, Houston claimed that the black community suffered from "petty jealousy, which came from a person thinking he is the whole show. In addition, those social features have no place in business. White people can be the most bitter enemies, yet these very enemies will come together on a business proposition, conduct the business in a friendly way and leave the meeting as big enemies." However, the editorial could also be positive. The *Savannah Tribune* applauded the Negro businesses and professional men who were planning to sponsor sport activities for school children.[343]

The paper printed the full report of an address J. C. Lindsay gave at St. Paul's C. M. E. Church, on March 26, entitled "Should Negroes Support Negro Enterprises?" Lindsay described the issue as "one of the most complex questions confronting the American business Negro today." Lindsay took pride in itemizing some black successes. There was "the pioneer Negro bank that started a few years ago with perhaps less than two hundred dollars in cash money and with no experience at all in this line of high-class business. Then there was the Scott Brothers Dry Goods Store, with its complete stock of shoes, and so forth." That haberdashery was said to be "well stocked and intelligently managed by men with twentieth century business ideas." The Savannah Pharmacy Company, the "only Negro drug emporium in the city," had two very able and competent registered pharmacists, Drs. Gant and Moody. These men served the fourteen medical doctors, and "look after our wants with the greatest care." Lindsay spoke about Handy and Turner in the tailoring business, Yelverton and Young brothers in the confectionary business whose competitors in large measure were "not only members of another race, but are people of another tongue."[344]

Lindsay saw another example in George S. Williams, the husband of Mamie George Williams, who had "planted right in the very heart of the commercial center of the city a three-story brick office building for the housing and encouragement of Negro business enterprises." He complained: "Our business men are losing golden opportunities by their failure to get together. "The time is now ripe. Get together; stay together."[345] A later editorial defended black Savannah against the *New York Age,* which criticized the role African Americans should play in an upcoming Exposition in Savannah.[346]

The *Savannah Tribune* praised Recorder Court Judge Schwartz for his efforts to break up the "black and tan resorts" of the city, which sheltered prostitution. Johnson hoped that the authorities "would ferret out at the same time all of the white women of the underworld who have migrated from the red light district in the northern section of the city to the peaceful communities of West Broad Street south of Gwinnet, which are inhabited by respectable Negro families."

Sol C. Johnson believed that the presence of these women made the "home surroundings of the above communities very obnoxious and very unsafe for the boys and girls growing up in these homes." In trying to both comfort and challenge the black community, editor Johnson was also aware of the fact that many of the "given limitations of black life, were beyond black control." An editorial outlined some of these obstacles. The editor bluntly stated the context of black life in Savannah:

> "History gives no record of any people who have succeeded who have failed to get together on common ground when the future welfare and maintenance of that people were at stake. Situated as we are, with prejudice, race discrimination and curtailment on every side, our people are now living in the most crucial period in their history. The lines are tightening on us every day. In politics, in business, in religion and every other avenue of activity we find that we are regarded as a separate and distinct people. We are being told in unmistakable terms and most frequently too, that we are not wanted here or there. The door is closed to us in many places.
>
> The so-called square deal has become a shadow in some instances, a memory in others. We are being told that we must fight for fight and ourselves we must. We are being shown no quarters. We must do or die. Shall we accept the former or the latter? To accept the former, is to work and work together. The sooner our people realize this the better for us...If we stand together we can survive the fierce competition and opposition of the day. If we stand apart from each other we shall soon succumb to the onslaughts of the enemy.[347]

Ever the realist/optimist, Johnson boasted triumphantly, "At no time in the history of our city has such great activity along building lines been noted among our people as now."[348] Small but lucrative business enterprises were plentiful. Sol Johnson lauded the formation of the *Savannah Boosters Club,* with its slogan "Boost Savannah. Do things now. Everybody boost everywhere and all the time."[349] Johnson found it necessary to rebuke his own people concerning the evils of social class enmity among them. He wrote "We have been exploited by designing and unfriendly interests in the past, because those interests could count on racial dissension, and capitalized the practice of putting one individual or one class of us against the other."[350]

In 1919, the paper had fourteen full time employees who not only printed the paper but also other printing jobs. The plant had a linotype machine and modern presses. Sol C. Johnson invested about $19,000 in new equipment, which included a new model 14-linotype machine and the latest improved flat bed web perfecting duplex newspaper press. These changes were said to make the paper "one of the largest if not the largest, individually owned Negro printing establishments in the country." F. B. Pettie planned to publish a local newspaper with offices at Gwinnett Street.[351]

The *Savannah Tribune* celebrated its thirty-sixth anniversary of continuous publication. Sol Johnson in an editorial reaffirmed the paper's intention to foster and encourage African Americans to enter business and to press for adequate educational facilities. Johnson thought that blacks had benefited educationally and that "in the acquisition of homes and property a record had been made." Finally, the editor felt that "the strong loyalty of its patrons is the main cause of the success. Its efforts will be redoubled along every constructive line for race betterment and especially the harmony of action in our community."[352]

When Solomon Charles Johnson died in 1954 an editor framed his remarkable by stating;

> "Sol C. Johnson has passed, and the community has lost a good citizen, his church a devoted member and sincere leader, and the Masons and their auxiliary and subsidiary bodies, a loyal brother and wise counselor. No civic movement within the last fifty years has been projected that did not have his encouragement and moral and financial support. His church, which he served as clerk and chairman of the trustees over a period of more than fifty years, will miss his ungrudged contributions of time, advice and money.
>
> The late Sol C. Johnson had several loves. Among them were his church, the Masons and the Savannah Tribune. All who knew him felt no doubt that these were close to his heart. He was Grand Secretary of the Most Worshipful Prince Hall Grand Lodge more than fifty years and was organizer of the Grand Chapter OES which he served as Grand Patron many years. As owner, editor and publisher of the Savannah Tribune, the Negro newspaper with the longest continuous publication in the country.
>
> Mr. Johnson was a quiet, modest benefactor of young people, especially those who were fortunate enough to serve him on the Tribune staff. For all the years the paper has been most of the time conservative, sometime becoming aggressive, but all the time a stabilizing influence in the community that he loved. His friendship was a tenacious and thoroughly dependable relationship worthy of anyone's possession. The First Congregational Church, the Masons, the Elks, the entire community, and we of the staff particularly, sustain an irreparable loss in the passing of Sol C. Johnson." [353]

Going Through The Storm

White Savannah's mood towards blacks in terms of race relations, changed ominously with the return of Democrats to power. The passage of the Civil Rights Act in 1875 signaled the abandonment of efforts by the Federal Government to reconstruct the South. Freed blacks were now at the mercy of an embittered and defeated white leadership. Gone was the old "paternalistic tokenism" of the "ancient regime." A new budding "disfranchisement virus" was on the horizon and would come to fruition with the enthronement of Jim Crow segregation. In 1891 the legislature passed its first Jim Crow law providing for the separation of the races in transportation facilities.

By 1896 the Supreme Court in *Plessy vs. Ferguson* provided for "equal but separate accommodations for white and colored races." This was a harbinger of officially sanctioned apartheid. For the next at least fifty years African Americans were doomed to "make bricks without straw," that is, eke out an existence in a social and legal context designed for their oppression. As of old, whites were determined to keep blacks "under due order and subjection." Never at their wits' end, African Americans tried to depend on their own resources as best they could.

The arrival of some 7,000 blacks within twenty years with blacks reaching 51% of the population in 1880, exacerbated the whites' ability to treat them as equals. Notions of white supremacy led to disbarring blacks from the ballot box, jury duty and equal education.

Blacks faced an increasingly uphill struggle for economic survival and had to rely on the limited skills they learned in slavery time. In 1870 black men held down 58 different occupations and ten years later that number increased to 92. They accounted for "more than half of the draymen, porters, bricklayers, coopers" from 1870 to 1880. Blacks cornered a majority of the shoemakers, butchers, barbers, and blacksmiths in 1880.[354] By the end of the 1870's, Savannah's neighborhoods became more racially defined with blacks concentrated in Yamacraw. During August of 1886 Savannah experienced a severe earthquake.[355]

According to historian John W. Blassingame, housing segregation seemed to have been based more on social class than race.[356] Blacks were confined to low paying jobs, about 3,000 children lacked school places. All they had was the hope of a better future largely dependent on their own resources. Savannah experienced an over 18 percent population increase in 1910.[357]

Charles Middleton (1825-1910) was born in Savannah in 1825. At age thirteen he was employed by the quartermaster's department of the army in conveying supplies to troops engaged in the Seminole war. In 1842 he enlisted in the navy and served for one year on the United States ships Mississippi and Vincennes. In

1848 Middleton went to Mexico with commissioner A.H. Sevier and was present at the signing of the treaty of peace with Mexico. When Sevier became ill, he entrusted Middleton with the custody of the American copy of the treaty for delivery to a special messenger sent from Washington.

From 1855 until he died, Middleton was attached to the Navy Department in various capacities, first as a messenger and later as a clerk. From 1864 he had been continuously employed in the Naval Bureau of Ordinance and was highly regarded by the officials of the Bureau. President Lincoln was found of him and secured his appointment to the regular position in the Navy Department. Middleton often referred with pride to the times when President Lincoln took him to the white lot to engage in target practice. Middleton had charge of the rifle, which the President borrowed from the Navy Department for the practice. Charles Middleton died in 1911. He was the uncle of L. G. Middleton of Savannah.[358]

Mrs. Celia Anderson (1819-1889) was born in Savannah about 1819 and was the wife of James Anderson, longtime sexton of Christ Episcopal Church. She experienced a house fire in October 1878, which "destroyed the homes of a number of our most respectable colored people." Celia Anderson was a "well and favorably known as a caterer for parties and receptions of our wealthier citizens, had in her house the night of the fire, the weeks wash of seven families." She and her husband James Anderson were able to "save the property of others entrusted to her care." When the wash was delivered "not one article being missing, and their fidelity cost them nearly one half of their own household effects, the savings of a life time of hard and honest labor."[359] She was "well known by all the old families of our city." She died in 1889 at her residence on Taylor Street near Price Street.[360]

Jackson B. Sheftall was born free,[361] in Savannah in 1836. A light skin mulatto butcher, he aided the Confederate cause by selling meat to the troops. He later claimed that he was forced to perform that function. Sheftall also worked at Fort Pulaski.[362]. He married a slave in 1855 and bought her freedom in 1862. Sheftall was "an old and respected citizen. He was one of the oldest butchers and green grocers in the city.

By his frugal habits he accumulated much property and was considered as one of our solid citizens. He was well known especially by the older citizens." Sheftall was a Mason "of high standing." He died in 1905 and his funeral took place from his residence on Park Avenue and Abercorn Street. It was "largely attended by his numerous friends." A wife, three daughters, Mrs. Sarah A. Jackson, Mrs. Maria Jackson and Miss Mamie Sheftall, one a son, Charles A. Sheftall survived him.[363] The *Georgia Baptist* reported that Sheftall was "highly regarded in business circles as well as in social circles."[364]

Anthony K. Desverney (1831-1892) was born in Charleston, S.C., in April, 1831. His father was French and his mother was African.[365] Charles Elmore claims that Desverney was born December 11, 1831.[366] Desverney came to Savannah in the mid 1860's and later married Rachel L. Jaleneau daughter of J. R. Jaleneau, and sister of Col. William H. Woodhouse's wife. The couple had a son, Edward, and a daughter, Rachel. Desverney eventually became a professional cotton shipper with Alex Hardee, Amzi Neely & Co., William Trenno, Kopps & Co. At the time of his death he was reputed to be the "oldest shipper on the Bay and was considered an expert at the business."

Desverney was actively involved in and attained the rank of Adjutant in the First Battalion Georgia Volunteers Colored. He was a Past Grand Master of the Most Worshipful Grand Lodge of A. P. & A. M. and was the second grand treasurer. He served as past master of Eureka Lodge No 1, A. F. & A. M. and was treasurer and was past Grand Master of the Most Worshipful Grand Lodge of A.F. and A.M., and was treasurer at the time of his death. He was ex-president of the Social Club and treasurer/secretary. Desverney also served as president of the Mutuals Benevolent Society and was treasurer at the time of his death. He was a Vestryman of St. Stephen's Episcopal Church for many years.[367] In all his activities, Desverney "was looked upon as being beyond reproach, among both classes of citizens he maintained this feeling."

A prominent member of black Savannah's mulatto "light skin elite," along with the Spauldings, Toomers, Deveauxs, Scarboroughs and others,[368] he lived on 4 Taylor Street and was listed as "a colored cotton shipper."[369] Three years later his address was listed as 10 ° Taylor Street.[370] The City Directory of 1877 listed him as living at 4 Taylor Street with his place of business at 84 Bay Street.[371] He was reputed to be the "wealthiest Negro in Savannah." The *Savannah Tribune's* report on his death was entitled, "One more Landmark Gone." It stated, "There has not been a death in a long while to have caused so general sorrow as was the demise of Adjutant Anthony K. Desverney."

After the funeral, conducted by the Rev. Richard Bright, rector of St. Stephen's Episcopal Church, the Most Worshipful Union Grand Lodge, the First Battalion Georgia Volunteers and friends, proceeded to Laurel Grove cemetery accompanied by a musical band. C. C. Leslie of Charleston, Dr. William Pollard, T. A. Morel, S. F. Spaulding, Louis B. Toomer and N. A. Cuyler were honorary pallbearers. The "pieces played by the bands caused many eyes to be dampened with tears." At the grave the Battalion fired its last salute. The return to the city "was made with a heavy heart, with the thoughts of one who has been honored among us."[372]

Mrs. Rachael Desverney died in October 1892. She had been ailing since the death of her husband and never regained her health. She lived at the home of her sister, Mrs. William Woodhouse. She belonged to "one of the first families of the city and was married about twenty-odd years ago, and they lived happily together until death parted them." While Rachael was still a young girl, her mother died and Col. and Mrs. Woodhouse raised her. A sister, a brother, a son and a daughter survived her. [373]

Edward E. DesVerney (1868-1915) was born in Savannah, October 5, 1868 and was educated in the public schools, Beach Institute, and later Hampton Institute. He was born into a family of very financially successful black Episcopalians, and was considered "an astute businessman." He later married Zella Desverney. They had three children, Louise, Richard and Edward Jr.[374] Desverney was a Director of the Wage Earners and Mechanic Banks, President of the Board of Trustees of Charity Hospital. He was a member of the Board of curators and librarian of Carnegie Colored Library. He was a member of the Mutual Benevolent Society, the Armour Lodge, Odd Fellows and supreme grand temple, U.B. of A. The *Savannah Tribune* listed the name as "DesVerney" in the death notice in 1915, [375] though the paper, listed his father's name as Desverney in 1892.

DesVerney was employed as a clerk for more than twenty years with cotton brokers Shearson and Hamlin. He was said to be "a model citizen, a devoted husband, an affectionate father." He amassed a substantial fortune, valued at about $50,000, in his 46 years of life and was regarded as "one of the city's substantial citizens."[376] His will stipulated that, after paying his debts and the necessary upkeep of his wife and children, the remainder was to be held in trust until all of the testator's children shall have reached the age of 21, at which time it is to be divided equally among the children and the testator's wife. Provision was made in the will to forfeit the wife's portion should she remarry. The children were to be "sent to Hampton Normal and Agricultural Institute there to learn some useful trade." Charity Hospital and Training School was given $30 per year "as long as Mary W. Long shall be connected with that Hospital as head nurse or matron." Beside his wife, Sadie Desverney, three children, one sister, Florida Desverney, and a nephew, Anthony Desverney survived the deceased.[377]

Moscow Jackson, a sleeping car porter, was "the oldest colored employee of a railroad in Georgia, if not the entire country." Jackson began working for the company "almost with the invention of railroads." He started off, while "quite a small boy," as a "track walker" in 1833. His owner "hired him to the old Monroe Railroad Company, afterwards known as the Macon and Western Railroad." In those days, the railroad used "strap" or flat iron placed on wooden strips. These strips tended to curl up at their ends and cause accidents. Moscow had the job of nailing down these "snake heads." These snakeheads could injure passengers by "tearing through the cars doors and taking off the legs of unexpectant passengers."

Moscow was sold to the Macon and Western Railroad and was "put down among the valuable assets of that corporation for eighteen years." In due course Moscow was promoted through different levels of track hand, to locomotive fireman. In that role he helped carry "many thousands of Confederate soldiers to the front," and then, after fifty years, he was elevated to the most lucrative position of porter of a sleeping car. When freedom came, Moscow dropped his owner's name, Carter, and took the surname Jackson. He was described as "not a dude, but has rather a ministerial appearance." Rail passengers reportedly had "a kindly regard for its worthy colored sleeping car porters, who like the gentlemanly conductors of the line, appear to have no other thought than to keep up the well established reputation of the road."[378]

J. H. Butler, associate editor of the *Savannah Tribune,* was arrested and charged with violating city and state law by "sending labor out of the state." The paper paid his $1,500 bail bond. Butler had arranged, with the New York office of the National League on Urban Conditions Among Negroes, to find jobs for college students. Mayor Pierpont sent city detectives to investigate the labor activities of J. H. Butler. Twenty-six of the boys had boarded the Steamer before the detectives arrived. At the same time, "seventeen college boys who were waiting at the New York Steamer's dock ready to sail were apprehended by the city detectives and held at the barracks as witnesses." Sol Johnson thought it was a "needless detention of the boys and was evidently done to inconvenience and intimidate them." The city fathers were once again responding to that decades old urge to keep blacks "under due order and subjection."

The *Savannah Tribune* carried the headline: "2,000 Laborers Disappointed." Hundreds of men and women wishing to go up north in search of jobs had expected two trains to arrive in the city. The paper reported that: "Four miles on the Augusta road, Sunday night and early Morning there was a sufficient number present to fill a train of fifteen coaches." Many had sold their furniture and given up their homes. About "four thousand were there viewing the expectant travelers and wishing them good luck." The county and city police were on the scene in full force. The crowd remained at the scene overnight and about seven in the morning.[379] Sol Johnson regarded the whole scene as "the outcome of the labor agitation which has risen here this summer caused by the departure of about 3,5000 laborers for the north." Editor Johnson "obtained an opinion of Assistant City Attorney Atkinson on the matter and was advised by him that the forwarding of students from this port to the tobacco fields of Connecticut did not in any way conflict with the labor laws of the city or state." Historian John Dittmer credits this exodus of black labor from Savannah as the beginning of the Great Migration of blacks to the north.[380]

A committee felt that the low wage paid blacks in the city was a contributing cause of the exodus. Among the members of this committee were black Episcopalians, Attorney J.H.Kinckle and Walter S. Scott. The *Savannah Tribune* gave its assessment of the black exodus to the North as "mob violence, poor housing, poor wages, educational disadvantages, inequality of employment, etc."

Butler was born in Savannah February 14, 1884. His parents were "J. H. C. Butler and Mrs. Sarah Flemister Butler who were among the first teachers at West Broad Street School." Jim as he was called attended local schools, Atlanta University and Chicago University. In 1910 he became associate editor of the *Savannah Tribune* and remained at that position til a few months before his death. His "front page layouts were among his most treasured duties," and his editorial against boledo "have been given credit in helping to rid the city of this vice." He died in 1959 and was a member of St. Matthews's Episcopal Church.[381]

Edward Howard Burke was a printer by profession and worked at Delamotta and Brown who operated a small job print shop and book store on Broughton Street near Barnard Street. Sol John employed him shortly after taking over the *Savannah Tribune.* In 1916, Johnson appointed him city editor. Burke was "The best known club man in the city. He was one of the founders of the Savannah Home Association and its president for fifteen years." He also served as president of the Fox Club, "being probably the only man in the city to hold the distinction of being head of two such civic organizations."

In 1920, while on vacation in New York City he "gathered together about twenty former Georgians and out of this nucleus grew the United Sons of Georgia, one of the strongest and most influential civic organizations in that city among our group." Burke was a member of P.N.F. of Armstrong Lodge, Odd Fellows; a past Chancellor of Hilton Lodge, K. of P. and a member of Pythagoras lodge Masons.

Edward H. Burke died at his residence, 307° West Henry Street. Editor Johnson stated that Burke's death, "Removed from Savannah one of its best known citizens." Burked worked for the *Savannah Tribune* for thirty-six years, first as a printer then for ten years as city editor. He was "a man of unusual ability, strength of character and a forceful speaker."[382]

George H. Bowen of Waycross, a "man of unusual energy and a most pleasing personality," was employed in the Railway Postal service of that city and engaged in the manufacture of soda water. Following a work-related accident, he resigned from the service around 1904. In 1906, he entered the real estate and insurance business in Waycross and became a very successful and well-known businessman. Bowen came to Savannah in 1911, and accepted a position with the General Agency for Central Park Land Corporation of Savannah. During those boom years, Bowen "caught hold of the spirit and rapidly forged to the front." Within months, Bowen sold about 800 lots, "practically selling the entire tract of Cann Park," 42nd and Florence Streets.

Bowen moved into new offices from 500 to 457 West Broad Street. The entire ground floor was taken over by him and the upper floor was let for offices. He had three large and well-equipped rooms for his business. George H. Bowen, "the hustling Negro real estate dealer of this city," closed a $40,000 deal for Oatland Island, near Thunderbolt bounded by Wilmington and St. Augustine Rivers and Richardson's Creek. In 1913, a black cigar factory opened at 458 West Broad Street.

Through this activity, Bowen was able to make an "opening for two other salesmen." Later, he decided to go into business for himself; as the *Savannah Tribune* of April 6, 1912, stated Bowen decided to handle "all classes of property," at his office at 605 West Broad Street. His home on Park Avenue between Lincoln and

Abercorn Streets was "one of the most beautiful cottages in the city owned by Negroes." Bowen had a slogan: "There is no better investment on earth than the earth itself. I can sell the earth." His office on West Broad Street was said to handle "all kinds of real estate, improved and unimproved." He was regarded as "highly respected and admired by both white and black and is fair and upright in his dealings with the people."

Bowen was said to have been a principal agent in the establishment of the Union Development Company, which was capitalized at $50,000.[383] In 1916, he bought a beautiful 40-acre tract of land near Isle of Hope, which he hoped to develop into a Negro settlement. Three years later George Bowen was "The leading Negro real estate dealer of the city, in great demand by both races. His success during the past five years has been one of the main topics of discussion in real estate circles."

His first big local success was the sale of the Central Park, four and a half miles on White Bluff Road then the Cann Park lots on the southwestern section of the city, which he sold in record time. Next came Hope Crest Amusement Park. Bowen also sold the brick building occupied by the Savannah Pharmacy and the adjoining building occupied by the Mechanic Savings Bank.

Bowen was working on the sale of Cherokee Heights, a subdivision on Bay Street extension. He later moved his office to the Wage Earners bank building. His last location was at the Dunbar building. He was a director of the Wage Earners Savings Bank, "the largest Negro banking institution in the country."

George H. Bowen was the "leading spirit" in the movement to establish the Union Development Company, a real estate stock company on northern half of the property on the northeastern corner of Alice and West Broad Streets, which the Wage Earners Loan and Investment Company had recently acquired. The plan was to erect a "modern three story brick building on the first floor of which will be two stores and on the second and third floors apartments or offices." The building was to be located one block south of the Union Station on a "most desirable piece of property to remain in possession of the Negroes of the city." In September, the group was officially constituted with a capital of $50,000. Shares were sold at $10 each and were available from Bowen's office at 458 West Broad Street.

In 1919, Bowen bought a piece of property on the southwest corner of Liberty and Price Streets from Solomon Sheftall. The property was said to be advantageously located, "being in a select white section of the city in which property values are increasing at a marvelous rate." Bowen was the first black to buy property in that area. The price was around $30,000. In 1924, George Bowen, feeling that there was "a good chance for his advancement in the North," sold his real estate business to Howard Stiles and left for Philadelphia, where he entered the real estate field. Within months, Bowen left for New Jersey to work with the Northeastern Life Insurance Company then in the process of formation. In time, Bowen's division became the leading branch of the Company. Bowen died in 1934.

Walter Sanford Scott Jr., was born in Savannah July 24, 1877,[384] the son of Duncan S. and Susie M. Scott. Duncan S. Scott Sr., was born in Savannah September 6, 1840,[385] and is listed as a mulatto in the 1860 Census of Chatham County.[386] He was a barber and private school teacher.[387] In 1871 his barbershop was located at 8 Whitaker Street and he lived at 8° Taylor Street.[388] Duncan Scott Sr died July 31, 1885. The family was one of the founders of St. Stephen's Episcopal Church.

Young Duncan Scott was educated in the public schools of Savannah and then at Tuskegee Institute, under Booker T. Washington. Scott graduated from the Academic Department and from the Trade Department ofTuskegee Institute in 1895. On his return to Savannah he worked at the Cotton Exchange. In 1902, he was Secretary/Treasurer of the Wage Earner's Loan and Investment Company. In 1903, he opened an ice cream parlor and a dry goods store. Sol Johnson was obviously very gratified. An editorial stated:

> "The opening of a business of this kind is what the Tribune has been encouraging for some time and takes pleasure in announcing this one. With his ability and business experience it is felt that Mr. Scott will conduct this successfully. The inaugurating of this the first business of its kind by one of our young men, should be hailed with delight and every minister, superintendent of Sunday schools and heads of other institutions should take delight in the making of it."[389]

The store was located at 120 State Street near Barnard Street. Scott was regarded as "a young man of business sagacity and experience." Scott had previously worked for some years in Montgomery, Alabama, at J. W. Adams, "one of the largest stores in that city. This has helped him considerably and in inaugurating his business it will not be new to him." Johnson hoped that Scott would receive "the undivided support of every colored person in the city and surrounding community." He also hoped that with this support, Scott would "be enabled to give employment to a number of our young ladies and men."[390] Some months later, a delegate to the Annual Conference visited Scott's store and wrote the editor on his visit. The writer found that "the stock he had in was all it had been recommended. All of the colored people should patronize him. He is a fine young man. I also called at the Wage Earners Loan and Investment Company's office. It is also a valuable enterprise for our race and demands the patronage of the entire race."[391]

Scott's dry goods store moved to 462 West Broad Street. His brother, Duncan J. Scott, joined him in the business in 1904 and the business changed its name to Scott Brothers. Duncan Scott returned home after an absence of several years. His many friends were glad to welcome him home.[392] The *Savannah Tribune* chirped:

"These are worthy young men and are deserving of the public patronage."[393] In 1906, he was treasurer of Royall Undertaking Company and by 1914, was President of the company. On December 27, 1910, he married Miss Laura McDowell of Savannah.[394] They had three children, Laura, Gertrude and Walter S. Jr. In 1915 Scott was one of the founders of the Savannah Savings and Real Estate Corporation and President of the Bank.

The Scotts put 429 lots, known as Scottland, situated at the intersection of Middle Ground Road and De Renne Avenue on the market. Walter S. Scott was President, Robert E. Scott first Vice-President and Lachlan M. Pollard was Secretary-Treasurer. Duncan Scott was the seller and George W. Jacobs and C.A.R.McDowell were the agents.[395]

Walter S. Scott Jr., died in 1951. His car rammed into an oak tree at the corner of Bull and Anderson Streets, as he was on his way to his home at 1511 Price Street. The 34-year-old Scott was transported to Candler hospital but then transferred to the Georgia Infirmary and finally to Charity hospital where he died. A strong tradition of black folk history has it that when the Candler authorities discovered that the light skin Scott was in fact a Negro, he was removed to the Georgia Infirmary, and this delay probably precipitated his death.

Scott was co-owner of the Acme Insurance Company and was connected with the Guaranty Life Insurance Company. His wife Grethel Harris Scott and his parents Mr. and Mrs. Walter S. Scott Sr., among others, mourned his loss.[396]

The 4-H Club members of Georgia honored Walter Scott Sr., president of Guarantee Life Insurance Company, as "one of their closest friends." He was made an honorary member of the organization. Accepting the honor Scott replied that he had "Faith in 4-H Club work and any worthwhile work that will help youth to improve." Agent Alexander Hurse said Scott stood out "among the many Georgia leaders who have contributed liberally to the promotion of the 4-H program." From the earliest days of Agricultural Extension Service work, Scott had "given prizes and awards for outstanding achievement and has generally encouraged the Extension program with Negro farm Families."[397]

During the upsurge of urban renewal in Savannah, Walter Scott wrote a letter to the editor of the *Savannah Morning News* in which he chided the editor for having, "Failed to endorse a plan to eliminate the slums we have and prevent a growth of others." The area in question was Hull and River Streets and west of West Broad Street to the Ogeechee Canal. Scott pointed out that the "area is almost completely occupied by Negro residents and changing the use of the land from a residential to a business community will cause the present occupants to be pushed into substandard housing in other portions of the city."

Scott reminded the editor that this form of "gentrification " was "used in the Old Fort where hundreds of Negro families were removed and replaced by white families." West Broad Street School in the same area had been "condemned as a fire trap and not suitable for school purposes." Scott wrote that the area ought to be developed as "a low-rental project similar to Yamacraw Village, setting aside about ten acres for a new West Broad Street School and finding more housing for our group."[398]

In 1904 Scott founded an insurance company.[399] This company was "established and developed by Savannah men and Savannah capital." It had its own home office and was under state regulation.[400] By the 1950's the company had total assets of $950, 000 and outstanding insurance of $8,000,000. The company boasted of forty-six years of "constructive history in the building of estate and in life protection for thrifty patrons."[401] In the 1960's his Guaranty Insurance Company was "one of the largest black-owned insurance companies in Georgia." Scott also owned the old Star Theater on West Broad Street.[402]

His bank, the Savannah Savings and Real Estate Association failed in 1930 even though strenuous efforts were made to save the institution.[403] He was vice-president of the National Negro Bankers Association. The Governor of Georgia appointed him as a director of the Y.M.C.A. He was a Mason, Odd Fellow and a member of the Knights of Pythias. A well-known philanthropist, Scott was very interested in the education of young blacks and was one of the founders of the local branch of the NAACP when it was established in the city. He served the organization as chairman of its education committee.[404] Walter S. Scott, Sr., died November 21, 1961 at Charity Hospital. He lived at 212 East Walburg Street. His wife Laura McDowell Scott who was born January 16, 1887, preceded him in death. She died May 12, 1958.[405] Two daughters, Mrs. Harold W. Calhoun of Bluefield, West Virginia and Mrs. Louis S. Martin of Chicago, a sister and a brother, and 10 grandchildren survived him.[406]

Duncan J. Scott was born in Savannah in 1881 and was educated locally before going to Fisk University from which he graduated in 1903. He joined his brother Walter in many business enterprises in Savannah including the Scott Brothers Dry Goods Store at West Broad and Gwinnett Streets. He was one of the officers of Royall Undertaking and Vice-President of the Guaranty Life and Health Insurance Company. He was a Trustee and Treasurer of Carnegie Free Library. Scott was also "actively engaged in many movements which were instrumental in improving the welfare of the Negro."

It was Duncan Scott who made the motion to get his fellow black Episcopalians to press for a black bishop. He held several positions in St. Stephen's Episcopal Church and was a Vestryman for more than 25 years. He was Treasurer of the Council of Colored Churchmen, a segregated grouping of all the African American Episcopal congregations in the Diocese, for more than 20 years.

Duncan J. Scott wrote a letter to the editor of the *Savannah Tribune* commenting on an article in the previous issue of the paper. In that issue, an individual had questioned the wisdom of supporting black businesses. Scott recalled the shabby treatment a black woman received from a white store on Broughton Street when she was finally asked to leave the store. He then related the incident in which a young man who had been trading with a well-established house for ten years had occasion to return an article that proved to be rotten. The upshot was that the clerk called the manager who "insulted him and told him his patronage was not wanted."[407]

Scott asked the rhetorical question, whether that same person had "ever gone to a colored store, (Scott Bros. For instance) where he was not treated politely? .... Did he ever give Scott Bros a chance to accommodate him by getting a desired article." Duncan Scott claimed: "Scott Bros have been trying for seven years to treat its patrons politely, hoping that in addition to giving value for every cent, good treatment and accommodation would bring business." In 1917, Duncan Scott and his wife lost their 16-month-old daughter.[408] Scott died January 7, 1934, at his residence at 2101 Ogeechee Avenue. His was a member of one of the founding families of St. Stephen's Episcopal Church, in 1855.

Cyrus Campfield Sr. lived on Jones Street in 1868. Living with him were Laura, Henry and Louis[409] He was a practical jeweler and worked for S. P. Hamilton. Campfield later opened his own shop at 11 Whitaker Street.[410] In 1877 Cyrus Campfield and L. Giles were delegates to Diocesan Convention and represented St. Stephen's parish with vote and voice.[411] He was elected senior warden of St. Stephen's Episcopal Church in 1887,[412] and was a delegate to the Diocesan Convention in 1891.[413] Campfield was badly burned as a can of alcohol exploded in his workplace. Lucy Campfield, daughter of Cyrus Campfield Sr., married George Price at her father's residence in 1889, "in the presence of a large number of invited guests. The bride and groom stood under a tastefully arranged horseshoe made of evergreens, while they were being made one. The bride was the recipient of a large assortment of useful and valuable presents."[414] Cyrus Campfield, Sr., died in June 1891.[415]

The younger Cyrus Campfield was born in Savannah, November 27, 1881. He received his early schooling in the city, and then went to the Tuskegee Institute from which he graduated in 1901. For some years he was principal of the Schofield School in Aiken, South Carolina. His many friends regretted to see him leave.[416] He was "singularly honored at the golden anniversary celebration of his class in November 1951." Campfield began his career at Atlanta Life Insurance Company "upon the recommendation of founder A. F. Herndon in September of 1923." His progress with the company was "steady and beneficent." He became a member of the Board of Directors and eventually attained the office of Assistant Agency Director in cage of the state of Georgia. Campfield organized several "One Hundred Year Clubs" throughout the system. These clubs eventually developed into the company's Life Extension Department.

Campfield greatly influenced the auditing practices of the company. He had the distinction of being the company's only Educational Director. President

Herndon presented Campfield with a signed "citation of felicitation and appreciation." For 32 years, his life was said to have been "an inspiration to all who know him. He was full of energy and vitality and this spirit was injected into the men and women under his supervision." The company instituted an annual Cyrus Campfield Week in memory of his contribution to the company.

Mrs. Rosa Lula Barnes (1868-1918) was born in Huntsville, Alabama, August 22, 1868, and faced "many difficulties" in obtaining and education at Huntsville Normal and Industrial Institute before coming to Savannah in search of opportunity. She married Richard Barnes August 16, 1884 and operated a grocery store on Price Street, and had "ten good years in the business." She subsequently also engaged other business enterprises. She found her grocery business "very confining," closed her grocery in 1893, and devoted the rest of her days to lodge work. Her husband died on September 2, 1911.

Her investments proved to be very profitable. She owned five vacant lots, had twelve rented houses, and investments in several businesses such as the Wage Earners Bank, the Standard Life Insurance Company and the Union Development Company.[417]

Rosa Barnes was one of the most active women in the city in the area of business, social work and lodge activity. Barnes held the offices of Grand Worthy Counselor of the Court of Calanthe of Georgia, Past Grand Worthy Superior of the Household of Ruth, of the Eastern Star, of the Good Samaritan, and of the Knights of Pythias. She was regarded as "perhaps the most widely known and most popular secret order woman in the state." She was one of the original members of the Household of Ruth in the state and "served the order with distinction." She was "one of the leading church workers of this city, being an untiring worker in the activities of St. Philip A. M. E. Church.[418] Barnes engaged white architect Percy Sugden to draw the plans for her two-storey brick building at 525 East Henry Street, in the Dixon Park area of the city, the locus of the black bourgeoisie.

African American contractor William Judson Ayers did the work. Ayers reportedly also drew plans for many houses he built in Savannah and other parts of Georgia, especially Ashburn. Another black contractor, William McKelvey, built a two-story neoclassical revival house for himself at 523 East Henry Street. For the next seven years, he built many houses on West 38th and 41st Streets. The Wage Earners Bank financed many of these houses. The *Savannah Tribune* printed a photo of the Barnes house and described the new residence "the second finest residence in the state owned by a Negro." It was said to occupy "an imposing position opposite the park."[419]

The two-story building was divided into twelve rooms. The woodwork was white enamel finished and the rooms were of the finest mahogany. The first floor consisted of a large reception hall, parlor, sitting room, dining room, library and kitchen, while the upper floor had four large bedrooms and bath. The back bedroom opened to a large convenient sleeping porch. On completion, he house was opened for public viewing from 2 to 6 o'clock. The reporter noted that "Scores of friends Inspect and Praise New Home of Mrs. Barnes."

The palatial residence at 525 East Henry Street was said to bring "words of praise" for contractor Ayers for "the excellence of the workmanship in every detail."[420] The Rev. A. L. Singleton assisted by the Revs, A. L. Sampson and William Cash, solemnly blessed the new home. Barnes owned twelve rental houses, which provided her an ample income. She was a director in the Wage Earners Bank, the Standard Life Insurance Company, the Afro-American Company and the Union Development Company.

Mrs. Rosa Lula Barnes died in New York in 1918.[421] She had gone to New York with Mrs Aurelia E. Allen to seek medical attention. The *Savannah Tribune* reported that she was "better known than any other in Georgia, and none was more beloved and highly respected." The body was to be sent to the city for burial. Her remains lay in state at her home until the day of her funeral at St. Philip's A.M.E. Church. An editorial in the *Savannah Tribune* was of the opinion that Mrs. Barnes's life illustrated "the tremendous possibilities for racial advancement, moral uplift and economic advantage, which lie within the reach of women of such splendid ambition and industry."[422] The editor thought Mrs. Barnes "learned to meet the obstacles and disappointments of life."

The paper reported that her holdings were sold for $21, 558. She had shares in the Union Development Co., the Standard Life Insurance Company and the sale of here personal effects brought in $5,000. She was also said to have had "considerable cash on deposit in several banks." The Wage Earners Bank shares were also sold. The *Savannah Tribune* claimed, "This is the first time any stock of the Wage Earners Savings has ever been offered at public outcry, and the high price it brought was very gratifying to the officers of the bank." Dr. J. W. Jamerson, Sr., bought her home for $8,500.

Mrs. George 'Mamie' Williams, the daughter of the Rev. James and Sarah E. Miller, was born in Savannah. She lived at 1212 East Broad Street.[423] She was the treasurer of the Toussaint L'Overture section of the local Red Cross. During World War 1, she worked for the Liberty Loan Drives, and the War Camp Community Service. She was Republican National Committeewoman for Georgia, 1928-32,[424] and was Grand Worthy Inspector of Courts of Calanthe of Georgia: President of Georgia Federation of Colored Women's Clubs.

She was the organizer for the twelve states of Southeastern Federation. She a was a Trustee for Georgia, Daughter Elks; Member Educational Committee of Savannah; Member Interracial Commissions of Georgia; Director Georgia State Savings and Realty Corporation. She was the leader of the movement that resulted in the establishment of Colored Recreation Center and Swimming Pool.[425] For several years she was Matron-in-charge, Chatham Protective Home for Girls in Thunderbolt and President, Chatham County Colored Citizens Council.

Editor Sol Johnson had this to say about the life of Mamie George Williams:

> "In the passing of Mrs. (Mamie) George S. Williams, Savannah has lost another citizen, native of the city, loyal to it to the core, and a tireless champion of her people. She was vice-president of the Carver Savings Bank. She was a member of the First Congregational church and took part during her membership in many of its activities. Perhaps, none of her activities gave her more satisfaction than her work with the Chatham Protective Home for Negro girls, and her work with the Girl Scouts. Many children whom she mothered bear eloquent testimony to her devotion to a cause to which she gave the latter years of her life."[426]

Burying the Dead

On April 7, 1763, the Assembly passed an Act requiring "200 feet square on the Common toward the five acre lots should be laid out as a burial place for Negroes."[427] Seven years later, the *Georgia Gazette* reported that slaves were burying other deceased slaves.[428] The city bought the former Springfield Plantation from the heirs of Joseph Stiles and named it Laurel Grove Cemetery. The property was laid out and drained.[429] On July 1, 1853, the old cemetery, the potter's field and the Negro cemetery were closed. Four acres, later increased to fifteen acres were set aside for the burial of blacks in the south section of Laurel Grove Cemetery.[430] In early 1855 all blacks buried in the Negro cemetery were exhumed and reburied in Laurel Grove South.[431]

A *Savannah the Morning News* reporter visited Laurel Grove Cemetery south and reported: "the student of African character will not have completed his researches until he has visited one of their burying grounds." The reporter found that "to a very large extent there is a neglect of the cheap wooden enclosures, and the elements have, in many instances obliterated the rude lettering on the plain boards that mark the greater number of graves." He observed that many "tokens of affection that are laid on the graves are as varied as the African character." A wash-bowl and a pitcher were very popular as were oil lamps, shaving mugs, snuff bottles and casts of animals. The old cemetery sexton reported that the shallow depth of the grave and the rapid decomposition of the bodies perhaps suggested that bodies should be burnt rather than buried.

William Harden reported that the black cemetery did not have any tombstones but grave mounds with ornaments laid on them, "such as are always found on graves of that race."[432] Sarah, a twenty-year-old slave drowned on the steamer *Pulaski* the night of June 14, 1838. Her owner, who had her from the age of eleven years, claimed that she "was never known to tell a falsehood, to take the most trifling article which did not belong to her, or for a moment to lose sight of her habitual good temper. Always cheerful, affectionate, intelligent and trusty, she was the very model of a faithful servant and enjoyed, as she deserved, the respect, kindness and affection of each member of the family, to whose service she was devoted." Another headstone was erected for Phoebe Ann Wright, who died October 29, 1874 at age 68 years. She was remembered as "Our faithful servant and true friend."

Efforts were made to improve access to the black cemetery. In 1889 the *Savannah Tribune* expressed the hope that "the health and cemetery committee will not fail to see the propriety and convenience it would afford a large number of citizens by placing a plank walk from the railroad track to the colored cemetery. It would be but right and just if it is done."[433] In 1890 Health Officer Brunner described the part of the cemetery used by the colored population as, "a disgrace to the city, the land being too low to admit of deep internments and several bodies being at times disturbed to inter one." In 1892, mayor McDonough referred to Laurel Grove South as "a menace to public health."[434] Richard Barnes was elected keeper of the colored cemetery to succeed S. S. McFall. H. D. Davis was his assistant.[435] City Council introduced a resolution to erect a booth at Laurel Grove cemetery for protection against rain and extension of a two-mile water main.[436]

James M. Simms located this cemetery in the vicinity of St. Joseph's Hospital.[437] Editor Sol Johnson stated that during the colonial epoch, blacks were buried in a cemetery "six blocks south of the Colonial cemetery, bordering South Broad and Abercorn Streets." Johnson thought that "proper consideration was not given these remains," as they were moved to Laurel Grove South. They "were buried with headstones and other tablets placed in a helter-skelter manner. Soon many head stones were "either covered by sand or trampled over by vehicles."[438] The Park and Tree Commission in 1901 appointed a keeper of the colored cemetery.[439] In 1896 a Mr. E. B. Bastow set apart 30 acres on Skidaway Road as a cemetery for colored people.[440] In 1899 the health officer found that "the death rate in the neighborhood of the cemetery is greater than in any other section of the city, and it is his opinion that the cemetery is responsible to some degree for these health conditions."[441]

William H. Royall (1842-1905), a charter member of the Mutual Benevolent Society, and a prominent deacon at First Bryan Baptist Church, was born in Savannah January 3, 1848. Mutual historian Frank Bynes states that Royall worked with Henderson Brothers, a white firm that carted away the bodies of blacks, who died during the yellow fever epidemic of 1876. By 1878, with the financial assistance of Albert Jackson, Royall became the first black in the city to operate his own coffin, casket and cooling board company at 22° Whitaker Street. Frank Bynes informed the author that before the modern day vascular injection was used to embalm bodies, the deceased was placed on a wooden board two feet wide by seven feet long. Then a 300-pound block of ice was placed in a tin container and finally the body was placed on the board over the ice. Hence the cryptic prayer of our elders: "Thank God when I got up this morning, my bed was not a cooling board."

Royall eventually moved his cooling board business in 1888 to 315 South Broad Street, now Oglethorpe Avenue. Major Royall added "a couple of handsome grey horses to his establishment."[442] A Mutual Aid Society, a burial society, was founded to assist people in providing for the burial expenses of loved ones. He was very active in the colored militia and was Captain of the Savannah Light Infantry Company D. He was "the moving spirit in the organization and did much for the perpetuation of the colored military companies in this city." Royall was among the first commissioned officers of the Savannah Light Infantry, which he commanded for years until he was elected Major of the First Battalion. He was one of the first commissioned officers of the First Battalion Georgia Troops Colored, but was placed on the retired list in 1903.[443]

When Major William H. Royall died March 30, 1905, he was: "the oldest undertaker in the city," and conducted "a flourishing business on West Oglethorpe Avenue." He was a member of Eureka Lodge No. 1, Armenia Lodge of Odd Fellows and a charter member of the Mutual Benevolent Society.[444] He was "a race man truly and many are the unfortunate ones that he has assisted while in trouble. If it were not for his liberality he would have left a fortune second to but a few in this County."[445]

Royall's funeral took place from First Bryan Church on a Sunday afternoon. Long before the funeral procession arrived at the church, the building was crowded and people lined all the streets around the church. The Rev. George W. Griffin, the church's pastor, and Dr. Cornelius McKane delivered eulogies during the service. As the remains left the church, they were received with full military honors while a band played a dirge. The Union band headed the procession to the cemetery, followed by three companies of the Battalion. Olympia Lodge, K. of P., Armenia Lodge of Masons formed the civic escort. Hundreds of on-lookers thronged both sides of the streets as they paid their respects to the deceased.

As the cortege entered the cemetery, a massive crowd surrounded the gravesite. Captain Dr. J. H. Bugg commanded the Savannah Light Infantry, which lined up and gave the usual military salute. A bugler of the Company sounded taps. A reporter noted "It was effective in the extreme." He also stated that the funeral was "the largest that has ever occurred in this city." The procession with the carriages was a mile long. The deceased left a valuable estate, including several parcels of property in the city as well as in the county and a good amount of insurance.

His son, Charles H. Royall, inherited the business.[446]

Ever mindful of its critical role as arbiter of the values and advancement of the black community, the paper harshly condemned the custom, "rampant among us for gorgeous and unnecessarily expensive funeral displays." While allowing for expressions of love towards the deceased, the *Savannah Tribune* saw the origin of this custom in the fact that there was growing among blacks "a class of people who might be termed professional mourners or funeral attendants."[447] The paper agonized over this "fast growing custom among us that ought to be condemned, that is, the Sunday funeral." The reporter commented on a funeral held the previous week during which, "those of us who happened to be on West Broad Street during the afternoon and early evening were made to bow our heads in shame at the unusual and unnecessary display of funeral finery and show that was exhibited to our gaze." Bands played and the funeral cortège "flanked on both sides by the habitués of the Streets, who formed themselves into marching clubs." Almost in exasperation the writer stated, "We do not know of any people, save ours, who are so much given to unnecessary elaborate funeral displays."[448]

Within weeks the paper's editorial was back again with another aspect of black funeral customs. The paper claimed to have been "on the verge of congratulating ourselves on witnessing the fading away of the custom when it suddenly boomed up again."[449]

J.C. Lindsay wrote a letter to the editor in which he called the paper the "watchman upon the wall endeavoring to guard each and every interest of our people." He thought the wholesale desecration of the Sabbath, "as practiced by us in this regard should be stopped." He felt that some burials were kept over "from Tuesday or Wednesday of the previous week, so as to have a big, jolly crowd to keep steps to the sweet music furnished by one of our well trained bands." Finally, he appealed to "our recognized leaders, the ministry, to break up this growing evil."[450] Lindsay thought the custom was wrong and those who engage in it "should be made to feel that it is wrong."[451]

Twenty-three years later, in 1935, another *Savannah Tribune* editorial castigated churches for holding funeral services for over an hour "catering mostly to those who wish to display oratorical and musical ability." As it happened at that time the health officer decided to refuse to grant permits for long delays of burial. The editorial continued: "Most of our more prominent citizens are buried the day after death and with service as simple and short as possible."[452]

Andrew M. Monroe (1856-1924) was born in Savannah in 1856.[453] After completing his elementary education in Savannah he attended Atlanta University. On his return to Savannah the Merchants National Bank employed him for some 47 years. When that bank folded Monroe went to work for the Federal Reserve Bank for three years retiring in 1922 with 55 years of continuous service to banking houses in the city. Monroe "became known in the financial circles of the city as perhaps no other Negro has."[454] According to Frank Bynes Monroe operated an ice cream parlor at Abercorn and Broughton Streets on a site later occupied by First Federal Bank. In 1897 Monroe bought the home of Mrs. Belle Nash at 607 West Broad Street.[455] He married Matilda M. Monroe in 1872 and they had five children. Matilda Monroe died in 1912.

By 1910 he had accumulated enough funds to open Monroe Funeral Home on the east side of West Broad Street between Huntington and Minis Streets. When he died in 1924, he was "interred in a Mausoleum, the first such interment for a black in Savannah." Andrew Monroe was a charter member of the Mutual Benevolent Society. Monroe Funeral Home had added a Studebaker service wagon to their fleet.[456] The business was said to be "well equipped, having three vehicles, two hearses and several carriages. It also carried a large assortment of caskets and robes which will be added to by the new owners." S. A. Grant headed the company and F. A. Curtright was manager. The reported sale was denied the following week.[457]

Lachlan "Lach" McIntosh Pollard (1867-1941) was born in Savannah December 12, 1867. He was the youngest son of Dr. William Pollard and was educated in the public schools and at Beach Institute. In 1890, he joined the civil service as a letter carrier and worked there for twelve years. On November 28, 1901, he married Eleanor "Nellie" Reid Scott, the second oldest daughter of Duncan S. and Susie M. Scott.

This "society wedding" was a grand affair. St. Stephen's Episcopal Church was "prettily decorated with palms and potted plants." Joseph L. Jackson and Frank L. Curly were ushers and Sidney M. Jackson was the groomsman. Susie M. Scott, the youngest sister of the bride, was the bridesmaid. She was dressed in "white fringed organdie, trimmed with insertion, lace and white satin ribbon. Her bouquet consisted of pink roses and maiden hair ferns, tied with white satin ribbon." Anna Scott, maid of honor, was "gowned in pink organdie, trimmed with satin ribbon. She carried a bouquet of pink roses and maiden hair ferns, tied with pink satin ribbon." L. M. Campfield was the best man. The bride's mother "was beautifully attired in tan broadcloth, trimmed with silk and C.C. Deveaux, sister of the groom, wore black silk."

Promptly at 8:30 p.m. the bride entered the church on the arm of her elder brother, Walter S. Scott, to the strains of the Lohengrin wedding march. She was dressed in "white satin entrained, trimmed with silk applique," and wore "a beautiful diamond sunburnt, a gift from the groom." Her "veil was artistically arranged and held in place with orange blossoms. She carried a bouquet of bride's roses and maiden hair ferns." The church's rector, the Rev. Richard Bright, officiated. After the ceremony the guests "repaired to the home of the bride's mother where a bounteous repast was served." The gifts "were numerous as well as costly." At the end of the festivities "the bride and groom were driven to their elegant home on Whitaker and 37th Streets."[458] The couple had two daughters, Eleanor and Susan, who were educated in Savannah and New York.

Lachlan Pollard took over the operation of Royall Undertaking Company and renovated the establishment, increased the stock, and had "everything on hand that is needed by the patrons of the company." The company was doing business at 319 West Oglethorpe Avenue. Working under him were, J.H. Ulmer, Paul Steele and W.H. Burgess.[459] Towards the end of 1908 plans were finalized "for the consolidation of the Royall Undertaking Establishment and the Johnson's Undertaking Establishment, the consolidation being under the name of the Royall Undertaking Company." The business was under the "direct management of Messrs L. M. Pollard and W. R. Fields. Both of these gentlemen are citizens of excellent repute, well known and liked, and the interest of all patrons will be safe in their hands."[460]

Pollard served on the Board of Directors of the Wage Earners Bank and in 1915, was a charter member of the Savannah Savings and Realty Corporation and was Treasurer of the Guaranty Mutual Life Insurance Company. Lachlan Pollard was an ardent churchman. From 1896, when he was Junior Warden of St. Stephen's Episcopal Church, to a few years before his death in 1941, he remained an official of the church. Father Gustave H. Caution, rector of the congregation for 28 years, informed the author that "many a Sunday" Lachlan Pollard provided his Sunday meal.

Lachlan M. Pollard, his brother-in-law Walter S. Scott, and Lucius E. Williams, bought the Royall Funeral Home from the Royall family in 1905[461] Black attorney J. H. Kinckle drew up the legal documents.[462] They combined it with the Johnson and Fields Funeral Services, established in 1900. The following week the owners announced that the active management of the company would be Charles H. Royall and W. S. Roundfield, "and we assure the public prompt and courteous attention."[463] The new operation was moved to 327 Jefferson Street under the name Royall Undertaking with Lachlan M. Pollard as manager. In 1914, Royall Undertaking Establishment had a rolling stock that compared favorably with "that of any similar business in the city and the stock of caskets, coffins and robes is large." Prior to the 1920's Royall Funeral Home was the only place in the city where black morticians could receive training, apprenticeship and licenses in mortuary science.[464]

The Company moved again in 1919, to the Globe Theatre at 501 West Broad Street. Manager Pollard was said to be "one of the most widely known men in Savannah and had occupied many positions of trust and honor." He was a Mason and a member of Ezra Consistory, No. 27, Scottish Rite Masons, Thirty Second Degree, and was Treasurer of Omar Temple No. 21, Nobles of Mystic Shrine. Pollard was also a member of Pythagoras Lodge and the Order of Eastern Stars and past worthy patron of Electra Chapter and of the Grand Chapter for more than 25 years. He was a member of the Mutual Benevolent Society.

When Pollard died in August 1941, funeral directors Paul J. Steele of Steele Undertaking and Al Roberts of Roberts Funeral Home were in charge of arrangements. Sol C. Johnson in an editorial remarked that Pollard was:

> "An ardent worker in his church not for a few, but for many years. There he was a main stay and a dependant. In the business field his integrity was unquestioned, adding much to the stability of concerns connected with causing the ones under his direction to have an improved conception of life. Fraternally he was beloved. He had the opportunity of displaying the innermost workings of his noble character.
>
> He was responsive to each worthy appeal, many times going out of his way to favor others and helping in needful causes. At times some of his friends felt that advantage was taken of his kindness, but he seemed to have secured pleasure there from. He was positive and scorned deception.... He was always the same good-natured and cheerful "Lach" Pollard. His passing is mourned, but his life has been of the greatest benefit to the community. Gentlemanly, refined, his memory will be always kept green." [465]

The Weldon Lodge, No. 26, published a Memorial To Brother L. M. Pollard, which stated: "Few colored men have attained a greater recognition within a lifetime than Brother L. M. Pollard." The article went on to conclude that his was a life "whose history is both an example and an inspiration."[466] His widow, Nellie Scott Pollard, two daughters Susan Pollard Waters, Eleanor Pollard Corneliuson of Brooklyn, New York, a sister, Eliza Pollard Deveaux, and two grandchildren were left to cherish his memory.

Dr. William Pollard (1824-1897), prominent Mutual charter member, was born in Savannah July 13, 1824. He was a mulatto, a free person of color, and the son of Eliza McIntosh. He was most likely educated in one of the underground black schools of his day. Later he studied at Ohio State University obtaining his doctorate in Veterinary Surgery. Pollard returned to the city and owned and operated a drayage company in addition to his veterinary practice. He was credited with being a "veterinary surgeon of great skill and made an enviable reputation in that capacity." In the 1860 census Pollard was listed as a 36-year-old dray master with $3,000 in real property and $600 in personal property[467] He was "the leading drayman" in 1870. He lost his son William Pollard, Jr., "son of our old and esteemed fellow citizen Mr. William Pollard." William Jr., was "frank and manly" and possessed "fine traits of character.[468]

In 1891 Dr. Pollard accidentally fell from his buggy and "was painfully injured."[469] He was one of the first blacks to pressure the Savannah /Chatham County Board of Education to provide for the education of black children. Pollard was known as "a man of the strongest convictions, brave, fearless, yet kind and courteous, and took an active interest looking to the elevation of our people." Dr. William Pollard died in 1897. He was a member of St. Stephen's Episcopal Church and was buried from the church.

Pollard made "a reputation as a veterinary surgeon. He was a man of excellent character and always devoted to the interest of his home." During reconstruction "his influence was considerable at that time with the leading city officials, and his efforts were approved by Col. E. C. Anderson and other active workers in the cause of education during that period." According to the white paper Deveaux left: "a name and record that his people may be well proud of."[470] His two children Mrs. C. C. Deveaux and Lachlan Pollard survived him.[471]

Captain Edward Seabrook (1869-1920) was regarded as one of "the most progressive and most substantial Negroes in Savannah." Born November 6,1869, in Aiken, South Carolina, he came to the city when quite a young man and in 1890, married Miss Nena Trayus. As a youth, he loved the water as "a duck takes to water." He worked on various steamboats plying the waters of South Carolina and Georgia and became so proficient that he was eventually granted a first class pilot's license. At the time, he was perhaps the youngest pilot in the area.[472] He also traveled up and down the coast from the St. Lawrence to the Gulf of Mexico. After some years, a bout of malaria forced him to take upriver steamer work, but eventually he had to give up the water entirely.

Around 1906 he entered the undertaking business. Seabrook held extensive real estate in the city and was a director of the Wage Earners bank. In this endeavor he was very successful and was able to "build up one of the most remarkable business enterprises in this city." He began the construction of a ten thousand dollar funeral home, at the corner of West Broad and Minis Streets. The three-story building was of red pressed bricks. The first floor was used as the funeral home, with a front display room and office, together with a chapel with seating capacity for 100.[473] The rear of the building contained a stable to accommodate 18 horses. Seabrook's living quarters were in the front while the rear was quarters for a carriage elevator. The third floor was taken up entirely with two large rooms, which were used as meeting places for societies. The building was one of the "best in the city owned by Negroes." Seabrook Undertaking Establishment added an ambulance, "the first motor power to be owned by a Negro undertaking establishment in this state." It was a highly polished car, gray in color and roomy.

In May 1918 the *Savannah Tribune* carried the headline, "Undertakers Seabrook and Pollard in Street Fisticuf." The affair, which attracted a large crowd in front of Undertaker Seabrook's office, "occurred over a dead body which he had at his establishment and which he refused to surrender to undertaker Pollard." After an exchange of words "undertaker Pollard and his assistant, D. J. Scott, took a few punches at undertaker Seabrook." One of Seabrook's assistants joined the fray "which lasted about five minutes." After the affair ended Mrs. Seabrook "took a throw at her husband's adversaries as they were passing the office. It was reported that undertaker Pollard wheeled suddenly and slapped her face." The incident was settled in police court.[474]

Seven months before his death, Seabrook retired from the business and sold all his stock to the Savannah Undertaking Company. Captain Seabrook was a Director of the Consolidated Realty Corporation. He was a member of the Progressive Lodge, K.of P., and Mt. Moriah Lodge, Masons, Georgia Home Boys Association, and the Good Samaritans, and a Trustee of St. Phillip's A.M.E. Church. An editorial in the *Savannah Tribune* stated: "Few men, in the short space of fifty years, have achieved so admirably in the field of the worlds business, considering the trying obstacles, which must be overcome." Seabrook was said to be a man with a "cordial and charming personality, a friend and fellow worker without guile." His funeral was "one of the largest funerals seen here for some time," and the deceased was reported to have left an estate valued at more than $50,000. Seabrook's wife, Nena Trayus Seabrook erected a granite obelisk at his grave.[475]

Savannah Undertaking Establishment bought out the Seabrook's Undertaking Establishment for about $23,000. Attorney J.G.Lemon handled the legal matters of the transaction.[476] The business was "one of the most up-to-date and best equipped businesses of the kind in the state."[477] Nathan Roberts, President, headed the new company with William Simmons Vice-President; T. H. Hamilton Secretary, M.H.Nichols Treasurer and J.B.Brooks Assistant Manager. James M.Ferrebee, General Manager and was reported to be "well known and popular among all classes." He had been a letter carrier for more than twenty-five years. Chatham Undertaking Company bought out the Monroe Undertaking Company.[478] The following week A. M. Monroe denied that he had sold out his business but had rented it.

And Are We Yet Alive

Music

In 1753, schoolmaster Joseph Ottolenghe observed that several of his slave students had "good voices" and sang during the services at Christ church.[479] Newspaper advertisements indicate that slaves played the violin and fifes during the period. Five slave musicians ran away and their owners advertised in the local pres for their return. One owner advertised the sale of Joe, a good cook and waiting man who played a "good" violin.[480] Another desired to buy two slave boys capable of learning to play the trumpet for the Troop of Horse band.[481]

Historian Donald Grant reports that during the Revolutionary War in Savannah, black fifers and drummers played for the British troops and Hessian mercenaries.[482] A syndicate in 1810, owned "boy Chatham," a slave bugler, who was rented out to military groups The *Columbian Museum and Savannah Advertiser* carried the notice: "Attention: The members of Chatham Troop of Light Dragons will appear tomorrow at 6 o'clock a.m. in front of the Court House in uniform, completely armed and provided with eight rounds of blank cartridges for the purpose of celebrating the anniversary of the Independence of the United States of America.[483] A picture of a Negro bugler was placed on top of the notice.

In the early nineteenth century, "the buglers and members of the military bands of the State of Georgia's armed forces were members of the Negro race." The slave bugler was rented out to military groups and they met once each year the investors gathered to divide the profit.[484] Lucy Smith reported that musically gifted slaves were "in great demand as musicians on the estates on town houses of owners."[485] Emily Burke observed that white troops had "colored men," as their musicians. Whites considered it beneath their status to play music on such instruments. Burke also found that these blacks were dressed in the full uniform of their companies.[486]

Joseph Burke of First African Baptist Church, William Rose and Frank Keating of Second African Baptist Church were the best-known African American singers in Savannah in the 1850's. The "Forest City Band, composed of colored musicians, discoursed most excellent music, contributing not a little to the soul-stirring animation of the scene." The mass meeting, comprising all classes of our citizens," of some three thousand persons, listened to the music.[487] In 1868, the black Washington Cornet Band headed a group of black conservatives on their way to Johnson Square.[488] Some African Americans made their own musical instruments.[489] The Braham String Band and the Skidmore Club String Band played for parades, parties picnics, outings, rail or boat rides, sponsored by civic groups or the Masons.

The Rev. John B. Deveaux organized the "Old One Hundred Society of Sacred Music," on May 28, 1817.[490] Charles F. Waters claimed that the Old One Hundred "was the best this city and state offered." Many in this original group were former house slaves or free persons of color during the dark days of slavery, and were exposed to some elements of formal musical education.[491] This was undoubtedly one of the first, if not the first, black organized musical group in the city. In 1857, Sturdevant a white man trained a "colored class of vocalists" and presented them in concert at St. Andrew's Hall.[492] During slavery, blacks were known for their "peculiar melodies."

James Porter, senior warden and organist at St. Stephen's Episcopal Church, and his daughter were the leaders of music in black Savannah from the 1850's.[493] William Rivers, Peter Duncan, King S. Thomas, George Gibbons, David Waters,

Lewis Glenn, Henry Field, F. J. Keaton, Levy Moore, the Habershams, the Deveaux Sisters, Alberta Finezy Erwin, Janie C. Houston, Sarah Burke and all the Burkes followed them. The "Old Fort Church, Second African Baptist Church" and the "little Bryan Street Jerusalem Church," gloried in the "thrilling strains of the Deveaux sisters, Finezys, Grants, Fields and Waters. Over at First African Baptist Church a choir of female voices: "had no equal." From 1861 to 1868, Jennie Currell Houston, Elizabeth Crittenden, George Noble Bonaparte and William Ctittenden "had no superior." This musical upsurge at what is now First Bryan Baptist Church led to the formation of similar groups in other churches.

Second African Baptist Church was the first black church in the city to own an organ. Unfortunately, this organ was subsequently destroyed by water and another built in Boston was acquired. The metal pipes were of zinc, lead and silver and the wood pipes were made of well-seasoned northern pine. Among the original One Hundreds were the Rev. William Rose, famous as a bass violin player; David Waters, who was considered one of the best tenors of his day; Hosea Maxwell, Frank Keton, Peter Duncan, Dr. Taylor, Henry Fields, Leroy Moore, Mesdames Jane Deveaux, Margaret L. Loyd, Elberta Erwin, Vastasha Duncan, Mary Wright, Rebecca DeLyons and Henrietta Cooper.

The Old One Hundred existed from 1817 to 1883 and was followed by the "Braham Musical Club," named in honor of David Braham, "the great songwriter of Harragan and Heart fame." William Rivers directed this group of young men, made up of "the best young men of Savannah." The group was in great demand especially as entertainers and often sang for "aristocratic white people." Their singing was reported to be "inspiring and uplifting." R.L. Gibbs, Lem Burke, Gordon Battle, Ed. Carter, Charles Waters, Henry Benton, William Williams, James Monroe, and John Boiffeuillette, famous song and dance artist, were part of the group. The "Broads Vocal Club" next came into prominence in the city. They were named after South Broad Street, as present day Oglethorpe was called. This group lacked formal training in music, but became famous as "serenaders." They produced a level of harmony that was "something wonderful."

John F. Thompson, William Harris, A.A.Colman, John Canaon, Richard Brownfield, John Franklin, Simon Mack and Charles Waters, were the main members of this group. First Bryan Baptist church choir, under the direction of a Mr. Taylor, was one of the outstanding church choirs of the day. Charles F. Waters regretted that "we are now accepted in choirs and similar organizations regardless of our ability. As a result more than 95 per cent know absolutely nothing about music." Waters feared that unless someone stepped in to save the day, all this fine tradition of musical achievement would, musically speaking, like the Old Hundred, "be a thing of the past."

The Chicora Cornet Band of Charleston visited the Washington Cornet Band of Savannah, "whose members are among our most respectable colored citizens."[494] Over the years the city had many famous bands among them Middleton's Band. The Braham Club, "composed of some of the worthiest colored young men in this city," serenaded the *Savannah Morning News.* The "solos were very fine and showed considerable cultivation, whilst the choruses were excellent. The club undoubtedly possess fine musical talent." The paper commented "This respectable class of our colored people is appreciated, and we tender the club our best wishes for their success and prosperity."[495]

Prof Samuel B. Morse was born McIntosh County in 1852, but spent most of his life in Savannah. He graduated from Atlanta University in 1876 and taught school in Athens, Savannah and Brunswick. In 1880 he entered the customs service. He bought a garden outside the city and farmed there for some years. Ten years later he rejoined the government service as a gauger for the city.[496] In 1892, Prof. Samuel B. Morse organized and directed a 40-voice, Savannah Choral Association Choir, composed of members of "various churches and others of musical fame." The object of the association was to "assist every charitable project." Prof A. O. Carter assisted Prof. Morse and Miss C. M. Campbell was the principal accompanist.[497] Morse was also a member of the *Old One-Hundred Society of Choral Music.* The choir made its debut in a concert at Beach Institute Monday May 16, 1892. The chapel was "comfortably filled with an appreciative audience."

Charles F. Waters sang, "What ere betide" and "needless to say it took the audience." Miss Clementine Campbell assisted Prof. A. O. Carter at the piano. The success of the program was "due to the indefatigable efforts of Prof Carter."[498] Morse owned a laundry and was a delegate to the Republican convention on three occasions.[499] In October 1892 Col. John H. Deveaux collector of customs re-appointed Prof Morse "United States gauger of Savannah."[500] Prof Morse found it necessary in 1896 to write a letter to the editor reminding the readers that even through the existing economic hard times he was still teaching music at 26 Gwinnett Street, "even if no signs are hung out."[501] A devoted Congregational Church member, Morse chaired the building committee that erected the new church and served as chairman of the trustees for many years. Morse wrote a very long obituary on his former music teacher, James Porter, in November 1895. Prof. Morse accumulated considerable property and left an estate "valued at about $20,000."

He provided for a scholarship "for the education each year of one worthy boy at Atlanta University to be recommended by the First Congregational Church."[502] A Concert and Soiree was given at the Ford Opera House, Whitaker and St. Julian Streets, for the benefit of McKane Hospital, then under the direct control of colored physicians of the city.[503] Mrs. Patience Morse, mother of Prof Morse, died in 1903. She was born in McIntosh County in 1830, the youngest of three sisters. Early in 1862 she, her husband and their only son, escaped from Darien and reached the Yankee gunboats at Doboy and St. Simons Islands and finally to Beaufort, South Carolina. Samuel G. Morse, Sr., enlisted in the U. S. Army at Beaufort, South Carolina on January 1, 1863, in the first colored regiment organized in the South, known as the First South Carolina Volunteers, and later the 33rd U. S. Colored Troops. The family accompanied the father during battle with the mother "passing" as a laundress. In February 1865 they came to Savannah. Her husband died in 1875.

The Rev. John Cox, pastor of Second Baptist Church, baptized Patience Morse "in the river at the foot of the gas house." She had "never been disciplined nor reprimanded by her church. And was a lady of great kindness of heart, given to much charity." She was a woman of "exceedingly strong mind and persuasive influence," and was "exceedingly concise and punctual; very out spoken and greatly opposed to all kinds of impurity, whether in man or woman, and she strove to impress these principles upon her son."[504]

Charles F. Waters, one of Savannah's great musicians, was a cornetist "with very few equals," and a vocalist of "the first order." He was one who could register C above the staff, and E below, full, clear and distinct. He composed the "Dark Side of Love and "A Mother's Request," which he dedicated to his only son and "Suffer The Children."[505] His father, William Waters, was drum Sergeant of the Republican Blues during the Civil War.[506] Charles Waters claimed that before the Civil War and just after it, Savannah and Augusta were known all over this state "for men and women of our race who read music at sight, and whose rendition of music was far above the average."[507]

During this time, quartets of colored singers from Savannah to Augusta made excursions to contest for the musical Palm. Prof. James Porter and his daughter held the scepter, followed by such stalwarts as William Rivers, Peter Duncan, and King S. Thomas, George Gibbons, David Waters, Lewis Glenn, Henry Fields, F.J.Keaton. Levy Moore, the Habershams, the Deveaux Sisters, Alberta Finzy Erwin, Janie C. Houston, Sarah Burke, and all the Burkes.

Talented singers, such as Anna Savoy, Sussie Denslow, Margaret Wallace, Henry Williams, I.R.Allen, Thos. Wilson and J.H.C.Butler, all made invaluable contributions to the musical climate of black Savannah. They exhibited that level of training and acquaintance with the subject. The writer, Pertina City, ended his article with almost a prayer that this tradition would somehow be kept. He wrote "Give us good teachers in these arts, wherever found, regardless of color, as that is merely secondary," expressed great satisfaction that the students in the public schools. With the coming of the First World War, and the influx of the competitive jazz orchestras, along with the change in musical tastes, other forms of music supplanted the old bands and eventually forced them from the scene. Savannah's "musical genius, Charles Waters," died in 1935. A *Savannah Tribune* editorial stated: "There was none more gifted in the lure of that art than he was." His love of music was inborn, "with a pleasing tenor voice from which he could readily change to bass or other variations with the slightest effort. Though self taught he mastered the fundamentals of music." In order to learn new songs he would attend the theatre and memorize the melodies.

Mathilda M. Monroe (1857-1912) was born in Savannah September 5, 1857.[508] She received her early education in the city, probably in one of the underground black schools, and then went on to Atlanta University. Soon after she completed her study there, she married Andrew M. Monroe, "a modest but sturdy specimen of nature's true ability." He worked as "a responsible clerk in one of the leading banks of the city for more than thirty years."

For many years, Matilda Monroe conducted "a large and successful private school for children in the day, and carried on a school for adults at night." One of her annual concerts was held at Ford Opera House in 1888. The cost of admission was 25 cents.[509] Several local ministers, "desiring to make better literary preparations for their work of ministry, availed themselves of the advantages offered in this school and thus prepared themselves for larger usefulness." At her funeral the Rev. William Gray, pastor of St. Johns Baptist Church, "one of the largest churches in the city," testified that he "received his start and inspiration in this school and owed largely what he is and what he has accomplished to Mrs. Monroe."[510]

Monroe was organist of First African Baptist church for more than seventeen years. She was a Sunday school teacher and was the first colored woman to represent the women of her church at the National Baptist Convention in Indianapolis, where she presented a paper entitled "The Gospel the only means of true Civilization."[511] During the week she also conducted the A. M. Monroe Funeral Home and was regarded as a "very astute business woman."[512] Her three daughters were "cultured musicians of high rank" while her two sons were performers "of splendid ability." One daughter, Mrs. J.G. Curtright, was the "cultured wife of Rev. Curtright, pastor of a large Baptist Church in Joliet, Illinois. She was educated at Fisk University. Essie L. Monroe graduated from Georgia State Industrial College and studied at the Conservatory of music in Chicago and was organist of Second Baptist Church in Savannah and a bookkeeper at the family business.[513] A son, James A. Monroe, a graduate of Georgia State Industrial College, was employed by the U. S. postal service as a mailman in Savannah. Andrew, the youngest, was still at school.

Matilda Monroe died in February 1912 at her home, 605, West Broad Street. Her funeral was "one of the largest, which occurred in this city in recent years and was witnessed by thousands of persons."[514] The church was "crowded to its utmost capacity." Crowds lined the streets from her church Second Baptist, to the cemetery to pay their respects to a remarkable teacher, organist and businesswoman. The *Savannah Tribune* regarded the casket as "one of the most expensive ever seen in this city, being one of the variety known as the McKinley state casket with extension handles." Her husband and five children survived her.

Struggle for Rights

Richard W. White, clerk elect of Superior Court, "indicted by the Grand Jury of the Superior Court Tuesday, for larceny," was arrested and jailed. He appeared before the Superior Court yesterday and gave bond in the sum of $2,000 for future appearance. James Porter and David Waters, colored, paid the bond of $2,000."[515] Richard W. White (sometimes written Richard M. White), a free mulatto, was born in Sumter, South Carolina, probably in 1840. He attended Oberlin College in 1858, and then taught school in Salem, Ohio. In the 1860's, White served in a Kansas Calvary Regiment and enlisted as a private in Company D, Fifty-fifth Massachusetts Infantry. He was promoted to Sergeant May 31, 1863 and to Regimental Commissary Sergeant, December 12, 1863. He was mustered out August 29, 1865.[516]

In 1868, White lived in Savannah and was instrumental in establishing the local Republican Party. He was included in the Radical County Ticket as candidate for clerk of the Superior Court.[517] In 1869 the *Savannah Morning News* corrected the *New York Tribune*, which claimed that Richard M. White was appointed Clerk of the Superior Court. The people of Savannah elected White in 1868. Dr. J. J. Waring, a white, was "being prosecuted by the Georgia Medical Society" the paper hinted, because he supported Richard M. White.[518] Judge Schley granted a writ of quo warranto against Richard M. White, Clerk of the Superior Court, February 4, 1869. White was in part: "alleged to be a person of color having in his veins one-eight or more of African or Negro blood, to show, twenty days after the service on him of a copy of said quo warranto."[519] The charge stated that "One Richard W. White, a person of color, having in his veins one-eight or more of Negro or African blood, received more votes than said Clements, but that said White was and is ineligible and disqualified from holding said office by reason of his being as aforesaid, a person of color…" [520]

The question of whether a person of color could hold the office of Clerk of the Superior Court, was before the court. Albert Jackson testified that he had "always regarded White as a colored man."[521] Richard M. White read the Fifteenth Amendment to the Constitution at a celebration of the Fifteenth Amendment.[522] Judge William Schley issued his judgment that declared in part, "the right to hold office in Georgia does not belong to any person of color. The demurrer is, therefore, overruled. W. Schley."[523] White appealed the judgment to the Superior Court of Georgia. The Supreme Court ruled in his favor.[524]

The Republican Party later nominated White for Congress but he was defeated. Foner claims that "white Democrats" indicted White for larceny but the case was dismissed.[525] White ran for Congress in 1870 and for sheriff in 1874, but was

official, true to his people and faithful to the Government."[536]

Louis (Lewis) M. Pleasant "an ex-collector of internal Revenue, was tried in the United States district Court yesterday for retailing liquor without having paid the special tax."[537] He was acquitted. Pleasant was chairman of the Republican Convention of the First Congressional district executive committee. In 1888 he failed to win a seat in the state legislature.[538] Pleasant was appointed deputy internal revenue collector, under Walter Johnson, for the thirteenth division or Brunswick District.[539] Pleasant also served as collector for the internal revenue for the Savannah District. He had the distinction of being the first Negro "appointed in the United States as a railway mail collector and railway mail clerk."[540] In February 1890 he was "the first colored appointee under the new administration"[541]

In July he chaired the meeting of the Republican Executive Committee of Chatham County at the colored Odd Fellows Hall.[542] That same year he chaired a meeting of the Republican Convention of the First Congressional District in Waycross,[543] and two years later was elected chairman of the Republican District Convention, which met at Waynesboro. Prof. Morse was elected secretary.[544] He attended the Republican National Convention in 1896 and again in 1900. Pleasant served as a keeper of the Congressional election.[545] Pleasant attained the rank of captain in the colored troops.[546] In 1896 he repudiated the "rump" convention led by Prof. Richard R. Wright in Atlanta.[547] In 1901, Col. Deveaux appointed Captain L. M. Pleasant a "customs inspector." This act brought the number of blacks in the custom office to seven. Pleasant had previously occupied this office and was "thoroughly conversant with its duties."[548]

The Pursuit of Justice

In the 1870's former state Senator Aaron Alpeoria Bradley, who reportedly practiced law in South Carolina, applied to be admitted to the local bar but was refused.[549] Attorney J. Robert Love of Atlanta was apparently planning to "hang out his shingle here in a few weeks," however he never made the move.[550] Sol Johnson was not one to easily give up. In December 1892 he was pressing the need for more black lawyers. He wrote: "Wanted; Savannah is badly in need of an able and energetic colored lawyer, one who will be attentive to his practice. This is an excellent field for the right man."[551]

John H. Kinckle was born in Lynchburg, Virginia, and was the first African American attorney to be licensed to practice law in the city. The 30-year-old Howard University Law School graduate sought admission to the local bar and appeared before Judge Faligant and a committee in 1891. The *Savannah Tribune* commented that "feeling was intense against such a move." Major P.W. Meldrim, Messrs. S. B. Adams and W. W. Osborne and solicitor general Fraser examined the candidate in the presence of Judge Faligant. The candidate underwent "a severe test" but "to the glory of Major Meldrim (later judge) he was recommended." The other two members of the committee refused to do so. Judge Faligant who had listened to the examination "was well satisfied and readily admitted him."[552]

Kinckle began his practice at a time when such a field was "unfavorable to the success of a colored man in this hard line." He "nevertheless made a success of the practice of law." His wife and son arrived in the city from Lynchburg, Virginia in July 1892.[553] The white press gave Kinckle some 'notoriety' when in 1903 when it reported his defence of a client before Recorder's Court, judge Myrick. Kinckle is reported to have suggested that "It is a well known axiom that a blow on the head of a Caucasian will cause death where in the case of a colored man there will be no serious results." Kinckle recommended that the case be tried as a misdemeanor or a felony rather than an assault. The recorder did not "see the logic of Kinckle's argument" and the case was remanded for trial.[554]

Attorney Kinckle was regarded as "Savannah's oldest practicing attorney," and "one the most widely known of the local attorneys, having practiced here for more than thirty-five years." Editor Sol Johnson recorded that Kinckle was: "a pioneer among Negro attorneys in the south," who "upheld the highest traditions of the law and the courts." The members of the bar, white and black, were uniform in their estimate "of his ability and fitness." Attorney Kinckle served until about four weeks before his death at his residence at 514 East Henry Street. He was a member of St. Stephen's Episcopal Church and was buried from the church.[555]

Abraham L. Tucker graduated from the law Department of Allen University in South Carolina in 1896, and won a prize for excelling in study and was admitted to the bar of that state. He applied to the Georgia authorities and judge Falligant appointed Messrs. A. H. McDonell and A. L. Alexander to examine him. The judge complimented Tucker on successfully completing the examination. Tucker was reportedly "a gentleman of no mean ability, and is bound to make an excellent record as a lawyer."[556] Within months John H. Kinckle and Abraham L. Tucker formed Savannah's first black law firm, Kinckle & Tucker, at 110 West Bryan Street.

The *Savannah Tribune* described the firm as "a deserving capable firm. The senior member has been a practitioner for a number of years and the excellent examination he stood before he was admitted to this bar is still fresh in the minds of the people and he has kept up this record ever since." Tucker, the junior partner, was described as a "close law student for a number of years, graduating from a law school about a year ago with the highest possible honors." When he took the local bar examination, an examining Chatham Superior Court judge commended him on his replies to questions. The paper concluded, "Both of these gentlemen are able lawyers and will give satisfaction to their clients. We expect much from them, and at the same time commend them to the public."[557]

Col. E. M. Morse, a recent graduate of Shaw University, Raleigh, North Carolina, was admitted to the Georgia bar after standing satisfactorily the required examination, which was very rigid and catchy.[558] Attorney Morse served for a time with the law firn of Kinckle & Tucker but left to form his own firm and had his offices in the Tribune building. He was described as "a lawyer of no mean ability and is destined to be one of the leaders at the bar."[559] Attorney Morse gave an address at the installation of officers of the Colored American Friendly Society.[560] Attorney Morse's health failed him and he went to Athens to recuperate. He died in 1905, after "about two years in the city." [561]

Prof. James Garfield Lemon of the Georgia Industrial College For Colored Youths passed the Georgia,"[562] bar exam[563] and soon resigned from the College to practice law in the city. The freshman class presented him with a "loving cup." In 1938, Lemon celebrated the 25th anniversary of his admission to the Georgia bar, with a gala reception at his home at 511 East Henry Street. He was said to have rendered "conspicuous service to the community and has been a staunch defender of human liberties." He taught at LeMoyne College in Memphis, Tennessee shortly after graduation from Atlanta University.[564] In 1938, Lemon wrote a long article entitled, What the Savannah Negro Is Doing and What Progress Has He Made? Published in the *Savannah Morning News.* [565] The following year Lemon wrote, Savannah's Negro Population Is Vital To City's Welfare.[566] And following year he wrote The Savannah Negro, published in the *Savannah Morning News.*[567] His last article entitled, Chatham County Negro Prospers, Has Built Splendid Businesses, published in the *Savannah Morning News.*[568]

Lemon was married to Callie McKinley Lemon and practiced law in Savannah for forty years before his retirement.[569] Attorney Lemon contributed an article in Kermit Smalls' book in 1934.[570] Attorney J. G. Lemon Jr. was born in Savannah and attended the local schools before going to Atlanta University from which he graduated in 1931. In 1934 he graduated from the Northwestern University School of Law and then taught for a while at Haven Home School in Savannah. Young Lemon practiced law in Chicago.[571]

Fleming D. Tucker, "the efficient cashier of the Mechanics Savings bank," and son of Attorney Abraham Tucker, passed the Georgia bar exam. Young Tucker graduated from the college Department of Atlanta University and the commercial department of two business colleges of Boston, Massachusetts.[572]

Attorney Foster B. Pettie, a Howard University Law school graduate, relocated to Savannah in 1906. The *Savannah Tribune* was obviously pleased with his choice. The paper headlined an article: Another Lawyer for us. He had been admitted to the bar in Georgia having "passed a creditable examination. He has been practicing in Macon." He was the brother of the well-known Edward Pettie of Savannah. The article concluded: "There is no reason why Mr. Pettie can not succeed here. We have a large population and with the ability that he has, he should win."[573]

Attorney Pettie ran a very successful law practice at 116 St. Julian Street, over the Savannah Tribune Office,[574] and was also active in the real estate business having bought out Howard Stiles Real Estate Company. Pettie practiced law here for many years until his untimely death in a motorcar accident in 1930. In "a quiet, modest manner he made his way into the confidence of the citizens of Savannah and caused a feeling of deep respect and high regard." He was "one of the best liked professional men in the city and had a wide circle of friends throughout the state."

He was a man of "unusual frankness and ability," and "enjoyed a high degree of confidence by his clients and friends." Editor Sol Johnson regarded attorney Foster B. Pettie as a "great asset" to the African American community of Savannah.[575] Five blacks were imprisoned for thirty days at the Brown farm for reading aloud the poem "Bound for the Promised Land, " a poem dealing with migration. The court found the matter "handling written matter which may incite a riot among the colored people of the city, as well as over Georgia."[576]

Mrs. Fannie C. Pettie, Attorney Pettie's widow lived in Savannah for more than fifty years. She lived with her daughter Augusta Pettie at 2313 Florence Street. She was an active member of the First Congregational Church, serving as deaconess for a number of years. She was also a member of Prince Hall Chapter No. 258, Order of Eastern Star; Charity Hospital auxiliary and Brownsville Community Club. During World War 1, she served with the local chapter of the American Red Cross. Mrs. Pettie died in 1956.[577]

Gordon Dingle finished his law course at Howard University.[578] Dingle passed the local bar examination.[579] There were three black lawyers in Savannah in 1918.[580]

Endnotes – Chapter 4

[1] Thomas Gamble, 79.

[2] *Savannah Morning News,* September 8, 1880.

[3] Mary Sowell, "A Social and Economic History of Savannah, Georgia During the Revolutionary War," (MA thesis, University of Georgia, 1952), 36.

[4] Joseph I. Waring, M.D., "The Yellow Fever Epidemic of Savannah in 1820, With a Sketch of Dr. William Coffee Daniell," *Georgia Historical Quarterly,* 52(December 1968): 398-404.

[5] *Acts of the General Assembly*, 1832, 177-179.

[6] *Daily Georgian,* August 5, 1823.

[7] Donald Grant, 42.

[8] Carter Woodson, *The Negro Professional Man and The Community, With Special Emphasis on the Physician and the Lawyer*, Washington, D.C. 1934, 8.

[9] Haunton, 319.

[10] William Harden, 48.

[11] *Savannah Tribune,* May 7, 1887.

[12] William Harden, 47.

[13] *Savannah Council Minutes,* August 9, 1865.

[14] *Drums and Shadows: Survival Studies Among The Georgia Coastal Negroes,* Georgia Writers' Project, 1940, 41.

[15] Thomas Gamble, 314.

[16] Thomas Gamble, 342.

[17] *Savannah Tribune,* September 2, 1876.

[18]*Savannah Tribune,* September 16, 1876.

[19] *Savannah Tribune,* September 9, 1876.

[20] John W. Blassingame, "Before The Ghetto: The Making of the Black Community in Savannah, Georgia, 1865-1880," *Journal of Southern History,* 6(Summer 1973): 469.

[21] Victor J. Ceryanec, *The History of Candler General Hospital,* Savannah, no date of publication, 11.

[22] *Savannah Tribune,* January 10, 1891.

[23] *Haddocks, Savannah, Ga. Directory,* 1871, 438.

[24] *Savannah Morning News,* October 6, 1870.

[25] *Savannah Tribune,* October 23, 1886.

[26] *Savannah Tribune,* October 23, 1886.

[27] Thomas Gamble, 343.

[28] *Savannah Tribune,* July 9, 1887.

[29] *Savannah Tribune,* July 21, 1888.

[30]*Savannah Tribune,* September 15, 1888. .

[31] *Savannah Tribune,* September 23, 1876.

[32] *Savannah Tribune,* January 10, 1891

[33] *Savannah Tribune,* February 13, 1892.

[34] *Savannah Tribune,* January 14, 1893.

[35] *Savannah Tribune,* January 23, 1893.

[36] *Savannah Tribune,* January 9, 1892.

[37] *Savannah Tribune,* November 26, 1892.

[38] Savannah Tribune, May 28, 1892.

[39] *Savannah Tribune,* July 30, 1892

[40] *Savannah Tribune,* December 17, 1892.

[41] *Savannah Tribune,* February 4, 1893.

[42] *Savannah Tribune,* February 2, 1895.

[43] *Savannah Tribune,* June 24, 1893.

[44] *Savannah Tribune,* November 24, 1894.

[45] Clarence Bacote, "Some Aspects of Negro Life in Georgia, 1880-1908," *Journal of Negro History*, 43(July 1958):197.

[46] Thomas Gamble, 346.

[47] *Savannah Tribune,* November 16, 1895.

[48] Thomas Gamble, 348.

[49] Thomas Gamble, 350.

[50] *Savannah Morning News,* October 31, 1940.

[51] *Savannah Tribune,* September 2, 1893.

[52] *Savannah Tribune,* September 9, 1893.

[53] *Savannah Tribune,* September 23, 1893.

[54] *Savannah Tribune*, May 4, 1895.

[55] *Savannah Tribune,* February 28, 1935.

[56] *Savannah Morning News,* October 31, 1940.

[57] *Savannah Tribune,* May 18, 1895.

[58] *Savannah Tribune,* May 30, 1896.

[59] *Savannah Tribune,* June 22, 1895.

[60] *Savannah Tribune,* October 9, 1930.

[61] *Savannah Tribune,* October 26, 1895.

[62] *Savannah Tribune,* February 8, 1896.

[63] *Savannah Tribune,* February 22, 1896.

[64] *Savannah Tribune,* February 29, 1896.

[65] Savannah Tribune, June 6, 1896.

[66] *Savannah Tribune,* August *1, 1896.*

[67] *Savannah Tribune,* June 27, 1896.

[68] Savannah Tribune, August 1, 1896.

[69] *Savannah Tribune,* August 22, 1896.

[70] *Savannah Tribune,* August 15, 1896.

[71] *Savannah Tribune,* September 5, 1896.

[72] *Savannah Tribune,* September 12, 1896.

[73] *Savannah Tribune,* November 7, 1896.

[74] Savannah Tribune, April 17, 1897.

[75] *Savannah Tribune,* October 24, 1896.

[76] *Savannah Tribune,* October 16, 1897.

[77] *Savannah Tribune*, June 19, 1897.

[78] *Savannah Tribune*, July 8, 1897.

[79] *Savannah Tribune,* April 23, 1898.

[80] *Savannah Tribune,* April 30, 1898.

[81] Savannah Tribune, July 2, 1898.

[82] *Savannah Tribune* of December 28, 1901.

[83] *Savannah Tribune,* February 16, 1901.

[84] *Savannah Tribune,* February 16, 1901.

[85] *Savannah Tribune,* February 28, 1935.

[86] *Savannah Tribune,* February 16, 1901.

[87] *Savannah Tribune,* May 25, 1901.

[88] *Savannah Tribune,* December 21, 1901.

[89] *Savannah Tribune,* March 9, 1912.

[90] *Savannah Tribune,* March 9, 1912.

[91] *Savannah tribune,* July 20, 1939.

[92] *Savannah Tribune,* May 3, 1919.

[93] *Savannah Tribune,* January 31, 1920.

[94] *Savannah tribune,* March 28, 1896.

[95] *Savannah Tribune,* January 31, 1903.

[96] *Savannah Tribune*, January 12, 1907.

[97] Savannah Tribune, May 14, 1942.

[98] Charles Elmore, 23.

[99] *Savannah Tribune,* November 7, 1903.

[100] *Savannah Tribune,* September 23, 1893.

[101] *Savannah Tribune,* July 30, 1892.

[102] *Savannah Tribune,* November 7, 1903.

[103] *Savannah Tribune,* August 24, 1957.

[104] *Savannah tribune,* October 19, 1957.

[105] *Savannah Tribune,* May 31, 1958.

[106] *Laurel Grove records.*

[107] From John B. Collier's Family Papers, which he graciously shared with the author, January 20, 2001.

[108] A.B. Caldwell, 94-96.

[109] *Savannah Tribune,* October 20, 1915.

[110] *Savannah Tribune,* August 16, 1918.

[111] John B. Collier Family Papers.

[112] A.B. Caldwell, 94-96.

[113] *Savannah Tribune,* October 12, 1950.

[114] *Savannah Tribune,* December 13, 1951.

[115] *Savannah Morning News,* November 23, 1961.

[116] *Funeral Program,* November 1961.

[117] *Savannah Tribune,* February 25, 1954.

[118] *Savannah Tribune,* May 1, 1952.

[119] *The Herald,* May 1, 1952.

[120] *Savannah Tribune,* February 25, 1954.

[121] Letter from Richard R. Wright, President of Citizens & Southern Bank And Trust Company, Philadelphia, June 3, 1935.John B. Collier Family Papers.

[122] Kermit O. Smalls, *Year Book of Colored Savannah,* Savannah, 1934, 43-44.

[123] *The Herald,* April 24, 1955.

[124] *Savannah Tribune,* June, 17, 1943.

[125] *Savannah Tribune,* July 22, 1943.

[126] *Savannah Tribune,* November 2, 1950.

[127] *The Herald,* May 26, 1955.

[128] *The Herald,* December 4, 1952.

[129] *Savannah Tribune,* July 17, 1952.

[130] *Funeral Program,* July 1989.

[131] *Savannah Tribune,* March 1, 1958.

[132] Charles L. Hoskins, 1983, 61.

[133] A. B. Caldwell, 195.

[134] *Savannah Tribune,* October 22, 1904.

[135] Savannah Tribune, May 14, 1910.

[136] A. B. Caldwell, 198-199.

[137] *Funeral Program,* First African Baptist, September 12, 1956.

[138] *Savannah Tribune,* November 1, 1951.

[139] *Savannah Tribune,* September 15, 1956.

[140] *Savannah Tribune,* August 31, 1918.

[141] *Savannah Tribune,* January 11, 1913.

[142] *Savannah Tribune,* April 25, 1935.

[143] A. B. Caldwell, 123-125.

[144] Jamerson Family Papers.

[145] Charles Elmore, 28.

[146] Note from Dr. J.W.Jamerson 111, October 10, 2000.

[147] *Savannah Tribune,* September 11, 1909.

[148] *Savannah Tribune,* May 14, 1910.

[149] *Savannah Tribune,* September 24, 1910.

[150] Note from Dr. J.W.Jamerson 111.

[151] Jamerson Family Papers.

[152] Charles L. Hoskins, 1995, 79.

[153] *Savannah Morning News,* January 6, 1999.

[154] Charles L. Hoskins, 1983, 66.

[155] Jamerson Family Papers.

[156] *Savannah Tribune,* October 25, 1951.

[157] *Savannah Morning News,* January 9, 1995.

[158] *Savannah Morning News,* January 9, 1995.

[159] *The Herald*, December 21, 1963.

[160] Savannah Morning News, November 1, 1964.

[161] *Savannah Tribune,* November 13, 1895

[162] *Savannah Morning News,* November 27, 1999.

[163] Walter Simmons in conversation with the author, October 17, 2000.

[164] *Savannah Tribune,* July 20, 1950.

[165] *Savannah Tribune,* July 20, 1950.

[166] *Savannah Tribune,* September 25, 1955.

[167] Memories of Yester Year, Savannah, 1970.

[168] *Savannah Morning News,* November 16, 1975.

[169] *Savannah Morning News,* June 12, 1980.

[170] *Savannah Morning News,* July 29, 1980.

[171] *Savannah Morning News,* November 16, 1975.

[172] *Savannah Morning News,* June 12, 1980.

[173] A. B. Caldwell, 85-87.

[174] A.B. Caldwell, 188-190.

[175] *Savannah Tribune,* October 19, 1912.

[176] *Savannah Tribune,* July 1, 1926.

[177] *Savannah Tribune,* March 21, 1935.

[178] *Savannah Tribune,* April 20, 1933.

[179] *Savannah Tribune,* March 14, 1935.

[180] *Savannah Tribune,* November 2, 1957.

[181] *The Herald,* February 1, 1958.

[182] *Savannah Tribune,* April 1, 1893.

[183] *Savannah Tribune,* April 22, 1893.

[184] *Savannah Tribune,* March 31, 1894.

[185] *Savannah Tribune,* June 9, 1894.

[186] *Savannah Tribune,* June 24, 1893.

[187] *Savannah Tribune,* January 14, 1905.

[188] *Savannah Tribune,* April 15, 1911.

[189] *Savannah Tribune,* May 17, 1913.

[190] *Savannah Tribune,* June 7, 1913.

[191] Savannah Tribune, ...

[193] *Savannah Tribune,* May 23, 1914.

[194] *Savannah Tribune,* October 3, 1914.

[195] *Savannah Tribune,* September 11, 1915.

[196] *Savannah Tribune,* December 2, 1916.

[197] *Savannah Tribune,* November 11, 1916.

[198] *Savannah Tribune* of March 15, 1919.

[199] *Savannah Tribune,* April 22, 1918.

[200] *Savannah Tribune,* September 6, 1919.

[201] *Savannah Tribune,* June 26, 1924.

[202] *Savannah Tribune,* October 14, 1926.

[203] *Savannah Tribune,* January 19, 1939.

[204] *Savannah tribune,* June 3, 1943.

[205] Savannah Tribune, July 17, 1952.

[206] *Savannah Tribune*, March 4, 1954.

[207] *Savannah Tribune,* March 4, 1954.

[208] Savannah Tribune, July 12, 1956.

[209] Blassingame, 468.

[210] Savannah Morning News, August 2, 1881.

[211] *Savannah Tribune,* January 17, 1891.

[212] *Savannah Tribune,* February 6, 1892.

[213] *Savannah Tribune*, January 16, 1892.

[214] *Savannah Tribune,* January 23, 1892.

[215] *Savannah Tribune,* March 12, 1892.

[216] *Savannah Tribune,* March 19, 1892.

[217] *Savannah Tribune,* March 26, 1892.

[218] *Savannah Tribune,* May 21, 1892.

[219] *Savannah Tribune,* May 7, 1892.

[220] Savannah Tribune, June 18, 1892.

[221] *Savannah Tribune,* December 24, 1892.

[222] Savannah Tribune, July 6, 1901.

[223] *Savannah Tribune,* April 20, 1901.

[224] *Daily News Herald,* June 20, 1867.

[225] *Savannah Tribune,* April 20, 1901.

[226] *Savannah Morning News,* September, 1872.

[227] *Savannah Morning News,* September 26, 1872.

[228] St.Stephen's Church Register, 104.

[229] *Deed Book,* 4, Folio 310.

[230] *Federal Census,* 1900.

[231] Charles L. Hoskins, 1983, 33.

[232] *Savannah Morning News,* April 7, 1874.

[233] *Savannah Morning News,* December 13, 1876.

[234] *Savannah Tribune,* September 9, 1876.

[235] *Savannah Morning News,* January 11, 1872.

[236] *Savannah Morning News*, October 14, 1884.

[237] *Savannah Tribune*, December 17, 1892.

[238] Will Book, R, 131.

[238] *Savannah Tribune,* May 11, 1901.

[239] *Savannah Tribune,* April 27, 1901.

[241] *Savannah Tribune,* May 11, 1901

[242] *Savannah Tribune,* April 20, 1901.

[243] *Savannah Tribune*, December 21, 1901.

[244] Savannah Tribune, March 1, 1902.

[245] Savannah Tribune, June 14, 1902.

[246] *Savannah Tribune,* August 2, 1902.

[247] *Savannah Tribune,* November 10, 1906.

[248] *Savannah Tribune,* August 30, 1902.

[249] *Savannah Tribune,* August 30, 1902.

[250] *Savannah Tribune,* November 8, 1902.

[251] *Savannah Tribune,* April 11, 1903.

[252] *Savannah Tribune,* April 11, 1903.

[253] *Savannah tribune,* October 24, 1903.

[254] *Savannah Tribune,* October 24, 1903.

[255] *Savannah Tribune,* April 30, 1904.

[256] Savannah Tribune, March 3, 1906.

[257] *Savannah Tribune,* September 8, 1906.

[258] *Savannah Tribune,* November 10, 1906.

[259] *Savannah Tribune,* June 8, 1907.

[260] *Robert W. Gadsden Papers.*

[261] *Savannah Tribune*, May 4, 1907.

[262] *Savannah Tribune,* May 25, 1912.

[263] *Savannah Tribune* of January 16, 1915.

[264] Savannah Tribune, July 13, 1912.

[265] *Savannah Tribune*, March 7, 1914

[266] *Savannah Tribune,* August 16, 1919.

[267] Savannah Tribune, March 7, 1914.

[268] *Savannah Tribune,* October 9, 1915.

[269] *Savannah Tribune,* December 22, 1917.

[270] *Savannah Tribune,* January 19, 1918.

[271] *Savannah Tribune,* June 8, 1918.

[272] Savannah Tribune, June 22, 1918.

[273] *Savannah Tribune* of November 9, 1918.

[274] *Savannah Tribune,* July 19, 1919.

[275] *Savannah Tribune,* August 9, 1919.

[276] *Savannah Tribune,* March 13, 1920.

[277] *Savannah Tribune,* August 7, 1920.

[278] *Savannah Evening Press* of August 10, 1920.

[279] *Savannah Tribune*, August 7, 1920.

[280] *Savannah Tribune,* September 11, 1920.

[281] *Savannah Tribune,* October 9, 1920.

[282] *Savannah Tribune,* October 23, 1920.

[283] *Savannah Tribune,* May 10, 1918.

[284] *Savannah Tribune,* July 19, 1919.

[285] Savannah Tribune, May10, 1918.

[286] *Savannah Tribune,* October 2, 1915.

[287] *Savannah Tribune,* March 6, 1920.

[288] *Savannah Tribune,* April 22, 1922.

[289] *Savannah Morning News,* October 31, 1941.

[290] *Savannah Tribune* of January 22, 1916,

[291] *Savannah Tribune,* April 22, 1926.

[292] *Savannah Republican,* June 6, 1849.

[293] *Savannah Tribune,* May 4, 1912.

[294] *Savannah Tribune,* September 22, 1938.

[295] *Savannah Tribune,* October 26, 1957.

[296] *Savannah Tribune,* November 23, 1939.

[297] *Savannah Tribune,* October 26, 1957.

[298] *Savannah Tribune,* October 26, 1957.

[299] Savannah Tribune, March 8, 1958.

[300] *Savannah Tribune,* September 9, 1916.

[301] *Savannah Tribune,* September 16, 1916.

[302] *Savannah Tribune,* March 8, 1958.

[303] *Savannah Tribune,* August 18, 1927.

[304] *Savannah Tribune,* August 18, 1927.

[305] *Savannah Tribune,* September 14, 1932.

[306] *Savannah Tribune,* May 10, 1934.

[307] *Savannah Tribune,* April 30, 1936.

[308] *Savannah Tribune* of May 7, 1936.

[309] *Savannah Morning News,* October 27, 1938.

[310] *Savannah Tribune,* June 21, 1950.

[311] *Savannah Morning News* of October 27, 1938.

[312] *Savannah Tribune,* April 1, 1937.

[313] *Savannah Morning News,* October 27, 1938.

[314] *Daily Morning News*, November 11, 1854.

[315] *Daily News Herald*, June 11, 1867.

[316] *Savannah Tribune*, October 14, 1914.

[317] *Colored Tribune*, December 4, 1875.

[318] *Colored Tribune,* March 26, 1876

[319] *Colored Tribune,* April 2, 1876.

[320] *Colored Tribune,* June 3, 1876.

[321] *Colored Tribune,* June 10, 1876.

[322] *Colored Tribune,* June 10, 1876.

[323] *Savannah Tribune,* November 4, 1876.

[324] *Savannah Tribune,* December 23, 1876.

[325] *Savannah Tribune,* March 11, 1954.

[326] *Savannah Tribune,* October 23, 1886.

[327] *Savannah Tribune,* October 2, 1930.

[328] Henritze, 40.

[329] Barbara K.Henritze, Bibliographic Checklist of African American Newspapers, Genealogical publishing Co. 1995, 40.

[330] *Savannah Tribune,* September 8, 1894.

[331] Henritze, 40.

[332] Henritze, 40.

[333] The *Johnson Explorer*, Student Publication, Johnson High School, December, 1958.

[334] A. B. Caldwell, 348-349.

[335] *Savannah Tribune,* March 2, 1889.

[336] *Savannah Tribune,* January 13, 1893.

[337] *Savannah Tribune,* April 30, 1892.

[338] *Savannah Tribune,* June 4, 1892.

[339] *Savannah Tribune,* June 11, 1892.

[340] *Savannah Tribune,* January 6, 1912.

[341] *Savannah Tribune,* January 13, 1912.

[342] *Savannah Tribune,* January 27, 1912.

[343] *Savannah Tribune,* March 30, 1912.

[344] Savannah Tribune, March, 1912.

[345] *Savannah Tribune,* April 13, 1912.

[346] *Savannah Tribune,* April 6, 1912.

[347] Savannah Tribune, August 24, 1912.

[348] *Savannah Tribune,* March 29, 1913.

[349] *Savannah Tribune,* November 20, 1913.

[350] *Savannah Tribune,* March 17, 1917.

[351] Savannah Tribune, May 18, 1918.

[352] *Savannah Tribune,* October 16, 1920.

[353] *Savannah Tribune,* March 4, 1954.

[354] Blassingame, 465-467.

[355] *Savannah Tribune,* September 3, 1892.

[356] John W. Blassingame, 481.

[357] *Negro Population in the United States, 1790-1915,* 93.

[358] *Savannah Tribune,* January 14, 1910.

[359] *Savannah Morning News,* October 10, 1878.

[360] *Savannah Tribune,* December 7, 1889.

[361] Whittington B. Johnson, 117.

[362] Whittington Johnson, 157

[363] *Savannah Tribune,* April 1, 1905.

[364] Savannah Tribune, April 8, 1905.

[365] *Savannah Tribune,* July 16, 1892.

[366] Charles J. Elmore, 5.

[367] Charles L. Hoskins, *Black Episcopalians in Savannah,* Savannah, 1983, 26.

[368] Robert E. Perdue, *The Negro In Savannah, 1865-1900,* New York Exposition Press, New York, 1973, 91.

[369] *Haddock's Savannah, Ga. Directory,* 1871, 58.

[370] *Abrams Savannah Directory,* 1876, 44.

[371] *Rogers City Directory, 1877, 77.*

[372] *Savannah Tribune,* July 16, 1892.

[373] *Savannah Tribune,* October 8, 1892.

[374] Charles Elmore, 5.

[375] *Savannah Tribune,* June 5, 1915.

[376] *Savannah Tribune,* June 12, 1915.

[377] Savannah Tribune, June 12, 1915.

[378] Savannah Morning News, May 14, 1888.

[379] *Savannah Tribune,* August 19, 1916.

[380] John Dittmer, *Black Georgia in the Progressive Era 1900-1920,* University of Illinois Press, Chicago, 1977, 186.

[381] *Savannah Tribune,* December 19, 1959.

[382] *Savannah Tribune,* October 21, 1926.

[383] *Savannah Tribune* of October 3, 1914.

[384] *St. Stephen's Register,* 1868, 84.

[385] Charles L. Hoskins, 1983, 26.

[386] *The 1860 Census of Chatham County, Georgia,* Georgia Historical Society, 1979, 335.

[387] Charles L. Hoskins, 1983, 26.

[388] T. M. Haddock, *Savannah, Ga. Directory,* Savannah, 1871, 352.

[389] *Savannah Tribune,* September 19, 1903.

[390] *Savannah Tribune,* September 19, 1903.

[391] *Savannah Tribune,* January 23, 1904.

[392] *Savannah Tribune,* October 29, 1904.

[393] *Savannah tribune,* November 12, 1904.

[394] *St. Stephen's Register,* 1868, 116

[395] Charles L. Hoskins, 1983, 44-45.

[396] *Savannah Tribune,* June 28, 1951.

[397] *The Herald,* April 21, 1955.

[398] *Savannah Tribune,* April 12, 1958.

[399] *Savannah Morning News,* January 15, 1950.

[400] *Savannah Morning News,* October 27, 1938.

[401] *Savannah Morning News,* January 15, 1950.

[402] *Savannah Morning News,* February 18, 1996.

[403] Charles L. Hoskins, 1983, 45.

[404] *Savannah Morning News,* February 18, 1996.

[405] *Bynes Royal Funeral Home Records.* May 12, 1958,

[406] *Savannah Morning News,* November 22, 1961.

[407] *Savannah Tribune*, March 18, 1911.

[408] *Savannah Tribune,* January 13, 1917.

[409] *St. Stephen's Register,* 1868, 13.

[410] *Savannah Tribune,* February 26, 1887.

[411] *Journal of the Diocese of Georgia,* 1877,

[412] *Savannah Tribune,* April 16, 1887.

[413] Charles L. Hoskins, 1983, 27.

[414] *Savannah Tribune,* February 2, 1889.

[415] *Savannah Tribune,* June 3, 1891.

[416] *Savannah Tribune,* January 5, 1928.

[417] Cyclopedia of The Colored Race, …)

[418] Savannah Tribune, July 31, 1915.

[419] *Savannah Tribune,* October 2, 1916.

[420]*Savannah Tribune,* October 28, 1916.

[421] *Savannah Tribune,* November 11, 1918.

[422] *Savannah Tribune,* November 16, 1918.

[423] *Who's Who In Colored America*, Brooklyn, New York, 1942, 565.

[424] Kermit Smalls, 49-50.

[425] *Savannah Morning News,* October 27, 1938.

[426] *Savannah Tribune,* July 12, 1951.

[427] Gamble, 61.

[428] Quoted in, Harold E. Davis, *The Fledging Province Social and Cultural Life in Colonial Georgia, 1733-1776,* University of North Carolina Press, 1976, 140.

[429] Sieg, 61.

[430] Gamble, 207.

[431] Gamble 207.

[432] William Harden, 57.

[433] *Savannah Tribune,* February 9, 1889.

[434] Thomas Gamble, 383.

[435] *Savannah Tribune,* April 11, 1896.

[436]*Savannah Tribune,* May 23, 1896.

[437] James Simms, 73.

[438] *Savannah Tribune,* November 23, 1939.

[439] Gamble, 387.

[440] *Savannah Tribune,* August 4, 1896.

[441] Thomas Gamble, 385.

[442] *Savannah Tribune,* January 25, 1896.

[443] Charles Elmore, 21.

[444] *Savannah Tribune,* April 1, 1905.

[445] Savannah Tribune, April 8, 1905.

[446] Savannah Tribune, April 8, 1905.

[447] Savannah Tribune, July 6, 1912.

[448] *Savannah Tribune,* September 14, 1912.

[449] Savannah Tribune, September 14, 1912.

[450] *Savannah Tribune,* September 21, 1912.

[451] *Savannah Tribune,* September 21, 1912.

[452] *Savannah Tribune,* September 12, 1935.

[453] Charles Elmore, 23.

[454] *Savannah Tribune,* January 24, 1924.

[455] *Savannah Tribune,* September 11, 1897.

[456] *Savannah Tribune* of January 19, 1918.

[457] *Savannah Tribune,* August 30, 1919.

[458] *Savannah Tribune,* November 30, 1901.

[459] *Savannah Tribune,* December 5, 1908.

[460] *Savannah Tribune,* January 2, 1909.

[461] *Savannah Tribune,* June 30, 1976.

[462] *Savannah Tribune,* July 21, 1906.

[463] *Savannah Tribune,* July 28, 1906.

[464] *Savannah Tribune*, June 30, 1976.

[465] *Savannah Tribune,* August 28, 1941.

[466] *Savannah Tribune,* September 25, 1941.

[467] Sweet, 159.

[468] *Savannah Tribune,* November 4, 1876.

[469] *Savannah Tribune,* February 21, 1891.

[470] *Savannah Morning News*, April 4, 1897.

[471] *Savannah Tribune,* April 10, 1897.

[472] A. B. Caldwell, 192.

[473] *Savannah Tribune,* June 6, 1912.

[474] *Savannah Tribune,* May 25, 1918.

[475] *Savannah Morning News,* February 8, 1999.

[476] *Savannah Tribune,* July 12, 1919.

[477] *Savannah Tribune,* July 7, 1919.

[478] *Savannah Tribune,* August 23, 1919.

[479] James Lawrence, 41-57.

[480] *Georgia Gazette,* May 13, 1767.

[481] *Columbian Museum & Savannah Advertiser,* August 3, 1798.

[482] Donald Grant, ...

[483] Columbian Museum and Savannah Advertiser, July 3, 1809.

[484] G. Noble Jones, "Boy Chatham, Bugler, *Georgia Historical Quarterly,* 25(June 1941): 184.

[485] Lucy Smith, "Music of the Early Colonies, *Daughters of the American Revolution Magazine,* 93(June July, 1959): 557-558.

[486] Emily Burke, *Pleasure and Pain.* Beehive Press, 1974, 26.

[487] *Daily News Herald,* March 25, 1868.

[488] *Daily News Herald,* May 8, 1868.

[489] William Harden, 48.

[490] Kermit O. Smalls, 47-48.

[491] *Savannah Tribune,* December 4, 1915.

[492] *Daily Morning News,* November 26, 1857.

[493] *Savannah Tribune,* November 13, 1896.

[494] *Savannah Morning News,* October 28, 1873.

[495] Savannah Morning News, October 2, 1875.

[496] *Savannah Tribune,* April 16, 1892.

[497] *Savannah Tribune, May* 7, 1892.

[498] Savannah Tribune, May 21, 1892.

[499] Charles Elmore, 25.

[500] *Savannah Tribune,* October 8, 1892.

[501] *Savannah Tribune,* February 1, 1896.

[502] *Savannah Tribune,* June 5, 1909.

[503] *Savannah Tribune,* January 26, 1901.

[504] *Savannah Tribune,* December 5, 1903.

[505] *WPA-Savannah Writers Project,* coll. # 1355, item 118, Georgia Historical Society.

[506] Kermit Smalls, 47.

[507] *Savannah Tribune,* December 4, 1915.

[508] Charles Elmore, 23.

[509] *Savannah Tribune,* April 28, 1888.

[510] *Savannah Tribune,* February 10, 1912.

[511] *Savannah Tribune,* September 28, 1889.

[512] *Savannah Tribune,* February 10, 1912.

[513] *Savannah Tribune,* February 10, 1912.

[514] *Savannah Tribune* of February 3, 1912.

[515] *Daily News Herald,* May 14, 1868.

[516] Record Of The Service Of The Fifty-fifth Regiment Of The Massachusetts Volunteer Infantry, Reprint Edition, 1991, Ayer Company Publishers, 1991, 109, 114126130.

[517] *Daily News Herald,* April 20, 1868.

CHAPTER 4: WHEN JIM CROW WAS KING

[518] Savannah Morning News, February 3, 1869.

[519] *Savannah Morning News,* February 9, 1869.

[520] Savannah Morning News, February 13, 1869.

[521] *Savannah Morning News,* March 27, 1869.

[522] *Savannah Morning News,* April 13, 1870.

[523] Savannah Morning News, March 27, 1869.

[524] Allen Candler, *The Confederate Record of the State of Georgia,* Atlanta, 1909, 5, 21.

[525] Eric Foner, 228.

[526] *Savannah Morning News,* January 11, 1872.

[527] Eric Foner, 228-229.

[528] *Colored Tribune,* January 15, 1876.

[529] *Savannah Tribune,* March 11, 1905.

[530] Eric Foner, 211.

[531] *Savannah Morning News,* May 15, 1887.

[532] William Harden, 124.

[533] *Savannah Tribune,* May 21, 1887.

[534] Eric Foner, 211.

[535] Frank Bynes, *History of the Mutuals,* unpublished document.

[536] *Colored Tribune,* April 15, 1876.

[537] *Savannah Morning News,* March 2, 1887.

[538] Kenneth Coleman and Charles S. Gurr, *Dictionary of Georgia Biography,* University of Georgia Press, Athens, 1983, vol. 11, 802: *Savannah Morning News,* August 23, 1888.

[539] Savannah Morning News, September 29, 1889.

[540] *Savannah Morning News,* December 20, 1889.

[541] *Savannah Morning News*, February 15, 1890.

[542] *Savannah Morning News,* July 15, 1890.

[543] *Savannah Morning News,* September 17, 1890.

[544] *Savannah Tribune,* September 10, 1892.

[545] *Savannah Morning News,* October 31, 1890.

[546] *Savannah Morning News,* November 6, 1888.

[547] *Savannah Tribune,* May 9, 1896.

[548] *Savannah Tribune,* February 23., 1901.

[549] *Savannah Tribune,* April 18, 1891.

[550] *Savannah Tribune,* February 20, 1892.

[551] *Savannah Tribune,* December 24, 1892.

[552] *Savannah Tribune,* April 18, 1891.

[553] *Savannah Tribune,* July 7, 1892

[554] Savannah Morning News, December 3, 1903.

[555] *Savannah Tribune,* March 9, 1922.

[556] Savannah Tribune, July 23, 1898.

[557] *Savannah Tribune,* August 6, 1898.

not elected. In 1872 he and John H. Deveaux were charged with rioting.[526] While working for the U. S. post office, White convinced the postmaster to remove the Jim Crow "white only" signs from water fountains.[527] White was one of the publishers of the *Colored Tribune* in 1876.[528] Captain Richard W. White, "an old line Republican," died in 1905 and was buried from St. Benedict Church. Among the politicians, "he was known as the Indian Dick."[529]

King Solomon Thomas was born in Savannah in 1835 and was "greatly esteemed by all who knew him." He was elected magistrate of the 4th. District G. M. in 1868 and served for four years. He was later appointed a Night Inspector of Customs for the port of Savannah, "discharging the duties of both positions with credit to himself." He was past master of Eureka Lodge, Past Deputy Grand Master of the Grand Lodge of Free and Accepted Masons for the State of Georgia, and a member of the Royal Arch Chapter and Encampment, "recently organized in this city."

In 1867, he served as a registrar of the city and in 1869 was justice of the peace. [530] King Solomon Thomas was a "great lover of the Order and could always be found when duty called him." King Solomon Thomas died in May 15, 1887.[531] Reflecting on Thomas from the white perspective, William Harden wrote "of him I need say nothing; his name alone indicated his character and intellect."[532] Thomas was buried from Second Baptist Church. The Nightingale Society and the Grand Lodge escorted the remains to Laurel Grove cemetery south.

The Rev. Alexander Harris paid "a very high tribute to the deceased, who had in past years labored faithfully for the building up of the Sunday school and choir of his church."[533] Thomas was nominated for County constable for Chatham County but apparently did not obtain that position. Later he was appointed Justice of the Peace and in April 1869, he was elected to the position. Judge Schley of the Superior Court appointed Thomas as Notary Public in May 10, 1870. That same year the Radical Republican Party nominated Thomas as candidate for sheriff. Thomas served as registrar and was a notary public in Savannah in 1869. He had $200 worth of property in 1870.[534] He was a harness maker by trade.

Louis M. Pleasant, a charter member of the Mutuals, was born in Savannah January 6, 1819. He was most likely educated in one of the underground schools in Savannah. In 1876, Pleasant lived on Charlton Street near East Broad Street.[535] Pleasant was an Inspector of Mails in the local Post Office. He was one of the founders of the *Colored Tribune* later the *Savannah Tribune.* Bynes claims that after Pleasant left the *Savannah Tribune,* he started his own paper, the *Savannah Advocate.* An ardent Republican he served as chairman of the Georgia delegation in 1878. Pleasant was not much involved in local Republican politics, but played a critical role in the Republican convention of 1880. In 1876, he was appointed a route agent on the A & G. R. R. between Dupont and Albany. Pleasant was described as a "bold and fearless Republican, as well as a courteous and obliging

[558] *Savannah Tribune.* January 10, 1903.

[559] *Savannah Tribune,* April 9, 1904.

[560] *Savannah Tribune,* April 23, 1904.

[561] *Savannah Tribune,* April 22, 1905.

[562] *Savannah Tribune* of January 6, 1917.

[563] *Savannah Tribune,* July 5, 1913.

[564] *Savannah Tribune,* June 23, 1938.

[565] *Savannah Morning News,* October 27, 1938.

[566] *Savannah Morning News,* October 26, 1939.

[567] *Savannah Morning News,* October 31, 1940.

[568] *Savannah Evening Press,* November 19, 1941.

[569] *Savannah Tribune,* January 22, 1953.

[570] Kermit O. Smalls, 50.

[571] *Savannah Tribune,* January 22, 1953.

[572] *Savannah Tribune,* January 1, 1916.

[573] *Savannah Tribune,* August 4, 1906.

[574] *Savannah Tribune,* December 1, 1906.

[575] *Savannah Tribune,* January 2, 1930.

[576] Savannah Morning News,….

[577] *Savannah Tribune,* October 28, 1956.

[578] *Savannah Tribune,* June 15, 1918.

[579] *Savannah Tribune,* July 20, 1918.

[580] Savannah Tribune, …..

Photo Credits

Front Cover:

Top Row left-Griot Eleanor "Nellie" Pollard
right-Editor Sol C. Johnson
Second Row left-Col. John H. Deveaux
right-Rosa Lula Barnes
Third Row left-Amanda Parker
right-Anthony Desverney
Fourth Row left-Charles Waters
right-Principal Emma Quinney

Back Cover:

Center-Thomas J. Goodall
Top center-Andrew C. Marshall
First Top left- Andrew Bryan
Second Top left-George Gibbons
Next right- James W. Carr
W.L. Jones, Emanuel K. Love
William J. Campbell

Pages 147-156

Fig. 1-Royall Funeral Home-Frank Bynes
Fig. 2-Lachlan Pollard-Savannah Tribune
Fig. 3-Royall Funeral Home
Fig. 4-Seabrook Ambulance-Savannah Tribune
Fig. 5-Captain Seabrook-Savannah Tribune
Fig. 6-Wage Earners Bank-Savannah Tribune
Fig. 7-Lucius Williams-Savannah Tribune
Fig. 8-Madam Carrie Cargo-Willis Hakim Jones Collection
Fig. 9-Typical 1920 summer outfit-Evalena Hoskins
Fig. 10-George Bowen-Savannah Tribune
Fig. 11- Daniel Simmons- Savannah Tribune
Fig. 12-St. Philip's Monumental A.M.E.-Savannah Tribune

Index

CHAPTER 1
TRAILBLAZERS

CHAPTER 2
MAAFA in Savannah

CHAPTER 3
Stuggle Begins

Index

CHAPTER 3 (con't)

CHAPTER 4
When Jim Crow Was King....

CHAPTER 4 (con't)

Index